The Strategic Alliance Handbook

Dedicated to my wife Gill for her unwavering support for over 30 years; without her constructive criticism and support throughout the whole tortuous process, this book would never have been written. Thank you. I love you more than words can say – 20 September 1980 was the best strategic alliance I ever instigated!

The Strategic Alliance Handbook

A Practitioners Guide to Business-to-Business Collaborations

MIKE NEVIN

Routledge
Taylor & Francis Group

LONDON AND NEW YORK

First published 2014 by Gower Publishing Limited

2 Park Square, Milton Park, Abingdon, Oxon OX14 4RN
711 Third Avenue, New York, NY 10017, USA

Routledge is an imprint of the Taylor & Francis Group, an informa business

First issued in paperback 2016

British Library Cataloguing in Publication Data
A catalogue record for this book is available from the British Library.

The Library of Congress has cataloged the printed edition as follows:
Nevin, Mike.
    The strategic alliance handbook : a practitioners guide to business-to-business collaborations / by Mike Nevin.
        pages cm
    Includes bibliographical references and index.
    ISBN 978-0-566-08779-0 (hardback : alk. paper) – ISBN 978-0-7546-8142-7 (ebook) – ISBN 978-1-4094-7136-3 (epub)
    1. Strategic alliances (Business) I. Title.

    HD69.S8N4926 2014
    658'.046–dc23

                                                                        2014011281

ISBN 978-0-566-08779-0 (hbk)
ISBN 978-1-138-21276-3 (pbk)

Contents

List of Figures

List of Tables

List of Case Studies

About the Author

Mike Nevin is a co-founder and former chairman of the Association of Strategic Alliance Professionals (ASAP). He now runs his own consultancy firm, Alliance Best Practice Ltd, a specialist strategic alliance and partnership consultancy operating principally in Europe. The consultancy uses proven best practice methodologies and tools to help clients initiate and manage alliances. The company has worked with over 300 leading alliance companies, including: Accenture, Adobe, Air France, AirPlus, Alcatel Lucent, Arqiva, AstraZeneca, AT+T, Atos, Bank of America, BASF, Bayer Schering Pharma, Bristol-Myers Squibb, British Library, BT, CA Technologies, Capgemini, Cardinal Health, CGI, Cisco, Cognizant, Colt Telecom, Dell, Delta Airlines, Disney, Dupont, Eli Lilly, EMC^2 Experian, Fujitsu, GlaxoSmithKline, Hewlett Packard, IBM, Infosys, Juniper Networks, Kaspersky, Laing O'Rourke, Lufthansa, Marks and Spencer, McAfee, Merck, Micro Focus, Microsoft, Motorola, NetApp, Nokia, O2, Oracle, PwC – PricewaterhouseCoopers, Qliktech, Reckitt Benckiser, Ricoh, Rolls Royce, Samsung, SAP, Schering Plough, Schneider-Electric, Siemens, Singapore Airlines, Star Alliance, Starbucks, Tieto, TNT Express, Unisys, United Airlines and VMware.

Reviews of The Strategic Alliance Handbook

The methodology that the author describes in this book matches exactly the processes that an experienced alliance manager would recognise as best practice. By identifying this with his 52 common success factors, the author has described a template that can be used by any alliance manager to build a successful alliance and to diagnose where there are weaknesses in the relationship.

Jim Whitehurst, Alliance VP, SAP and
former UK President of Association of Strategic Alliance Professionals

At last, the one book which accelerates an Alliance program between companies using a common methodology. Creates an aurora between Alliance partners where each has the desire to work together delivering exceptional joint propositions. This book will be utilised by Canon worldwide.

Frank Steggall, Canon UK and Ireland

This book takes a comprehensive and critical view of alliance best practices and presents a structured and practical system for both analysis and intervention. Importantly, it has been thoroughly road-tested through Mike Nevin's vast experience of assisting companies to improve their partnering capabilities. A key strength is its applicability across different industry sectors. A must for any serious partnership professional!

Peter Thurlby, Principal Consultant, Phase7

Foreword

In today's turbulent and fast moving business environment, different companies face different challenges, but one factor remains common to them all: no company (whatever its size) can go it alone. Alliances are no longer a peripheral activity on the outskirts of marketing, sales and corporate planning; they have become a vital necessity in creating explosive business growth and delivering world-class products and services to an ever more demanding set of global customers.

Not only have alliances become necessary to secure transitory business opportunities, they have become central to the corporate strategies of many of the most well-established and fastest-growing organisations on the planet.

External market pressures are further driving this increasing focus on business-to-business collaboration through factors like the global recession, the need for organisational agility, the innovation imperative and the desire for world-class status. In addition, many of the major initiatives with which we are familiar today rely on effective collaboration for success – initiatives like cloud computing in information technology, Software as a Service in software companies, code and ticket sharing in the aviation industry, cost reduction in supply chains, creative excellence in the media and broadcasting industry, and 'Smarter Technologies' in power supply and city planning.

However, the reality is that creating strategic alliances efficiently and effectively is still a notoriously difficult thing to do. It relies not only on clear processes and activities, but also on the attitudes, behaviours and characteristics of the people involved. At its heart, an effective strategic alliance is a relationship, often between two large and egocentric organisations. Successful promulgation of alliances requires the participants to practise some uncomfortable new behaviours and adopt some unpopular business beliefs, such as: seeing the other person's point of view, making sure that while you are winning your partner is winning too, one plus one equals three, and collaborative negotiation. These concepts and associated language are not usually found in the majority of boardrooms around the world!

To combat these difficulties, organisations need to invest in new processes and standards and teach their executive teams new skills and behaviours, because one thing is certain: the number of global strategic alliances is growing year by year, and those companies that can get alliances right are enjoying extraordinary success. At its heart, the alliance model is simple and yet powerful – leverage resources you don't own (and don't have to pay for) to achieve exponential business benefit.

I was delighted when I was asked to write a foreword to this book because I believe that only by increasing standards and developing competencies in this new area can we hope to be successful in our alliances. Indeed, I would go further and say that organisations that can develop business-to-business partnering as an organisational competence are developing a critical competitive advantage for the twenty-first century.

This book gives you what you need to know to start that journey of alliance excellence. In it you will find clear and objective research into the common success factors in successful strategic alliances, and in addition templates and tools that will help you to put this research into practice quickly and easily. If that wasn't enough, you can read case study after case study illustrating how alliance-excellent companies (both large and small) have put these alliance best practices into action.

I think that this book is destined to become essential reading for any professional alliance manager. I see it as a teaching tool for business school courses, and at the same time a field manual that practising alliance managers use on the job; like me, I think you will come back to this book time and time again to solve thorny alliance problems and accelerate the conduct of your collaborative relationships.

In the future I believe we will see more alliances rather than less, and I believe the degree of dependence that companies place on alliances will grow rather than diminish. In that environment, a handbook that allows you to chart your progress through this complex area is a must, A handbook that is both easy to read and has great practical value is a luxury. Thankfully, I believe that Mike Nevin has achieved both of these objectives. Best practices work, and if you want your alliances to be more successful, I can't think of a better way than following the advice in this book.

Russ Buchanan
Chairman, The Association of Strategic Alliance Professionals
Boston, MA

The Association of Strategic Alliance Professionals (ASAP)

The Association of Strategic Alliance Professionals (ASAP) supports the drive to develop alliance best processes and standards by providing training, research, publications, webinars and conferences. Our network of local chapters around the world provides an opportunity for like-minded professionals to meet together to discuss best practices and learn about the latest trends in alliances and partnering. ASAP is the only association to offer a professional certificate of strategic alliance management, known as CAAM (the Certificate of Advanced Alliance Management).[1]

---

1   To learn out more about ASAP, visit www.strategic-alliances.org.

Preface: How It All Began

If All Strategic Alliances are the Same, Why are Some More Successful than Others?

From 1994 to 2002 I worked in the information technology (IT) industry, first as an IT director of a large financial services company, then as the director of consulting for a systems integration business. In both organisations I faced the practical challenge of how to get multiple companies to collaborate for the common good (that is, client or customer value).

In every case I felt like I was making it up as I went along. Some things seem to work well in certain situations, and then less so in others. There seemed to be no common approaches, not even a common agreement as to what everyday phrases meant. Some people talked about alliances, and others talked about partnerships. Some emphasised personal behaviours and organisational culture, others stressed processes, metrics and business models.

At one point much earlier in my career I was a performance improvement consultant with Ernst & Young, and the experience left me with an abiding admiration for, and fascination with, business processes. Ernst & Young taught us that there were two aspects to business performance improvement: process improvement (largely based on H. James Harrington's excellent 1991 work *Business Process Improvement*) and process innovation (based on Tom Davenport's equally excellent 1993 work *Process Innovation*). What I was searching for was *the* book on alliance processes, but I couldn't find it.

That might have been the end of the story right there were it not for the fact that in June 2001 I attended the inaugural conference of the Association of Strategic Alliance Professionals (ASAP) in Scottsdale, Arizona. It was a three-day conference filled with nothing but a discussion and exploration of this new and (to me at least!) exciting new business model of strategic alliances.

I was bombarded with differing points of view and seemingly contradictory case studies – far from clarifying the area for me, it made me even more confused! I determined to try and make sense of this new and possibly powerful fledgling management science.

The reason I was so fascinated was that successful strategic alliances appear almost magical. In essence, you borrow resources that you don't own (and therefore don't have to pay for) and leverage them using the efforts of partners (that again you don't need to hire) to produce outstanding value which both sides share. The cost to value ratio can sometimes appear off the scale.

As soon as I got back to the UK I contacted ASAP, the organisers of the conference, and told them that I'd like to join their organisation and if possible promote strategic alliance management standards and ideals in Europe. Setting up a European 'chapter' of an American not-for-profit association was not without its challenges, but I was convinced that the world would need more, not fewer, alliances and that as a consequence organisations should be encouraged to 'do it right'. We finally launched ASAP Europe Ltd in March 2002 at a conference at Cranfield Business School just outside Milton Keynes in the UK.

From the very first day the idea struck a chord with business leaders and operational practitioners alike, and membership grew quickly to over 150 within a year. Members liked the fact that they could come together and discuss 'what works' in alliances. They liked even better the fact that they could learn from their peers so that they didn't need to make the same mistakes that others had made before.

But something else happened that I hadn't foreseen: from day one, the members came back to me time and time again and said: 'We like this talk about best practices as they apply to strategic alliances but could you help us actually execute them in practice?'

I took this request back to ASAP, and was told that providing direct advice wasn't possible as they were incorporated as a not-for-profit educational charity. In practice, this meant that they could only offer meetings to members as a way of discussing alliance issues; they couldn't offer active advice on what best practices to pursue or how to execute known best practices. As a consequence, in August 2002 I started a research and benchmarking company focusing exclusively on business-to-business collaborations (alliances and partnerships). I called the business Alliance Best Practice Ltd, and I took as my visionary tag line the famous words of Sir Isaac Newton, 'Standing on the Shoulders of Giants' ('If I have seen further than other men it is because I have been standing on the shoulders of giants).

The quote and the name summed up all that I was trying to achieve. I wanted to understand what works in strategic alliances and to codify it in such a way that everyday practitioners could execute alliances using a best practice approach.

The questions I set out to answer were the ones that had fascinated and frustrated me in equal measure when I was doing the job:

- How is it that two organisations in a strategic alliance relationship can be astoundingly successful in one country and miserably failing across the border in the country next door?
- How is it that one alliance can flourish with a total absence of trust when in another it is absolutely crucial to success?
- What part does personal chemistry play in the business model, and does it outweigh process?
- Is the only value worth recognising in alliance relationships commercial value?
- What part does vision and planning play in overall success, and how should we avoid the 'ready, fire, aim!' syndrome?
- What about the complex fit of both companies' products and services and the way they take them to market – surely this is key?
- Perhaps the most fundamental question of all – why is it that the majority of alliances fail?

These and other questions had puzzled me for years, and have subsequently become the object of an extensive, ongoing and focused personal research crusade since that conference in Arizona. I resolved there and then to research this area thoroughly and to test my research with companies that were active in practising business-to-business partnering.

This book is not intended as an academic tome. This is a book founded on conclusions from the practical observation of alliances in action (both good and bad). I constructed hypotheses and then tested them by actively consulting with alliance practitioners, academics and other consultants. I developed tools, methodologies and systems to support my approach along the way.

Above all, this book is based on best practice; it seeks to answer fundamental questions of collaboration, such as:

- What factors recur time and again in successful alliances?
- What behaviours and attitudes contribute to success?
- How can one replicate alliance success regardless of market conditions, business sector or business proposition?
- How can you optimise your alliance relationships to derive the greatest value for the lowest cost?
- Why is it that some combinations of partners are more successful than others?
- How can alliance success be planned and delivered on time in a coherent and integrated way?

I couldn't find a definitive best practice text on how to instigate, design, develop and execute strategic alliances when I needed it, but it is my fervent desire that this book will provide that service for you.

I hope you enjoy discovering and applying alliance best practices as much as I have, and in the true nature of continuous improvement, if you feel you have a best practice to offer in this area, please feel free to suggest it on our website, www.alliancebestpractice. com, or email us at info@alliancebestpractice.com.

Conventions Used in This Book

The Use of the Phrase 'Alliance Best Practice'

The phrase 'alliance best practice' is used in a dual context in this book. When the phrase is in lower case it refers to a general observation of some commonly understood business-to-business partnering practice or practices, as in: 'The current standards in alliance best practice have increased markedly in Europe during the last five years.'

When the phrase is used with initial capital letters ('Alliance Best Practice') or when it is shortened to the acronym ABP it refers to the organisation created to discover, develop and disseminate alliance best practice principles and practices, as in: 'Alliance Best Practice Ltd (ABP) is a research and consultancy organisation with a number of associate partners based in the United Kingdom.'

The Database

During the course of the research and codification of results conducted by ABP over the last ten years, I have constructed a useful framework for alliance practitioners. This framework lies at the heart of this book and contains the accumulated insights that our clients and I have generated. As a simplification, I refer to this framework throughout the book as 'the Database' or 'the ABP Database'.[1]

Definition of Terms

Where a common term or phrase is used in a particular context, then it is included in Appendix 4, 'Definition of Terms').

As a convention, most alliance relationships described in this book refer to bilateral collaborative relationships – that is, between two parties – although in practice the conventions can equally refer to multiple interactive alliance partners in so-called alliance ecosystems.

Alliance executives are invariably referred to as 'he' in this book. This is only partly a convention, as the vast majority of alliance executives practising their art in multiple industries today are males. There are some extremely effective female alliance executives, but they are very much in the small minority (in our experience less than 15% approximately).

---

1   Further information about the Database is available at www.alliancebestpractice.com.

As an aside, there is some research which suggests that the feminine psyche is actually better suited to alliance management as it has been suggested that women are generally more nurturing of individual and group personalities than their masculine counterparts!

Although collaborative relationships can take many forms and be described in multiple ways, to aid simplicity and the learning process I have used the term 'alliance' throughout the book to denote a relationship between two or more organisations to achieve some joint objectives which they could not achieve alone. Further, I have used the term 'strategic alliance' to denote an alliance of business-critical importance with a high degree of business intimacy.

There is confusion in the market generally regarding the use of the two interlinked terms 'alliance' and 'partnership', which is less than helpful. In this book I refer to the entity 'alliance' to connote a business-to-business relationship with a high degree of collaboration Likewise, I refer to the act of creating such relationships as 'partnering'.

The reason I choose to use such language is for simplicity and ease of reading alone. I am well aware that there is a considerable body of research and application regarding the investigation of partnering as a business model, and I believe that the principles and approaches advocated in this book have equal relevance to that group of relationships as well as to those of alliances.

Views Expressed

Throughout this book, observations by the author alone are prefaced by 'I', as in: 'I believe that the following factor is important.' Such observations represent the personal views of the author and are attributable to no other source. The majority of the observations, however, have come from interactive discussions between Alliance Best Practice Ltd associates, partners or clients who between them have come to a common agreement about the point under discussion, thus these observations are prefaced by 'we', as in: 'We believe that trust is an important factor in strategic alliance relationships.'

Common Success Factor Coding

The ABP research has discovered a number of common success factors present in successful strategic alliances. Much of our subsequent work has involved the clarification and codification of these factors. In doing so, I have observed that the factors naturally fall into five distinct categories: Commercial, Technical, Strategic, Cultural and Operational.

These factors are coded in the Database according to their type and position as follows:

- **Commercial** – Co1–Co10
- **Technical** – T11–T19
- **Strategic** – S20–S30
- **Cultural** – Cu31–Cu38
- **Operational** – O39–O52.

How to Read This Book

This book has been designed for a range of readers and also to be read in a number of different ways.

Types of Readers

PRACTITIONERS

First and foremost, this book has been written for active alliance practitioners. These are typically people who are responsible for one or multiple alliance or partnership relationships, and their prime concern will be to use the book as an aid to improving the performance of their selected relationships.

ACADEMICS

Academics may include practising professors or research students with an interest in the area of business-to-business collaboration. It is hoped that they will find research, methodologies, frameworks, insights and references in this book to further their own studies.

CONSULTANTS

It is our hope that business consultants advising companies on their strategic relationship management issues will use the resources the book provides to benchmark and objectively assess those relationships against a suitable industry standard prior to advising their clients on the most appropriate improvement strategies and action plans.

How to Read This Book

Firstly, you may want to dip in and out of the book to help you better understand and deal with a critical issue you are currently facing. This would typically be the case for alliance practitioners who have little time for additional theoretical study. They require practical and sound advice concerning an issue which is giving them problems now. If this is the case, then a good starting point would be to read a general description of the alliance best practice common success factors (CSFs) found in Part I.

Secondly, you may wish to read the book from beginning to end in order to understand the best practice framework employed, its origins and evolution over time. This is most likely to be the case for alliance researchers who wish to understand not only the conclusions and key insights of the research on which the book is based, but also the manner in which that research was conducted.

Finally, you may have purchased this book simply because you wanted to get to the practical stuff – in this case, the Appendices are for you! These are referenced in the text throughout, but can also be read by themselves as a standalone description of useful tools along with examples of their CSF applications. Business consultants in particular will value these resources.

Whatever your role, interest or preferred manner of reading, I hope you will find practical insights in this book that will help you understand the complex and often bewildering field of business-to-business collaboration.

Emerging Alliance Best Practice

1 *Alliance Success Factors*

Background/Research Methodology

This book is founded on extensive research that has identified a list of common success factors (CSFs) that consistently feature in successful strategic alliances (successful as defined by both or all partners in the relationship).

The original secondary research was conducted by Alliance Best Practice Ltd (ABP) during 2002–3. The research was called secondary because it examined the literature available at the time regarding successful strategic alliances.

The research methodology was relatively simple:

- identification of any research that focused on why alliances succeed;
- identification of any common factors in successful alliances.

ABP identified over 27,000 instances of international (different countries) and domestic (same-country) alliances. These instances came from a wide range of published material by practitioners, academics and consultants.

Having identified over 27,000 instances of alliances, ABP went on to assess how many of these relationships were deemed successful. The ABP definition of success was simple: all parties to the relationship agreed that the alliances delivered the expected or hoped-for results, or better.

ABP found less than 3,000 alliances that satisfied these criteria (the actual figure was 2,840, or 10.52%).

ABP then asked the follow-up question – Why? Why were these relationships successful? We then collected all the reasons for success and found that some reasons seemed to feature in a statistically significant manner, meaning that their occurrence could not be explained by luck or coincidence alone.

An example may help to make this clearer. In our research we discovered that trust was a success factor that was a feature of successful alliances. That is not to say that all successful alliances have a high degree of trust; but it is to say that a high proportion of successful alliances did have a high degree of business-to-business trust.

We designated these recurring success factors as common, hence the term 'common success factors', and its acronym, CSF.

Somewhat later in our research, while I was teaching a class of alliance managers for Oracle in Geneva, I was offered another interpretation of the acronym which I also feel holds true: 'common sense factors'!

It is important to note that not all CSFs are present in all successful relationships.

Having conducted the original secondary research, we then turned our attention to primary research and shared our findings with over 340 members of the Association of

Strategic Alliance Professionals in order to validate the original findings. What we wanted to know was:

- Do these results make sense?
- Do they resonate with you?
- Do you recognise these factors as desirable in your alliance relationships?

The answer in all cases was a resounding 'Yes.'

ABP has since used the resulting framework to analyse and diagnose alliance health and effectiveness, and has developed a benchmarking database (the Database) which allows us to score the degree of CSF use in alliance relationships. This scale is graduated 0–100, with 0 representing a situation in which there is no evidence of any CSF usage in the alliance and 100 representing a situation in which all the CSFs are present and working perfectly.

So far over 340 organisations have contributed to the research, which is ongoing. (For a full list of contributing companies identified by business sector please see Appendix 3 – List of Companies).

As of June 2014, the ABP Database of findings from the research contained over 200,000 entries from organisations in multiple sectors. In each case at least three key stakeholders were interviewed in detail:

- **executive sponsors** – usually responsible for setting strategic direction and primarily concerned with cost benefit analysis;
- **alliance executives** – usually responsible for managing more than one alliance and principally concerned with managing multiple alliances as efficiently as possible;
- **alliance managers** – usually responsible for the day-to-day running of a single alliance and most concerned with a specific relationship and its operational challenges.

The research was conducted by telephone and face-to-face interviews with alliance professionals in the following sectors: IT software, IT hardware, systems integration, airlines, manufacturing, logistics, pharmaceutical, financial services, telecommunications and fast-moving consumer goods.

ABP found that there were recurring and consistent common success factors in strategic alliances. The 52 CSFs fall into one of five dimensions or categories:

1. Commercial
2. Technical
3. Strategic
4. Cultural
5. Operational.

All of these dimensions are at play in all strategic alliances, although the degree to which they are important is dependent on geography, business sector, the purpose of the relationship and the stage of maturity of the alliance: (1) opportunistic, (2) systematic or (3) endemic (see Chapters 4 and 15 for explanations of these stages).

Table 1.1 identifies the appropriate dimensions for the full list of CSFs.

Table 1.1   Common success factor list

Commercial	Technical	Strategic	Cultural	Operational
Co1: Business value proposition	T11: Valuation of assets	S20: Shared objectives	Cu31: Business-to-business trust	O39: Alliance processes
Co2: Due diligence	T12: Partner company market position	S21: Relationship scope	Cu32: Collaborative corporate mindset	O40: Speed of progress so far
Co3: Optimum legal/business structure	T13: Host company market position	S22: Tactical and strategic risk	Cu33: Collaboration skills	O41: Distance from revenue
Co4: Alliance audit/ healthcheck	T14: Market fit of proposed solution	S23: Risk sharing	Cu34: Dedicated alliance managers	O42: Formal joint business plan
Co5: Key metrics	T15: Product fit with partners' offerings	S24: Exit strategies	Cu35: Alliance centre of excellence	O43: Communication
Co6: Alliance reward system	T16: Identified mutual needs in the relationship	S25: Senior executive support	Cu36: Joint decision making process	O44: Quality review
Co7: Commercial cost	T17: Process for joint problem solving	S26: Business-to-business strategic alignment	Cu37: Other cultural issues	O45: Memorandum of understanding and principles or alliance charter
Co8: Commercial benefit	T18: Shared control	S27: Fit with strategic business path	Cu38: Business-to-business cultural alignment	O46: Relationship change management
Co9: Process for negotiation	T19: Partner accountability	S28: Multiple relationships with same partner(s)		O47: Operational metrics
Co10: Expected cost/value ratio		S29: Common strategic ground rules		O48: Business-to-business operational alignment
		S30: Common vision		O49: Exponential breakthroughs or innovation
				O50: Internal alignment
				O51: Relationship development plan
				O52: Issue escalation

As mentioned above, not all factors appear in all successful relationships (indeed, it would be remarkable if they did), but Table 1.1 serves to illustrate why some alliance relationships are successful while others are not.

For example, it is entirely possible to have a high degree of synergy and trust in the relationship without generating an equally high degree of commercial value. This is because the commercial proposition has not been identified with appropriate rigour. In such cases organisations get on very well together, but the alliance underperforms in commercial terms because inadequate attention has been given to the commercial or technical factors. Equally, it is possible for two or more partners to hate working together, but for the relationship to be reasonably successful because of the power of the breakthrough value proposition of the product or service being provided by the relationship.

In both cases it can be observed that attention to the missing dimensions would pay significant dividends. The list of factors allows us to develop a number of pragmatic insights:

- Best practice(s) can be developed by combining various CSFs in the most appropriate combination for the situation in which the relationship finds itself.
- The use of a common framework of CSFs allows organisations to initiate and manage alliances more easily since they are all talking a common best practice alliance language which is derived from real life and is synthesised common sense (best practice).
- Further sophistication is possible by combining disparate elements in the model at different lifecycle stages (for example, start-up, ramp to revenue, maturity, extension, decline/renewal).
- The framework allows people to understand that all alliances are unique, but their uniqueness comes from the way individual alliances use the individual elements. Thus the situation can be likened to the human DNA: all people have the same constituent factors, but how they are combined dictates whether people are male or female, light- or dark-skinned, have blue eyes or brown eyes and are right- or left-handed.

This final insight allows alliance professionals to be far more sophisticated in their diagnosis and management of strategic alliances. Until now the tendency was to apply a 'one size fits all' solution (we need trust; we need to make money in this relationship; we need a defined process; we need to improve our ability to execute, and so on). Now very flexible long- and short-term action plans can be constructed from the constituent factors.

A Short Explanation of Each of the Common Success Factors

Below is a brief list of the common success factors we found in our research. A longer and more detailed discussion of each of the factors is included in Part III.

COMMERCIAL COMMON SUCCESS FACTORS

Co1: Business value proposition

All parties to the relationship must have a very clear and common understanding of the business value proposition (BVP). In the best cases the BVP is a breakthrough value proposition (that is, a product or service customers cannot currently obtain from other suppliers or combinations of suppliers). Leading companies take great pains to ensure that as far as possible the partnership BVP is difficult to replicate by other consortia. In this way they extend the period during which they can expect to enjoy a market-leading position. The existence of a BVP is critical to alliance success. Although all the other factors may be in place, if you and your partner are not offering customers something they can't get elsewhere (or offering it for a price at a quality that they can't get elsewhere), then your relationship is critically hamstrung from the outset. It is a must-have success factor in all your relationships. Those organisations in the Database that do not have this element in place show a very high correlation with failure.

Co2: Due diligence

In many cases a full and formal due diligence process may be inappropriate in the early days of an alliance relationship. However, in the best relationships both parties understand that an assessment of how they will work together before they try is of enormous value. Commonly, organisations perform some form of internal or external diligence around the areas of commercial factors, technical alignment of prospective partners' products and services, a strategic understanding of where prospective partners are heading, a cultural assessment of the organisations involved, and finally, an assessment of how they will co-operate operationally.

Co3: Optimum legal/business structure

Different alliances have different purposes, and it is important to recognise that a structure that works well for one relationship may not work well for another. Questions such as whether the relationship should be formal or informal and whether the structure should include or exclude an equity element are all important in deciding the best structure. However, bear in mind that the business negotiators on both sides should draw up the overall structure of the relationship before it is finalised by each party's lawyers.

Co4: Alliance audit/healthcheck

Alliances are typically reassessed regularly to identify dynamic changes in day-to-day operations or because of key personnel changes. However, this CSF refers to the practice of a formal alliance review over an agreed timescale. Typically, this review will be formal in nature and be attended by the full nominated stakeholder teams on both/all sides. This review usually takes place annually and is the means by which original expectations and assumptions are challenged.

Co5: Key metrics

Many organisations are finding that the selection and appropriate support of a balanced set of key metrics is critical to the success of their relationships. When deciding on their set of measurements, best practice companies bear the following factors in mind:

- Commercial success tends to be an effect rather than a cause.
- Causes tend to be leading indicators, and effects tend to be lagging indicators.

In a balanced set, not only do organisations consider the different dimensions (Commercial, Technical, Strategic, Cultural and Operational), but they also consider short-term and long-term influences.

Co6: Alliance reward system

This point is very closely allied to factor Co5 above. Only after they have decided on the important aspects to measure do best practice companies embed the right behaviours for those key metrics. Always remember that the operational level is where the grandest partnering schemes and strategies need to be implemented. At this most basic level it has never been truer that 'what gets measured gets done'. It is no use an executive team for either partner talking a good game of alliance inter-operation while rewarding direct sales and confrontational behaviour.

Co7: Commercial cost

Most organisations have no idea how much their alliance relationships cost. Many organisations are now looking actively at this area to identify first line costs, such as the cost of the staff employed by both sides to manage the relationship, the joint marketing funds available to both organisations to achieve common goals, and the direct costs of interaction (for example, buildings, R&D and training). However, leading-edge organisations are now going one step further and identifying the second-line 'add-on' costs of such things as the time of line managers taken up by alliance initiatives, the opportunity costs of not pursuing suitable initiatives or pursuing them in an ineffective manner, and the costs of knowledge leakage to one's partner.

Co8: Commercial benefit

It may appear to be stating the obvious that organisations should be clear about the value they receive from their alliance relationships, but in fact many organisations are insufficiently exact when identifying the commercial value they receive. Most can identify new sales and new market share which they would not have received were it not for the partnership. However, many do not allocate value to such aspects as knowledge of new markets or technological services, the innovative opportunities available to them through interaction with their partners, or access to clients which would not otherwise be available. Best practice companies are now trying hard to allocate commercial value to some non-tangible factors. The reason they are doing this is to better understand the full value of their relationships in terms of the only commonly available measure – cash revenue!

Co9: Process for negotiation

It could be argued that good negotiating practice would be best positioned in the 'Cultural Common Success Factors' section below. But in the ABP methodology it appears here because it has such a powerful effect on the commercial value of the deals which are agreed. Typically, when negotiating a deal both parties take an adversarial position and believe that for either of them to win, the other must 'lose a little'. However, in true collaborative relationships both partners understand that they are not looking to strengthen their personal position per se, but rather they are trying to strengthen the value and effectiveness of the relationship. This leads to some interesting insights into what constitutes good negotiating practice in alliance relationships. ABP calls this unusual type of negotiating 'co-collaborative negotiating', to emphasise the aspect of understanding and strengthening one's partner's commercial position and the role that such a view plays in outstanding alliances.

Co10: Expected cost/value ratio

As discussed earlier, best practice companies are increasingly looking in more detail and with more exactitude at the twin elements of commercial cost and commercial benefit. This allows them to develop cogent views around the cost/value return ratio of selected relationships or alliance programmes. However, this success factor goes slightly deeper than this simple observation. Increasingly, best practice companies are conducting their own internal research to identify similar classes or families of alliances which can be directly compared. When they do so, they discover that increasingly they can start to set expected standards for such relationships; when they do so, the best indicator of success is the expected cost/income ratio. If relationships are not performing to the norms established for good alliance performance, then they are quickly dissolved to save scarce collaborative resources to be used for other and better-performing relationships.

TECHNICAL COMMON SUCCESS FACTORS

T11: Valuation of assets

It is important for both partners to feel that they are receiving equal and reciprocal amounts of value in any balanced collaboration. Consequently, many leading-edge organisations are now beginning to put a monetary value on the assets in the relationship. This is usually a two-stage process. The first stage identifies and quantifies the hard assets (for example, marketing funds, R&D facilities and personnel), and the second usually includes aspects such as intellectual property rights, client mindshare and knowledge transfer. Identifying any actual or perceived differences in value provision in the relationship in this way avoids deep-seated but unspoken disquiet fermenting into active discouragement and sabotage.

T12: Partner company market position

Many partnering organisations do not take enough time to critically examine the current and future market positioning of their prospective partners. They take the view (sometimes erroneously) that what has gone before will continue into the future. However, this is very often not the case, and it behoves every organisation to understand carefully its prospective partners' market positions and the impact that such positioning has on its own operations.

T13: Host company market position

Clearly of equal value in a collaborative relationship is being able to explain with clarity, simplicity and exactitude one's own market positioning, particularly as it will apply to the partner. Without this key explanation the partner will not be able to assess your own organisation as a prospective partner, and valuable time will be lost in potentially confusing and conflicting messages from multiple executives from both (or all) companies.

T14: Market fit of proposed solution

We have alluded to this common success factor above in the section on Co1, 'Business value proposition'. Organisations need to understand how their combined offering with a partner will fit with the existing market. Ideally, such a fit will be good, allowing both partners to bring something new and of added value to the customer. In this way both parties will beat their traditional competition, but also beat the competition of other collaborations open to the final consumer.

T15: Product fit with partners' offerings

If your organisation's products or services overlap with your partners' in any way, there will always be the possibility of conflict no matter how many and how varied the control mechanisms you put in place. Ideally, you should choose partners which have no overlap, but increasingly in the real world such an ideal situation is rare. The best most organisations can hope for is a reduced amount of overlap to reduce the risk of conflict. When facing such overlap, it is always best to acknowledge the fact as soon as possible and to develop joint protocols with your partner to deal with the situation.

T16: Identified mutual needs in the relationship

Best practice organisations strive to find partnerships that genuinely satisfy a long-lasting mutual need for both partners. Most regard 'making more money' or 'saving considerable revenue' as merely the starting point for such a conversation. The range of mutual needs covered is as wide as the number of alliance relationships itself. However, all the best examples have a number of elements in common:

- The needs satisfied are considerably different, but tend to be structural to the organisation in question.
- The needs tend to be ones which no partner could easily satisfy on its own.
- Generally the needs represent considerable commercial value to the receiving party, but paradoxically represent extremely low value to the delivering organisation.
- In general, the wider the diversity of needs satisfied, the greater the value leveraged.

T17: Process for joint problem solving

Strategic alliances are first and foremost active collaborations. Consequently, alliance managers on both sides should be encouraged not to think in terms of 'my problem' or 'your problem', but 'our problem'. In this way the relationship will benefit from a higher quality of problem solving as both organisations combine their best efforts to solve problems.

T18: Shared control

We mentioned above the value of balance in the best alliance collaborations. There is no better example of the power of balance than in the area of shared control. If organisations can master the sharing of this critical feature of the relationship, then the chances of success are massively enhanced. Note that this does not necessarily mean that both sides always exercise the same degree of control in the relationship, but rather that the control is exercised by the most appropriate partner at the most appropriate time. This could mean conceding control at key moments in the relationship to a partner who has a better grasp of the current situation or a better ability to effect meaningful breakthroughs. Organisations do this because they expect (and receive) the same courtesy from their partners when the need arises later in the relationship.

T19: Partner accountability

Partners need to be absolutely clear as to the scope and degree of their accountability in the alliance relationships. Best practice companies jointly develop clear ground rules to leave all parties in no doubt as to what is expected of each of them. In many cases these rules are in no way legally binding, but rather reside in charters or codes of behaviour or memorandums of understanding and principles (MOUPs). Wherever they reside, they contribute to a clarity of expectation from all parties that obviates the damage of misaligned expectations.

STRATEGIC COMMON SUCCESS FACTORS

S20: Shared objectives

It is critically important that the high-level (or strategic) objectives of both or all contributors to a partnership are shared and understood by all. Although seemingly obvious, it is remarkable how often this basic tenet is flouted. In many cases one or all of the partners have strategic intentions which are not shared with their partners. Although this situation may be tolerable in the short term (18 months), in the longer term the differing strategic intentions of the partners will cause an increasing amount of tension in the relationship which will inevitably initiate a downward vicious spiral. The reverse of this is also true, in that common strategic objectives act like a magnet, drawing the relationship on ever-faster towards shared goals.

S21: Relationship scope

In all relationships considered by ABP in this research, the scope of the relationship was a factor which was poorly understood in a significant minority of cases. It was rare to find an MOUP (see O45 below) which explicitly stated and defined the current and ongoing scope of the relationship.

In those cases in which scope was defined, it was articulated in multiple ways: geographic, technical, functional, departmental, and so on. But in all cases the clear articulation of suitable boundaries improved the focus of the relationship.

S22: Tactical and strategic risk

Factors S22 and S23 are clearly intimately linked, but ABP found it useful to separate them in its analysis because so often organisations had one but not the other. Many organisations identified risk in their collaborative relationships (79%), but fewer further refined their understanding to encompass tactical and strategic (64%), and fewer still had a formal risk mitigation process in place to deal with the different types (32%). The factor most often cited as commonly understood risk was 'the risk of losing money or wasting time'.

S23: Risk sharing

Of those organisations that did recognise risk as a problem, relatively few actually initiated risk sharing strategies (13%). Interestingly, of those organisations that did share risk, their Business-to business trust score (see Cu31 below) was significantly higher by a factor of over 40%.

Risk sharing was observed to be a principal driver in the area of 'business intimacy', and was crucial for late Stage II (systematic) and Stage III (endemic) companies (see Chapters 4 and 15 for an explanation of these stages of alliance maturity). It contributed greatly to the development of trust, and was observed to be a key influencer on this factor (as was the style of negotiation).

S24: Exit strategies

A great deal of confusion exists in companies regarding this practice, and many liken it to a pre-nuptial agreement before marriage. In ABP's opinion, this analogy is both flawed and damaging. Those who support this view maintain that discussing what might go wrong before it has gone wrong introduces a discordant note into the relationship, and in addition reduces the degree of trust assumed by both/all parties.

We at ABP disagree. We believe that a sensible discussion of events which are not currently planned or foreseen, but which if they actually happen will have a significant adversarial impact on the relationship, is a sensible practice. The analogy we would draw is with the legal condition of 'fundamental breach' in English contract law. This condition allows that despite the best intentions of both parties something might happen which renders the relationship 'null and void', and in such circumstances one or both parties are entitled to invoke the exit clause(s) previously agreed between them.

S25: Senior executive support

The vast majority of relationships researched revealed the need to secure senior executive support (93%). However, the majority of senior executives interviewed paid only lip service to the role of executive sponsor. There were very few organisations that adopted a formal job description for the role (9%), and of those that did, only a handful required the senior executive to sign off on the objectives, duties and responsibilities that such a job description contained.

At the same time we identified a number of natural 'alliance champions' who felt great frustration because they were unaware of how to contribute to the success of the relationships in question.

All too often senior executive support was reduced to personal 'chemistry' between top executives on both/all sides of the relationships. The best examples of senior executive support seemed to go hand in hand with regular (six-monthly) 'executive briefings' at which the senior executive of one or sometimes both sides drove a formal agenda which included not just operational, but also strategic issues for discussion. It was observed that in these cases there was a greater sense of integration and coherence between the operational teams on both sides of the relationship. The practice also developed a virtuous (though threatening) circle. Typically, this was demonstrated by the operational teams on both sides contributing more and more planning time for these meetings (10–15 days was not unusual), so as not to be caught out in front of their own senior executive and thus personally and professionally embarrassed.

S26: Business-to-business strategic alignment

This is a critical factor with one of the lowest instances in the Database. It is typified by organisations sharing strategic direction with each other on such issues as technical/business direction, research and development, and market research. Most organisations had a timeframe of only 12–18 months, and if they had a strategic plan for the relationship it was constructed from significant initiatives rather than a consideration of classical strategy affecting issues: political, economic, social, technological, and so on.

Evidence from the Database suggests that pharmaceutical alliances tend to score higher here (+35% on the Database average). This is possibly a result of the particular nature and longevity of typical pharma alliances and the practice of being able to exploit new drug development under licence for a relatively long period before being exposed to open market competition.

S27: Fit with strategic business path

Just as strategic alignment between both partners was a relatively little understood or practised concept, the concept of key alignment between the aims of the alliance and the stated corporate objectives of both companies was rare (< 9%).

Organisations seemed to view the effort of aligning the goals and objectives of the relationship with the corporate objectives of both companies as simply too hard to achieve. However, in the few instances were this was achieved it was clear that there was a resulting improvement/increase in such factors as senior executive support, securing suitable resources for the alliance, joint marketing statements, and the preparedness of both organisations to support the other in public.

S28: Multiple relationships with same partner(s)

In those situations in which a significant relationship had multiple instances with the same partner, the overall effectiveness of each instance was improved (40–50% better). This appears to be the result of the 'natural' and instinctive sharing of experiences from the teams on both sides of the relationship.

S29: Common strategic ground rules

Those organisations that took the trouble to identify, articulate and document their understanding of commonly binding strategic guidelines enjoyed a better return on their relationships. Very often there was no common or consistent description of such a document (for example, an MOUP, charter, rules of engagement, behavioural code, standards manual or code of ethics). The reason appeared to be that documenting the commonly agreed processes significantly accelerated the planning and operationalising of the relationship, so both parties 'got to the money' quicker with less organisational or personal posturing.

As soon as we agreed a simple set of relationship principles then wrote them down, managers on both sides felt that they could call out their opposite numbers on any behaviours or actions that weren't in sync with the charter. This stopped people damaging the relationship through inappropriate behaviours and sped things up considerably!

S30: Common vision

A defined vision was absent in the majority of cases examined. In fact, it was present (formally) in less than 12% of the relationships in the Database. However, that is not to say that individuals on both sides of the relationships couldn't articulate in their own words what the relationship was all about. Best practice in this area suggests that the existence of a compelling vision can have a galvanising effect on the mechanics of the relationship.

CULTURAL COMMON SUCCESS FACTORS

Cu31: Business-to-business trust

In a large majority of the relationships examined trust was clearly recognised as being of paramount importance (87%). However, the subtle but important distinction between personal and organisational trust was less clear. There were many instances in which two or more individuals from both sides developed a powerful rapport and personal chemistry. This rapport seemed to have little to do with national or ethnic considerations, and there were many instances of strong personal friendships resulting from such rapport.

Indeed, in some cases the rapport was so strong that individuals were seen as 'going native', meaning that they favoured the objectives and intentions of their partner's organisation rather than their own.

The incidence of business-to-business trust was far less common, and no organisations identified in the Database have a formal or credible business-to-business trust building model. This is due in no small part to the fact that the essence of organisational trust is misunderstood.

Paradoxically, the impact trust can have on relationships was almost universally identified as a common success factor (94%), with many individuals able to cite quite clearly the commercial value of developing trust. For example: 'It helps you negotiate the natural ups and downs of the relationship more easily. Your partner doesn't immediately reach for the contract when you don't deliver, and he looks to see why this problem might have occurred rather than blaming individuals.'

There has been an increasing degree of attention paid to this important area in the recent literature on alliance management.[1] There is no doubt that many organisations are

---

1   See particularly Fons Trompenaars and Peter Woolliams, 'Getting the Measure of Culture: From Values to Business Performance': www.thtconsulting.com/articles/getting_the_measure_of_culture%20july05.pdf (accessed 8 April 2014); Khaled Abdou and Simone Kliche, 'The Strategic Alliances between the American and German Companies: A Cultural

now beginning to wake up to the hidden impact that cultural misalignment can have, and many organisations are developing a language to describe organisational diversity in a way which allows them to address the differences (for example, British Telecom, SAP, Siemens Communications, Air France, Delta and Capgemini).

Cu32: Collaborative corporate mindset

Many individual alliance managers cited this aspect as being the most difficult to deal with. Quotations such as this from a senior executive at Atos were typical: 'We don't do alliances very well. This is due in no small part to our historical growth. If we see an organisation that we would like to work with, we don't ally with them, we buy them!'

Organisations that exhibited an immature or nascent organisational collaborative mindset tended to fall into the Stage I (opportunistic) alliance maturity category (see Chapters 4 and 15). This means that they would pursue collaborations only in so far as they helped them to secure particular opportunities which were too large or too complex for them to win alone. When that particular opportunity was secured they would then pursue another one, but there was no co-ordination of alliance activities other than those necessary to win deals.

In comparison, those organisations that had reached Stage III (endemic) saw partnering not as a separate function, but rather as 'the way we do things around here'. Such organisations regarded partnering as the core of their business, and took great pains to ensure that partnering ethics and behaviours were practised throughout their organisations (for example, Starbucks, Eli Lilly, Dow Corning and Siebel).

Cu33: Collaboration skills

No organisations in the Database had a coherent and integrated structure for collaboration skills development, although many had individual training courses for aspects of the collaboration skill set (such as negotiation, interpersonal skills, 360-degree review, project management, influencing skills, and mediation).

This is in many respects surprising given that there is a clear and strong causal link between the collaboration skills of key stakeholders and the success of collaborative relationships. It appears that the reason might be that no association or trade body has sufficiently articulated a comprehensive framework of skills to describe the competencies of professional collaboration. However, evidence suggests that such initiatives are now gaining ground.

Cu34: Dedicated alliance managers

In many respects this is the simplest and easiest best practice factor to track. There is empirical evidence that when dedicated resources are allocated to a strategic relationship, that relationship improves by 50–80% defined in the success terms of the individual relationship (for example, more products sold, greater influence with introducers, quicker time to market, better profit margin, greater gross sales or higher revenue).

Perspective', *European Business Review* 16(1), 2004, pp. 8–27; Pablo C. Biggs, 'Managing Cultural Differences in Alliances', Scarborough, Ontario: Strategic Triangle, 2006.

Given this fact, it is surprising that so many organisations continue to expect individual managers to run multiple alliances. The reason appears to be a damaging 'Catch-22' situation. When a manager asks to be allocated full-time to a relationship, the common answer from executive management appears to be: 'When you can generate x amount of increased revenue, I will allow you to go full-time on the relationship.' However, the problem is that without being full-time, the individual manager will never have the time available to produce x revenue, let alone develop a coherent long-term growth plan for the relationship: 'I spend all my time running from one of my three so-called strategic alliances to the next desperately fire-fighting operational issues which arise, and then I get criticised by my manager because I haven't developed a coherent strategy for each!'

Cu35: Alliance centre of excellence

There was overwhelming evidence from the Database that when organisations started to share alliance knowledge among practitioners, performance improved (incidence 46%, with an average performance improvement increase of 87%).

These centres were by no means all physical entities; some were virtual groups of multiple disciplines. Furthermore, not all were formally established; some were clearly operationally started as a common observation of need:

> We started a regular teleconference call once a month to share experiences on our alliances. To be honest, at first it was just a chance to share frustrations, but pretty soon people began to share experiences or tips and tricks that had worked well for them that others could use. We started to share documents and templates, and it really helped with our day-to-day jobs!

There was a common misconception in high-tech alliances that the technical centres of excellence that were formed to test technical solutions were the same as alliance centres of excellence; this was clearly erroneous, although there were aspects of technical collaboration that shared common best practices with alliances (for example, communication models, operating protocols or budgetary sign-off procedures).

Cu36: Joint decision making process

One aspect of an organisation's culture which was seen as extremely influential in the Database (> 84%) was reflected in its decision making process. Very often this is a point of significant friction between collaborating organisations. For example, generally in a large multinational organisation a significant decision needs to be vetted and validated by a number of management levels, whereas in a small organisation the same decision can be made quickly by a handful of senior executives sitting together or communicating remotely via telephone.

The problem is not so much that both organisations take different timeframes to make decisions; it is that both sides misunderstand the nature of the other organisation. In the large organisation (not unreasonably), managers have been told to generate a traceable audit trail of authorisation thoroughly through multiple levels of senior executives, whereas in the smaller, more agile company, risk taking and entrepreneurship are generally encouraged.

The manner in which this factor affects relationships stems from misconceptions on either side about the pace and depth of consensus needed to make a successful decision. In at least one example in the Database this factor was the one aspect that consistently held back the relationship. On the one hand was a large multinational organisation which managed very much by consensus, and on the other was a much smaller, much more agile, high-tech start-up that could make decisions quickly.

Cu37: Other cultural issues

In every strategic alliance relationship examined there existed some specific aspect of both organisations' cultures which led to problems with the relationship. Sometimes this might involve the nature of communication, in others it might be an organisational reflection of arrogance or aggression; in yet others it might be the attitude of organisations towards escalating problems (in some organisations this seems perfectly reasonable, while in others it is seen as a fast track to proving that you can't do your job and leads directly to an early exit from the organisation); whatever the particular instance, there was a high occurrence in the Database of specific cultural issues causing specific problems (over 86%).

Cu38: Business-to-business cultural alignment

In those organisations that recognise organisational culture as an in-house enabler or barrier to progress with partnership, many of them have developed their own language to describe their own cultural norms. They use this language as a framework to identify to potential partners the culture with which those partners will be aligning, and they actively encourage partners to consider their own organisations' culture along similar lines. There is good evidence that such an active and early cultural alignment helps minimise the delays, misconceptions and damaging perceptions commonly found in the Cultural dimension.

In those organisations that do not already have a cultural alignment language or framework, many are now actively turning to external advisers to help them with the situation. For example, Siemens Communications and SAP conducted a five-day cultural alignment exercise which was attended by 13 executives from each organisation. The output was a range of three to five new initiatives which the partnership believed could be inculcated into the product set of both organisations within 18 months. Another example is that of Air France and Delta airlines, in which both organisations recognised after three to four years of the alliance relationship that the disparate cultures of both organisations was getting in the way of a successful relationship. In that case both organisations jointly commissioned a cultural assessment of the relationship each partner could explain to the other – this was how things got done around here.

OPERATIONAL COMMON SUCCESS FACTORS

O39: Alliance processes

There appears little doubt from the Database that the adoption of any common process between two or more partners will produce a corresponding improvement in both the efficiency and effectiveness of the relationship (> 87% likelihood). Such a process does not necessarily need to be 'best practice'; the very fact that both sides are working to a common process helps to match expectations, reduce tension, and make accurate and coherent progress reporting more achievable. Organisations which have such an alliance process reported a 60–70% increase in the efficiency of those relationships which used the approach. In at least one case a senior executive sponsor put the point succinctly: 'It's very simple guys, when we follow a process that we have already agreed we do better than when we don't. So from now on, if you don't follow agreed processes in alliance management, I will sack you!'

Obviously, while any process is an advancement, the fact that two or more parties to a strategic relationship will have their own practical processes for managing alliances brings its own problems of integration and translation. Hence the power of a best practice approach in which both organisations agree the effectiveness of a best practice set of factors, principles and methodologies which are then inculcated in a defined joint process which can be explained with equal ease to both organisations.

O40: Speed of progress so far

While not in itself a defined best practice factor, it is extremely valuable for alliance partners to define the state of progress of their relationship, if no other reason than it prevents damaging misconceptions which can blow up into significant problems in the not too distant future. For example, if one organisation thinks that it has made significant progress and the other thinks that it has made little progress, then it won't be long before these two misconceptions express themselves as extreme dissatisfaction, possibly leading to strife and relationship breakdown.

The aspect of this factor which is valuable to collaborative organisations is to match the speed of progress achieved in the relationship to some form of common plan; only by doing so can both parties objectively report to their senior management that planned progress is being made.

O41: Distance from revenue

The planned or anticipated distance from revenue versus the actual distance from revenue is a significant factor in a successful relationship. In some instances (for example, the software industry) the distance may be very short (less than 90 days); in others it can be disproportionately long (in the pharmaceutical sector, five to seven years). Whatever the empirical distance from revenue, it is important that both parties have a clear understanding and genuine acknowledgement of what it is; if clarity is not achieved on this particular success factor, then the chances are that at least one if not both senior executive teams responsible for the provision of resources and budget will quickly become disillusioned and there will be a consequent reduction in attention, support and budget for the relationship.

O42: Formal joint business plan

In those relationships that had a business plan, it was noticed that the corresponding Commercial CSF scores were significantly higher (73%). In addition, this was a success factor which was very often misconstrued. For example, in the high-tech sector many alliance professionals who claimed to have formal business plans in fact had forecasts for new business rather than a balanced plan showing both investment and revenue returns.

The existence of a well-defined and formal business plan appeared in a relative minority of those relationships examined (< 23%).

O43: Communication

Communication was generally acknowledged to be one of the most important common success factors in the Operational dimension. Very often there was regular and effective communication between the two individuals specifically responsible for the relationship. However, more often than not, that communication did not extend beyond those two individuals. In the best relationships, both organisations recognised the value of both internal and external communication, and developed suitable and appropriate communication programmes for both internal and external consumption. Such communication programmes included an identification of the key stakeholders on each side and a description of their relative roles and responsibilities, along with a formal diary or current chart of the meetings that were to be held. In addition, the communication programmes gave individuals an understanding of what information they should expect to receive as a result of those meetings.

The best communication programmes identified at least three key categories of stakeholder: (1) operational management, (2) multi-relationship management and (3) strategic management. Not only was the communication good between all three levels within each organisation, but equally communication was good (that is, appropriate) between the various levels in the partnership. In this way the senior executive sponsor was able to have a good overall view of the relationship, which was fundamentally in sync with the day-to-day feelings of the operational management team responsible for the relationship.

The best communication programmes generated a communication matrix, which was used as the backbone for the governance model: issues were passed up the structure, and guidance and direction was passed down. Within each organisation such common communications were passed across to the partner simultaneously, as they were generated in both partners.

O44: Quality review

This common success factor was one of the most rapidly expanding of all those identified in the operational area. As little as three or four years ago the idea of reviewing the quality or effectiveness of a relationship was seen as potentially very damaging because it conveyed a message that one or both of the partners was remiss in certain key aspects. However, there is clear evidence from the Database that the adoption of a formal quality review process – sometimes called a healthcheck or even an audit – is now rapidly becoming the norm. This development appears to be driven by both internal and external factors. The internal factor is the desire of senior management to check on the appropriateness of the actions to generate commercial return. The external factors appear to be based on the need to regularly audit key relationships as a result of Sarbanes Oxley, Enron and other high-profile audit failures.

It is evident from the annual conferences of ASAP that a regular healthcheck enacted through a formal quality review meeting (usually held annually) is becoming standard practice in a wide range of diverse sectors (for example, the 2014 ASAP and metrics track contributed to by Procter & Gamble, Eli Lilly and Cisco Systems).

O45: Memorandum of understanding and principles or alliance charter

The existence of an MOUP in strategic alliance relationships is a surprisingly good litmus test of both the effectiveness and the maturity of the relationship. Such a document (which is variously described as a charter, a code of behaviour, a partner plan or a partner programme) should not be legally binding and should concern itself with those factors which form the backbone of a significant strategic alliance relationship (governance structure, communication, key stakeholders, vision, business value proposition, communication matrix, project-specific issues, business value proposition, and so on).

The existence of an MOUP is one of the most common success factors in the Operational dimension. In addition, it is the one that is most welcomed by all levels of management. Operational managers welcome it because it gives them a context within which to perform their day-to-day duties and a set of rules to live by, and senior executives welcome it because it gives them an easy-to-read way of understanding where the relationship is currently up to (say, a five-page document).

O46: Relationship change management

While most relationships had a defined change management process for the initiatives of projects that were run as part of the relationship, very few (< 15%) had a defined change management process for the relationship itself. Consequently, issues such as changing personnel, changing strategies, acquisitions and mergers or new product launches all took the relationship by surprise. When questioned, individuals from such relationships had no means of articulating what progress the relationships had made other than stating team generalities such as 'I think we are better now than we were before,' or 'I think key people understand each other better.'

In a small minority of relationships in which a formal or informal relationship change management process was in existence, it was noticed that the relationships enjoyed elongation or extension of the value they delivered, and in general were valuable for longer. It appears that this factor is the one most responsible for enabling relationships to endure the stresses and strains of the dynamics of modern-day business life.

O47: Operational metrics

It was noticed that in some organisations, while there were sets of strategic or cultural metrics which were used to measure the relationship generally, a separate and often simpler set of operational metrics was also in use. This is most often noticed in high-tech relationships in which such factors as number of days trained on the partner's products or services, the number of opportunities in the pipeline, leads generated by the partner and proposal wins were all recognised as specific operational indicators of the success of the relationship.

O48: Business-to-business operational alignment

As with cultural alignment, many organisations did not pay sufficient attention to the integration of the intent of the relationship into both organisations' operational units. In the most outstanding cases the relationship resulted in a 'zippered' interaction between very many different operational levels in both partners.

However, in the more poorly performing relationships there was a good alignment between the intent or desire of both alliance partnership teams, but this hardly ever reached the operational units necessary to execute on the relationship.

O49: Exponential breakthroughs or innovation

This common success factor is the one most often associated with the new management buzzword 'innovation and business sustainability'. It refers to the ability of organisations to generate new and exciting business value propositions through a defined and repeatable process within the context of the relationship. It was observed that a very small minority of organisations had anything closely resembling a formal process for this up until two or three years ago. However, this factor is another which is rapidly gaining prominence in the better-performing organisations (see, for example, Reckitt Benckiser, Procter & Gamble, SAP and IBM). Many organisations are now looking to external third-party advisers to help them shape a breakthrough process which will allow them to bring new products and new services to market more quickly and more effectively.

O50: Internal alignment

This factor is most often closely associated with the business-to-business operational alignment factor, and very often goes hand-in-hand with it. Whereas business-to-business operational alignment looks at the alignment between both parties to a relationship, internal alignment looks at the efforts organisations make to align their own organisation to take advantage of the products and services generated by the relationship more effectively within their own go-to-market processes.

Organisations which had devoted specific resources to this area showed a high leverage of value to effort (that is, the amount of effort they put into communicating internally, making presentations, persuading both verbally and also by adapting compensation plans, paid for itself very many times over in terms of extra products and services sold). This was seen as a high leverage point by a large number of senior executive sponsors when questioned (> 67%).

O51: Relationship development plan

There was a marked absence of any formal project plan in the relationships examined (< 13%). This in part appears to be the result of the maturity of alliance professionals' thinking. Many alliance professionals believed that collaboration and partnering was based around personal contact and regular interaction with key stakeholders in the partner organisation, and that a project plan would simply be a barrier to the necessary fluid and nebulous networking necessary for success. There was also a second and more pragmatic reason why many alliance professionals felt that they could not develop a defined project plan. Many of them felt that the majority of their role was taken up with tactical efforts of doing rather than planning (this was particularly true of those alliance professionals who were handling more than one strategic alliance at a time).

Whatever the reason, there is clear evidence that the existence of a formal project plan, no matter how brief and no matter how prescribed, contributed very greatly to the operational success of strategic relationships. Such a plan very often went hand-in-hand with be the communication matrix mentioned earlier. Indeed, in those relationships examined in which there was a project plan, in the overwhelming majority of cases there significant attention was also devoted to communication (> 97%).

O52: Issue escalation

Issue escalation appears to be a well-understood and well-practised procedure in most project management relationships, and more specifically in high-tech projects. However, it is seldom formally recognised in strategic alliance management. In the majority of cases where strategic alliance professionals were questioned about this factor, the most common answer was: 'That is part of my job. It is my job to make sure that issues are resolved.'

Where relationship issue escalation processes were in place, they usually reflected the types of issues that arose: technical issues would be escalated to the appropriate technical channels, commercial issues would be escalated to executive sponsors, and relationship issues would be escalated to strategic alliance managers. Most organisations did not have a formal issue escalation process in their strategic alliance relationships. In those relationships where issue escalation took place effectively, there was usually evidence of senior executive support, good communication and a formal quality review.

2 *Common Challenges*

In subsequent chapters of this book we will explore the concept of individual common success factors which, if followed, increase your organisation's chances of success in relationship initiation and management.

However, before doing so it will be useful to identify some themes and challenges which appear common to many alliances and which you will need to consider before applying any of the best practices described in this book.

Categorisation of Strategic Alliances

The first challenge is to establish whether the relationship under consideration is in fact a strategic alliance relationship at all. In very many situations organisations apply the titles 'strategic' or 'alliance' apparently at random. Consider Case Study 1.

Case Study 1: British Telecom and Cisco

British Telecom (BT) is a traditional fixed-line data telecommunications company based in the UK. Over the past fifteen years it has been transforming into an information communications and telecommunications provider by offering its customers a new wave of products and services, generally referred to as ICT (information and communications technology), including broadband, mobile and managed services.

BT has developed world-class strategic partnerships and joint R&D initiatives to offer businesses and other consumers a wide choice of innovative, inspirational and integrated solutions. At the time of ABP's involvement, BT's strategic partners included Accenture, Cisco, CSC, Hewlett-Packard (HP), Intel, Microsoft and Nortel.

Cisco Systems Inc. is the worldwide leader in networking products and solutions for the Internet. It provides industry-leading products and solutions in the company's core development areas of routing and switching. Cisco sells its products through a complex series of value-added resellers (VARs) and marketing partners.

Both companies have a very successful and profitable relationship. BT buys routers from Cisco that it needs to sell to its own customers, and because it buys a lot of products it gets them at a good price. Cisco buys data bandwidth from BT to allow its customers to use the routers it manufactures, and again because it buys a lot of bandwidth it gets a very good price.

So far so good, but note that this is not a strategic alliance relationship. Although it satisfies our first criterion, that of 'strategic importance' (the relationship represents many billions of dollars of value to both companies), there is no element of collaboration; rather, both sides represent a buyer or a seller, depending on who is purchasing what volume from whom at what time. (Actually, this buyer–seller equation is even more complex, depending on geographical location – BT is the major customer in Europe and Cisco is the major customer in the USA, and both want to exploit the pre-eminent position of the other in their home markets.) The flow of value can best be described as a 'balance of trade' in a 'buy from' and 'sell to' relationship.

But now let's imagine that as a result of trading together for some time both organisations decide that they would like to explore a joint go-to-market proposition together.

In practice, what might happen is that Cisco makes the routers and BT badges them with its brand logo, then incorporates these products into a more general marketing campaign to get households in Europe to accept home-based broadband services (BT Total Broadband).

In return, Cisco puts many millions of dollars of marketing budget at the disposal of the relationship to drive the adoption of this new service. Notice that there would be no service without the combined efforts of both parties. Also notice that we now have a high degree of collaboration between both organisations.

(In actual fact the relationship is more complex than this since both BT and Cisco both need content providers to be part of the relationship to provide digital television, games playing, videoconferencing calls and so on, and both parties also need other infrastructure partners to ensure speed, security, wireless capability and remote updating).

This case study provides a powerful lesson: you need to categorise your alliance relationships carefully to ensure that you apply the right resource to the right situation. Most organisations will have a multiplicity of business-to-business relationships, but only a small fraction of them will be strategic alliances. Let's highlight this point by considering two further cases illustrating the damage that inappropriate categorisation can cause.

The first situation is straightforward: Company A is a global systems integrator which uses the desktop computers and servers that Company B makes to provide integration services to clients. Because of the volume of valuable trade which passes between them, Company A deems Company B to be a strategic alliance partner (and says so publicly on its website).

However, in trying to categorise the relationship, problems arise early. Company B seems to have little or no appetite for the strategic planning or go-to-market discussions that Company A wishes to initiate with its partner. Despite numerous attempts over a lengthy period, Company A finally has to reluctantly concede privately that it will need to downgrade Company B to the status of merely a supplier of products and services rather than that of a partner. Discussions follow long into the night as to the most courteous way to do this without offending Company B (remember that this relationship is extremely valuable to Company A), but finally a senior executive is dispatched to break the bad news to Company B.

The response is not quite the reaction that Company A was expecting:

Thank goodness for that! All we want to do is sell you things, and you guys were pulling us into more and more complicated discussions about things that didn't interest us. We didn't want to say 'no' because you represented a very good customer to us, but I have to tell you we feel we have wasted lots of time in useless meetings over the course of the last eighteen months. I'm glad it's all over now and we can just supply you with a good set of products and services.

The damage here was 'only' wasted senior executive time in meetings (which in itself accounted for many hundreds of thousands of dollars), but consider the following more damaging Case Study 2.

Case Study 2: Ford and Firestone

Ford and Firestone initiated a strategic alliance relationship. It appeared to be a match made in heaven: Ford had no interest in manufacturing tyres, and Firestone had no interest in making cars. Both concentrated on what they were good at and provided exceptional value to the other.

Joint research and development labs were set up, and a profitable time was had by both for many years. After twelve years, however, things changed, and Ford found the competitive environment suddenly got much tougher. A new management team was sent in to 'sort things out', and (as such teams do) it examined critically the practices and agreements of the previous incumbents.

The new team demanded cost savings from Firestone, which it erroneously concluded was a mere 'supplier'. Firestone pointed out that the relationship had never been based on cost, and that the relationship was about intimacy and knowing each other's future plans so that new products could be developed to accommodate future markets. Ford held firm and demanded cost reductions, and used its pre-eminent position with Firestone to force it to supply tyres at a reduced cost. Firestone felt it was being treated like a supplier, so it acted like a supplier (by reducing the quality of the product it supplied).

The result? Ford fitted lower-quality tyres provided by Firestone to its high-performance off-road vehicles such as the Ford Explorer. The tyres were not up to the job, and a spectacular series of high-profile (and high-speed) blow-outs ensued. The Ford Explorer was renamed by the American public the 'Ford Exploder'. The legal claims suffered by both companies escalated to many hundreds of millions of dollars, and the damage done to the brands of both organisations has been estimated in the billions of dollars – all because two organisations didn't categorise their relationship accurately and jointly.

BARNEY ALLIANCES

I have no idea who Barney was, but I do know that he has a lot to answer for in the alliance world. His name has become synonymous with those empty press releases we saw so much of in the dot.com boom of the late 1990s. You know the type:

ABC Ltd [a leading-edge systems integration and services company] is proud to announce that it has forged a breakthrough strategic alliance with XYZ Inc. [the world's leading software company]. A spokesperson for the alliance said last night: 'Both organisations are very excited by this groundbreaking relationship. The synergistic combination of ABC's services and XYZ's products will enable us to dominate the Asia Pacific business sector for the next ten years.'

The capital markets love the combination, and the share prices of both companies jump up 20 points overnight. The market analysts rave about the leverageable synergies of both organisations. Lots of pictures are taken and lots of words are used to describe a meaningless press release. The logos of both organisations appear on each other's websites, and eighteen months later the whole affair is quietly scrapped.

Although this scenario was common in the dot.com boom, don't imagine it doesn't equally exist today. There is still a large degree of this thinking in the minds of many senior executives. The thought logic appears to be: 'We are both strong players in a particular sector. We don't challenge each other in terms of services or products (we are complementary), consequently we should get together and make lots of money.'

The problem with this logic is that it fails to appreciate that *relationships need to be managed actively to provide value.*

Of course it's important to have good products and services (although nowadays this is a starting prerequisite for all companies, rather than a distinguishing feature of the best). Of course it's important that there should be a good degree of complementarity on both/all sides, but in addition all partners need to provide energy, effort, focus, structure and resources to make the relationship work. It won't suddenly grow spontaneously just because all the right ingredients are put into the same place at the same time.

UNDERDOG ALLIANCES

Regardless of the size of your organisation, as an alliance executive you will be faced with the problem of disparate partner size. This means that both/all of the partners in the relationship are of different sizes or have a different degree of influence or power in the current situation. If the degree of dissimilarity is great, then such partnerships are often called 'underdog alliances'. The genre features a number of specific issues which mark it out in the partnering field:

- getting on the larger partner's radar;
- developing identified business value propositions for the relationship;
- convincing the larger partner that both/all sides should conduct a formal alliance audit once a year;
- adopting a collaborative negotiating style;
- identifying clear mutual needs;
- developing a clear understanding of partner accountability on both sides;
- risk sharing in the relationship;
- engaging senior executive support from the larger partner;
- ensuring decision making compatibility;
- managing internal and external communications.

Getting on the larger partner's radar

The first problem smaller organisations experience in initiating a new alliance relationship with larger partners is 'getting on the radar' – in other words, finding a way to make their voices heard above the hubbub of other potential partners screaming for the attention of the larger organisations.

This is a very real problem, both for the smaller organisations and for their prospective larger partners, who value the innovation, flexibility and speed smaller players can offer. Many smaller organisations have tried developing white papers or pilot solutions which are then vetted by industry analysts; only then do they take the evidence of the proposition to their potential larger partner.

The problem with this approach is that it is time-consuming. Consequently, some organisations have turned to hosting an initial workshop to brainstorm new propositions which will create value for both sides. One approach is to base such workshops on the value migration concepts originally developed by Adrian Slywotzsky of Harvard Business School.[1] This approach has a number of identified benefits:

- It provides a framework for managing multiple alliance initiatives in a single relationship.
- It helps provide flexibility in an environment of rapid change.
- It helps to create a shared vision for all alliance team members.
- It positions alliance initiatives for high-impact competitive advantage.
- It tailors a relationship growth strategy to reduce risk.
- It translates strategy into executable and cost-justified action plans.

While the workshop itself is attended by mostly operational-level practitioners, crucially a senior executive sponsor of the larger organisation is usually asked to appear for a short time to hear the initial results of where the relationship is heading. In this way senior executive support can be created for the proposed actions.

The scale and extent of this problem is well summarised by Jay Ennesser of IBM:

> *I tell any small prospective partner that they need to be prepared to invest at least one million dollars upfront before IBM will take them seriously. This figure may be slightly incorrect, but if it is, it isn't out by much, and it sure focuses the smaller organisation's mind on what it's like to partner with a powerhouse like IBM.*

Case Study 3 describes how Micro Focus addressed these issues in its alliance with Accenture.

---

1   See, for example, Adrian J. Slywotzky, *Value Migration: How to Think Several Moves Ahead of the Competition*, Boston, MA: Harvard Business School Press, 1996.

Case Study 3: Accenture and Micro Focus in the UK

In 2006 Micro Focus (a UK software company with a turnover of £150 million) wanted to deepen its relationship with Accenture (a global systems integration firm based in the USA). The problem, according to Tony Hill, the UK Managing Director of Micro Focus was simple: 'We can't get on their radar. They see us as a software company with interesting software, so they come to us when they want to buy our software to help them with a deal that's going down. The problem is that by then they already have the deal in mind, so every penny they pay us comes off their margin on the business, so they are extremely aggressive in negotiating big discounts on the licences they buy. They simply won't let us "in" to a joint and equal relationship where we identify and approach the customer together.'

The solution was to look at the problem from the partner's point of view.

Typically, Micro Focus had been selling Accenture on the idea that Micro Focus's software was good and that it had the best designers of this type of software in the industry, but seeing the solution only from the Micro Focus perspective missed at least two other significant parties to the prospective alliance relationship: Accenture and the clients they served.

When Micro Focus looked at the issue from its partner's perspective, it was able to discern a different value proposition which ticked all the above boxes. The solution was migration management.

Up until the time of the alliance, the way large organisations had replaced their IT systems had been colloquially called 'rip and replace' – in other words, rip out the old stuff and replace it with the new stuff.

But that model had become increasingly unattractive to clients because of the disruption and the high business cost of hiring large teams of systems integrators (like Accenture) to rip out the old and put in the new. Consequently, systems integration firms like Accenture were finding that they had lots of traditional old-style 'rip and replace' staff unemployed, and this was a major internal cost for them.

The solution Micro Focus suggested was a 'list and shift' approach to reduce business disruption, using Micro Focus software to migrate older systems to newer platforms with less business disruption.

The idea was attractive to Accenture because it helped to explain how it would get the unemployed consultants back out working again. So attractive was it, in fact, that Accenture built specific IT migration practices within its business to accommodate the demand, and both sides developed joint and integrated offerings to provide the consultants to conduct the 'list and shift exercises successfully.

Developing identified business value propositions for the relationship

It is human nature, I suppose, to focus on the advantages and features of one's own products and/or services when considering an alliance. However, our research shows that the best alliances are those in which synergistic business value propositions are created. In such propositions, the value to three key stakeholder groups is clearly articulated:

1. the organisation initiating the alliance;
2. the selected partner;

3. the customer or consumer of the offering(s) of the alliance.

In underdog alliances it is all too easy for a smaller partner to subsume its own desires in deference to the requirements of the larger player. This would be a mistake, since it is some aspect of the smaller organisation's offerings or capabilities that the larger player wishes to leverage.

The example in Case Study 4 might make this conundrum clearer.

Case Study 4: IBM and Intentia

In 2001 IBM and Intentia (a Swedish software company) announced a strategic alliance. The partnership would deliver an integrated hardware/software offering built around Intentia's business tools. Analysts like *Computer Reseller News* suggested that the move represented IBM's latest efforts to develop integrated server offerings targeted at small and medium-sized businesses.

The integrated solution was called the IBM eServer iSeries for Intentia. The solution included a specially configured IBM eServer i270 server, WebSphere Internet e-business software and the Intentia Movex eBusiness 4.1 solutions – a set of enterprise resource planning and customer relationship management applications.

'We're trying to work with our independent software vendor partners to tie their software and our hardware together into a turnkey package,' said Kim Stevenson, Vice President of IBM eServer iSeries marketing operations. 'We want to reach small business customers by developing these customer-ready boxes, which will be much more attractive than the idea of buying the hardware and software and then spending the money for someone to do the integration and setup.'

However, not unreasonably, Intentia was, nervous about the arrangement, believing that IBM was partnering simply as an early step in a process designed to eventually buy Intentia. As one IBM executive put it to me: 'The hardest part about that relationship was that we had to start every meeting for four years stating once again that IBM had (a) no intention of buying Intentia and (b) no intention of developing competing software.'

The relationship developed well, and was valuable for both companies. Intentia helped IBM to gain market share in the Nordic market, particularly for its WebSphere software product, and IBM helped Intentia to win business beyond the boundaries of its local market (for example, in Iberia – Spain and Portugal) and to increase the average size of its proposals.

The relationship had a paradoxical conclusion, because in June 2005 Lawson Software (another IBM strategic alliance partner) announced its intention to buy Intentia. Would Lawson have bought Intentia if they weren't both already strong partners of IBM? Maybe, but the technical integration was certainly easier because they were both in the IBM partner programme, and the deal had the tacit backing of IBM, which saw further opportunities for tighter integration of a connected software suite and even more inroads into the commercially valuable small to medium-sized enterprise (SME) market in Europe.

Such examples are not limited to the high-tech business space alone, as Case Study 5 illustrates.

Case Study 5: AstraZeneca and Cambridge Antibody Technology

In November 2004 AstraZeneca (AZ) announced a strategic alliance with Cambridge Antibody Technology (CAT) to discover and develop human antibody therapeutics for inflammatory disorders.

The partnership was a five-year research and development alliance in monoclonal antibody research, principally in the field of inflammatory disorders, including respiratory diseases. AstraZeneca paid £75 million in cash for an issue of 10,217,983 new ordinary shares in CAT, representing a 19.9% shareholding.

Both parties were happy with the arrangement: 'The alliance offers an excellent balance and fit between CAT's established expertise and capabilities in monoclonal antibody generation and optimisation, together with its process technology and early clinical skills, with AstraZeneca's drug development capabilities and global market strength and representation.'

In other words, CAT had a promising compound that would plug a gap in the AZ drug portfolio, and AZ had the marketing muscle to sell the resulting product worldwide.

Sir Tom McKillop, Chief Executive of AstraZeneca, said at the time: 'I see this alliance with CAT as a major component of AstraZeneca's strategy to develop new therapeutics for inflammatory and respiratory diseases. Both partners are combining their expertise and making a significant commitment of resources to the alliance.'

Peter Chambré, Chief Executive Officer of CAT, commented: 'This innovative alliance with a world leader in the field of inflammatory diseases represents a major strategic move by both companies. Not only will it enable CAT to deploy its full range of capabilities and expertise in the early stages of product development, but it will also allow us to enhance our capabilities in the later stages and, for the first time, potentially participate in product commercialisation. Most significantly, CAT will share directly in the successes of products which result from the collaboration, and it is therefore an important and exciting opportunity for us to make a significant advance in our transition to a product-based biopharmaceutical company. The creation of this alliance with AstraZeneca is a tribute to its vision in seeing the opportunity for a new model of collaboration between a major pharmaceutical company and a leading biotechnology company.'

Dr John Patterson, Executive Vice President Product Strategy and Licensing for AstraZeneca, said: 'We are delighted to be joining other shareholders in this innovative biopharmaceutical company and are underpinning the closeness of the alliance and strategic importance to both parties by making a significant equity investment in CAT.'

However the two companies could hardly have been more dissimilar, as Table 2.1 shows.

Table 2.1   Comparison of AstraZeneca and Cambridge Antibody Technology

AstraZeneca	Cambridge Antibody Technology
AZ is a major international healthcare business engaged in the research, development, manufacture and marketing of prescription pharmaceuticals and the supply of healthcare services. It is one of the world's leading pharmaceutical companies, with healthcare sales of over $18.8 billion at the time of the alliance in 2004 and leading positions in sales of gastrointestinal, oncology, cardiovascular, neuroscience and respiratory products. AZ is listed in the Dow Jones Sustainability Index (Global) as well as the FTSE4Good Index.	CAT is a biopharmaceutical company using its proprietary technologies and capabilities in human monoclonal antibodies for drug discovery and drug development. Based near Cambridge in England, CAT currently employs around 270 people. CAT is a leader in the discovery and development of human therapeutic antibodies and has an advanced proprietary platform technology for rapidly isolating human monoclonal antibodies using phage display and ribosome display systems. CAT has extensive phage antibody libraries, currently incorporating more than 100 billion distinct antibodies. These libraries form the basis for the company's strategy to develop a portfolio of antibody-based drugs.

The alliance was a raging success, with both parties very clear about the distinct differences in their offerings and the customers and markets they were serving.

In fact, so successful was the alliance that AZ recognised the value the relationship had created and didn't want that value to fall into anyone else's hands, so in May 2005 AZ announced its intention to buy CAT outright for £702 million – which is interesting, because the BBC reported on 15 May 2006 that: 'CAT shares were trading at 796.5 pence when markets closed on Friday, meaning the firm was worth £420m. This latest transaction represents a 67% increase on that price.'

So why did AZ pay 67% above the odds for CAT? And where did the added value come from?

The answer may lie in the subsequent development of a string of successful drugs coming from the original agreement. By October 2007 AZ's strategic intentions for CAT became somewhat clearer: 'AstraZeneca is merging UK-based Cambridge Antibody Technology into MedImmune in Gaithersburg, MD as it creates a new subsidiary that will focus on the development of biologics. The move follows AstraZeneca's decision to lay off about 10 percent of CAT's workforce, including CEO Hamish Cameron and research chief Alex Duncan.

'A spokesperson for AstraZeneca told The Times that its acquisition of CAT and MedImmune has led to some redundancies at each of the two biotech companies but that no cuts were expected in their research operations. And she added that the combination of CAT and MedImmune would lead to the creation of one of the largest biotech companies in the world.'[2]

2   Source: 'AstraZeneca Merges MedImmune, CAT', *FierceBiotech*, 22 October 2007: www.fiercebiotech.com/story/astrazeneca-merges-medimmune-cat/2007-10-22 (accessed 8 April 2014).

Clearly, the original alliance with CAT featured heavily in the alliance strategy of AZ, and we will see later in the book that in successful alliances not only are the partners' day-to-day activities aligned, but so are their strategic market directions.

Convincing the larger partner that both sides should conduct a formal alliance audit once a year

This is not easy. Typically, the larger partner will have more alliances than its smaller counterpart and thus will see the exercise as an administrative burden. However, conducting a formal appraisal is crucial to the continuing health and success of the relationship.

We can see from the examples above that things change quite quickly in business life, and the factors affecting change are myriad: market conditions, economic recession/expansion, differing strategies, changing management teams, and so on.

To deal with these changes it is imperative that both teams sit down together at least once every year and review the strategic intentions of both sides so that each can reconfirm that the strategic alignment is still strong.

As can be seen from Case Study 2 above involving Ford and Firestone, if strategic alignment is lacking then it is better to redesign the alliance or even to abandon it rather than continue with a relationship with significant differences of intent.

Adopting a collaborative negotiating style

Some people erroneously consider that negotiating is something that only happens when the original alliance deal is being constructed, but this is not the case. The truth is that alliance executives are negotiating almost every day of their lives. A quick consideration of the structure of the vast majority of alliances in existence today reveals the reason for this. Remember that we said in our definition that in an alliance (as opposed to a merger or a takeover) both sides retain their own independence. This means that neither side can order the other to take any particular course of action. Both need to negotiate the outcomes they desire.

Consequently, negotiating technique is one of the most critical skills an alliance manager can develop.

When considering negotiating style, it's important to draw a distinction between adversarial negotiation and collaborative negotiation. In the adversarial style, each party will think first of 'what's best for me in this situation', while in the collaborative style they are thinking 'what's best for the relationship in this situation'. This distinction, though subtle, is important because the first style (adversarial) damages the relationship, while the latter (collaborative) enhances it.

However, non-alliance personnel may see the accommodation of one's partners' views and aspirations as a sign of weakness, and a typical phrase they use to disparage such an approach is 'going native', meaning that the alliance executive in question is favouring the partner's views and position rather more than his own company's. This charge is often a difficult one to counter because to answer it fully entails a deeper understanding of the value of the relationship and a recognition that 'what is right for the relationship is not always right for our organisation'.

An amusing technique ABP uses in its workshops to illustrate this point is to introduce the collaborative arm wrestling completion. The class is split into teams of two equally matched 'opponent' collaborators and the rules are clearly explained:

- Points are scored when the back of the hand of either party touches the table.
- Elbows cannot leave the table.
- Points must be scored sequentially by *both* parties. This means that when one hand has touched the desk, the only way for another point to be scored is if the back of the hand of the partner next touches the table.
- The winning team is the one that has scored the most points in 30 seconds.

Observing such exercises is illuminating. Even though the rules have been clearly explained and even though all the sets of two people (or teams) know that they should be acting together to beat the other teams, it still seems difficult for some people to 'allow' their hand to touch the table first.

The approach seems to be: 'I don't mind my hand touching the table, but I want the satisfaction of seeing yours touch the table first!'

When I observe this exercise in my classes, I can see some common themes:

- The more senior the executives in the teams, the less they like to be the first to concede an individual point. Indeed, in many cases I have observed two equally senior people straining every last sinew so as to not be the person to touch the table first.
- Losing teams typically try to push their team member's hand down.
- Winning teams tend to pull their team member's hand over so that they voluntarily allow their hand to touch the desk first.
- The lower the combined egos of the participants, the more successful the team.

A key implication of this for negotiating technique in alliances seems to be this: *The person who concedes first in negotiations wins!*

Indeed, I have seen experienced alliance collaborative negotiators actually look for opportunities to concede minor points in discussions as early as possible so that they can demonstrate to their partners that they have their partner's views in the forefront of their minds.

Obviously, this concession technique cannot go on for ever (or indeed, even very long) because as soon as one side concedes, it will be looking for similar concessions from the other side to establish balance in the relationship. If such a balance is not forthcoming then the conceding side needs to demonstrate strength in the discussion to avoid giving its alliance partner the impression that it is weak and will allow the partner to win on every point.

This and other similar negotiation points are made in a good book by Danny Ertel and Mark Gordon called *The Point of the Deal*,[3] in which the authors stress that the point of a deal (the point in time when the deal is struck) is not the point (or purpose) of the deal. The purpose of the deal is to negotiate a workable alliance arrangement that leads to value for both sides. So negotiating the best deal possible for one side as opposed to the

---

3   Danny Ertel and Mark Gordon. *The Point of the Deal*, Cambridge, MA: Harvard University Press, 2007.

other might in fact be counterproductive, particularly if the other side cannot live with the deal that's been agreed.

This point may seem somewhat self-evident, but it's amazing how many companies fail to take it into account in their alliance processes. Many pharmaceutical and biotech firms, for example, split their alliance functions such that one part (business development) is responsible for negotiating the deal while another function entirely (operations) is responsible for the ongoing management of the deal which has been struck.

The damage stems from what parameters are used to measure each side. The development teams are measured in terms of how many commercially advantageous deals they can create. They don't have to worry about running them afterwards. The natural consequence of this is that many alliance deals need to be painfully unpicked and rebuilt over many months, which is costly both in time lost and also in legal fees.

The better partnering organisations recognise that the teams that negotiate the deal should be the same ones that will live with the deal they have negotiated.

A good exercise to test this thinking is to arrange a two-day workshop and explain to the group being coached that the first day will be spent negotiating the deal and the second day will be spent in thinking through how the deal will be put into practice or executed.

On the first day, hand out two sets of tee-shirts to the group, one coloured red and one coloured blue, and explain to the two sets of people that the blue team is one partner and the red team is the other. Allow both teams to negotiate whatever terms they like between themselves. Then on day two insist that everyone swap tee-shirts so that the red team becomes blue and the blue team becomes red. In this way both sides will be compelled to live with the deal they have negotiated.

The results are often enlightening!

Identifying clear mutual needs

While truly mutual needs are not always necessary in alliance relationships, their presence is a powerful driver of success, as Case Study 6 shows.

Case Study 6: Unisys and Microsoft

In the mid-1990s Unisys decided that it wanted to enter a new market: the data centres (or mainframe rooms) of large corporate organisations. Accordingly, it developed a new enterprise-strength server called the ES 9000 range and prepared to go to market. Unisys allocated R&D and marketing budgets and ramped up its business development efforts to identify potential customers.

Just before it went to market, however, one bright executive spark posed an interesting question: 'This campaign is going to cost us a lot of effort and a lot of money. Is there anyone else that wants to get into this area that we could partner with to offset costs and improve our chances of success?'

Amazingly, relatively quickly they identified such a partner, a software company that had previously supplied operating systems for personal computers (PCs) and was now hungry to get into corporate clients' data centres. The prospective partner had a great brand image and lots of marketing budget and stamina for the exercise. What it didn't have was hardware to run its operating system.

The partner's name was Microsoft, and the alliance very quickly became strategic (critical for the future business direction) for both partners. In addition, it was very cost-effective for both of them.

As Irv Epstein, Senior Vice President of Unisys, put it: 'As an alliance we virtually doubled our marketing budget and manpower overnight because both companies were fully committed to doing this. But the greater size of teams and the greater degree of resources meant that we were successful far faster than we would have been otherwise.'

In this case the identification of a compatible and complementary mutual need – entry into the data centres of large corporate clients – was a powerful driver of success. Other mutual needs can be more prosaic. For example, two second-tier competitors in a market could come together to beat the number one, or more critically two organisations struggling to survive in a moribund market sector could come together to develop a new and radical business model impossible to achieve otherwise.

The example of mutual needs in Case Study 7 may help to illustrate this factor in action.

Case Study 7: Hoover and Procter & Gamble

In the latter half of the 1980s American home owners started to favour hardwood floors as opposed to carpets in their homes. This was bad news for the Hoover corporation, whose staple offering was vacuum cleaners.

The market was declining rapidly and Hoover could see that it needed to get into the hardwood floor business. But all its expertise and capability was in the vacuum cleaner industry. It had neither the expertise nor the experience to develop a hardwood floor cleaner itself.

The solution came in the form of an innovation alliance with Procter & Gamble (P&G). P&G prides itself on its ability to make a wide range of domestic cleaning products developed as a result of its deep and enduring understanding of chemical detergent production.

In the case of the approach from Hoover, P&G was able to offer a compound that had proved too astringent for an alternative application it was trialling, so in fact the alliance made use of a 'failed' product which when put into a different context became a winner.

In this case Hoover provided the mechanics of a machine that could clean hardwood floors and P&G provided the detergent to do the actual cleaning. Both parties were able to derive additional commercial sales from a 'failed' product (P&G's) and a complementary product line (Hoover's).

Such situations are by no means isolated examples, as the following selection shows:

- Philips and Douwe Egberts introduced the Senseo, the first single-cup coffee machine for household consumption, achieving immediate market penetration and dominance that has lasted to this day. In this case Philips made the machine and Douwe Egberts provided the coffee.
- Reckitt Benckiser and the Bosch Corporation recommend Calgon dishwasher cleaning tablets in all Bosch dishwashers.
- Toshiba and Wella partnered to produce a high-performance portable hair dryer for salons in the USA. This example was interesting because sales of the original Hitachi hair dryer were very poor until Wella lent its brand awareness to the product and sales rocketed.
- Philips and Biersdorf GmbH combined to produce a cordless electric shaver which also deploys Nivea skin cream as an aid to smoother shaving.

Developing a clear understanding of partner accountability on both sides

Partner accountability is an important CSF in any alliance relationship since both/all parties need to know what their partners are committed to and what they themselves are accountable for. But the situation is exacerbated when there is a large size difference between the two parties. In this situation it's very difficult for the smaller party to demand accountability from the larger player, but such clarity is important in the governance model for the effective operation of the alliance.

The solution to this dilemma lies in the concept of voluntary governance models. This means that both sides agree to be bound by some mutually agreed rules or conventions even though the rules will restrict (to some extent) the activities of either of them.

The key point to remember here is that it is the effectiveness and operability of the alliance that matters, not the freedom of action of either or both of the partners.

Risk sharing in the relationship

All alliance relationships carry some degree of risk, whether it be commercial, brand, reputation, impact on other activities or just simply the risk of failure. In the best relationships the risks are identified, then risk sharing strategies are developed to address them.

It is no coincidence that in many major pharmaceutical alliance relationships the degree of investment and expected return is split 50/50. Such a sharing of both risk and reward powerfully illustrates that both sides are sharing the risks equally.

Unfortunately, in underdog alliances this is not always the case since the degree of disparity between partner resources can be extreme. In such cases both sides should pay special attention to the allocation of risk consummate with the size and undertakings of the partner concerned. The more both sides can see that each is taking a sizeable risk (appropriate to the relative size of the organisation concerned), the better the chances for success in the alliance relationship.

Engaging senior executive support from the larger partner

Senior executive support is one of the most important of the CSFs in the best practice framework, and we will see later how its importance plays out in alliances between organisations of similar sizes. However, the problem is made even more acute when one partner is considerably larger than the other. In such cases there is a disparity between the relative roles of the senior executives in both organisations. In the smaller organisation, for example, the senior executive sponsor might be the chief executive of the company, whereas in the larger organisation it might be the divisional director of a particular unit.

It is unrealistic for the smaller organisation to expect the chief executive (or an executive board member) to spend considerable time on the relationship; but similarly, the larger organisation must demonstrate respect for the smaller partner to the extent that the relative roles and responsibilities of the executive sponsors concerned are spelled out in full. It is tempting to believe that some form of mathematical equation could be developed to match the relative importance of both sides, but in our experience this simply isn't possible and the best that both sides can hope for is an honest and open discussion of the situation, with neither side afraid to demand the most senior sponsor it can secure from its partner.

Ensuring decision making compatibility

Clearly, if the two partner organisations are of very different sizes then the decision making process in both will be vastly different. Whereas members of one partner might be able to walk down the hall to speak to the key executive stakeholders in a strategic alliance, members of the other partner might have to communicate across continents and upwards through multiple levels of management seniority.

Such a disparate pace of decision making can cause considerable problems in the relationship. Once again the answer lies in openness and honesty from the beginning. It does neither side any good (much less the relationship itself) if either party pretends that it can make binding decisions faster than is actually possible.

It is far preferable for both sides to understand the reality of the situation and be able to allocate the appropriate time for such decisions in their relationship governance model.

Managing internal and external communications

The reality of underdog alliances means that sometimes the larger organisation cannot share certain information that affects the relationship with its partner. These situations need to be handled very carefully if they are not to result in complete relationship breakdown.

For example, imagine a situation in which a small biotech company with 15 scientific staff partners with a large multinational pharmaceutical company to co-develop a compound which might (in time) prove to be a blockbuster drug in a medical field crucial to both.

On the face of it the alliance is built on strong foundations: the small biotech has developed a promising compound but doesn't have the necessary funds to take the compound through the complexities and expenses of regulatory approval; the large pharmaceutical company does have the funds available, and if the compound is successful it has a large marketing machine to offer global sales as a way to derive maximum value from the developed drug.

Now let's further assume that the alliance in question is located in the USA, with both partner teams resident in that country. It is entirely possible (and has happened more than once) that the larger company may be backing more than one horse in this particular alliance race by supporting another such relationship with very similar goals located in, let's say, Japan. It would be unreasonable (and possibly illegal) for the larger organisation to make either of the two competing partner teams (even in its own organisation) aware of the other's existence. In such a situation the problem will surface when one or the other team makes a critical breakthrough and the larger company is forced to make a decision as to which team to continue supporting.

Such situations are by no means uncommon, but they are exceedingly hard to manage in underdog alliances because an executive in the smaller partner may assume that his immediate counterpart and partnering executive knew of the competing partnership all along and was actively withholding this information.

Even if there is no other alliance relationship, large organisations make decisions that affect local alliances every day, and the job of the larger organisation alliance executive is to manage these messages carefully to ensure that the partner for whom he is responsible suffers no collateral damage as a result.

Damaging Alliance Myths that are Holding Back Progress

The *Oxford English Dictionary* defines a myth as 'a widely held but false idea'. There are a number of alliance myths or misconceptions that are holding back alliance professionals and hindering their collaboration efforts. Some of the more common ones we have found are discussed below.

COLLABORATION IS AN UNNATURAL ACT

This point of view most often leads us into a philosophical consideration of the nature of humanity itself (Is man naturally good or bad? Is he naturally disposed towards collaboration or competition?). The argument supporting this assertion is founded on the idea that since all natural resources are by definition finite, it is a 'natural' act to fight to secure a greater share of those limited resources for oneself rather than sharing them.

The answer from the ABP research appears to be that while collaboration is very difficult for some personalities, it is extremely easy (and the interaction of choice) for others. In addition, the law of scarce resources actually acts in favour of good collaboration, since successful collaborators know that they need to offer something they have a lot of (or that costs them very little) in return for something they have a little of (or that costs them a lot to obtain).

There is also a great deal of evidence from nature itself that collaboration is not just a 'natural' act, but in many instances a necessary one.

ALLIANCES ARE ABOUT PEOPLE, PURE AND SIMPLE

The essence of this view is that collaborations between companies ultimately come down to the relationship between a finite number of people, hence alliances are fundamentally concerned with whether people get along.

While it is perfectly true that chemistry is an important and catalytic element in most strategic alliances and that the Cultural dimension is important in the CSF framework, it is also evident from the research we have conducted that it is only one of many such important considerations. Furthermore, it is evident that in two relationships, both with an equally strong bond between the participants, the relationship with the added advantage of Commercial, Technical, Strategic and Operational CSFs will have a vastly enhanced chance of success.

IF THE MONEY IS GOOD ENOUGH, THEN PEOPLE WILL PRETEND TO GET ALONG

This is, in a sense, the converse argument to the one above that 'It's all about people.' Once again the answer is similar: although the money (or commercial return) is important, there are a whole host of other factors (actually, there are 51 other factors!) which can contribute to a successful relationship.

In fact, evidence from the Database strongly suggests that commercial return is an effect rather than a cause of strategic alliance success, meaning that if the underlying causes are in place (all other things being equal), then increased commercial value will flow as a natural consequence.

THERE CAN BE NO SINGLE BEST PRACTICE: ALL ALLIANCES ARE UNIQUE

It is entirely true that one cannot isolate a single CSF, or indeed a small group of CSFs, and say with any confidence that such a small group represents best practice. In addition, it is equally true to say that all alliances are different and unique in their makeup, context, results and positioning. However, statistically it is possible to identify those CSFs that feature on a regular basis in successful strategic alliances and to identify those factors in all alliances regardless of type, intent, sector or background.

The analogy is akin to that of human DNA, in that the range and complexity of individual humans is infinite, with each one being unique. However, we now know that all humans (whatever their sex, colour, physical makeup or ethnicity) are built from a common set of DNA strands. The best practice Database maintained by ABP represents a collection of the DNA strands of strategic alliances from which many types can be observed.

ALLIANCES ARE NOT 'SEXY' BUSINESS MODELS

A recent edition of *Forbes* business magazine devoted over a hundred pages to intense consideration of the alliance model, concluding with the deceptively insightful comment that 'strategic alliances are not sexy', meaning that mergers, takeovers, grabbing market share, beating the competition and so on are all phrases which are considered 'sexy' by male and female CEOs, whereas collaboration, seeing others' point of view, 'one plus one equals three' and so on are seen as aspirations of non-commercially minded people.

In our experience there is a tipping point in the understanding and deployment of strategic alliance models. If a CEO can hang in there long enough with a genuinely strategic relationship, then the long-term commercial results will justify the model's adoption. However, it is also true that those organisations that have a predominantly short-term vision for their business relationships struggle to find the stamina required to successfully adopt a strategic alliance mindset. This is reflected in those organisations that have stable senior executive teams rather than those that have a high degree of senior management turnover (success models include Microsoft, Cisco, Dell, Eli Lilly, Siebel and Starbucks, all of which have at one time or another had stable senior management teams prepared to take a longer-term view of business success).

NO ORGANISATION IS GOING TO WILLINGLY COMMIT TO A LIMITED NUMBER OF PARTNERS

The argument here is that organisations will want to deal with as many organisations as possible to give them the best chance of commercial success. However, evidence from our research suggests otherwise.

Firstly, any organisation (of whatever size) has a limited bandwidth available in terms of people, skills, technology platforms and so on, which makes dealing with more than a handful of truly strategic partners impossible.

Secondly, the act of allying with one organisation necessarily alienates that organisation from a relationship with others. This is principally the reason why 'alliance fortresses' or 'islands' are growing, with competition developing not between individual organisations, but between competing collaborations.

Finally, our research shows that the commercial benefits of a successful alliance chosen with the right partner in the right sector which has a high degree of organisational intimacy between the players outweigh the alternative benefits of allying in a non-proprietary manner with a large number of less intimate partners.

THERE ARE TOO MANY VARIABLES IN ANY COLLABORATIVE RELATIONSHIP TO ALLOW MEANINGFUL ANALYSIS

While it is true that the primary and secondary variables generated by collaborations are complex and can at times appear bewildering, organisations which have used the framework generated by the ABP research report good results which are practical, applicable, relevant and insightful.

In part this is because what the ABP framework teaches them is in sync with their intuition. This in itself is not surprising, since the research contains systematised common sense from a large number of appropriate observations, hence it would be surprising indeed if the data were not relevant and immediately practical.

PART II

Alliance Analysis

3 *Benchmarking Alliance Relationships*

There is no doubt that for many people the most pragmatic use of the alliance best practice framework is the ability it gives them to benchmark their relationships against an objective standard, answering such questions as:

1. How is the individual relationship performing?
2. What is going well?
3. What is going badly?
4. How do we compare with our industry?
5. How do we compare with best in class?
6. What would we have to do to improve?

For those organisations that benchmark their relationships regularly, additional questions can be asked and answered:

1. What is the change (good or bad) since the last benchmark?
2. What has been the commercial impact (on our bottom line) of the changes in the benchmark score?
3. What effort have we had to expend to achieve the commercial results?
4. Cost/value – was the effort worthwhile in commercial terms?

To help practitioners decide whether an alliance benchmarking programme would be useful for their organisations, this chapter discusses the following questions:

1. Why is it important to benchmark your alliance relationships?
2. What should the process of benchmarking include?
3. What should the output look like?
4. What are some of the practical issues in benchmarking alliances?
5. What are the benefits of instigating an alliance benchmarking programme?

Why is it Important to Benchmark Your Alliance Relationships?

As far back as 2002, research was conducted by Ard-Pieter de Man and Geert Duysters (both at the time at the University of Eindhoven) to assess the impact measuring alliances can have on their performance.[1] The research gave an insight into the most valuable tools alliance managers can use. Their list (in order of importance) is replicated below. Companies with alliance success rates of 60% or higher reported using these tools, whereas companies reporting success rates lower than 40% did not.

1. alliance database;
2. joint evaluation of alliances with the partner;
3. standard partner selection approach;
4. intranet – employees have access to company specific alliance resources;
5. responsibility for alliances lies with the strategy function;
6. transfer of knowledge about national differences to international alliances;
7. alliance managers exchange experiences;
8. alliance department;
9. alliance managers;
10. evaluation of individual alliances;
11. alliance metrics.

You can see that joint evaluation of alliance performance with the partner is rated as the second highest factor contributing to success (incidentally, the highest-rated factor was the existence or otherwise of an alliance database). You might also notice that the definition of the measuring process includes the phrase 'joint' – in other words, it is important to discuss and agree the scores with your partner(s) before taking any remedial action.

The reason this is important is that the process elicits the hidden areas of misalignment in the relationship, where one partner has a markedly different view of the relationship to the other. Left unattended, these areas of misalignment will damage the relationship because both/all parties will have a different view of what constitutes reality.

An example might help to make this clearer. Imagine that two partners agree to assess their alliance relationship and that they both agree that trust will be an important criterion in this measurement process. What happens if one partner scores trust as high (let's say 80/100) and the other scores trust low (let's say 15/100). The reality is that without an objective assessment of the factor, both partners might assume that the other sees the relationship as they do, in which case in the present circumstance one partner is sharing information openly and trusting the other partner's attitudes and behaviours, while the other is more suspicious and is not sharing anything like as much information with the trusting partner.

In such a situation the relationship will progress at the pace of the lesser score. What is required is a process by which both parties agree to make public their feelings and discuss the implications of the widely differing scores. Indeed, this is the first stage in assessing benchmark scores that ABP would recommend (see later in this chapter).

Should any further evidence that benchmarking is important be necessary, a cursory examination of the literature available on the Internet shows without doubt that benchmarking is an important tool in an ongoing business improvement programme.

---

1   Ard-Pieter de Man and Geert Duysters, with the assistance of Koen Heimeriks, 'The State of Alliance Management: The Effect of Alliance Management Tools and Processes on Alliance Success', presentation to ASAP Summit Chicago, 11–13 March 2002: www.duysters.com/downloads%20presentations/ASAPpresentation02.pdf (accessed 8 April 2014).

Also referred to as 'best practice benchmarking' or 'process benchmarking', this process is used in management, and particularly strategic management, in which organisations evaluate various aspects of their processes in relation to best practice companies' processes, usually within a peer group defined for the purposes of comparison. This then allows organisations to develop plans for how to make improvements or adapt specific best practices, usually with the aim of increasing some aspect of performance. Benchmarking may be a one-off event, but is often treated as a continuous process in which organisations continually seek to improve their practices.

In 2008 The Global Benchmarking Network, a network of benchmarking centres representing 22 countries, commissioned a comprehensive survey on benchmarking. Over 450 organisations from over forty countries responded. The results showed that:

1. Of 20 improvement tools, mission and vision statements and customer (client) surveys were the most frequently used (by 77% of organisations), followed by SWOT analysis (72%) and informal benchmarking (68%). Performance benchmarking was used by 49% and best practice benchmarking by 39%.
2. The tools that were likely to increase in popularity the most over the next three years were performance benchmarking, informal benchmarking, SWOT analysis and best practice benchmarking. Over 60% of organisations that were not currently using these tools indicated they were likely to use them over the next three years.

There seems little doubt, then, that benchmarking processes and performance in general business areas is a beneficial action that leads to improved performance. ABP's contention is that the same applies in the alliance management field, and that companies should benchmark their relationships regularly (at least once a year).

What Should the Process of Benchmarking Include?

If we agree that benchmarking our alliances is a beneficial and productive exercise to complete, then naturally our attention as practitioners turns to the question, 'How should we design and execute the benchmarking exercise?'

There is no single benchmarking process that has been universally adopted. The wide appeal and acceptance of benchmarking has led to the emergence of a variety of benchmarking methodologies. One seminal book is Robert Boxwell Jr's *Benchmarking for Competitive Advantage*.[2] Robert Camp (who wrote one of the earliest books on benchmarking in 1989[3]) developed a 12-stage approach to benchmarking:

1. Select the subject.
2. Define the process.
3. Identify potential partners.
4. Identify data sources.
5. Collect data and select partners.

---

2   Robert J. Boxwell Jr, *Benchmarking for Competitive Advantage*, New York: McGraw-Hill, 1994.

3   Robert Camp, *The Search for Industry Best Practices that Lead to Superior Performance*, New York: Productivity Press, 1989.

6. Determine the gap.
7. Establish process differences.
8. Target future performance.
9. Communicate.
10. Adjust the goals.
11. Implement.
12. Review and recalibrate.

Looking at the list above, you can see that it represents a considerable effort on the part of individual organisations. This is why they turn to the ABP Database, in which steps 1, 2, 4, 5 and 6 have already been determined for them.

Looking at the list above also helps to highlight the distinction between conducting healthchecks and conducting benchmarks. Most organisations that are reasonably serious about conducting alliance programmes will perform some form of regular healthcheck of their alliances, but the critical factor in benchmarking is the capture and collation of external performance data – something that is very difficult for individual companies to accomplish.

Let's now consider how the alliance best practice benchmarking process works with reference to the standard process identified above.

1. SELECT SUBJECT

This is relatively easy because the subject is the alliance relationship in question. However, care must be exercised here to determine with clarity what is the agreed scope of the relationship. For example, many organisations have alliance relationships in place in multiple geographic locations or individual countries; while it is possible to conduct a global benchmark for the relationship, the results are generally less valuable than conducting a benchmark country-by-country. This is because the particular aspects of the relationship under review will vary dramatically from country to country.

2. DEFINE THE PROCESS

Again, this is relatively easy if the company is using the ABP approach, in which case the process is as follows:

a) Decide the scope.
b) Decide the key stakeholders to provide data from both/all sides of the relationship.
c) Decide the range of CSFs to be measured.
d) Capture the data, either by interview or online questionnaires.
e) Benchmark the results against the ABP Database.
f) Produce the benchmarking report.

3. IDENTIFY POTENTIAL PARTNERS

This should be simplicity itself, because presumably the exercise is being conducted partnership-by-partnership.

4. IDENTIFY DATA SOURCES

The identification of suitable data sources is important in order to capture balanced data. It is likely that the data will be captured at three levels: Strategic, Managerial and Operational.

5. COLLECT DATA AND SELECT PARTNERS

This can be done either online or by telephone or face-to-face interviews. Face-to-face interviews usually provide the highest-quality data but take the longest (and are therefore more costly), whereas online data capture is quick and easy (but note that interviewees completing online questionnaires may need guidance in advance to help them understand the answering process).

6. DETERMINE THE GAP

This gap represents the difference in scores between the relationship in question and the comparator set (either industry best in class or world class).

7. ESTABLISH PROCESS DIFFERENCES

This step involves a deeper understanding of 'What is the comparator doing that we are not doing to achieve such higher scores?'

8. TARGET FUTURE PERFORMANCE

Given a good understanding of current resources and the ability to deploy those resources, it should be possible to target certain performance improvements and to plan accordingly. Obviously, the lower the relative score, the greater the degree of possible improvement.

9. COMMUNICATE

Communication should involve the whole team completing the benchmark questionnaire and those affected by the proposed improvement actions. A useful additional tool here is the RACI process or RACI charting.

10. ADJUST THE GOALS

Obviously, part of the benchmarking process involves adaptation for future improvement, so this stage identifies and documents clear goals that both sides will strive to achieve. Clearly, these goals may need adjustment if they are either (a) achieved or (b) prove too difficult to achieve.

11. IMPLEMENT

In the benchmarking context, this means that the new approach or process to the CSF in question needs to be incorporated into the working practices of the relationship in question.

12. REVIEW AND RECALIBRATE

Although companies don't always conduct benchmarking exercises on an ongoing basis (usually annually), there is evidence that it would be a beneficial to do so. In essence, this creates a continuous improvement process that continually improves alliance performance and focuses annually on the lesser-performing areas.

A NOTE ON SCORING

Obviously the accuracy of the scoring in benchmarks is extremely important. In the ABP scoring model, scores are allocated from '0 = Not in existence, zero, none' and so on to '100 = Perfection'. We have found that scoring in such a way allows individuals to exercise suitable sophistication and nuance between different aspects of the issue in question which is missing in more simplistic scoring systems (for example, '1–5' or 'Totally Unsatisfactory–Fully Satisfactory').

Giving interviewees a set of texts to represent each of the scores also improves the objectivity of the scoring.

Finally, it is useful to have some way of assessing data integrity in the scores posted (it would be useful, for example, to know whether the benchmark questionnaire was completed in 30 minutes or three minutes!).

The ABP system incorporates a series of data validation techniques to identify a data integrity score. This score represents the degree to which the organisation can rely on the data captured, and is usually expressed as a number adjacent to 100%. So, for example, a score of 100% data accuracy (somewhat unlikely) indicates that there is no conflict in any of the answers given. A score of 85% data integrity indicates that some answers may be questionable based on a comparison with a paired set of control questions in the questionnaire. Experience has shown us that data with a score of greater than 80% can reliably be used for key decisions.

For an example of an ABP benchmarking questionnaire, see Appendix 6, 'Useful Additional Resources'.

What Should the Output Look Like?

We at ABP believe that to be useful, a measuring process (and set of questions) should:

- be holistic and integrated, representing all aspects of the relationship;
- be simple to understand (intuitive);
- provide striking insights;
- reflect multiple dimensions of the relationship;
- reflect both/all sides' views;

- be objective and numeric;
- be rigorously researched;
- be applicable to action planning;
- be capable of being used for benchmarking;
- enable action to be taken linked to the insights;
- be simple to operate;
- encourage involvement and commitment from all key stakeholders;
- be amenable to regular refreshing.

As a consequence, we have designed our most common output graph to demonstrate benchmark findings as shown in Figure 3.1.

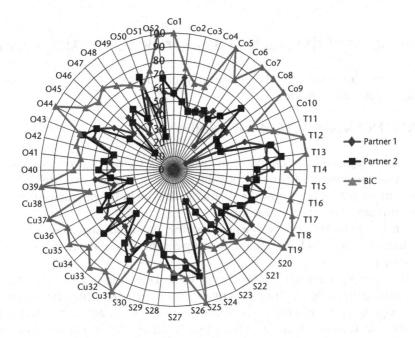

Figure 3.1   Example of an ABP benchmarking chart

The chart can be produced simply enough using Microsoft's Excel program, and it is commonly known as a spider chart or spider diagram due to its resemblance to a spider's web.

What the chart shows is the 52 common success factors measured on a scale of 0–100, with 0 at the centre and 100 at the outer rim.

The different dimensions of the benchmark are shown by the coding letter:

- Co = Commercial
- T = Technical
- S = Strategic
- Cu = Cultural
- O = Operational.

The two lines show the scores of two partners in the same relationship, with the areas of alignment and misalignment clearly identifiable. The third outer line shows a chosen comparator assessment from the Database which represents best in class for that particular industry (the best example of an alliance type which is most closely comparable to the relationship under examination in the ABP Database).

Areas for potential improvement can be clearly seen, and improvement action plans can focus on one or more of the five dimensions, or could incorporate a range of the factors involved.

In practice, teams looking to develop improvement action plans would typically focus on the lower-scoring areas first.

For a full example of a typical ABP benchmarking report, please see Appendix 6, 'Additional Useful Resources'.

What are Some of the Practical Issues in Benchmarking Alliances?

A number of practical issues, challenges or questions usually arise when conducting an alliance benchmarking exercise.

CAN YOU BENCHMARK ACROSS INDUSTRIES?

One of the advantages of benchmarking alliances to a set series of predetermined criteria is that comparison across industries is possible. Thus an alliance executive in the high-tech sector can learn a lot from how his alliance colleague in the pharmaceutical industry establishes and develops trust, for example.

But care needs to be exercised when looking cross-industry because (of course) industry characteristics will have a major bearing on the appropriateness or otherwise of the comparison.

Take, for example, common success factor Co2, 'Due diligence'. This is the method by which organisations pick their prospective alliance partners; while the process is valid in both the high-tech and pharmaceutical business sectors, the actual conduct of the due diligence exercise, the complexity and the length of time it takes will vary dramatically.

THE DEBATE BETWEEN SUBJECTIVE AND OBJECTIVE

A common discussion point that arises when conducting a benchmarking exercise is the distinction between subjective and objective data capture. Detractors of the approach will claim that all the results are ultimately based on subjective data, and are thus flawed.

While it is true that the data captured are necessarily subjective (they are the individual views of the interviewees on which the assessments are based), it's not fair to say that the process is not objective. The inclusion of clear scoring guidelines and the request for examples of the behaviour, process, task or approach being examined mean that in practice the results are usually seen as valid and representative by the vast majority of interviewees who take part in these exercises.

Another important consideration in this area is encompassed by the phrase 'perception is reality' – this means that even though one partner might feel that a particular common success factor scores highly, if the other partner does not, then that partner will act accordingly and the lower score is 'the truth' as far as the second partner is concerned. This is a very important insight into managing alliance relationships, and alliance executives should be aware of its existence at all times. It is not enough to be doing a good job; your partner needs to *feel* that you are doing a good job.

IS THERE ANY INDUSTRY STANDARD DATA THAT CAN BE USED FOR COMPARISON PURPOSES?

This is a question clients frequently ask, the idea being that in the fast-moving consumer goods business sector the 'correct' or usual score for 'business-to-business alignment' is 65/100.

Unfortunately, it is almost impossible to create industry standard scores because the range of variable factors affecting the outcome is so broad. For example, it can encompass:

- the type of alliance concerned;
- the stage the alliance has reached;
- the relative maturity of both partnering organisations;
- the economic climate in the industry sector in question;
- the prime purpose of the alliance;
- the collaboration skills of the executives involved on both sides;
- the degree of senior executive support on both sides;
- the existence (or otherwise) of dedicated resources for the alliance;
- the degree of trust that is present in the relationship.

However, certain average scores can be identified for sectors as a whole for certain common success factors, which gives companies an opportunity to match their internal scores against industry standards, while also giving them insights into alliance maturity as expressed in that relationship.

WHAT SHOULD WE BENCHMARK AGAINST?

Another common question that clients ask is: 'Who or what should we benchmark our alliances against?' This question is easier to answer. An appropriate comparator set would be a group of alliances with the following characteristics:

- The alliances should be in your business sector.
- The prime purpose of the alliances should be the same as yours (for example, business development, growth, innovation or cost reduction).
- The alliances should be of a similar size and complexity to your own.
- The alliance set you use for comparison should include examples that are both better and worse than your situation.
- The alliances you use for comparison should be in the same geographic location or country, or at least the same region (for example, Asia-Pacific, the Americas, Africa, Latin America, Far East or Middle East).

4 *Organisational Alliance Maturity*

Is There Such a Thing as Organisational Alliance Maturity?

During the course of our work in identifying common success factors in individual alliance relationships we examined very many organisations. As a result we identified what appeared to be a repeating pattern of organisational attitudes to partnering. These stages will be examined in more detail in Chapter 15, but to summarise, we observed the following stages in what we came to call 'alliance maturity':

- **Stage I** – opportunistic
- **Stage II** – systematic
- **Stage III** – endemic.

All the organisations we have worked with appear to have progressed through each of the above three stages (although, to be sure, not all at the same pace).

Organisations typically (in our opinion) do not start out with a collaborative strategy in mind. Rather, they spot market opportunities that they can't secure alone (for example, through lack of skills, market knowledge, suitable products or services). Consequently, they partner with another company to take advantage of the opportunity. The situation is seen as a one-off initiative, so no deep systems or procedural thinking are required.

However, over time these individual collaborations grow, and at some point a senior executive in the organisation (typically from audit or the operations field) recognises that there is now a considerable amount of business the company is transacting which is 'off the books' – it is not entirely under the control of the organisation in question.

At this point, senior management begin efforts to systematise the instigation and operation of these relationships to exert a more predictable degree of control over them. Just like any other important business mega-process (for example, sales, marketing, human resources or auditing), a degree of systematisation is required, both to gain control and to produce more predictable (and better performance) results.

Organisations that invest suitably in these alliance systematisation programmes discover that business-to-business collaboration is a powerful and very cost-effective model when conducted correctly, thus some (though by no means all) move on to the final stage, which we call 'endemic'. In this stage the organisation has become good at partnering, or to put it another way, the organisation has developed partnering as an organisational competence.

As a development of our work with individual relationships, we started (approximately five years ago) to conduct alliance maturity assessments with a similar scoring system (0–100).

We noticed that organisations that were in the opportunistic phase typically scored 0–25 on their individual alliance relationships, organisations in the systematic phase scored 25–75, and organisations that scored 75–100 exhibited all the attributes of an alliance endemic organisation because they had established partnering as an organisational competence.

The next stage in the development of what we came to call the Alliance Maturity Model (AMM™) was the development of a series of questions taken from our earlier observations which seemed to us to indicate degrees of advancement in an organisation's approach to partnering.

Finally, we codified our questions into categories and constructed a thematic model of alliance maturity based on the earlier and well-respected Business Excellence Model which later became the foundation of the European Foundation for Quality Management.[1] We called this the Alliance Excellence Model, and used it as a way of explaining to businessmen the critical interaction between *alliance capability* (those things the organisation can put in place to improve the partnering process) and *alliance performance* (the results achieved from individual alliance relationships).

Later in this chapter we will discuss the Alliance Excellence Model in more detail, since we believe it is a key contribution to the partnering literature and gives organisations the ability to understand the partnering journey (from opportunistic to endemic) on which some of them are set.

We at Alliance Best Practice believe that there is such a thing as *alliance maturity*. We believe that it can be measured objectively with a score of 0–100, and we believe that it is useful to companies by allowing them to objectively assess their current position and the success strategies (drawn from others who have made the journey) to take them to where they want to go in the quickest and most efficient manner possible.

So let's move on to a consideration of the process of determining an organisation's alliance maturity and the practical implications of conducting such an exercise.

How Should You Construct an AMM™ Benchmark, and What are the Practical Challenges and Implications?

Clearly, as in any benchmarking exercise, what is required in the first instance is a set of benchmarking questions and a model so that practitioners can understand what they are building.

For a full set of AMM™ model questions, see Appendix 6, 'Useful Additional Resources'. These questions apply directly to the Alliance Excellence Model as developed by ABP (see Table 4.1).

---

1   See www.efqm.org.

Table 4.1   The Alliance Excellence Model

Alliance capability			Alliance performance	
1. Strategy	**2. Resources**	**3. Processes**	**4. Metrics**	**5. Results**
Leadership	People	Alliance processes	Commercial	Key performance business results
	Procedures		Technical	
	Programme		Strategic	
	Products		Cultural	
	Platform		Operational	
Internal benchmarking on an ongoing basis: continuous improvement cycle				
Alliance Maturity Model (AMM™)			Alliance Best Practice Index (ABPI™)	
External benchmarking: Alliance Best Practice Database (ABPD™)				

Before we examine each section of the model in turn, it may be worth making some general observations about the model itself and its structure:

- Developing alliance excellence should be approached in numerical order, as illustrated in Table 4.1:
  1. Identify and confirm organisational leadership.
  2. Identify suitable resources.
  3. Develop appropriate alliance processes.
  4. Design measurement systems – key metrics.
  5. Identify resultant business performance outcomes.
- The model is holistic – investment in one aspect of the model alone (for example, training) will not deliver the goal of organisational alliance competence.
- Individual alliance managers need ongoing support to produce the best results. All too often we in ABP see situations in which senior executives believe that individuals can do a good job with no resources. They are not given adequate job descriptions, they are given no overview of what is to be achieved, they are not allowed any suitable training, and so on. Indeed, it is a miracle that in these cases any progress is made at all!
- Building corporate capability is essential to delivering positive results. While an organisation may enjoy a brief period of good opportunistic results, in reality sustainable improvement and commercial competitive advantage relies on an ongoing programme of support in all five of the areas identified above.
- The achievement of a defined level of alliance capability will normally take two or three years. Many senior executives seem to think that alliance excellence can be achieved in a matter of months. This is not the case. It usually takes anything from 18 to 36 months to achieve progress from one level of alliance maturity to the next (for example, opportunistic to systematic), and progress becomes harder as results increase.
- In our view, relatively few companies worldwide can truly claim to have developed a high level of corporate alliance competence. Consequently, the achievement of a high level in this area will deliver considerable competitive business advantage.

1. IDENTIFY AND CONFIRM ORGANISATIONAL LEADERSHIP

Developing an alliance excellence programme or simply deciding to be better at organisational partnering starts at the top of the organisation with 'leadership'. It is not sufficient for the senior executives in the executive management team to pay lip service to the idea of collaborating with alliance partners; they must truly believe that partnering is essential to the success of the organisation.

To be fair, this is in large measure now happening worldwide. The stresses of the global recession and the increasing complexity and speed to market of new products and services mean that most senior executives concede that they can't go it alone and that they need powerful partners in order to be successful.

However, many executives still believe that simply signing the deal will mean that revenue will flow; they don't seem to understand that relationships need to be managed and that they need support from the very top levels of the organisation.

Organisations which have a history of partnering and have realised this lesson for themselves typically have formal structures in which senior executives become the sponsors of selected relationships. Examples include IBM, Capgemini, CSC, Microsoft, GSK, Eli Lilly, AstraZeneca, Rolls-Royce, Star Alliance and Starbucks.

Despite this obvious attention at or near board level, many organisations are content to view this area as one in which individual passion and attention will suffice. This is not the case, and ABP suggests that the following categories of leadership should be investigated, and if absent, created.

1A: Attitude

Serious thought should be given to assessing the attitude of senior executives to ensure that they are comfortable with the concept of collaboration and don't just see it as a 'kiss to kill' strategy.

1B: Commitment

You should point out to senior executive sponsors that the role of partner sponsor will demand a degree of planned and pragmatic effort as opposed to the usual situation of 'I was in your hometown so I thought I'd pay you a visit.' What is required is a planned series of senior executive meetings (at least once if not twice a year) to allow the partner sponsors to fully understand and be briefed on a whole range of their partner's strategic intentions: new products in the pipeline, attitude to common problems, expansion retraction in geographic areas, and so on.

1C: Guidance

All too often senior executives are expected to know what to do *because* they are senior executives. This is certainly not the case in the area of strategic alliances. Many business schools are now developing senior leadership programmes in which guidance in organisational partnering and the skills required to perform the activity well are playing a large part.

1D: Structure

Where the function of partnering and alliances is located in an organisation is an important consideration, and much can be understood from its placement. Is it located in the corporate strategy division? If so, is it seen as an inconsequential corporate function that has no bearing on business results? Or is it perhaps located in the procurement division, because obviously it concerns getting the most out of one's suppliers? Or is it located in sales because, after all, that's what the bottom line is? In reality, the decision as to where to locate the partnering and alliances function is a complex one and differs from industry to industry, reflecting the key purpose of alliances in a particular industry. In high-tech, for example, it is usually located in sales because that is its purpose. In the pharmaceutical and biotech sector it usually finds itself in R&D because its purpose is to source new products, compounds and other assets that may become drugs of the future.

Wherever the function is located, it is important that despite its relatively small size (very few multinational organisations will have more than a couple of hundred alliance managers worldwide) it is treated with the importance its capability demands.

Perhaps a brief example will make this point more clearly. At an alliance congress some years ago I was talking to the global head of alliances (at that time) of Cisco. He said that Cisco was keen to understand how effective and cost-efficient the company's sales force was. As a consequence, Cisco conducted an exercise in which it divided the amount of gross sales by the number of salesmen to arrive at an average 'sales per salesman' figure. The figure produced was in the multiple hundreds of thousands of US dollars, so the organisation was content. In other words, Cisco's salesmen were bringing in more monetary value in new sales than it was paying them, so the cost/value equation was favourable.

Cisco's head of alliances thought this was a great idea, so he conducted a similar exercise for alliance sales. He took all agreed alliance sales and divided the figure by the number of alliance managers in the company. He was careful to exclude direct sales which had already been counted in the earlier exercise. He was equally careful to count only those deals which had been brought to Cisco by partners, not those that had been created by the Cisco marketing function. The result was that average alliance sales were over US$4.3 million per alliance manager.

'Wow, that's fantastic!' I said. 'This will obviously mean that you'll be allowed to recruit more alliance managers and grow the alliances function worldwide. At last the alliances function will assume its true position as a major value creator for Cisco.'

'No,' he said. 'That's not going to happen, I'm afraid. You see, the problem is that no one believes the figures.'

To this day I am convinced that this is a major problem in many organisations – they truly don't understand the incredible amount of 'introduced' or partner-driven value being created by a handful of hardy alliance management souls in their organisations. As a result, the function of alliance management is very often relegated to the second tier of functions and excluded from the major decision making bodies of most large enterprises (the board).

If you are in any doubt, simply ask yourself the following question. You'll have heard of the chief executive officer (CEO) and chief financial officer (CFO); you'll have even heard of the chief marketing officer (CMO), but have you ever heard an organisation appoint a chief alliance officer (CAO)? Yet all the company literature trumpets that fact that 'alliances are key to our survival' and 'we need to be the partner of choice in our selected sector'.

1E: Global/regional interaction

Finally, the question of global and regional interaction comes to the fore as a challenge for organisations. We may agree that alliances are important and therefore need to be at or near to the seat of decision making power in the organisation, which usually means head office. However, in most multinationals budgetary control is devolved to country level. Let's imagine how this challenging scenario might play out.

A large software company with substantial business worldwide targets a systems integration business as a key partner. Discussions take place at the highest level of both companies, and a global enterprise agreement is signed which states that each will become the preferred partner of the other.

Many hundreds of thousands (if not millions) of dollars are spent in marketing the alliance relationship and developing new joint products and services which will be sold to the market.

The relationship is passed down to individual countries, and country general managers are asked to work with the preferred partner in their local regions. What could be simpler? The local managers just get on with establishing the new relationships, right?

Wrong! The local managers already have systems integrator relationships in place and they are not the preferred partner, so they carry on using their local favourites. The alliance 'strategy' (of who to partner with) is effectively being formulated at the local level and is fragmented into hundreds of partners worldwide.

When the global head of alliances visits a local country manager and demands to know why he is not working with the preferred supplier, the local manager says: 'Because I don't want to!' And because the country manager doesn't report to the head of alliances, there is no effective governance or control.

If you wish, you can also play this scenario out in reverse, which is equally damaging.

A global command and control consultancy, systems integration and outsourcing business decides in its head office (in the USA) that it will partner with a preferred software partner worldwide. This partner is one which the company has done lots of business with over the last ten years and has built up a large and extremely valuable relationship in the USA. As a consequence, it sends out an edict to local country managers that they now need to use this software company rather than local players. The result is a string of painful emails back to head office:

'The American model won't work in Europe.'

'That software company doesn't have any representation in my country.'

'I don't like that software company. A couple of years ago they cut us out of a really big deal.'

And so on and so forth – an endless stream of increasingly vituperative missives complaining about the newly selected partner.

In truth, the problem is a difficult one, and it requires very careful thought and a high degree of communication to solve. The ideal, of course, would be a combination of both approaches, but as many senior executives have found, very often the compromise middle ground of a little bit of both is the killing ground of indifferent performance.

This is recognised by the old adage, 'Better an imperfect strategy executed with conviction than a perfect strategy executed with confusion.'

2. IDENTIFY SUITABLE RESOURCES

If the organisation has generated the right kind of senior executive support in the leadership section, the second area it should turn its attention to is resources. It is surprising how few companies have a really good set of alliance resources for their staff to use.

If you are in any doubt about this, just ask yourself these questions about your own company or a company you know well:

- Is an alliance manager training programme available?
- Is there a data store of useful template documents that alliance managers can use when they are negotiating the relationship?
- Are there set procedures for how certain activities will be accomplished (for example, alliance meetings, reviews, partner promotions and demotions)?
- Is there an alliance programme with clear subsidiary projects to achieve the goals of the Alliance Excellence Model?
- Is there a partner relationship management technical platform that allows alliance activity, successes and sales to be logged effectively?

Very few (if any) organisations can boast such a full set of alliance resources that are easily available to their alliance managers.

3. DEVELOP APPROPRIATE ALLIANCE PROCESSES

Similar to the above point regarding resources, many organisations do not have defined alliance processes that managers can use to conduct day-to-day alliance business efficiently. Examples of such processes include:

- partner selection and due diligence checking;
- partner recruitment and onboarding;
- partner segmentation;
- knowledge exchange between alliance managers in the organisation;
- partner/alliance healthchecks;
- relationship reviews and optimisation;
- partner promotion and/or demotion or exit strategies.

4. DESIGN MEASUREMENT SYSTEMS – KEY METRICS

The issue of key metrics is covered extensively elsewhere in this book, so I don't intend to go into detail here. Suffice to say that when measuring alliances it is not just about the money alone – there are a number of factors which need to be taken into account to develop a balanced and effective alliance scorecard. In the ABP model these are based around the five critical dimensions of common success factors: Commercial, Technical, Strategic, Cultural and Operational.

5. IDENTIFY RESULTANT BUSINESS OUTCOMES

Finally, it must always be borne in mind that the reason the organisation is devoting effort to building an alliance excellence programme is because it feels that this is a cost-effective and necessary thing to do, so it is imperative that the alliance metrics measured in Section 4 of this model are equated and correlated with the key business metrics in Section 5. Organisations will obviously have their own key metrics which are important to them and in many senses help define the organisation, but here are some examples of benchmarking issues which can help to achieve this:

- **5A** – gross partner revenues;
- **5B** – partner of choice statistics;
- **5C** – cost of alliance sales;
- **5D** – cost/value ratios;
- alliance excellence programme milestones.

Do Mature Organisations Perform Better?

There is clear evidence in the Alliance Best Practice Database that mature organisations (those organisations scoring higher on the AMM™) perform better. This conclusion is further supported by additional research from elsewhere, most notably in the recent report *The State of Alliance Management: Past Present and Future* by Geert Duysters.[2] In addition to many other valuable insights, this report drew the following conclusions:

- Companies continue to differ widely in their alliance success rates – there is a considerable performance gap between high- and low-performing companies.
- Companies that invest more in alliance management perform better than those that think they can economise by scaling back their involvement in alliance management.
- Even though alliance success rates have increased, the proliferation of management tools has not completely closed the performance gap, indicating that other elements are relevant as well. Alliance culture (that is, maturity) may be one of those elements.

There is a clear connection between the concept of alliance maturity and common success factor Cu32, 'Collaborative corporate mindset'. What Cu32 is measuring is the desire of the organisation to enter into collaborative relationships. What alliance maturity is measuring is the degree, depth and sophistication of the organisation's attitude to partnering.

These results can be visualised as shown in Figure 4.1, which shows a number of organisations in the ABP Database at various stages of alliance maturity. As can be seen, the three conceptual stages of Opportunistic, Systematic and Endemic are also represented by various bandings in the scoring chart.

---

2   Geert Duysters, *The State of Alliance Management: Past Present and Future*, Eindhoven: Brabant Center of Entrepreneurship, 2012.

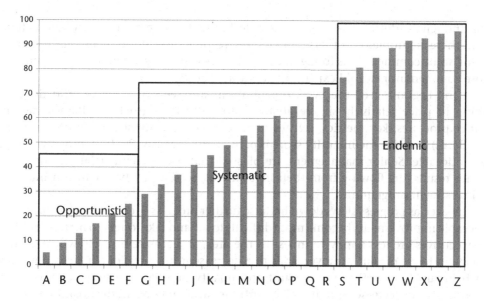

Figure 4.1   The three stages of alliance maturity

We hope that with a growing number of entries in the Database, we can offer increasingly sophisticated advice to participants regarding the 'correct' strategy to employ to make progress.

Clearly, a journey from a score of, say, 20 to 40 is not the same as a journey from 60 to 80. In the former case, certain basics are not yet in place, while in the latter the basics are all present but further attention needs to be paid to the more sophisticated aspects of collaborative management.

What Does the Future Hold for Alliance Maturity Management?

One of the interesting aspects of organisational alliance maturity we have observed is that it is not a static factor, but rather a dynamic one that fluctuates in response to internal and external pressures.

There are many examples of organisations that have developed advanced alliance partnering capabilities only to lose them through a period of inattention brought on by a series of commercial results that are less favourable than expected.

Nortel in Europe was a good example of this during the last decade. Previously, Nortel had built up a large and sophisticated central alliance function supported by a wealth of appropriate materials and a well-trained alliance management team. However, as the commercial challenges it faced increased, Nortel divested itself of these resources in a series of forced redundancies in a vain attempt to stave off Chapter 11 proceedings under the US Bankruptcy Code. As it turned out, these efforts were ultimately futile, but the damage done to the partnering capability of the organisation was severe. In many cases, individuals with enhanced partnering skills left the organisation, never to be replaced, and because there was no one there to manage and maintain them, the alliance processes themselves fell into disrepair and ultimate extinction.

Although Nortel is an extreme example brought about by a cataclysmic external event, there are numerous others of a kind of creeping dissolution of alliance capability, leading some commentators to suggest that alliance capability is a cyclical phenomenon. Those commentators would explain the cycle as follows.

At the beginning of the cycle organisations are keen to improve, and do so by putting in place relatively simple alliance capability tools (such as alliance training, alliance processes, key metrics, centres of excellence, and investment in processes and procedures). Because the maturity score is particularly low (say, 20/100), progress is rapid and noticeable. Senior management are pleased that better commercial returns (better alliance results) are flowing from their investments, so they are happy to continue with the investment programmes.

However, as progress slows down because further progress becomes harder and harder, noticeable improvements become more difficult to see and take longer to materialise. Now the executives are less happy to invest in the area, and seek returns elsewhere. Natural wastage in terms of staff turnover leads to a decrease in the level of alliance knowledge, which in turn means that the amount and quality of alliance insights in the central knowledge store decrease, and the cycle continues until once again the organisation finds itself back where it started on the journey in the first place.

Although this cycle takes a number of years to run its course (typically five to seven years), ABP has noticed it in a number of companies with which it has worked, notably IBM, Microsoft, SAP, Oracle, GSK, AstraZeneca, Starbucks and Eli Lilly. Given the obvious importance organisations place on collaborative partnering in the future, it is strange that these organisations did not stick to their guns and continue with progressive and ever-increasing best practice partnering programmes. It may be that such a cycle of boom and bust is inevitable; however, our observation is that many of the organisations with which we have worked have faced significant and severe external pressures that had nothing to do with their desire to partner effectively, but did lead them to compromise (through cost reduction) on the efforts they devoted to their partnering programmes.

It would be an interesting exercise to identify a relatively mature and large organisation in a stable market sector and analyse its alliance maturity scores over an extended period to see once and for all whether the boom and bust cycle is as inevitable as a number of commentators believe.

Despite the nature of the alliance maturity cycle discussed above, there seems little doubt that in future organisations will devote more effort to developing their alliance programmes and will look to external research, certification and benchmarking organisations to help them clarify, quantify and improve their organisational partnering competence. There will be more detailed discussion of this point in later chapters, but for now suffice to say that industry associations like ASAP and government-supported initiatives like BS 11000 on business collaborative relationships are driving a higher degree of professionalism in this area of management science.

5 *Alliance Optimisation*

Can an Alliance be Optimised?

Let us state from the very beginning that we in Alliance Best Practice believe very strongly (even passionately!) that alliance relationships can be optimised. What we mean by 'optimised' is that the alliance is performing well in two ways:

1. **Alliance effectiveness** – It is focusing on the right things (the correct combination of CSFs).
2. **Alliance efficiency** – It is performing those selected things very well.

Our contention is that a relationship is optimised when both of these factors are present to the highest degree possible given the available resources.

The concept of alliance optimisation is very closely allied to that of alliance benchmarking. Indeed, one could argue that benchmarking is the essential first step in an alliance optimisation exercise. But what exactly do we mean by 'optimisation', and how do we tell whether it has been achieved?

By now you will not be surprised to discover that in ABP's terms, optimisation relates to the existence or otherwise of a defined set of common success factors in successful collaborative relationships. Put simply, the more suitable CSFs are present and operating at maximum efficiency, the higher the level of optimisation in the relationship.

The level of operating efficiency of each CSF is measured on a scale of 0–100 which measures how well the CSF is operating (see Table 5.1).

Table 5.1   Scoring the common success factors

0	25	50	75	100
None	**Somewhat**	**Moderate**	**Very**	**Maximum**
The CSF is not in existence.	The CSF exists and is operating at a low level.	The CSF is in existence and is operating with a moderate degree of success.	The CSF is operating well.	The CSF is operating at maximum efficiency.

The scores are captured by interviewing three representative views of the alliance on each/all sides at the strategic, managerial and operational levels. A valid score is a number between 0 and 100 that ends in a 0 or a 5. Thus, for example, scores of 5, 25, 50, 70, 85 or 90 are acceptable, while scores of 21, 32, 43 or 54 are not acceptable.

This allows interviewees to place an individual CSF between two points on the scale. So, for example, they may say that trust is present in the alliance (effectiveness), and when asked how high a level of trust exists (efficiency), they may answer that it is somewhere between moderate and very high. When pushed further, they may say that it is closer to very high than moderate, so by a process of elimination a score of 65 is arrived at, with which the interviewee feels comfortable.

At an early stage in our development of the interviewing process we found it necessary (and useful) to include past interviewees' views in the scoring pattern. Thus, instead of talking in generalities about trust we were able to describe specific situations and descriptions of levels of trust which interviewees were able to relate to very well. In this way they were able to answer quickly and confidently that, for example, 'It's better than the first example you gave me, but not quite as good as the second one you gave me.' In this situation the interviewer was able to say that the two situations represented points 50 and 75 on the scale, thus a score of 65 seemed appropriate.

Being able to describe a situation at various levels for each CSF was very sector- or industry-specific, thus a number of questionnaires needed to be developed for each industrial sector being interviewed. Let's consider CSF Co2, 'Due diligence', to illustrate this. In one were to interview a high-tech company about the due diligence process for a hardware/software alliance relationship, an answer of two to three months of active assessment of the partner and its capabilities would be viewed as a very high score. But in the pharmaceutical sector, an answer of two to three months would be viewed as a very low score indeed. The influencing factors here are the industry sector, the speed with which the sector moves, the purpose of the alliance and the estimated lifetime of the relationship.

Note that optimisation does *not* mean a score of 100 for each CSF chosen. There is a law of diminishing returns at play here which suggests that the value organisations derive from moving a CSF from 25 to 45 is considerably greater than moving it from 75 to 95, because as the score increases it becomes increasingly difficult to secure a 'perfect' score, and more and more time and effort are needed to achieve progress. Therefore, our definition focuses on the best possible score from a defined set of available resources.

From the beginning, we in ABP recognised the subjective/objective nature of the scoring patterns, in that scores were subjective in nature because they were the views of individuals, but were objective because they were placed in context with other interviewees' views on an objective and measurable scale of 0–100.

Indeed, our initial research revealed that subjective views are very powerful in strategic alliance relationships. This is illustrated by the phrase 'perception is reality' – if someone thinks a CSF is scoring very low, then he will act as if that is the truth. Let's take the example of CSF Cu31, 'Business-to-business trust'. If interviewees feel that trust is low, they may score it at less than 25/100 (let's say 15/100). This means that they don't trust their partners with sensitive information regarding the relationships, so they hold back information the partners need to make appropriate partnership decisions. The result is that the relationships do not fulfil their maximum potential (optimisation), and when questioned, relationship personnel highlight lack of trust as a major factor.

The reverse is also true, and is sometimes called the 'halo effect'. In this case, because the interviewees feel that the degree of trust is high, they feel comfortable sharing important and sensitive information, which in turn leads to optimum decision making and a better-performing relationship. When questioned, interviewees typically say that the high level of trust was a major contributing fact to the alliance's success.

So who is right and who is wrong? What is the 'correct' score for trust in the example above? The answer is that the true score is what people think it is – in other words, it is a purely objective measure.

This manner of collecting scores from both/all the partners in a relationship has an immediate and beneficial effect since *each of the individual CSFs will operate at the level of efficiency of the lowest score.*

Using the trust example again, this means that if one side of the relationship scores the CSF very high and the other side scores it very low, then in reality it will be operating at the lowest common denominator – the lowest score. The opportunity this generates to allow both sides to engage in discussions about why each side has allocated a certain score is the first element of value derived from the exercise. This is what ABP calls 'alignment' or 'misalignment', and it is the first step in the optimisation workshop run after capturing the data (a full description of the relationship optimisation process appears later in this chapter).

The Connection between Scores and the Type of Alliance

In the early days of the development of the Database we in ABP contented ourselves with a simple binary scoring system: we simply asked whether or not a CSF was in existence in the alliance in question, and the answer was either 'yes' or 'no'. But as our data grew, we found that we could ask a subsidiary question of our interviewees: 'To what degree does the CSF exist?' – in other words, how well it was performing, from not at all (0) to perfection (100).

This and the depth and degree of our interviewing efforts began to give us insights into the types of alliance with which we were dealing, and we found a simple categorisation process helpful, which we refer to as the TECP (Transactional, Enhanced, Collaborative, Partnership) Model (see Table 5.2).[1]

Table 5.2   Types of alliance relationship in the TECP Model

Transactional	Enhanced	Collaborative	Partnership
0–25	25–50	50–75	75–100

When we conducted a full alliance benchmark, we interviewed three 'perspectives' from each organisation (the three levels identified earlier: strategic, managerial and operational). When we did so, we noticed that alliance relationships that scored 0–25 exhibited transactional tendencies and characteristics. Typically, in these alliances one partner had something of value but limited means to bring it to market, while the other had the means to bring it to market but not the product or service required. Consequently,

---

1   The early categorisation work was conducted in part with the help of Vantage Partners, LLC (www.vantagepartners.com), for which we are very grateful.

the nature of the relationship was rather transactional, meaning that each partner bought and sold capability from the other to make the alliance a success.

Examples of this type of relationship are common in the pharmaceutical field, for instance, in which one side has developed a promising compound, but lacks the ability (or often the funds) to take the compound through the necessary regulatory testing and then subsequently market the successful drug. The other partner (usually the larger distributor) lacks the original compound or asset, but does have a distribution and marketing network already in place.

Another example would be in the high-tech field, where one organisation may have a piece of software its partner needs to complete a large systems integration project. In this case, the systems integrator buys the software from the partner and resells it to the customer as part of the project. In fact, in high-tech circles this type of alliance is known as a 'reseller alliance'.

The reason why these relationships scored relatively low on the partnering spectrum is that many of the more advanced aspects of partnering were absent from the relationship because they were not needed. So, for example, questions regarding alliance vision and senior executive support and supporting business intentions and trust were meaningless. Much more important were questions regarding the cost of the offering, the go-to-market model and the technical capability of the products or services in question. Hence they scored low, typically 0–25.

But then we noticed that there were some alliances in the Database that scored 25–50, and these seemed to be making more use of the available CSFs: more CSFs were present, and the ones that were present were operating at a higher level of efficiency. When we examined these alliances we noticed a degree of 'enhancement' that had been applied to the original product, service or proposition. In other words, one partner or the other (or both) was actively using its own resources and efforts to improve the core offering of the alliance and make it more valuable. In fact, in the high-tech sector these types of alliances are called 'value-add', and partners who perform the function of adding value are known as 'value-add resellers'.

Similarly, we noticed that alliances that scored 50–75 were well on the way to being fully optimised partnership relationships. They didn't have all the characteristics of a true partnership, but they were certainly more valuable and more complex than enhanced alliances (those scoring 25–50). The term we coined for these relationships was 'collaborative alliances'.

Finally, we identified alliances that scored 75–100 and were to all intents and purposes acting as fully formed and well-optimised alliance partnerships.

This categorisation gave us a number of valuable insights which have proven useful to this day:

- There are at least four types of alliance relationship, and each has its own characteristics and operating principles.
- As the use of available CSFs increases, so does the degree of business intimacy, which in turn leads to increased value.
- Organisations need to allocate resources applicable to the type of alliance in question, so the concept of cost/value ratio becomes important in the conduct of the alliance.

- Optimisation in this context thus becomes a relative concept – for example, a transactional alliance scoring 25/100 is fully optimised if it is focusing on the right CSFs (effectiveness) and scoring at or near maximum on those CSFs, while a score of 25/100 for an alliance partnership is a bad one because not enough CSFs are in play and/or their average scores are very low.

Table 5.3 matches the CSF focus to the alliance categorisations.

Table 5.3   CSF focus in the TECP Model

Transactional	Enhanced	Collaborative	Partnership
1. Business value proposition (Co1)	1. Shared objectives (S20)	1. Process for negotiation (Co9)	1. Valuation of assets (T11)
2. Due diligence (Co2)	2. Multiple relationships with same partner(s) (S28)	2. Identified mutual needs in the relationship (T16)	2. Shared control (T18)
3. Commercial cost (Co7)			3. Risk sharing (S23)
4. Commercial benefit (Co8)	3. Relationship development plan (O51)	3. Process for joint problem solving (T17)	4. Business-to-business strategic alignment (S26)
5. Partner company market position (T12)	4. Issue escalation (O52)	4. Partner accountability (T19)	5. Fit with strategic business path (S27)
6. Host company market position (T13)	5. Relationship scope (S21)	5. Tactical and strategic risk (S22)	6. Common strategic ground rules (S29)
7. Market fit of proposed solution (T14)	6. Communication (O43)	6. Exit strategies (S24)	7. Common vision (S30)
	7. Quality review (O44)	7. Senior executive support (S25)	8. Collaboration skills (Cu33)
8. Product fit with partners' offerings (T15)	8. Memorandum of understanding and principles or alliance charter (O45)	8. Business-to-business trust (Cu31)	9. Dedicated alliance managers (Cu34)
9. Speed of progress so far (O40)		9. Collaborative corporate mindset (Cu32)	10. Alliance centre of excellence (Cu35)
10. Distance from revenue (O41)	9. Alliance reward system (Co6)		11. Business-to-business cultural alignment (Cu38)
11. Optimum legal/business structure (Co3)	10. Joint decision making process (Cu36)	10. Other cultural issues (Cu37)	
	11. Business-to-business operational alignment (O48)	11. Alliance processes (O39)	12. Relationship change management (O46)
12. Operational metrics (O47)		12. Formal joint business plan (O42)	
	12. Alliance audit/healthcheck (Co4)		13. Exponential breakthroughs or innovation (O49)
13. Expected cost/value ratio (Co10)	13. Key metrics (Co5)	13. Internal alignment (O50)	

What Table 5.3 shows is that if you want an optimised transactional alliance relationship, you only need to focus on 13 of the available 52 CSFs, whereas if you want an enhanced alliance relationship, you need to focus on the original 13 (transactional) and a further 13 (enhanced) CSFs – hence 26 factors – and so on until you come to a full partnership alliance in which you need to focus on the entire range of 52 CSFs.

This provides us with another insight into the optimisation process, since in our definition we focused on two quite specific elements. After conducting your benchmarking exercise for your given alliance (by asking all 52 questions) you might find that your alliance is underperforming because it is focusing on the wrong CSFs (effectiveness) or because the scores of the CSFs you are focusing on are too low (efficiency) – of course, in reality it could be a combination of both of these issues.

The model above allows organisations to understand (a) where they are now and (b) what CSFs they need to focus on to take them where they would like to go.

The Connection between Scores and Value

We have seen that there is now an effective model for optimising alliance relationships, but a key question remains: 'Does it matter? All this talk of best practice and optimisation is all very well and good, you might say, but does it actually achieve anything in practice?

This degree of scepticism was one that we endured for a number of years, and it was, to say the least, frustrating! We had many conversations with senior alliance executives that went along very similar lines:

> Q: *Do you believe that a defined group of alliance best practices exist?*
> A: *Yes.*
> Q: *Do you believe that by focusing on best practices and doing those things better you will get better results?*
> A: *Yes.*
> Q: *So will you instigate an optimisation process by instigating some benchmarks?*
> A: *No, because we don't have time. We're too busy running the alliances!*

There seemed to be a feeling that talking about alliance models and scoring patterns made the exercise too academic and classroom-related. But at the same time alliance executives at a number of levels couldn't seem to shake the feeling that if they did the 'right' things they would get the 'right' results.

This problem was compounded by the fact that many clients were unwilling (or unable) to quantify for us the base value of the alliance relationships in question.

It took many years before clients began to realise that benchmarking is an essential step in the overall process of alliance value optimisation.

Today in our assignments ABP insists on a baseline commercial value for an alliance engaged in an optimisation exercise: only by insisting on this can we prove that focusing on the right issues (the correct CSFs) will produce the right results (increased commercial value).

The breakthrough came slowly over a number of years, but one instance stands out as an 'Aha!' moment. I had developed a training course for Oracle, and was teaching its alliance and channel professionals the basics of alliance management and how to design and implement alliance optimisation programmes for themselves. An early attendee was an Indian lady who was responsible for the IBM alliance in Germany. She listened attentively and took copious notes, and I thought no more about it until a year later, when she appeared on my course again. I was somewhat puzzled because I thought she had grasped the concepts the first time round. In front of the entire class of 35 Oracle alliance professionals, I asked what she was doing back on the course (Note to self: When teaching, don't ask questions you don't know the answer to!).

She said that she had listened very carefully on the previous course and had put in place an optimisation programme with IBM in Germany. I held my breath as another class member asked the inevitable question: 'Did it work?'.

'Oh yes,' she said. 'We went from a best practice score of 32/100 to 73/100 in a year. But more importantly, our incremental or net new revenue from the partner went from €6 million to €23 million!'

Into the stunned silence, I asked: 'But if you've made such fantastic progress, what are you doing back on the course?' Her answer: 'We have had a terrific journey at great speed from low enhanced to high collaborative, but now need to understand how to design and implement a full partnership alliance running at optimum efficiency.'

As you might imagine, I had little difficulty ensuring class attention after that!

The anecdotal example above has now been played out many times with multiple alliances. Sometimes factors beyond the control of alliance managers prevent them from optimising their relationships beyond a certain point. Sometimes when both sides understand the commitment and business intimacy of a full partnership they express a different goal of wanting a collaborative alliance instead. Regardless of the external and internal factors at play, we have found that the concept and definition of alliance optimisation allows us to show clients how to get the best out of their alliances with the least possible effort.

How to Execute an Alliance Optimisation Programme

If it's so valuable to conduct an alliance optimisation exercise or programme, how exactly should you go about it? From our experiences with clients large and small, we would suggest the generic process set out in Table 5.4.

Table 5.4   Generic alliance optimisation process

Identifier	Stage 1	Stage 2	Stage 3	Stage 4	Stage 5
Description	Goal setting and scoping	Diagnostic	Action planning	Resource mapping	90-day review
Objective	To identify the currently projected commercial value of the relationship for the next 12 months	To generate an objective view of the relationship which shows 52 strengths and weaknesses identified as a score of 0–100	To generate with the partner a jointly agreed action plan to optimise the relationship	To map all identified actions to a RACI framework to identify key stakeholders' roles and responsibilities	To track the progress of the joint action plan towards target(s) and take remedial action as required

Table 5.4　**Generic alliance optimisation process** *continued*

Identifier	Stage 1	Stage 2	Stage 3	Stage 4	Stage 5
Activities	Contact all key stakeholders and draw up a strawman value projection Resolve conflicts and discrepancies with stakeholders Document the draft final value projection Obtain sign-off of the value projection from the senior executive sponsor	Agree on key stakeholders to provide data Gather data and send the results to ABP ABP benchmarks the data and produces a draft alliance efficiency report (AER) Discuss the AER with the other partner (and/or ABP) and decide whether to progress to action planning	Construct an agreed agenda from the draft report Analyse areas of misalignment (CSFs which show different scores for each partner) Agree with the partner common scores for all 52 areas Identify areas for action Identify short-term and long-term actions Identify the help required for long-term actions Produce an agreed action plan	Conduct RACI chart mapping for all identified improvement actions Communicate and agree roles of all stakeholders on the RACI chart Revise the RACI chart as necessary Agree on a single stakeholder from both/all organisations in each category Sign off the RACI chart with host and partner executives	Conduct a healthcheck assessment prior to the review meeting Construct an agenda and pre-meeting progress report Conduct the meeting, focusing on underperforming areas Agree the revised action plan with remedial actions Publish the revised action plan
Inputs	Relationship business plans Alliance strategy document Briefing Pack from ABP	Online diagnostic Briefing pack from ABP ABP coaching as required	Draft the AER Draft a suggested workshop agenda Agree on the workshop attendee list	Agreed action plan RACI resource mapping tool	Jointly greed action plan Jointly agreed stakeholder map MOUP Agenda
Outputs	Agreed scope Agreed initial commercial valuation	Draft alliance efficiency report (AER) from ABP Benchmarking report Decision to proceed	Jointly agreed action plan	Stakeholder map of agreed actions	Revised action plan

The process described in Table 5.4 is the one we have found gets the best results in the least possible time, and it is sufficiently simple to be used by an organisation of any size. In addition, it has sufficient logic to be scalable to alliances or organisations of any size. The process consists of five stages:

1. goal setting and scoping
2. benchmarking
3. action planning
4. resource mapping
5. 90-day review.

1. GOAL SETTING AND SCOPING

It is essential to identify the scope of the alliance to be benchmarked before you do anything else. This initial scoping exercise allows you to identify the key stakeholders who will need to be interviewed to secure the benchmark data. Also, don't forget that part of this stage is the value baselining, in which you identify the current commercial value of the scope in question.

2. BENCHMARKING

The second stage is to gather data from the key stakeholders about the CSFs you have chosen. The type of questionnaire you choose will be influenced by the type of relationship desired. If it's a transactional alliance, you only need to ask 13 questions, but if it's a full alliance partnership, you will need to assess all 52 areas.

3. ACTION PLANNING

Having gathered your data, now it's time to run a workshop with your partner. The great value here lies in identifying misaligned areas and agreeing on a joint alliance optimisation action plan. Note that there will be too many things that need attention for you to do them all at once, so take care to focus on achievable outcomes that have a defined payback. If you wish, you can combine short-term (this year) improvement activities and long-term (next year) improvement activities. If you repeat this process annually, then you create an ongoing continuous improvement cycle.

4. RESOURCE MAPPING

Having decided *what* you are going to do, be sure you know *who* is going to do it by mapping the available resources to the selected actions. This will tell you whether you are being too ambitious in your improvement plans given the available resources.

5. 90-DAY REVIEW

Finally, don't forget to instigate a formal process for reviewing the optimisation action plan at least every 90 days to allow for changes and unexpected challenges – this will keep you on track.

6 *Creating a New Strategic Alliance*

In all the examples in this chapter it is my intention to outline a generic best practice process which can be scaled as appropriate. There is no doubt that the eventual process used will be heavily influenced by multiple factors, such as the industry concerned, the size of the organisation, the organisational alliance maturity level and the value of the prospective opportunity.

The purpose in documenting the core processes outlined in this chapter is to provide alliance managers with robust and proven approaches which are equally viable in a variety of industries (for example, high-tech or pharmaceutical) and company sizes (for example, multinational enterprises or small to medium-sized organisations).

Let's assume that you're facing a situation in which you have been asked to develop an existing or new business opportunity using a strategic alliance. Where do you start? What do you focus on first? How does your planning and identification of possible partners merge into the later stages of start-up and growth?

We suggest the model shown in Table 6.1, based on the framework we introduced and developed in Chapter 5 (see Table 5.4 in particular).

Stage 1: Partner Selection

It's axiomatic, perhaps, but deserves mentioning here that for a strategic alliance to have the best chance of success, you need to choose the most appropriate partner. This may seem an overly simplistic statement, but in our experience this actually happens in a relatively small minority of cases. The reasons abound:

> *'We don't have a choice, we have to partner with Company X because it has a compound, product or service we want.'*

> *'We have to partner with Company Y to secure that attractive business opportunity.'*

> *'We have to partner with Company Z because if we don't, another company will, and they'll secure dominant market share.'*

Whatever the reasons, we see many instances where organisations set themselves mountains to climb by choosing inappropriate partners with which it is wildly difficult to form partnerships.

In ABP, we would say that the goal when choosing partners is to maximise the degree of alignment in your preferred areas.

Table 6.1 ABP Partner Selection Model

Description	Stage 1	Stage 2	Stage 3	Stage 4	Stage 5
Objective	To rationalise the alliance strategy and connect partner selection to business strategy	To create a partner list (long)	To create a partner list (short)	To interview partners and assess organisation fit	To review accumulated data and make partner selection
Tasks/ activities	Identify and secure organisational business plan, referencing the amount of business to be generated from indirect means Create partner segmentation model	Use the partner segmentation model to identify desired partner profile in each level of the segmentation plan, including critical criteria model Conduct public research using the desired criteria in the model and create partner selection list (long)	Share partner list with senior executives in the business and invite a scoring exercise driven by the scoring of appropriate criteria Compile, rationalise and summarise all input to create partner list (short)	Interview partner in accordance with agreed criteria list to ascertain relative scores criterion by criterion Prioritise partners in order of attractiveness, highlighting good and bad points	Present due diligence research findings to senior management and discuss Make recommendations to senior management based on prioritised list Communicate final decision to partners
Inputs	Business strategy	Alliance strategy	Partner criteria model	Partner criteria analysis	Partner interview notes
Outputs	Alliance strategy	Partner criteria model Partner possible list (long)	Partner list (short) Analysis of partners to criteria model	Interview notes from partner assessment interviews	Agreed prioritised list of partners

The key activities to achieve this in Stage 1 are:

1.1 building a partner criteria model for selection;
1.2 performing an appropriate amount of due diligence on the possible candidates;
1.3 creating a preferred partner shortlist;
1.4 mapping your own organisation against the partner criteria model to show prospective partners what they would be partnering with;
1.5 ranking the preferred partners;
1.6 documenting the partner choice.

STAGE 1.1: BUILDING A PARTNER CRITERIA MODEL FOR SELECTION

You need to decide how many of the possible CSFs to use as a partner criteria model. Too few and you will make bad decisions based on a lack of available evidence, too many and the process will become unwieldy and unworkable. ABP suggests that 15–20 CSFs spread across all five dimensions (Commercial, Technical, Strategic, Cultural and Operational) in a balanced manner is a good number.

The creation of a partner criteria model is an essential first step in choosing partners because it gives the organisation (or the division) the ability to realise what criteria are being used to judge partners in the current exercise. It is entirely possible for different criteria models to be developed for different alliance purposes.

The best way to decide on the criteria factors is to send a questionnaire including the full range of 52 CSFs to alliance key stakeholders in the organisation and ask them to rank the CSFs in order of importance (for consistency, a suitable scoring system might be 0–100, where 0 = not important at all and 100 = critical). Then collate all the answers and consider using all the CSFs that score more than 75/100, for example. In this way, not only do you gain the input of experienced alliance managers and key commercial stakeholders in your organisation into the partner selection process, but you also obtain a more balanced view from multiple perspectives.

STAGE 1.2: PERFORMING AN APPROPRIATE AMOUNT OF DUE DILIGENCE ON THE POSSIBLE CANDIDATES

Having identified the areas you will be using to assess your potential partners (the partner criteria model), the next step is to use that model to find possible partners. It is usually best to complete this activity in two steps:

1. assess the commercial and technical fit;
2. assess the strategic, cultural and operational fit.

This is because the first step of assessments can normally be carried out remotely with little or no input from the prospective partners, while step 2 will need their active co-operation.

Having completed Stage 1 above, you should by now have a preliminary list of prospective partners that satisfy the commercial and technical criteria you decided on earlier. Now it's time to rationalise that list into a preferred partner shortlist.

STAGE 1.3: CREATING A PREFERRED PARTNER SHORTLIST

The way to create this shortlist is by conducting interviews with the partners concerned using the criteria model you developed earlier in the process. This exercise should take no more than an hour, and can usually be conducted by telephone or a teleconference call.

We have heard the following objection from organisations we have worked with: 'Why should these organisations answer these questions? Isn't this an intrusion?' Our answer (which we have found true in all cases) is that when the situation is explained to the prospective partners appropriately, not only do they not object, they are enthusiastic participants. A suitable explanation might be along these lines:

> We are conducting a partner due diligence exercise, and I am delighted to tell you that you have been successful in passing a Stage 1 assessment (Commercial and Technical). However, we would now like to progress to a Stage 2 assessment (Strategic, Cultural and Operational) which will enable us to understand whether our two organisations could work together effectively and efficiently. The exercise can be completed by telephone and will take no more than one hour. No commercially sensitive information will be captured, and if you wish, we are happy to sign a mutually binding non-disclosure agreement.

Expressed like this, we find that potential partners are impressed by the professionalism of the firm reaching out to them and considering the partnership, rather than being put off.

STAGE 1.4: MAPPING YOUR OWN ORGANISATION AGAINST THE PARTNER CRITERIA MODEL TO SHOW PROSPECTIVE PARTNERS WHAT THEY WOULD BE PARTNERING WITH

Having gathered data from each of the shortlisted prospective partners, now it's time to map your own organisation against the same questions. The purpose here is to assess the degree of alignment in the criteria categories chosen, and an example might help to explain this.

In the following example, Company A (the organisation looking for partners) has decided on the CSFs set out in Table 6.2 to form its criteria model.

Table 6.2   Example of a partner criteria model

Commercial	Technical	Strategic	Cultural	Operational
Commercial benefit	Market fit of proposed solution	Senior executive support	Trust	Communication
Joint business value proposition	Partner accountability	Relationship scope	Dedicated partnering resources	Joint action plan
	Partner company market position	Business-to-business strategic alignment	Collaborative corporate mindset	Distance from revenue
	Host company market position	Shared objectives	Collaboration skills	Internal alignment
	Product fit with partners' offerings	Fit with strategic business path		Process for negotiation
	Identified mutual needs in the relationship			Business-to-business operational alignment
				Alliance/partnering process

In this example, the company has chosen 24 out of the possible 52 criteria; this is appropriate in size for the exercise being conducted, and also maintains a degree of balance in the criteria model between the five categories.

Company A interviews Company B, seeking to understand the importance Company B places on each factor, but also to determine how 'good' Company B is in terms of that factor (scored 0–100). Then Company A looks at its own organisation and assesses the same factors. Figure 6.1 shows the results, which are tabulated in Table 6.3.

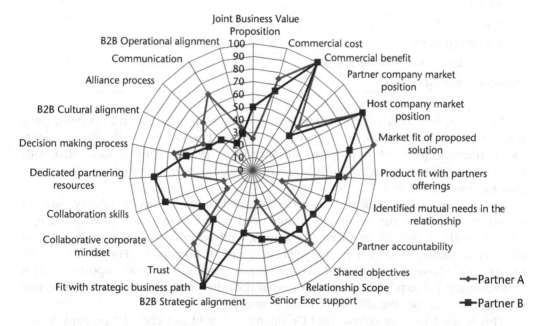

Figure 6.1   Partner criteria map

Table 6.3   Partner criteria mapping table

CSF in the criteria model	Partner A	Partner B
Commercial benefit	40	45
Joint business value proposition	30	25
Market fit of proposed solution	80	80
Partner accountability	20	40
Partner company market position	75	70
Host company market position	80	75
Product fit with partners' offerings	80	10
Identified mutual needs in the relationship	80	15
Senior executive support	90	90
Relationship scope	50	55
Business-to-business strategic alignment	65	60
Shared objectives	95	90
Fit with strategic business path	90	15
Trust	70	60
Dedicated partnering resources	90	15
Collaborative corporate mindset	90	20
Collaboration skills	80	75
Communication	100	95
Joint action plan	70	70
Distance from revenue	0	0
Internal alignment	80	25
Process for negotiation	90	85
Business-to-business operational alignment	15	15
Alliance/partnering process	80	10

As we can see, there is good alignment in areas such as commercial benefit, joint business value proposition, market fit of proposed solution, collaboration skills, communication, joint action plan and distance from revenue. This indicates that both sides view these areas in a similar way and have similar amounts of resources allocated to their successful outcomes.

But now let's take a look at some other factors, like partner accountability, product fit with partners' offerings, identified mutual needs in the relationship, fit with strategic business path, dedicated partnering resources, collaborative corporate mindset and alliance/partnering process. Here the picture is not so favourable. The scores suggest that there are large divergences between what one partner regards as important and is therefore prepared to pay attention to and what the other feels is important. These factors will make the prospective alliance difficult to manage.

This is not to say, of course, that Company A should not choose Company B as a partner – the actual choice will rely on the other partner criteria scoring models and the priority allocated to each criterion, but it does show the power of using such a visual alignment modelling tool to help in the selection process.

STAGE 1.5: RANKING THE PREFERRED PARTNERS

Having conducted the assessment phase and mapped all the scores, it's now possible to rank the preferred partners. Once again, the multidimensional nature of the ABP framework helps (see Table 6.4).

Table 6.4   Example rankings for three prospective partners

Example 1						
	Commercial	Technical	Strategic	Cultural	Operational	Totals
Prospective Partner 1	70	55	80	65	55	65
Weighting	1	1.3	0.8	0.6	1.5	
Rank	70	71.5	64	39	82.5	65.4
Example 2						
	Commercial	Technical	Strategic	Cultural	Operational	Totals
Prospective Partner 2	40	80	60	50	95	65
Weighting	1	1.3	0.8	0.6	1.5	
Rank	40	104	48	30	142.5	72.9
Example 3						
	Commercial	Technical	Strategic	Cultural	Operational	Totals
Prospective Partner 3	70	40	95	95	45	69
Weighting	1	1.3	0.8	0.6	1.5	
Rank	70	52	76	57	67.5	64.5

In the examples in Table 6.4, at first sight the scores might appear to be similar, but on closer inspection one can see that in Example 1 the raw score and the ranked score are very similar. However, in Example 2 the raw score is higher than the ranked score, and in Example 3 the ranked score is higher than the raw score. This is because in Example 3 the prospective partner scored highly in those areas (dimensions) that were important to the company conducting the exercise – in other words, the ranking was higher. In Example 2, although the prospective partner scored well on the raw scores, it didn't score particularly well in the preferred (highly ranked) areas, hence making the alignment decision easier.

STAGE 1.6: DOCUMENTING THE PARTNER CHOICE

The final stage is to document the partner choice. In many cases of partner selection, we see situations where companies go to great lengths to choose partners – in fact, they put considerable effort into the exercise – only to be challenged later when things do not always go to plan.

By documenting the process and the outcome, the company can create an audit trail of the decisions it made – and more importantly, why it made them. This is an extremely important factor in developing alliancing capability, because each exercise should feed into the next one so that the company's speed and efficiency in choosing the right partners can be improved over time.

Another good reason for keeping a record in this way is that sometimes (in our view, often) organisations go through a professional process and deliver their results to senior executives, only to have their analysis rejected in favour of 'gutfeel' or 'lowest cost provision'. Maintaining an audit trail of the process and its conclusions can help to reinforce the process itself by showing that a 'gutfeel' decision made in favour of a lower-scoring candidate can often lead to inferior results, which in itself strengthens the case for following the formal process next time.

Stage 2: Creating a Vision and a Strategy for the Alliance

Any significant relationship requires direction and an overarching goal to be achieved. I'm sure we're all familiar with the phrase 'Ready, fire, aim!' as opposed to the more usual 'Ready, aim, fire!' In this context, the phrase means that without a suitable degree of correct planning, the relationship will not achieve its goals.

Obviously, the skill of the alliance manager is involved in deciding the correct degree of planning to be applied to a relationship. The more complex and potentially valuable a relationship, the greater the degree of planning necessary to: (a) involve the correct number of stakeholders, (b) align all stakeholders behind a set of common objectives and (c) define key terms and terminology in a manner which is clear and transparent to all.

The key activities in Stage 2 are:

2.1 conducting an alliance readiness assessment;
2.2 agreeing on the current relationship type and value;
2.3 developing the relationship vision and strategy.

STAGE 2.1: CONDUCTING AN ALLIANCE READINESS ASSESSMENT

The first step in Stage 2 is to assess the organisation's readiness to partner. When we say 'organisation' in this context, we mean the agreed scope of the relationship, which may be specific to the country, function or business unit.

The readiness assessment should be simple to administer (usually by email and teleconference), yet comprehensive and detailed enough to give a suitable picture of the alliance-readiness of the unit being examined.

The ABP tool supporting this task is the ABP Alliance Readiness Assessment Questionnaire (see Appendix 6), which assesses the alliance capability in five dimensions:

1. **Leadership** – Is the leadership team in the organisation solidly behind the concept of partnering, and does the team understand the implications of the undertaking?

2. **Resources** – Does the unit have sufficient resources to make a success of the proposed alliance in terms of people, platform, products, procedures and programmes?

3. **Processes** – Does the organisation have suitable alliance processes to facilitate the efficient conduct of multiple alliance relationships (for example, an alliance launch process, a process for choosing suitable partners, a process for relationship optimisation or a process for developing new joint products and services)?

4. **Metrics** – Does the organisation measure the correct things when assessing the success or otherwise of its alliance relationships? In many cases, organisations measure only one or at best two dimensions of alliance operation (Commercial and Technical), while in reality they should measure at least five dimensions: Commercial, Technical, Strategic, Cultural and Operational.[1]

5. **Impact on business results** – Does the organisation have a clear 'line of sight' of the impact alliances have on its key business results? Only by understanding the current impact will the organisation be able to calculate the added-value impact further alliances might have.

In the ABP alliance readiness assessment process, scoring is conducted as follows:

- **Absent** – The area under examination is not in existence at all = 0/100.
- **Somewhat** – The area under examination is in partial existence in some places or has just started = 25/100.
- **Sporadic** – The area under examination is in existence in multiple places, but is not 'joined up' and cannot be seen as systematic = 50/100.
- **Common** – The area under examination is in common existence in multiple places in the organisation and is integrated = 75/100.
- **Comprehensive** – The area under examination is in extensive existence in multiple places and is universally accepted and followed = 50/100.

If any area scores less than 25/100, treat it as a potential weakness deserving of further examination.

If any area scores 75/100 or more, treat this as a potential strength worthy of further investigation.

If the overall assessment scores less than 25/100, advise the client not to proceed with the alliance relationship, but rather to address the weak areas of alliance capability first. For further information, see the ABP Alliance Excellence Model.[2]

Output of this task

The output of the alliance readiness assessment should be a report recommending a go/no go decision on the proposed alliance. This report should be supported by a summary presentation presented to the senior executive sponsor for the hosting organisation. There are multiple examples of such reports in the Alliance Best Practice Database.

---

1   See, for example, the ABP support tool 'Developing an Alliance Balanced Scorecard' on the Alliance Best Practice website under the 'Downloads' section www.alliancebestpractice.com/downloads.

2   Available for download on the Alliance Best Practice website under the Downloads Section at: www.alliancebestpractice.com/downloads.

Milestone

*   Senior executive support for the proposed alliance.

Having secured senior executive support and agreement to proceed, the next step is to determine the nature of the relationship to be constructed.

STAGE 2.2: AGREEING ON THE CURRENT RELATIONSHIP TYPE AND VALUE

In classifying relationship types, TECP is an acronym for transactional, enhanced, collaborative and partnership. These terms are defined as follows:

1. **Transactional relationships** – These types of relationships are commonly called vendor or supplier relationships. They are transactional in nature because the common interaction is adversarial, with both parties aiming for diametrically opposed objectives (for example, highest price/lowest price, greatest volume/greatest value add). Typically, while these types of relationships may be called 'partnerships' for public consumption, they are in fact simple vendor–supplier relationships. One party has a product or service it sells to the other party, which may then sell on the product or service to the eventual consumer. There is little or no collaboration or creativity/innovation between the parties.
2. **Enhanced relationships** – Sometimes a simple transactional supplier will add extra value to the relationship at its own cost and effort. These situations often concern specific products, services or business units, and are generally conducted as pilots. The key dynamic balance that needs to be maintained here is the ability to generate extra value for both parties.
3. **Collaborative relationships** – Assuming enhanced pilot projects have been conducted in the relationship, the next step is to combine these disparate activities into a co-ordinated and integrated whole. When this is achieved, we say that the relationship has reached collaborative status (that is, both parties are actively looking for collaboration opportunities to add to the existing enhanced projects).
4. **Partnership relationships** – Finally, it may be the case that a client enters into a full partnership with a supplier in which the defining characteristics are shared risk and reward. Typically (although not always), these relationships are highly structured and run as legally binding joint ventures.

Common success factors of different types of relationship

These are shown in Table 6.5.

Table 6.5   Common success factors of different types of relationship

Transactional	Enhanced	Collaborative	Partnership
Business value proposition (Co1)	Shared objectives (S20)	Process for negotiation (Co9)	Valuation of assets (T11)
Due diligence (Co2)	Multiple relationships with same partner(s) (S28)	Identified mutual needs in the relationship (T16)	Shared control (T18)
Commercial cost (Co7)			Risk sharing (S23)
Commercial benefit (Co8)	Project plan (O51)	Process for joint problem solving (T17)	Business-to-business strategic alignment (S26)
Partner company market position (T12)	Issue escalation (O52)	Partner accountability (T19)	Fit with strategic business path (S27)
Host company market position (T13)	Relationship scope (S21)	Tactical and strategic risk (S22)	Common strategic ground rules (S29)
Market fit of proposed solution (T14)	Communication (O43)	Exit strategies (S24)	Common vision (S30)
Product fit with partners' offerings (T15)	Quality review (O44)	Senior executive support (S25)	Collaboration skills (Cu33)
Speed of progress so far (O40)	Memorandum of understanding and principles or alliance charter (O45)	Business-to-business trust (Cu31)	Dedicated alliance managers (Cu34)
Distance from revenue (O41)	Alliance reward system (Co6)	Collaborative corporate mindset (Cu32)	Alliance centre of excellence (Cu35)
Optimum legal/ business structure (Co3)	Joint decision making process (Cu36)	Other cultural issues (Cu37)	Business-to-business cultural alignment (Cu38)
Operational metrics (O47)	Business-to-business operational alignment (O48)	Alliance processes (O39)	Relationship change management (O46)
Expected cost/value ratio (Co10)	Alliance audit/ healthcheck (Co4)	Formal joint business plan (O42)	Exponential breakthroughs or innovation (O49)
	Key metrics (Co5)	Internal alignment (O50)	

Running the workshop

The TECP workshop has two objectives:

1. To establish the type of relationship currently, and
2. To establish the type of relationship desired within the next 12 months.

The process for running the workshop is as follows.
   Prior to the workshop:

1. Establish the scope of the relationship.
2. From the scope, establish the current key stakeholders (see Appendix 4: Definition of Terms for a fuller explanation of key stakeholders).
3. Interview key stakeholders using a questionnaire using appropriately developed CSFs.
4. Combine all scores and aggregate them by dividing all gross scores by the number of CSFs used. The result will be a figure between 0 and 100.
5. The current relationship type is discovered as follows:

- transactional – score = 0–25;
- enhanced – score = 25–50;
- collaborative – score = 50–75;
- partnership – score = 75–100.

Having established the current score and relationship type, we can now progress to running the workshop itself. Using the questions and CSFs above as the agenda, the key stakeholders should now be invited to attend a TECP workshop at which the existing relationship type will be confirmed and the desired relationship type will be established.

At the workshop:

1. The first step is to discuss with the key stakeholders the current scores and situations and explore whether the conclusions resonate with the attendees. In essence, this is checking that the data capture stage was conducted accurately.
2. Having confirmed the present relationship type, the group can then pass on to a discussion of the desired relationship type by considering the next available stage in the relationship (for example, transactional to enhanced, or enhanced to collaborative).
3. The purpose of considering the CSFs in future desired states is to ascertain the appetite of both organisations for an increasingly complex and deep business-to-business relationship. All too often organisations declare that they want a partnership, but have no true understanding of the implications of that statement.
4. By focusing the conversations on the resources and requirements of each stage, both parties are able to develop an accurate impression of the effort required to establish the desired future state.

Output of this task

The output of the workshop is a report detailing the current relationship type, the strengths and weaknesses and the desired future state (with reference to the CSFs), and the degree of effort required to get there (again with reference to the CSFs).

The TECP report should not only identify the type of relationship desired, but also the effort required to make that a reality. The output of the TECP workshop will provide critical input to other tasks in Stage 1 (such as Stage 2.3).

Milestones

- Clarity around the current type of relationship.
- Joint team and key stakeholder support for the desired type of relationship.

STAGE 2.3: DEVELOPING THE RELATIONSHIP VISION AND STRATEGY

Supporting tools for this task[3]

- Various examples of completed MOUP documents;
- an MOUP pre-workshop briefing document;
- an MOUP questionnaire;
- MOUP briefing pack for senior executives;
- MOUP scoping template document;
- MOUP draft project plan;
- draft MOUP agenda;
- MOUP workshop factsheet;
- 'Initiating a Strategic Alliance Using an MOUP Workshop' (explanatory slide deck);
- 'Reviewing a Strategic Alliance Using an MOUP Workshop' (explanatory slide deck).

Having established the desired future type of the relationship, the next step is the heart of Stage 2: to developing an agreed vision for the relationship and an accompanying strategy to achieve that vision.

Note: 'Vision' and 'strategy' here refer to the relationship-specific vision and strategy for the relationship in question. These documents will obviously exist within the overall context of the broader organisational alliance vision and strategies of both/all organisations.

Some organisations are uncomfortable with the term 'memorandum of understanding and principles' because they believe such documents carry legal connotations which can inhibit creative thought. If this is the case, it is entirely acceptable to rename the event and stage using alternative terminology familiar to the organisations involved (for example, charter, guidance notes or relationship operating principles). However, for clarity and simplicity I will use the term or its acronym, MOUP, henceforth in this book.

The MOUP workshop is conducted in three stages:

1. pre-workshop activities;
2. activities at the workshop itself;
3. post-workshop activities.

These are conducted as shown in Table 6.6.

---

3   These tools are available from the Alliance Best Practice website at www.alliancebestpractice.com or from info@ alliancebestpractice.com.

Table 6.6   The three stages of the MOUP workshop

Pre-workshop activities	Workshop activities	Post-workshop activities
Send explanation of process to both/all partners. Arrange conference call to explain process to partners (if necessary). Send briefing materials to chosen stakeholders to complete the online pre-workshop questionnaire. Compile all responses and discuss with relationship managers.	Confirm workshop attendees with relationship managers. Brief all attendees on draft agenda and purpose of the workshop. Diary management – workshop date agreed.	Input transferred to MOUP template. Draft MOUP produced and circulated to all attendees for comment/revision. Revisions received and draft MOUP amended.
Milestone: Agree MOUP agenda	**Milestone: Workshop conducted and input captured**	**Milestone: Final version of MOUP signed off by attendees**

Running the workshop

We suggest the discussion points in Table 6.7 for the MOUP workshop.

Table 6.7   Discussion points for the MOUP workshop

Morning	Afternoon
Vision of the relationship	Key stakeholders
Business value proposition(s)	Business-to-business strategic alignment
Scope	Relationship development plan
Key metrics	Communication programme(s)
Alliance reward system(s)	Relationship change management
Market fit of proposed solutions	Internal alignment
Pilot geographies/roll-out	Business-to-business alignment
Governance	Key documents/contracts

We suggest that each of the points in Table 6.7 should represent at least a half-page paragraph in the completed MOUP document. While not all the topics need to be included, it is dangerous to leave out too many as this will considerably diminish the degree of consensus and clarity in the relationship in future.

Depending on the size and complexity of the relationship (scope), it may be necessary to conduct the workshop over two or even three days to accommodate a sufficient degree and depth of discussion.

Output of this task

The output of this task is an agreed MOUP document identifying the vision, strategy and scope of the relationship.

Milestone

• Clarity about all the items discussed at the workshop.

Agree current relationship value (baseline)

It must never be forgotten that the purpose of strategic alliances is to generate cost-effective income for both/all parties to the relationship. Consequently, it is important for the relationship managers to have a clear understanding at all times of current and proposed future commercial revenue. This allows them to build business cases for further investment and also to cost-justify the effort and activities involved in developing the relationship.

There is no doubt that many organisations find it difficult to produce agreed figures relating to relationship value; however, the relationship manager(s) must stand firm on this point and insist on a number which both sides can agree on as being a good clear indication of present relationship value.

Often one or both parties will not want to divulge this figure to their partners – this in itself is a worrying early indicator of lack of trust.

It is difficult to outline a specific process for developing this common baseline since the information will come from such a multiplicity of sources. However, the following activities are generally seen as key:

• Agree the scope with all key stakeholders.
• Identify both direct and indirect value figures with all key stakeholders.
• Review with executive sponsor(s) and increase the number of key stakeholders if necessary to capture more accurate data.
• Produce a current draft cost/value statement for the relationship.
• Review the draft with key stakeholders and validate it.
• Sign off current the baseline (cost/value ratio) with the senior executive sponsor(s).

Output of this task

The output of this task is an agreed baseline cost and value figure for the relationship scope in question.

Milestone

• A clear and mutually agreed commercial starting point.

Stage 3: Developing the Skills Necessary to Support the Alliance

The key activities in Stage 3 are:

3.1 agreeing on the go-to-market model and skills required;
3.2 developing and executing a skills training programme;
3.3 developing a scalable governance model.

STAGE 3.1: AGREEING ON THE GO-TO-MARKET MODEL AND SKILLS REQUIRED

Having identified the vision and strategy of the alliance (the *what*), we now need to develop the action plans to achieve the strategy (the *how*). This is achieved by developing suitable skills on both/all sides of the relationship and agreeing how both/all will carry out their intentions.

The first step in the process is agreeing the most appropriate go-to-market (GTM) model.

Supporting tools for this task[4]

- 'Running a Business Value Proposition (BVP) Workshop' (explanatory slide deck);
- sample BVP agenda;
- sample 'typical deal template' with participation rates;
- sample 'typical deal template' with illustratory example figures;
- sample 'customer analysis compelling reasons to buy template';
- sample 'market characteristics template';
- sample 'joint sales engagement and execution model';
- sample 'demand generation – sourcing and cost template';
- sample 'expected financial summary – year 1 template';
- sample 'action plan template';
- sample 'message summary template';
- sample 'BVP/opportunity prioritisation template;
- compensation structure for referral, influence, closing deal.

An alliance relationship is designed in order to allow joint service or product offerings to be sold to consumers. In the high-tech sector these are sometimes called joint service offerings (JSOs). ABP prefers the term 'business value propositions' because it encourages the parties to think of the three key communities involved in their construction: the client, the partner and the customer.

All too often alliances just sell the products or services each party produces. To be clear, this is not a partnership relationship. It is at best a transactional relationship in which a high degree of reselling takes place and one or all of the partners views the others as customers for their products and/or services.

It is imperative that both/all the partners in the relationship construct *joint* offerings which (when sold) offer good commercial value to all parties. These BVPs lie at the heart of the relationship, and tracking the number sold and the potential sales in the pipeline will constitute a key aspect of the construction of a key metrics set for the relationship.

Sometimes the nature of the relationship demands such a wide range of BVPs or such complexity involved in their construction that a separate BVP workshop is required to agree the products or services that the relationship will jointly sell.

Note: The output of the BVP workshop will still need to be included in the MOUP.

Generally, the process for conducting a BVP workshop to agree the products and/ or services the relationship will sell is the same as for running an MOUP workshop.

---

4   These tools are available from the Alliance Best Practice website at www.alliancebestpractice.com or from info@alliancebestpractice.com.

This similarity is deliberate and leads to greater simplicity in the overall process and a greater degree of comfort with the processes from the attendees.

Running a BVP and GTM workshop

Running a BVP and GTM workshop involves three stages, as shown in Table 6.8.

Table 6.8   The three stages of running a BVP and GTM workshop

Pre-workshop activities	Workshop activities	Post-workshop activities
Information gathering to identify: • What is the target market and business level we are looking for? • What is the solution portfolio and what role would both/all products and services play in that? • What is the proposed business plan? • What is the strategic difference/role that we would both/all contribute?	Refinement of the model Population of the model Action plan to execute	Document new BVPs and GTM model for review Circulate draft documents for approval Sign off all documentation and action plans
Milestones: **Draft list of BVPs** **Draft GTM model**	**Milestones:** **Agreed model** **Agreed GTM plan** **Action plan to execute**	**Milestones:** **Signed off BVPs** **Signed off GTM model**

Table 6.9 shows a typical agenda for a BVP workshop.

Table 6.9   Typical agenda for a BVP workshop

Morning	Afternoon
8.30–9.00: Opening	14.00–15.00: Go-to-market planning
Objectives and agenda	Sales engagement model
9.00–10.00: Alliance status presentation	Target geographies and accounts
Current relationship type	First draft of business case
Pre-workshop information for review	15.00–16.00: Action planning, for example:
10.00–13.00: Break into three tracks, for example:	• business plan and governance
1. financial services	• solution and services plan
2. public services	• sales execution
3. pharma and biotechnology.	• marketing and sales enablement.
Each track discusses:	16.00–17.00: Workshop review
• service/product offering	Review of stakeholders and action plan
• customer analysis	Next steps
• market characteristics.	17.00: Close meeting
13.00–14.00: Working lunch – revenue modelling	

Obviously, as with an MOUP workshop, this agenda flow can be expanded or contracted to adapt to the number of attendees if necessary. However, remember that the purpose of the exercise is to understand three critical aspects with absolute clarity:

1. What are we selling (BVPs)?
2. Who are we selling them to (target sectors or key accounts)?
3. How are we selling them (GTM model)?

Sign off MOUP BVP and GTM models

The final task in this stage is a milestone in itself: senior executive acceptance and support for the agreed direction, purpose and resource implications of the proposed alliance.

Note: 'Senior executive support' means support from the senior executive sponsor(s) on both/all sides of the relationship.

Supporting tools for this task[5]

•   Sample 'alliance business plan' template.

While it will be necessary to construct a document for senior executive approval, in all likelihood it will also be necessary to present the key aspects of the relationship and the implications to the individuals concerned.

The documents presented need to be high-level and should not be burdened with too much detail. The key sections should include:

•   **Vision, Strategy and Purpose**
    –   What is this relationship all about?
    –   What are we seeking to achieve?
    –   What is the scope? Where are we doing this?
•   **Business Value Proposition and Go-to-market Model**
    –   What are we selling?
    –   To whom are we selling it?
    –   How are we selling it to them?
•   **Forecasting Execution and Action Planning**
    –   What will it cost us to do this, and what benefits can we expect (cost/value ratio)?
    –   What are the current action plan milestones?
    –   What resource implications does this plan have?

STAGE 3.2: DEVELOPING AND EXECUTING A SKILLS TRAINING PROGRAMME

The details of the skills training programme will depend on those factors particular to the organisations involved (for example, hardware or software, complex or simple propositions). The following information is for guidance only, and should be used in conjunction with the organisation-specific training programmes already in place for partners.

---

5   These tools are available from the Alliance Best Practice website at www.alliancebestpractice.com or from info@ alliancebestpractice.com.

The training stage in our model will help partners to achieve the revenue goals in their business plan. It is in both/all parties' interest to ensure the appropriate resources are available in their respective organisations and that they have the correct skills in each other's products and services. The goal is for both/all partners to be able to deliver:

- a sales pitch;
- a demonstration;
- a proof of concept;
- successful implementation.

The training can be delivered in a number of ways, for example:

- face-to-face classroom education supported by trainers for one or both/all organisations;
- virtual classroom education supported by trainers from one or both/all organisations;
- self-paced online courses.

It is more than likely that some form of certification or accreditation will be necessary in the chosen hardware, software or services offered by both parties. In this case both/all parties in the alliance should provide training courses with a number of clearly defined objectives. As an example, these could be:

- designed to take the guesswork out of training for IT professionals in key job roles throughout the partner organisation(s);
- structured by job role and product, allowing trainees to advance from core product knowledge to advanced skills and on to full accreditation;
- focused on guiding partners through extensive training solutions, when and where they need training and at the lowest appropriate investment level.

The alliance managers from both/all organisations serve as guides through this process and are the key enablers of the system. It is their responsibility to ensure that the requisite training has been provided to ensure that partner staff are able to implement the chosen solutions successfully.

The alliance managers will also be involved in training and upskilling of partner staff on an ongoing basis to ensure that their level of competency rises over time rather than diminishes. Such ongoing activities could include:

- technical boot camps;
- sales boot camps;
- technical 'deep dive' workshops;
- outbound communication to the partner(s) to keep them informed (for example, newsletters and/or monthly community calls);
- organising a single access site for presentations, messaging, content, demos and so on;
- access to partner-related forums such as partner advisory councils and technical councils;
- access to beta programmes.

It is the alliance managers' responsibility to develop a training programme which is balanced both technically and also economically. This means that the partner(s) will not be subjected to the cost of attending expensive training courses without the prospect of business flowing from that training as a result of the joint business value propositions which are developed as part of the overall alliance.

Just as with the alliance readiness assessment, the alliance managers will have to use their skills to judge when, how and in what numbers to train up partner staff prior to a real or virtual engagement.

STAGE 3.3: DEVELOPING A SCALABLE GOVERNANCE MODEL

Supporting tools for this task[6]

- 'Trust model' template for high-tech companies.

Developing a scalable governance model means balancing the degree of partner accountability with the size and scope of the alliance envisaged.

There are no right and wrong answers here, much less defined processes, but it is likely that the alliance managers will build the governance model around three critical levels of key stakeholders at the strategic, managerial and operational levels.

The manner in which the alliance managers put the governance model together may vary. In some cases it might be appropriate to hold a joint workshop with the partner(s); in others it might be that the model could be put together as a series of email communications. Whatever form the development process takes, the outcome is the same: a defined document with a number of key sections which set self-imposed rules for both/all parties to the relationship to follow.

The sections in the document should include:

- a list of key stakeholders, including roles and responsibilities;
- contact details of all key stakeholders;
- a list of the documents in use (and their location);
- a description of partner accountabilities (for both/all sides);
- a meetings description (purpose, length, attendees, expected outcomes and so on);
- risk sharing (if appropriate);
- escalation procedures;
- governance bodies (for example, a steering group or joint operational task teams).

These issues are described in further detail below. The governance model should be signed off by the executive sponsors on both/all sides of the relationship.

Governance structures

Management of an alliance will be greatly facilitated when the basic governance structure established by the MOUP and/or procurement instrument is clearly defined.

---

6   This tool is available from the Alliance Best Practice website at www.alliancebestpractice.com or from info@alliancebestpractice.com.

It can be assumed that the partners have achieved a high level of trust and have a shared commitment to achieving results. They can maintain openness and accountability to one another by establishing clear agreements on governance procedures. At a minimum, it is desirable to address the following areas:

- specific roles and responsibilities of alliance partners, as well as of their relevant supporting units;
- key elements of governance, such as frequency of meetings, decision making processes, participants, the need for working groups, outreach to stakeholders/beneficiaries, and monitoring systems;
- how to resolve differences should these arise.

Addressing governance issues in writing at the outset of an alliance will prove invaluable as partner personnel rotate during the lifetime of the alliance or new partners are brought in. The document created might be equivalent to a mission order, though it does not need to be as formal. It should be a living document, to be amplified or modified as the parties gain more experience of working together.

Roles and responsibilities

- **Clarity of authority** – Who are the key stakeholders? Who is authorised to make decisions, convene meetings, address implementation issues and provide substantive technical information? It is a good idea to provide a formal list of names, contact information and level of authority to all relevant participants.
- **Representation** – Who has a supportive role, and how should they be kept in the loop (and by whom)? Decisions should be made on the mode and frequency of participation in, or information on, alliance issues.
- **Transparency and accountability** – Partners should agree on and practise direct communication on all aspects of alliance implementation, at all three working levels (strategic, managerial and operational). It is important to inform each other about the relevant internal processes of each partner, and any changes therein.

Governance structure and operations

Clear 'rules of the game' make it easier for alliance partners to focus on their role in implementation. Alliances comprised of many partners, or regional alliances serving as funding sources for sub-alliances or grants, may require the preparation of formal by-laws and the establishment of working committees, while less complex alliances can operate on a more informal basis. Where alliances include a number of corporate partners which may be competitors and accustomed to keeping each other at arm's length, provisions need to be made to keep essential information flowing smoothly.

Questions that could be addressed include:

- What is the frequency of meetings of the principal governing body of the alliance? Are teleconference meetings acceptable?
- Who convenes and who participates (actively, or with observer status) in meetings? Should there be working committees, and if so, what are their specific responsibilities?

Should periodic open meetings be convened for information sharing and gathering purposes with parties relevant to alliance progress (including beneficiaries)?

- Who is empowered to make binding decisions? Will decisions be made by consensus or by vote? Who is responsible for setting the agenda, preparing minutes and circulating them? Should minutes be signed by the principals?
- In alliances where partners are pooling their funding, what is the process for making funds available? The level and timing of funding needs should be discussed, as well as the likely burn rate of the activity.
- How will alliances work with beneficiaries, host governments and potential new partners? To what extent will partners inform each other when they have separate contacts with such groups? A voluntary code of conduct is one way alliance partners signal commitment to alliance precepts.
- What kind of public outreach is relevant, given the host country situation? Should the alliance develop a joint approach? Does each partner prefer to publicise its efforts separately? Should outreach be aimed at informing, garnering public support or satisfying host government concerns? In some countries, and for some alliances, outreach may need to be aimed at combating misinformation by others.
- How will partners monitor and report alliance progress? Is there a limited set of performance indicators or metrics that all partners are willing to adopt and use, notwithstanding any additional indicators they may wish to identify and track? Do partners have reporting requirements that the alliance can help them meet?

Resolving differences

Conflicts among partners in an alliance must be anticipated. In the interest of good governance it is appropriate to address the issue and identify, at a minimum, principles that should be followed in the event of disagreement. Such principles include:

- always proceeding with respect for the other party;
- clarifying underlying issues;
- identifying options for resolving disagreements;
- being inclusive, not exclusive, of stakeholders who might be able to propose solutions;
- agreeing at the outset on procedures for resolving disagreements;
- agreeing on time limits within which problems should be resolved.

Stage 4: Developing Trust to Grow the Alliance

The key activities in Stage 4 are:

4.1   developing a balanced set of alliance metrics;
4.2   developing a joint relationship development plan;
4.3   monitoring and amending the alliance as necessary.

STAGE 4.1: DEVELOPING A BALANCED SET OF ALLIANCE METRICS

Supporting tools for this task[7]

- ABP's sample 'Alliance Balanced Scorecard Dashboard';
- 'Alliance Balanced Scorecard Explanation' (explanatory slide deck);
- ABP's sample 'Alliance Balanced Scorecard for ABC Corporation;
- the ABP white paper 'How to Develop an Alliance Balanced Scorecard';
- 'Managing Alliances with the Balanced Scorecard' by Robert S. Kaplan, David P. Norton and Bjarne Rugelsjoen.[8]

There is a growing body of evidence to suggest that business-to-business trust is not just a factor involved in the ongoing development of a strategic alliance, it is the single most important factor and goal of ongoing alliance management.

Stage 4 in our model focuses in detail on this extremely important element of collaborative business relationships, and shows how (suitably supported by other measurement systems) the securing and subsequent improvement of trust in the relationship is a prime goal of the modern alliance manager.

The first task in Stage 4 is to develop an agreed set of metrics to measure the relationship. These measurement sets are sometimes called 'alliance scorecards', and ABP strongly believes that these scorecards should be 'balanced', as in Kaplan et al.'s 'Balanced Scorecard' approach. This is because alliance relationships are about more than just financial considerations; our research has led us to conclude that a healthy alliance can be measured in at least five dimensions or categories, each of which brings a different insight to the management and optimisation of alliance relationships. To recap, these dimensions are: Commercial, Technical, Strategic, Cultural and Operational.

One of the most significant obstacles to effectively managing and learning from alliances is the difficulty of comprehensively measuring partnership performance. Leading organisations establish a broad set of financial and strategic indicators to evaluate alliance performance, and conduct timely postmortem reviews to extract lessons learned from recently completed alliances.

Problems addressed

- **Insufficient metrics** – Companies tend to define and therefore measure alliance performance purely in financial terms. Yet traditional financial metrics fail to capture the 'soft' value generated by many alliances, nor do they adequately track development of the relationship itself.
- **Reluctance to scrutinise failures** – Companies rush to distance themselves from unsuccessful partnerships rather than capturing the learning opportunities inherent in a failed alliance.

---

7   These tools are available from the Alliance Best Practice website at www.alliancebestpractice.com or from info@alliancebestpractice.com.

8   Robert S. Kaplan, David P. Norton and Bjarne Rugelsjoen, 'Managing Alliances with the Balanced Scorecard', *Harvard Business Review* 88(1), January–February 2010, pp. 114–20.

Features

- **Holistic performance measures** – A customised set of financial and non-financial metrics for each alliance allows companies to measure progress towards monetary and strategic objectives as well as to assess the underlying health of the relationship.
- **Timely evaluation** – Regular monitoring of 'live' alliance performance allows managers to detect and address problems early, while prompt postmortem reviews ensure that participants contribute fresher, better-informed lessons learned.
- **Link to participant performance** – By establishing a direct link between the performance measures of an alliance and those of its participants, companies create transparency in terms of how participants will be evaluated and strengthen accountability for their involvement with the partnership.

Successful alliances provide a proven route to growth and profitability. They rely on a good value proposition, joint working, matching cultures and strong relationships. Having appropriate commercial arrangements, strategies, technology, culture and operational practices will make a major difference.

Yet when organisations come to manage alliance performance, most alliance measures don't inform or influence these factors. After revenue, they tend to concentrate on what is easily measured (such as marketing activity).

In contrast, companies want to know whether they are doing the right things, influencing the right behaviours and having the right results.

The Alliance Best Practice Balanced Scorecard helps to:

- focus attention on what matters so that alliance managers understand what is important to improve day-to-day alliance management;
- assess and demonstrate progress and performance;
- distinguish between causes and effects of success;
- focus attention on the underlying drivers of success – culture, styles of management, skills, relationships and knowledge – that make alliances work and will take clients to the next level;
- demonstrate the value that is being created.

Alliance measurement in Stage 4 concentrates on the operation of individual alliances, rather than the alliance strategy and the portfolio of alliances. However, it does have consequential value for both, as discussed below.

For your alliance portfolio

- Manage your portfolio as a whole.
- Build a clear view of all alliance activity across the business.
- Demonstrate where value is created.
- Maximise synergy across alliances.

For individual alliances

- Improve the visibility of alliance activity and performance.

- Help the alliance focus on what matters most.
- Address culture, behaviour, capability, activity and results.

Modern balanced scorecards start with a strategy map. This sets the context for the scorecard and ensures that you focus on what matters – that which is strategic rather than tactical. A key element is cause and effect: What capabilities will drive future performance? This also makes management meetings and reporting far more effective. Table 6.10 shows the structure of such a scorecard.

Table 6.10   The structure of an ABP alliance balanced scorecard

	Objective	Measure	Target	Initiative	Who
	What the strategy must achieve	How success will be measured	The level of performance required	Key investment programmes	Responsibilities
Commercial	Example: Develop a cost/value ratio for the alliance	Example: The commercial return for the financial investment in the relationship	Example: 2010 – 15:1 2011 – 25:1	Example: Improved joint financial reporting	Example: Alliance managers
Technical	Example: Improve market fit of alliance BVPs	Example: The degree to which the alliance BVPs are differentiated in the market	Example: Market share increase of 20% in current year	Example: Establish a BVP test centre and customer feedback groups	Example: chief technical officer and alliance sponsors
Strategic	Example: Develop other relationships with the same partner(s) over time	Example: A 'heat map' indication of relationship growth in both/all companies	Example: Increase number of countries where the relationship exists by five in current year	Example: Conduct country 'roadshows' illustrating the value of the relationship	Example: Alliance managers and country general managers
Cultural	Example: Increase the degree of business-to-business cultural alignment	Example: Output score of the 'Identity Compass' tool	Example: Increase degree by 30% in current year	Example: Design and adopt a jointly agreed 'Identity Compass'	Example: Alliance managers from both parties

Table 6.10   The structure of an ABP alliance balanced scorecard *continued*

	Objective	Measure	Target	Initiative	Who
	What the strategy must achieve	How success will be measured	The level of performance required	Key investment programmes	Responsibilities
Operational	Example: Increase the degree of business-to-business operational alignment	Example: The number of operational meetings held 'in-country'	Example: A minimum of four meetings per year with an agreed agenda	Example: Alliance management facilitation of early meetings	Example: Alliance manager

STAGE 4.2: DEVELOPING A JOINT RELATIONSHIP DEVELOPMENT PLAN

Supporting tools for this task[9]

- 'ABP RACI Process' (explanatory slide deck)
- 'ABP RACI' template (a blank template for client use)
- *Role & Responsibility Charting (RACI)* by Michael L. Smith and James Erwin[10]
- RACI Template by Sandra Diaferio.

The essence of Stage 4 is to support structured growth in the alliance relationship through agreed development activities. The added complication with alliance activity development and planning is the fact that many objectives and action plans require the help and support of multiple people from both/all partnering organisations. The result is the creation of a 'virtual' project team whose members need to work together effectively despite not being part of the same organisation or even being physically located in the same place.

The RACI approach to virtual project management activities is integral to the success of this stage.

Responsibility charting is a technique for identifying functional areas where there are process ambiguities, bringing the differences out into the open and resolving them through a cross-functional collaborative effort.

Responsibility charting enables managers from the same or different organisational levels, or indeed companies, to participate actively in a focused and systematic discussion about process-related descriptions of the actions that must be accomplished in order to deliver a successful end product or service.

---

9   These tools are available from the Alliance Best Practice website at www.alliancebestpractice.com or from info@alliancebestpractice.com.

10   Michael L. Smith and James Erwin, *Role & Responsibility Charting (RACI)*, Philadelphia, PA: Project Management Institute, 2011: https://pmicie.org/images/downloads/raci_r_web3_1.pdf (accessed 8 April 2014).

Approach definitions

Responsibility charting is a way to systematically clarify relationships pertaining to:

- alliances in and between different companies;
- internal stakeholders, divided into three levels of governance – strategic, managerial and operational;
- communication or actions required to deliver an acceptable product or service;
- functional roles or departmental positions (no personal names);
- participation expectations assigned to roles by decisions or actions.

Responsibility charting theory

Managers and supervisors are not accountable for everything in their organisation or alliances. Responsibility charting ensures that accountability is placed with the person who really can be accountable for specific work. This often results in accountability for actions being moved down to the most appropriate level, thus speeding up critical actions which in turn significantly improves alliance performance.

Everyone has some process role in their job. Because of differing perceptions, one person's view of his role may be quite different from another's. Role perceptions held today will change tomorrow even though the job activities remain the same. There are three basic assumptions in any role:

1. **Role conception** – What a person thinks his/her job is and how the person has been taught to do it. This thinking may well be influenced by many false assumptions (for example, misleading titles, or training received from a predecessor during his last week on the job).
2. **Role expectation** – What others in the organisation think the person is responsible for, and how he should carry out those responsibilities. Others' ideas may also be influenced by incorrect information (for example, the way tings were done at a former job, priority changes, assumptions, or inconsistent messages from leadership). The role expectation is usually based on the output of results expected from the role.
3. **Role behaviour** – What a person actually does in carrying out the job.

Responsibility charting reconciles *role conceptions* with *role expectations*, meaning that *role behaviour* becomes more predictable and productive. Ideally, what a person thinks his job is, what others expect of that job, and how the job is actually performed are all the same. The RACI process is a tool to lock all elements in place. Working with other process providers provides a real-time consensus that clarifies who is to do what, with whom and when. This is of great benefit for overall process performance.

A substandard product or process can often be tracked back to a fault in the chart. Common faults in the chart include an action which should be included in the chart being missing, a position failing to perform as assigned, or a missing or misapplied responsibility code. The highly visible and collaborative nature of the charting process promotes rapid and effective updates/corrections as well as better understanding by those involved in the work.

Diagnosing the need

The need for managers and supervisors to clarify roles and responsibilities does not end after the responsibility charting process is complete; it must be an ongoing activity. Alliance managers need to acquire a 'sixth sense' so they can recognise the symptoms of role confusion and determine when the process needs to be repeated. Perception drift is natural. The identification and elimination of such drift is important to the relationship's overall wellbeing as it relates to cost, service and quality.

The symptoms of role confusion include:

- concern over who makes decisions;
- blaming others for not getting the job done;
- out-of-balance workloads;
- lack of action because of ineffective communications;
- issues about who does what;
- a 'we–they' attitude;
- a 'not sure, so take no action' attitude;
- idle time;
- creation of and attention to non-essential work to fill time;
- a reactive work environment;
- poor morale;
- multiple 'stops' needed to find an answer to a question.

RACI charting definitions

- **Responsible (R): 'The doers'** – Doers are the individuals who actually complete the tasks. Doers are responsible for action/implementation. Responsibility can be shared. The degree of responsibility is determined by the accountable (A) individual.
- **Accountable (A): 'The buck stops here'** – The accountable individual is ultimately answerable for the activity or decision. This includes 'yes' or 'no' authority and veto power. Only one accountable individual can be assigned to an action.
- **Consult (C): 'In the loop'** – The consult role is undertaken by one or more individuals (typically subject matter experts) to be consulted prior to a final decision or action. There is a predetermined need for two-way communication. Input from the designated position is required.
- **Inform (I) – 'Keep in the picture'** – Individuals in this role need to be informed after a decision or action is taken. They may be required to take action themselves as a result of the outcome. This is one-way communication.

RACI charting: The six-step process

1. Identify actions that will develop the relationship. Start with high-impact areas first:
   - Don't chart processes that will soon change.
   - Work processes must be well-defined.
   - Fewer than ten activities implies the definition is too narrow.
   - More than 25 activities implies the definition is too broad.

2. Determine the decisions and activities to chart:
   - Avoid obvious, generic or ambiguous activities, such as 'attend meetings' or 'prepare reports'.
   - Each activity or decision should begin with a good action verb, for example:

Evaluate	Schedule	Write	Record	Determine
Operate	Monitor	Prepare	Update	Collect
Approve	Conduct	Develop	Inspect	Train
Publish	Report	Review	Authorise	Decide

3. Prepare a list of roles or people involved in those tasks. Roles can be individuals, groups or entire departments:
   - These can include people outside your department our outside the company.
   - Involve customers, suppliers and so on.
   - Roles are better than individual names. The RACI chart should be independent of personal relationships so that the chart would still be valid if new people filled all the roles tomorrow.
4. Develop the RACI chart. As a general rule, first assign the Rs then determine who has the A, then complete the Cs and Is.
   - For larger groups or more complex issues, an independent facilitator is required.
   - Meeting time can be significantly reduced if a 'straw model' list of decisions and activities is completed prior to the meeting.
5. Secure feedback and buy-in:
   - Distribute the RACI chart to everyone represented on the chart but not present at the development meeting.
   - Capture their changes and revise the chart as appropriate.
   - Issue the revised RACI chart.
   - Update as necessary on a ongoing basis.
   - The ideal group size is four to ten people.
   - A follow-up meeting may be necessary if significant changes are made.

Table 6.11 shows an extract from a relationship development plan RACI chart.

Table 6.11 RACI charting a relationship development plan (partial extract only)

Actions	Responsible	Accountable	Consulted	Informed
Research all key stakeholders	Global alliance manager	Country alliance manager Alliance administrative support (if available)	Country general managers from both/all partners	Global VP alliances
Run relationship development workshop	Regional VP alliances	Global alliance manager Country alliance manager	Country sales and account managers in target accounts	Country general manager

Table 6.11 **RACI charting a relationship development plan (partial extract only)** *continued*

Actions	Responsible	Accountable	Consulted	Informed
Agree relationship development action plan	Global alliance manager	Global alliance manager Country alliance manager	Global VP alliances	Country general manager
Agree joint investment and training plan	Regional VP alliances	Head of professional services training Country general managers from both/all partners	Head of professional services training Country general manager	Alliance executive sponsor Global VP alliances
Sign off relationship	Alliance executive sponsor	Country general manager Head of professional services training	Regional head of sales	Global head of direct and indirect sales

Note: While there might be multiple entries in the other boxes, there should only be one entry in the 'Responsible' box.

6. Develop the action plan. An important element of RACI charting involves developing the actions to be charted and agreed upon. The lists can be developed in several ways:
    – One effective way to gather information on functions, decisions, or activities is via a one-on-one interview. This interview is an analytical questioning process and ranges from broad questions such as 'What are the department's objectives?' or 'What must the team accomplish?' to very specific questions involving inputs and outputs of work, both to and from the participant.
    – An alternative to such an interview is a group 'brainstorm' or other idea generation technique with representatives from the process participant departments. A facilitator records the actions which can then be fine-tuned in subsequent group meetings.

The usefulness of RACI chart analysis

One of the important uses of the completed chart is to assess the reasonableness of the intended actions and plans. This can be accomplished in one of two ways: vertical analysis and horizontal analysis (see Table 6.12).

Table 6.12 RACI charting: vertical and horizontal analysis

Vertical analysis	
Observation	**Question**
Lots of Rs	Can this individual stay on top of so much?
No empty spaces	Does the individual need to be involved in so many activities?
Too many As	Can some of the accountability be 'pushed down' in the organisation?
No Rs or As	Is this a line position? Could it be expanded or eliminated?
Overall pattern	Does the pattern fit the personality and style of the role occupant? Does it go against the personality type of the role occupant (that is, either too much or too little involvement, and so on)?
Horizontal analysis	
Observation	**Question**
Lots of Rs	Will the task get done? Can activities or decisions be broken down into more specific tasks?
Lots of Cs	Do all these individuals really need to be consulted? Do the benefits of added input justify the time lost in consulting all these individuals?
Lots of Is	Do all these individuals really need to be routinely informed, or could they be informed only in exceptional circumstances?
No Rs	The job may not get done; everyone is waiting to approve, be consulted or informed; no one sees their role as taking the initiative to get the job done.
No As	There is no performance accountability, and therefore there is no personal consequence when the job doesn't get done. Rule no. 1 in RACI charting: There must be one, but only one A for each action or decision listed in the chart.
No Cs or Is	Is this because individuals or departments don't communicate? Does lack of communication between individuals or departments result in parallel or uninformed actions?

RACI closing guidelines

* Place accountability (A) and responsibility (R) at the lowest feasible level.
* There can be only one accountable individual per activity.
* Authority must accompany accountability.
* Minimise the number of consults (Cs) and informs (Is)
* All roles and responsibilities must be documented and communicated.
  - Discipline is needed to keep the roles and responsibilities clear. Drift happens. RACI has to be revisited periodically, especially when symptoms of role confusion reappear (see the section on 'Diagnosing the need' above).

When to use responsibility charting

* Use it to improve understanding of the roles and responsibilities regarding the work process:
  - 'as is' and
  - 'to be'.

- Use it to improve understanding of roles and responsibilities within a department.
- Use it to define the roles and responsibilities of team members on a project.
- Use it to improve internal alignment so that everyone within your company understands who does what and why.
- Use it to improve business-to-business alignment so that everyone in the partner organisations understands who does what and why.

Trying to get work done without clearly established roles and responsibilities is like trying to parallel park with one eye closed.

What about role behaviour?

The RACI chart shows who does what at a high level and individuals' RACI role. If more specificity is needed – and it often is – you can use process maps or list the steps or decisions and document the specifics of what needs to be and has been done.

You can go from process maps to RACI charts or RACI charts to process maps, or you can document your understanding of the role behaviour by taking the RACI chart and listing the steps or decisions and documenting the specifics of actions in simple terms: who, what, when, inputs and outputs. You can expect more resistance when clarifying the roles in this way than if you use RACI charting alone.

We now know who is to do what with whom and when in such a way that each person is truly accountable for their part of the overall process, and we can draw up a chart to assign roles and responsibilities – see a suggested layout below.

Task/ decision	RACI	Who	What	When	Inputs from	Outputs to

STAGE 4.3: MONITORING AND AMENDING THE ALLIANCE AS NECESSARY

Supporting tools for this task[11]

- 'The Alliance Relationship Change Management Process' (explanatory slide deck).
- 'The Relationship Change Management Agenda' (ABP template).
- 'How to Run Review Meetings' (ABP factsheet).
- 'Designing and Implementing a Key Metrics Set for Alliances' (an ABP common success factor).
- 'Designing and Implementing an Operational Metrics Set' (an ABP common success factor).
- 'How to Conduct an Alliance Strategy Review Meeting'.

---

11   These tools are available from the Alliance Best Practice website at www.alliancebestpractice.com or from info@alliancebestpractice.com.

The final task in Stage 4 is to monitor and amend the joint action plan. This is accomplished by conducting a regular and planned relationship change management process, a key part of which involves relationship change management meetings.

We all know that the only constant is change, therefore as alliance executives we need to be careful to factor change into our plans. However, change too often has a disruptive and disturbing effect both on alliance personnel and also on the processes designed to ensure success. Consequently, we recommend that relationship change management meetings be conducted no more frequently than every 90 days.

Care should be taken in this task to ensure that all appropriate decision makers are fully consulted before changes are made to the agreed joint action plan. In reality, it is unlikely that all the decision makers will be able to attend the meetings to discuss these points, so effective use needs to be made of teleconferencing and the circulation of the existing joint action plan and the proposed changes well in advance of the change management meeting.

Who should attend?

The purpose of the meeting will dictate who should attend, as shown in Table 6.13.

Table 6.13 Review meeting attendee criteria

Purpose	Attendees	Probable frequency
Operational reviews to ensure that the joint action plan is being followed and the development of any remedial actions	Operational representatives from both/all sides, with remote input from those who could not attend	Monthly Facilitated by the alliance managers
Managerial reviews assessing the degree of resources allocated and the accomplishment of key milestones	The alliance managers reporting to the alliance executive sponsors, either face-to-face or by teleconference	Quarterly Facilitated by the alliance managers from both/all sides.
Strategic annual assessments of the direction and long-term goals of the alliance and the consideration of any investment/ divestment decisions	The full alliance steering group and the alliance managers from both/all sides, with remote input from those who could not attend.	Annually Facilitated by the executive sponsors

What should be discussed?

We suggest that the points in Table 6.14 provide a sufficiently pragmatic guide when setting the agendas for review meetings.

Table 6.14 Review meeting agenda guide

Operational reviews	Managerial reviews	Strategic reviews
Personnel changes since the last meeting and assessment of their impact	Review of the key metrics set and discussion of any changes necessary	Review of the previous MOUP and assessment of any changes necessary
Review of the operational metrics set and discussion of any changes necessary	Discussion of overall targets and achievement rates, including any remedial action necessary	Consideration of any investment/disinvestment decisions as a result
Discussion of operational targets and achievement rate, including any remedial action necessary	Documentation of changes and circulation of proposed changes	Reassessment of market conditions and growth forecasts
Documentation of changes and circulation of proposed changes	Co-ordination of feedback and publishing of an agreed new joint relationship development plan	Amendment or restatement of the alliance strategy
Co-ordination of feedback and publishing of an agreed new joint operational plan		Documentation of all approved changes and circulation of these to key stakeholders
		Co-ordination of feedback and publishing of an agreed new joint alliance strategy

Applying the Methodology: Three Successful Case Examples

The following scenarios are three recent examples from partnerships in the high-tech sector in Europe. Their purpose is to illustrate that when you choose a new partner (or a partner new to a particular country), you should pay attention to a multiple set of business-to-business alignment factors. If you do so, success will follow.

PARTNER A AND PARTNER B IN POLAND

The client was Nordea bank in Poland. The joint service offering (JSO) was to deliver a high-availability data centre solution using optical disk storage technology and Partner A's systems integration skills.

Although Partner A had a good relationship with Partner B (the chosen partner) in other countries in Europe, this would be the first time the two had worked together in Poland.

The project was very well received, and the client chose the Partner A/Partner B combination because:

> The partnership was clearly harmonious from the start, both sides knew exactly what each contributed and how to leverage the skills and unique capabilities of the other. We had no hesitation in awarding the contract to the Partner A/Partner B collaboration.
>
> *CIO, Nordea EMEA*

For Partner B this was a breakthrough win involving a key enterprise client in the financial sector:

It couldn't have been done without support from the partner, I am really pleased about the quality of co-operation with our partner.

Territory Sales Leader, Partner B, Poland

Relationship ABP score: 84/100
Total contract value of the assignment: €2.75 million

PARTNER C AND PARTNER D IN SPAIN

The client was Banco Pastor in Spain, which has 655 branches and 4,500 staff. The opportunity was particularly important for Partner D as it would be the first time it had competed head-to-head in mainland Europe with Cisco (a traditional Partner C favourite) for a key client.

The project was the enterprise-wide implementation of Partner D's cloud-ready data centre solution. This solution was a combination of Partner C's services integration capabilities and implementation methods and Partner D's products.

The account was particularly important for Partner C as it represented a 'win back' client from a key competitor that had been targeted previously as a must-win account for 2012.

Although Partner C could have partnered with Cisco for the bid, it chose to go with Partner D:

We went with Partner D because they were the more hungry for the business. They listened to our concerns and worked with us to allow us to understand how we would support this implementation in the future. They were sensitive throughout to the strategic nature of the account to us.

VP Financial Markets Iberia, Partner C

The collaboration was successful in being chosen from among 39 other company offerings in a very intensive RFP procedure.

The result for the client was improved networking capability and reduced costs.

Relationship ABP score: 88/100
Total contract value of the assignment: €3.4 million

PARTNER E AND PARTNER F IN SWITZERLAND

The client was Novartis, with its head office in Switzerland. The account represented a key strategic account for both Partner E and Partner F. Both organisations offered power management hardware and service capability, and both had a troubled history of lack of co-operation in Europe prior to this account.

Both Partner E and Partner F had struggled to make any headway in the account on their own, and in fact both were facing meltdown and removal from the account.

A last-ditch effort was made by both sides to work together harmoniously. By combining their offerings and working together, they managed to retain the account, grow the account revenue and turn the account around:

We had to put personal considerations aside because we were falling off a cliff! We had to try to understand each other's position, and (whatever else happened in the rest of Europe) we had to trust each other in the relationship and work with the best interests of the client in mind.

VP Marketing, Partner F

Relationship ABP score: 87/100
Total contract value of the assignment: €3.5 million

III
Common Success Factors

7 *The Commercial Dimension*

Whichever way you look at it, strategic alliances of any kind have to start with an answer to the commercial question, 'What's in it for me/us?'

Co1: A Joint Business Value Proposition

All parties to the relationship must have a very clear and common understanding of the business value proposition.

It seems obvious that both/all parties to any collaborative relationship should have a clear understanding of the BVP created by the alliance, but this is by no means universally common. In many cases organisations collaborate because of a perception that each is a powerful player in a particular business sector, therefore getting together must be a good thing. However, consider the following case study.

Case Study 8: IBM and Siemens in Germany

Siemens, one of the world's largest electrical engineering and electronics companies, headquartered in Berlin and Munich, was looking to instigate a strategic alliance with a global systems integrator. The company was well positioned to be attractive to potential partners. It is one of the world's largest in its chosen business sector, and holds leading market positions in all its focused business areas.

The company has approximately 475,000 employees working to develop and manufacture products, design and install complex systems and projects, and tailor a wide range of services to individual requirements. It provides innovative technologies and comprehensive know-how to benefit customers in over 190 countries.

It was founded 160 years ago, and the company focuses on the areas of automation and control, power, transportation, medical, information and communications and lighting. In the financial year ended September 2006 it had sales of €87.325 billion and net income of €3.033 billion.

The particular division that was looking to partner was the Enterprise Communications division, which makes large telecommunications switching equipment essential, for example, in large call centres.

The executive head of this division in Germany had just had a very uncomfortable meeting with his global president at which it was made clear to the executive that his profit margin was not good enough. The margin was currently 7.3–8.6%, depending on the product line.

The executive concluded that he urgently needed an alliance to help transform his division from a products company to a services company, because in such a services company the margins are much higher (typically anywhere between 13% and 18%)

The division had a historical relationship with PricewaterhouseCoopers (PwC, part of which had been recently acquired by IBM and renamed IBM Global Services). Both organisations had worked together successfully in the past, and the senior executive had a good personal relationship with the ex-PwC senior partner based in Munich.

The result was that both men went out to dinner in one of Munich's fashionable gentlemen's clubs, and over coffee and port discussed the possibility of an alliance relationship.

The logic appeared impeccable. Both organisations worked well together. Both organisations were active in the enterprise telecommunications sector (indeed, it was a major focus area for both of them). Both organisations had a high regard and respect for the other based on a shared passion for technical engineering excellence. Combined, they had ready access to an overwhelming majority of their clients' boardrooms in Germany.

The deal was agreed within ten minutes, and close observers report that the defining moment came when the executive looking for the partnership said:

'Look, we're big in this sector and you're big in this sector, so combined we must represent a juggernaut! It makes strategic sense for us to combine our efforts, so let's establish an initial target for the alliance at, say, €50 million in the first year and let our respective staffs work out the precise details.'

Consequently, the following Monday a senior manager at Siemens arrived at his desk to find some 'good' news. The email essentially said:

'Congratulations you have been promoted to the newly created position of Strategic Alliance Manager with special responsibility for IBM Global Services. Your job is to exploit the rapidly expanding enterprise communications sector in Germany, and you have an initial target of €50 million in the first year. The executive vice president in charge of your division has negotiated this deal himself with a senior partner in IBM and will be taking a keen interest in your progress.'

The manager had a number of options, of course. He could:

- book an interview with the vice president and ask for the underlying logic of the relationship, and more specifically the business value proposition underpinning the collaboration;
- recognise that he had been given an impossible job (a 'poisoned chalice') and resign immediately;
- contact the partner and start to look busy, hoping that the logic of the commercial imperative would become clear over time.

Which would you have done?

Which one do you think the manager did?

Yes – absolutely right! He contacted the partner, to find that an equally bemused senior manager at IBM had received an equally disturbing email from the executive vice president in charge of large-scale telecommunications integrations. Together they planned meetings and enthusiastically talked about 'getting on' together and the close personal and organisational synergies that existed between both organisations.

They produced white papers that showed how both had an excellent track record in the area, and they both actively canvassed their respective organisations for opportunities to contact customers and explain their collaboration.

The story has a tragic ending, because the sales forces in both organisations asked the not unreasonable question of our two alliance professionals, 'What are we selling?' Unfortunately, neither could adequately describe the value proposition to the customer in a compelling manner. Consequently, they received little or no interest from prospective customers and no internal support from the field sales forces on both sides.

As the year progressed and the required sales failed to materialise, both individuals grew more and more frantic. By now they had used their senior executive support to secure budget to develop some concept architectures, and had even commandeered a building in the commercial sector in Munich to demo the solutions to prospective clients. This area was called a 'customer experience suite', and was expensively laid out to showcase the capabilities of both organisations. It didn't come cheap, obviously, because a large range of leading-edge technologies were deployed there, and a number of knowledgeable staff were employed to explain the breakthrough use of this technology.

In addition, a series of expensive roadshows was organised to take the solution from city to city in Germany to appeal to large corporate clients of both organisations.

In Berlin, a prospective customer was talking to a chief technologist from Siemens. His question was simple: 'Why is this a good solution for me?' The technologists answering this question talked about technical excellence and the combined reputations of both sides, and the customer went away shaking his head.

Inevitably, towards the end of the allotted first year the two alliance managers were called in front of their respective executives and castigated for their abject 'failure' in managing the relationship. Many hundreds of thousands of euros had been spent on a fruitless series of marketing campaigns, and no sales had been forthcoming. The two managers were reprimanded severely, and both subsequently left their respective companies after vowing never to be involved with strategic alliances again!

Tragic as this tale is, it is depressingly familiar to a large number of alliance professionals I speak to. But what really went wrong here? On the face of it there were many factors that should have contributed to success:

- There was a high degree of senior executive support.
- They had good access to customer boardrooms in the chosen geographic sector (Germany).
- Both organisations had very good reputations.
- There were good personal and organisational relationships at multiple levels.
- There was a large budget to market the chosen solutions.

The one thing missing, of course, was a business value proposition that made sense to the target customers.

Notice that the value to both partners was obvious and high. The products company gained the opportunity to sell expensive switching equipment and become involved in solutions (with the help of the systems integrator) so its margin increased (a prerequisite for the electronics vice president). The systems integrator gained the opportunity to work with good technical products to develop potential solutions that provide a high value multiplication factor. For every €1 spent on equipment it earned seven to twelve times that amount in integration services.

In the best cases, the BVP is actually a breakthrough value proposition (a product and/or service which customers cannot currently obtain from other suppliers or combinations of suppliers).

Good alliance managers know that any consideration of a strategic alliance has to start with the fundamental question, 'What's in it for the customer?' Unless the collaboration can answer this seemingly simple question quickly and obviously, then in very many cases the relationship is doomed from the outset.

Of course, the complication in a collaboration is that the customer is not the only stakeholder involved. Not only does the value to the customer need to be clear, the value to both/all parties to the collaboration needs to be equally clear, and ensuring this is not a trivial exercise. Notice that simple 'aggregation' of services and or products is not enough to differentiate a successful collaboration. In Case Study 8 both organisations had a leading position in the chosen sector, but simply coming together and hoping that something good would be developed was a fatally flawed plan.

Leading companies take great pains to ensure that before they start they are able to answer three critical questions:

- What's in it for us? – Why does the prospective solution represent good value?
- What's in it for the partner? – What will motivate the partner to do this as well?
- What's in it for the consumer? – Is the service offered substantially different from other offerings because of the nature of the partners in the relationship?

Simplistic as this scenario might sound, it sometimes becomes extremely complex, particularly in scenarios where one or more of the partners could be deemed to be in 'co-opetition'. Co-opetition is typically a situation in which one or more organisations collaborate to generate value for end consumers and/or to secure a business deal or opportunity. However, they are also partial or full competitors, either fully (all their functions compete) or in part (one small part of each organisation competes with the other partners).

This complicated and confusing landscape gives rise to such concepts as 'Chinese walls', or as IBM calls them, 'firewalls'. Consider a scenario in which a senior IBM account executive responsible for a very large customer may know that the customer needs some solution which requires IBM to partner with another company (for example, Accenture as a systems integrator) and that some business is possible with the target customer, and is trying to secure that business in collaboration with a global systems integrator (in this case Accenture).

The firewall in this scenario involves the organisation relying on the personal morality and ethics of the IBM executive to avoid notifying the IBM Global Services Division (a global systems integrator in its own right and a competitor of Accenture) that this opportunity exists. The difficulty in this scenario for Accenture involves whether it would secure the business anyway without the help of IBM (usually unlikely) and/or, if it is going to partner with IBM, how it can ensure that IBM Global Services (the competing division) does not hear about its critical unique selling propositions.

As far as possible, you should try and ensure that it is difficult for other consortiums to replicate the partnership BVP, so that you extend the period during which you can expect to enjoy a market-leading position.

The existence of a BVP is critical to alliance success. Although all the other factors may be in place, if you and your partner are not offering customers something they can't get elsewhere (or offering it for a price at a quality that they can't get elsewhere), then your relationship is critically hamstrung from the outset. It is a must-have success factor in all your relationships. Those organisations in the ABP Database that do not have this element in place show a very high correlation with failure.

Co2: Choosing a Partner (Due Diligence)

In many cases a full and formal due diligence process may be inappropriate in the early days of an alliance relationship. However, in the best relationships both parties understand that an assessment of how they will work together before they make the attempt is of enormous value. Commonly, organisations perform some form of internal or external diligence around the areas of commercial factors, technical alignment of both companies' products and services, a strategic understanding of where the other partner is heading, a cultural assessment of both organisations, and finally an assessment of how they will collaborate operationally.

It is a truism to say that in the most successful relationships both parties chose the right partners. The reality is somewhat more complex, however, since the research suggests that there is a bell-shaped curve on a graph of factors used to assess or choose a partner and partnership success.

What this means is that if you use too few factors to choose your alliance partners, your relationships will not be successful. As you increase the number and complexity of the factors you use to assess partners, the chances of success increase (sometimes quite sharply). However, this situation does not last for ever, and if you use too many factors, your due diligence process becomes unwieldy and counterproductive as it becomes too difficult to run the process effectively and you may miss out on the market opportunity you were hoping to exploit. This situation is visualised in Figure 7.1.

Organisations tend to differ quite markedly in the degree of time and attention they devote to the question of due diligence before they enter important strategic alliance relationships. This difference is probably most extreme in the cases of the pharmaceutical and biotechnology sector, where due diligence can take many months, if not as long as a year, and the high-tech sector, in which due diligence sometimes appears not to have taken place at all.

Alliance Best Practice has seen many instances in which a struggling relationship can be traced back to the fact that various successive alliance managers have inherited the relationship from their predecessors with no particular thought given to whether their organisation should be in this alliance relationship at all, or indeed any consideration of the suitability of the partnering organisation. In some cases this is because a prospective partner organisation represents a place in the market or has a range of products or services that are absolutely essential to a company seeking a partnership, so it believes it has no choice but to partner. However, in such cases no consideration appears to be given to the degree of difficulty involved in making such an alliance relationship work.

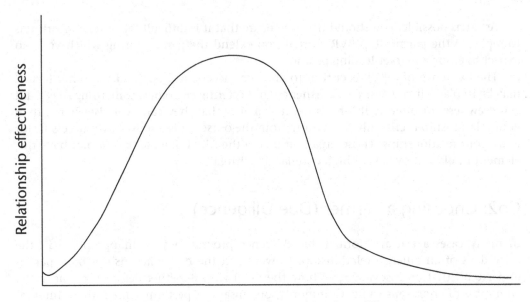

Number of discrete factors selected in due diligence process

Figure 7.1 Partner due diligence effectiveness bell curve

A good example is a situation in which a large US software company with a substantial business in Europe was partnering with a global systems integrator. When questioned, the senior executives in the software company said: 'They are one of the most successful systems integrators in the world and have a critical position in our chosen markets. We have to deal with them because they are ever-present in our chosen market sectors.' However, when the operational alliance managers were questioned, it was clear that the practical difficulties of maintaining the relationship on a day-to-day basis were extremely considerable, if not insurmountable. The systems integrator was arrogant and high-handed in its attitude to the software company, and believed that the software company was merely a supplier of products. This dismissive air was a consistent thread throughout the organisation, resulting in very bad feeling in the software company and a complete absence of any personal chemistry in any of the individual relationships necessary to drive a substantial relationship.

Compare this with a typical situation from a pharmaceutical alliance relationship. In this case, Schering Pharmaceutical developed a potentially valuable compound which could, in time, develop into a commercially attractive drug to combat breast cancer. However, the costs of developing such a compound proved so onerous that it started to look around for a suitable partner to assist it with the development costs and also to help market the drug effectively should it get to that viable stage.

The degree and complexity of Schering Pharmaceutical's due diligence exercises included a range of technical, pharmaceutical, and cultural aspects until at last it decided that AstraZeneca would be the most suitable candidate partner to align with. In this case the due diligence process took some four to six months and was undertaken by a team of five people from Schering Pharmaceutical.

Despite the fact that Bayer HealthCare merged with Schering during this process (some would say acquired it), the relationship continued to flourish and there was a high degree of interaction between both teams. This was further strengthened by the existence of a common purpose: 'beating breast cancer together'. The compound currently under development, and indeed all future activities in the relationship, was shared 50–50, with both sides taking on 50% of the costs and, should they arise, 50% of the future revenues.

In this case, because of the care taken in choosing the partner, the relationship had such a firm foundation that it has survived significant challenges and changes in management teams on both sides. In addition, there is a high degree of mutual respect between the organisations, and although an escalation process exists, it has never been invoked. This is an excellent example of an organisation spending enough time to make a suitable decision so that no time is lost as the relationship develops because the initial choice ends up being fundamentally flawed.

Therefore, assuming you are going to conduct a due diligence exercise with regard to strategic alliances, what aspects should you consider? Many organisations consider only two fundamental types of alignment or interaction in their due diligence exercises:

1. **Commercial due diligence** – Is the prospective partner commercially strong, and will it be in existence over the course of the next five to ten years?
2. **Technical due diligence** – Do our products and services match well with the partner's products and services?

However, there are at least three other areas that should be given serious consideration in any alliance due diligence exercise, as described below.

STRATEGIC DIRECTION

Is the partner generally heading in the same strategic direction as we are? If two organisations have a fundamentally different direction in which they are heading with regard to their business ambitions, this will inevitably cause stresses and strains that will eventually lead to a divergence of purpose and intent in the relationship. Such a situation is unsustainable in the long term.

CULTURAL DIRECTION

Is the organisational culture of our partner well suited to our own? Many organisations fail to consider this aspect at all when initiating their strategic alliances. However, the degree to which prospective partner organisations think in the same way is extremely important in developing that nebulous but extremely powerful concept of 'organisational chemistry'.

Consideration of cultural similarities or differences between organisations is extremely powerful when considering collaborative relationships. This is not to say that both/all organisations need to think exactly the same on all issues. Some degree of diversity is to be welcomed, since this diversity can lead to a high degree of leverage. However, it is important that both/all organisations understand each other's cultural attitudes.

This cultural examination should not be confused with national or geographic cultural attributes (although, of course, these have a part to play). Rather, what we are discussing here are those aspects of the organisation's day-to-day operations that define 'the way we work around here'.

For example, some of the cultural alignment features measured could be aspects such as the personal values illustrated by the perspective of the individuals involved. In other words, are they strongly committed to what is important to the relationship (irrespective of what is important to them or their own organisations)? Can they and their organisations easily view a scenario from another's perspective and see the world through their eyes? What is the speed of the organisations' decision-making capabilities, and is there a significant difference? Whether the organisations make decisions quickly or slowly matters less than a significant *difference* between the speed with which they make decisions.

This is quite obviously one of the stress points in alliances between very large and very small organisations, in which the larger organisation values the fleet-footedness and dynamism of the small organisation but is totally unable to make meaningful decisions at the same pace. What about the organisations' tolerance of change and attitude to risk? Do they have a degree of arrogance allied to some deeply held belief regarding their own organisation's capabilities – for example, technical arrogance in high-tech companies, or quality or engineering arrogance in established manufacturing companies?

A good example of this cultural misalignment that can cause problems is the Air France and Delta Airlines strategic alliance which lies at the heart of SkyTeam. Both companies had been in a genuinely strategic alliance for a number of years, and the strategic and business imperatives of such a relationship were extremely clear and powerful. Both airlines operate from key hub airports in their respective continents – Air France from Charles De Gaulle, and Delta from Atlanta. Both companies have a code-sharing relationship, which means that each can sell seats on the other airline for complementary trips to the same destinations and they even go to the extent of sharing ground crew resources to save on costs (Air France ground crew support and maintain Delta Airlines at Charles De Gaulle, and Delta ground crew support and maintain Air France aircraft at Atlanta).

However, both organisations are fundamentally different in their organisational culture. These differences are best illustrated by two critical examples.

The first concerns the willingness of the organisation (or indeed, individuals in the organisation) to escalate problems. In Air France the junior and middle managers have no difficulty escalating any issues to their line managers. This is seen as an entirely appropriate thing to do, and the quickest way to ensure progress on difficult issues. However, in Delta escalation was generally viewed as a sign of weakness, and an individual who escalated problems too frequently was viewed with deep suspicion about his ability to perform the job role.

This led to damaging situations in which junior members of the alliance relationship on both sides would discuss an issue, and it would become clear to the Air France operatives that it should be escalated. The advisability of such escalation might even have been discussed during a meeting, with the Air France personnel leaving it with a clear impression that an escalation would take place. When their progress was observed some time later (typically within 90 days, which was the usual review period for this relationship), the Air France individuals were not unnaturally angry at such lack of progress and could not understand the seemingly 'diversionary excuses' Delta Airlines' operatives resorted to in order to explain the failure to escalate.

A linked but completely disparate organisational cultural problem was that of the degree of 'politeness' in the organisation. The middle and senior management operatives in the relationship at Air France were typically direct and blunt in their observations. They saw no problems with this as they simply saw themselves as straight-talking individuals. However, Delta's middle and senior management had been born and grown up (in the main) in the deep South of the USA, where courtesy and conversational politeness were essential aspects of their culture.

This led to problems at difficult meetings, where the Air France personnel would express their dissatisfaction with a situation and suggest a course of action, and the Delta individuals would find it hard to disagree or challenge these perceptions with the same degree of forthrightness and bluntness used by their French counterparts. Consequently, although Air France might believe that a decision had been made to rectify a certain situation and that Delta had agreed to a course of action, Delta had merely not voiced disagreement. So once again damaging delays occurred which were inexplicable to either partner.

In the case of Air France and Delta, the chosen remedy was to employ an external cultural alignment consultant to run a series of cultural awareness workshops to illustrate and explore with both partners how each operated in its own organisation. This did not necessarily solve the problem in the sense that both partners changed their attitudes and approaches, but it did mean that both partners now had a clearer understanding of each other's organisational perspectives. Indeed, it developed to such a degree that both felt able to inject humour into the situation and challenge various statements at public meetings with comments like 'Are you being very "Air France" about that?' or 'Are you really happy with that, or are you just being polite to me?'

OPERATIONAL ALIGNMENT

The final dimension that should be considered in due diligence is operational alignment: To what extent will our various operating divisions/countries/functions be able to inter-operate effectively and efficiently in the alliance?

Significant difficulties may arise from something as simple as differences in organisational structure. It would have been extremely easy to observe these differences in advance and predict the consequent difficulties of inter-operation.

For example, if one organisation is structured hierarchically around countries and the other is structured hierarchically around service lines or product sets and both organisations choose to enter into a strategic alliance relationship, then it will only be a matter of time before the stresses and strains of the misaligned organisational structures prove extremely challenging to the success of the relationship. A visual analogy is that one organisation is organised around vertical lines, and the other is organised around horizontal lines. Trying to get the two lines into a degree of alignment is extremely difficult, if not impossible. Such scenarios may play out as follows.

Let's say, for example, that Oracle is structured in Europe around countries (UK, France, Germany, Netherlands, Benelux and so on). It needs an alliance relationship with a large and capable global systems integrator (let's say Accenture).

Both organisations are originally American in inception. Both are extremely commercially aggressive, and both value very highly technical excellence, rigour and the desire to win. So on the face of it they have an excellent opportunity for good alignment. However, although Oracle is organised around country lines, Accenture is organised around practice areas – meaning service lines.

Now let's imagine a meeting between the Accenture executive responsible for logistics practice in Europe and the similarly senior Oracle executive responsible for France. The Accenture executive wants to talk about opportunities and joint development and research spanning the whole of Europe, whereas the Oracle executive simply wants to talk about his own country, France.

The Accenture executive feels there is not enough business in France to warrant his exclusive focus on that country, whereas the Oracle executive knows that Accenture in only one among five or six global integrators he wants to engage with. However, he wants to engage with them all in France alone, and certainly doesn't want to spend time, energy and/or money developing initiatives in other countries for which he has no responsibility and will not be remunerated. The typical tensions such situations produce are as follows.

Both sides agree that while France is not large enough (as a country, as a sector) to warrant exclusive focus, a suitable and significant pilot project can be initiated in France. All is sweetness and light for a significant period as both sides throw their energies into the pilot. From Oracle's point of view, it is seeing good business being conducted in France; from Accenture's point of view, it is seeing a good pilot exercise in the area of logistics. But both sides have to devote considerable amounts of time and effort to the pilot relationship.

Assuming the exercise is a success (which in many cases it is), the Accenture executive returns to the Oracle executive quite quickly to say: 'Good, we've made a success of France, now let's expand or leverage that scenario into other countries.'

This is where the problems begin, because the Oracle executive has no control over the other countries, so he is in no position to commit his colleagues to leveraging the initiative, and the Accenture executive finds himself in the invidious situation of having commit a lot of time, energy and effort to get a successful alliance collaboration off the ground to sell good-quality services and products to a well-satisfied customer set, only to find that he can't leverage that situation.

In many cases one or both/all partners leave what may essentially be a successful relationship quite early on because of a sense of complete discouragement as a result of one or the other's inability to leverage such a good situation into other geographic or technical sectors.

At its heart the problem was one of organisational structure and misalignment, and both parties should have considered the impact of such differences in organisational structure before they even developed the first idea of the pilot. Notice that neither organisation is in a position to change its own organisational structure, which has been developed over a lengthy period and is now embedded in the company DNA.

Co3: Optimum Legal/business Structure

Different alliances have different purposes, and it is important to recognise that a structure that works well for one relationship may not works so well for another. Questions such as whether the relationship should be formal or informal and whether the structure should include or exclude an equity element are all-important in deciding on the best structure. However, bear in mind that each partner's business negotiators should draw up the overall structure of the relationship before it is finalised by their lawyers.

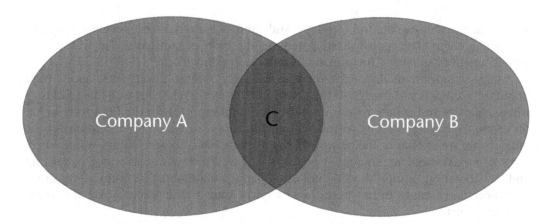

Figure 7.2 Typical alliance interaction zone

One of the many confusing things about strategic alliances, particularly those at the international level, is the lack of a standard format for business or legal structures. The multiplicity of forms which relationships can take is as much a testament to the ingenuity of the alliance professionals practising the collaboration as it is a damning indictment of the lack of standardisation of this rapidly growing commercial business model.

However, a quick glance at an extremely simple diagnostic model of an alliance relationship will deliver some clues about the practical problems involved. Figure 7.2 represents two organisations which are partnering for common competitive advantage.

Because neither organisation wants to own the other, nor indeed be owned by the other, the construction, management structure and organisation of the relationship (see the shaded area C in Figure 7.2) represents the desire of both companies to interact in an efficient and effective manner.

However, notice that neither organisation will change its internal rules or operating protocols to accommodate the other. It is extremely unusual for organisations to enter into a formal joint venture from the outset. Such relationships usually begin as an opportunistic exploitation of a particular commercial opportunity. Only later, as the opportunity grows, or as more opportunities are identified, does the relationship become more formal.

Until the relationship is more formal and until it is regarded as a separate entity, it has to exist within the context of its own organisational rules and structures. These rules and structures apply only in area C in Figure 7.2, and are developed by both partners' alliance executives, heavily influenced by the operating protocols and company culture of the host organisation (Company A or B).

This is the aspect that makes integration and inter-operation so complex. Neither organisation is willing to adopt or accommodate the other's operating protocols (Why should they, because even in relatively junior partners or smaller organisations these processes and protocols have been developed over a lengthy period?), and even if they were prepared to accept the other's operating procedures, they would not be able to persuade the rest of their organisation to accommodate those procedures.

Consequently, what we have is an informal, fluid, flexible structure which has no formal shape, hierarchy or governance model, and all the operating procedures, governance, structure, control, strategy and guidance need to be developed by the individuals themselves, constructed purely on the basis of consensus. No wonder the establishment of suitable structures and models is so difficult!

Many organisations fall back on the relatively safe solution: they apply their 'standard' contracts and models to the situation. This works relatively well in an industry where alliances and collaborations are relatively commonplace (in the high-tech sector, for example), but less well when the relationship is new or where the intentions of the relationship are unclear or the purpose of the relationship is to develop new value where none had existed before. Equally, it performs less well in those areas where partnering and collaboration is not a well-understood and well-established form of business operation (for example, in the professional services arena in the public sector, and in the healthcare sectors).

The development of suitable models, cost structures, and management or governance structures in this area is a growth industry. Many consultants and external advisers currently advise their clients on suitable structures and/or approaches to apply in this area.

However, the problem goes deeper than this, in that in today's modern flexible economies, the problem is not simply bilateral, but rather multidimensional. Figure 7.3 explains this fluidity and dynamism.

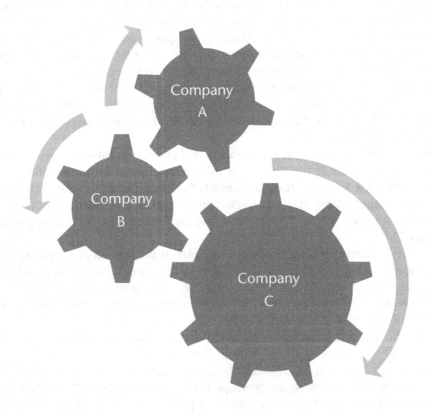

Figure 7.3   Example of an alliance ecosystem interaction

As we can see from Figure 7.3, not only do organisations want to interact with each other, but they also want to interact with other partners or groups of partners to establish common value or to resolve industry- or sector-specific issues. This development is possibly most advanced in the high-tech sector, in which a technical format and standardisation for inter-operability have already been developed (for example, the Open Group organisation monitors, controls and develops open source resources to promote technical inter-operability between organisations).

An excellent book which explores this area in some depth is *The Network Economy* by Ard-Pieter de Man, Professor of Organisation Science at the Free Trade University of Amsterdam, The Netherlands.[1] De Man explores in some depth the landscape of the new network economy, both past and present, the strategies necessary for companies that wish to be successful in the new landscape, and the impacts, both internal and external, of such an approach.

It is clear in an era when increased specialisation is delivering a greater degree of quality and excellence at an ever-reducing price to the consumer that such models will become increasingly important in the future. Indeed, a sub-branch of strategic alliance research already concerns itself very deeply with a consideration of the concept of 'alliance eco-systems'. Although it is not within the remit of this book to explore this important area in any depth (it would take too long and would be an inappropriate degree of specific focus), it is worth noting that some of these alliance eco-systems are becoming extremely powerful (see, for example, the agility alliance championed by EDS Corporation, the extended enterprise developed and co-ordinated by Deloitte Consulting LRC, and the service-orientated enterprise concept championed by, among others, Capgemini, IBM and Oracle).

Co4: A Formal Alliance Audit/healthcheck

Alliances (particularly strategic ones) are typically reassessed regularly to detect dynamic changes in day-to-day operations or key personnel changes. However, Co4 refers to the practice of a formal alliance review following an agreed timescale. Typically, this review will be formal in nature and be attended by the full nominated stakeholder teams on both sides. This review usually takes place annually, and provides the means to challenge the original expectations and assumptions.

The concept of auditing one's alliance relationships may be distasteful to many alliance executives, bearing connotations, as it does, of 'catching people out' or 'checking up on people'. However, bearing in mind that such a high degree of value is wrapped up in strategic alliance relationships, leading-edge companies are now beginning to realise that for most alliance relationships, a formal assessment of the aims and intentions at a strategic level and progress at an operational level is an absolute necessity.

This alliance audit is typically performed formally once a year (in all but the very smallest alliance relationships). It is usually attended by the senior executive sponsor of both/all partners, and follows a structured format and agenda. In the pharmaceutical sector, such a meeting or process is called a 'governance committee review' or 'steering

1   Ard-Pieter de Man, *The Network Economy: Strategy, Structure and Management*, Cheltenham: Edward Elgar, 2006.

committee review'. Its purpose is to ensure that the alliance relationship is on track and delivering on its identified goals.

Running such meetings and balancing the discussions of strategic, managerial and operational needs of the alliance relationship can be somewhat challenging. These meetings are also extremely expensive, since many executives from both/all sides of the relationship will wish to attend. Consequently, many organisations allocate a set number of days (two or three) for the exercise, which is normally hosted at a neutral venue and sometimes facilitated by external advisers.

Whatever approach is used to run such meetings and to embed them into the review process and the alliance in general, the process should have clearly understood and defined outcomes which move the relationship forward. The purpose should be to track progress in multiple dimensions, to discuss the degree of progress that has been achieved, to achieve a consensus between one or both/all partners, then to agree what needs to happen in the future to improve that progress further.

There is no doubt that the health of the relationship and its efficiency and effectiveness in delivering on established goals, targets and objectives is directly related to the commercial value generated by the relationship. Studies by Booz Allen Hamilton have shown very clearly that organisations which actively review their procedures and attempt to incorporate best practice procedures from outside perform statistically significantly better than organisations which simply use internally developed procedures and methodologies. The degree of difference is exponential rather than incremental – see, for example, the research by Peter Pekar Jr and John Harbison for Booz Allen Hamilton during 1996–2002, estimating that relationships run according to best practice methodologies and protocols will perform seven times better than ones that are not.[2] The commercial impact of such a high degree of improvement is also clear. Pekar and Harbison cross-referenced the degree of progress made by organisations that followed best practice to estimates of their return on capital employed (ROCE), and found that best practice companies averaged 25.6% ROCE, while non-best practice companies averaged 5–6%.

Co5: Key Metrics (What Should You Measure in a Strategic Alliance Relationship?)

Many organisations are finding that the selection and appropriate support of a balanced set of key metrics is critical to the success of their relationships. Such constructs are often called 'alliance scorecards', or in the case of the more advanced versions, 'alliance balanced scorecards'.[3]

When constructing their sets of measurements, best practice companies bear the following factors in mind:

- Commercial success tends to be an effect rather than a cause.
- Causes tend to be leading indicators, and effects tend to be lagging indicators.

---

2   John R. Harbison, Jr. and Peter Pekar, *Smart Alliances: A Practical Guide to Repeatable Success*, San Francisco: Jossey-Bass, 1998.

3   For a more detailed discussion of this topic, see Robert S. Kaplan, David P. Norton and Bjarne Rugelsjoen, 'Managing Alliances with the Balanced Scorecard', *Harvard Business Review*, January–February 2010, pp. 114–20.

In a balanced set, not only does the organisation consider different dimensions (for example, Commercial, Strategic, Operational, Cultural and Operational), but it also considers short- and long-term influencers.

One of the most keenly debated and topical areas of discussion in the strategic alliance management field is the question, 'What should I measure?' This is not simply because of the old adage, 'What gets measured gets done,' it is a reflection of the advancement in thinking in this area, which suggests that it is not simply about the commercial value. The research ABP has conducted suggests that to be effective in this area, organisations need to employ a balanced scorecard approach, as illustrated in Figure 7.4.

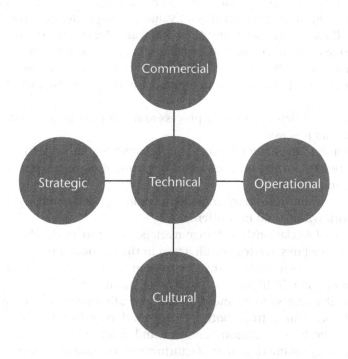

Figure 7.4   Example of an alliance balanced scorecard showing the five dimensions

This balance of measuring sets shows that to be effective, alliance measurement systems need to reflect complementary and/or diverse dimensions. This is reflected in Figure 7.4, in which the strategic elements are balanced by operational considerations, and the commercial value and desire to make money are balanced by the cultural elements. The whole is kept in check by the integrative effect of the technical alignment of both partners' products and services.

Strategic

It should go without saying that one has to measure the strategic aspects and impacts of a strategic alliance relationship, otherwise the relationship simply becomes an opportunistic or a tactical one. The very nature of a strategic relationship suggests a degree of sustainability and future progression and value generation that is negated if this important area is not explored. Examples of aspects to be measured in this area include degree of future strategic alignment, congruence of both/all partners' view of the market, senior executive support from all parties to the relationship, and vision for the relationship.

Operational

Strategic considerations are all well and good, and will give the relationship a high degree of long-term focus, but operational measures are essential to ensure that the alliance relationship stays on track while the greater value is being generated. The nature, degree and extent of these operational measures will vary depending on the sector under consideration (measures in the pharmaceutical sector, for example, will be significantly different from those in the high-tech sector, or indeed the professional services or manufacturing sectors). However, some common aspects of measurement in this area are:

- the existence of a defined alliance process and the progress both/all partners have made using that process;
- the expectation of commercial value (Is it the same on both sides?);
- the existence of a formal business plan, operational plan or sales forecast plan for the relationship;
- the degree of communication and identification of stakeholders (Who will have meetings with whom, and how often?);
- the existence of a relationship change management process to allow for changes of personnel, procedures, strategy or direction in the relationship;
- the extent to which collaborative behaviour is rewarded (sometimes called a 'compensation plan' in high-tech collective relationships;
- the degree of business-to-business operational alignment that exists outside the specific alliance teams from both/all organisations (How well do the operating functions of both organisations connect and inter-operate – for example, sales, marketing, R&D, production, manufacturing and technological/technical?).

Commercial

There is absolutely no doubt that this is something which, almost without exception, every strategic alliance measures in some form or another. Whether the commercial value is represented in terms of revenue generated from new products and services developed, or from extra income received from exploring new market sectors, or from generating a higher degree of market share in existing sectors, or whether it comes from cost reduction or quality enhancements in the value chain/supplier chain made possible by the interaction of multiple partners, all credible collaborating organisations that have any pretensions to being effective in this area will obviously measure this dimension in some detail. The measures they employ vary, but include:

- an estimate of the value of the identified business value proposition for the alliance;
- the commercial cost of the relationship so far;

- the commercial benefit of the relationship so far (indeed, some companies are now moving to a cost/value ratio measurement, which shows the amount of revenue as a factor compared to the financial investment in the relationship).

Other less obvious measures of value include intellectual property rights (IPR), access to clients/customers, knowledge of a new sector, and knowledge gained about new products and procedures. It is interesting to note the growth and sophistication of the measurement of risk that is beginning to be applied to the commercial area of measurement.

Many organisations are now actively recognising that risk is a significant factor in these relationships. In collaborative relationships no partner controls the other(s), therefore the degree of risk is that much higher since the direction, purpose and intent of the relationship is not under the full control of any one partner. This has led to the development of risk registers and the systematisation and codification of both tactical and strategic risk, along with the development of risk mitigation strategies. These are probably most advanced in the pharmaceutical and biotech sectors.

Cultural

Although the Cultural dimension is not entirely at odds with the Commercial dimension, it is often felt that one can either have a good commercial return or a good relationship, but one cannot have both. The logic of this thinking is based on the fact that to obtain the best possible commercial return, organisations need to be very aggressive in their negotiating techniques. This in turn creates bad feeling' among their partners, which produces undesirable side effects such as lack of trust, lack of open communication and lack of mutual respect.

However, a deeper consideration of this apparent trade-off reveals that the opposite is very often true, and that the better the focus on the cultural aspects, the better the commercial deal that can be negotiated.

The US consulting firm Vantage Partners, LLC is currently possibly the pre-eminent practitioner in this area in the world. Its deep and enduring research into the area of conflict resolution began with the seminal work *Getting to Yes*.[4] The research Vantage has conducted with a number of clients over more than twenty years suggests that paying attention to the cultural aspects of being able to secure what you want while not preventing your partner from securing what it wants is an extremely powerful aspect of collaborative negotiation.

The key distinction between collaborative negotiation and adversarial negotiation lies in the active consideration by each partner of the wants, desires and needs of the other, and the recognition that what is best for the relationship may not always be optimal for a particular partner in isolation at each point in time. Such a negotiating mindset is extremely difficult to apply in practice, although many organisations are now spending large amounts of money to ensure that their procurement departments are beginning to think in such a pro-collaborative manner. For example, this type of thinking underpinned the breakthroughs and performance enabled in Toyota when it was able to

---

4   Roger Fischer, William Ury and Bruce Patton, *Getting to Yes: Negotiating Agreement Without Giving In*, New York: Penguin Books, 1991.

collaborate openly with non-proprietary suppliers, even taking the risk of its proprietary knowledge being disseminated to its competitors.[5]

Regardless of which balanced scorecard organisations employ, it seems relatively accepted best practice that one should regularly measure one's alliance relationships (see for example Andy Eibling and Dave McCamey, PhD Associate Directors of Global Alliance Management at Eli Lilly). Eibling and McCaney presented a compelling argument for regularly measuring one's alliance relationships at the annual ASAP Conference on 8 February 2005.[6] Eli Lilly use a tool developed in-house called The VOA Survey. VOA in this context stands for 'Voice of the Alliance', and is borrowed from six sigma terminology and lore that refers to the 'voice of the customer'.

McCamey and Eibling looked at three major dimensions of alliance effectiveness: cultural fit, operational fit and strategic fit.[7] In doing so, on the strategic side they considered such issues as commitment, strategy, and trust and fairness; on the operational side they focused on communication, conflict management, decision making, leadership, performance measurement, roles, skills and competencies and team co-ordination, and on the cultural side they considered flexibility and knowledge management. Their internal analysis clearly suggests that those relationships within Eli Lilly which had the higher overall scores and were more balanced in their consideration of more than one dimension were commercially more successful and performed better. The Eli Lilly research had a clear set of conclusions:

- If both parties to a relationship regularly assess alliance performance and implement improvements, they can deliver results above expectations and ahead of schedule.
- Successful balanced assessment programmes:
  - reveal an overall perspective of the alliance relationship (critical to establishing balance) highlighting aspects that are working well;
  - identify areas that may represent barriers to future progress;
  - provide data to create an improvement plan.

The Eli Lilly study suggests that there may be a number of key points to be borne in mind in developing a successful assessment process:

- Leaders from both/all partners agree on the need for assessment and initiate the work.
- They lead the team in discovering the improvements.
- They focus on one or two high-impact changes.
- They conduct regular progress reviews to drive adoption of the improvements.
- They enable continuous improvement in alliance effectiveness.
- They use a joint assessment tool enabling a 360-degree assessment, and also encouraging involvement, focus and agreement of a joint action plan.

---

5   For an excellent examination of this situation, see Jeffrey H. Dyer, *Collaborative Advantage: Winning Through Extended Enterprise Supplier Networks*, Oxford: Oxford University Press, 2000.

6   For further details of the VOA Survey please see the ASAP website at www.strategic-alliances.org, materials are available from the downloads section.

7   Such thinking pays due homage to the earlier work of Robert Porter-Lynch and the Warren Company: www.warrenco.com.

In the pharmaceutical sector, regular measurement of one's alliances has become a major factor in improving alliance programmes. At the ASAP conference in 2005 Greg Fox, the Director of Strategic Alliances Marketing for Cisco Systems, reiterated Eli Lilly's findings by emphasising six 'must do' features any assessment programme:

1. the existence of a shared strategic map;
2. the establishment of an agreed alliance governance framework;
3. a series of agreed gated phases (based on budgetary control and allowances);
4. early customer wins;
5. early field alignment;
6. constant measurement.

Cisco has been actively measuring its alliance relationships (particularly the strategic ones) over a relatively long period . The initial studies began in 2000, and were revisited in 2002 and 2006, since when the assessments have continued annually. The assessments have a number of objectives:

- to identify areas of improvement for the strategic alliance organisation overall, and to give insights into specific issues at the alliance level;
- to determine actions and resources needed to achieve 'satisfaction' as defined by Cisco and its alliance partners;
- to provide recommendations for prioritising and optimising improvements.

Cisco uses a three-pronged approach to deliver a balanced and realistic assessment process:

1. qualitative phone interviews with alliance executives to assess strategic performance;
2. a quantitative Web survey involving the alliance's functional managers to assess tactical execution;
3. a quantitative Web survey involving Cisco's directors and managers to judge the accuracy of self-assessment and alliance predictions.

These assessments take a month to conduct, and are designed to assess the predictive behaviour of partners as influenced strongly by the degree of partner loyalty. Partner loyalty in itself is affected by the quality of the alliance relationship, which in turn is underpinned by a number of elements:

- Cisco's image;
- strategic programme elements;
- communication;
- alliance management;
- business development.

These elements generally break down into attraction qualities and retention qualities, with Cisco's image and the strategic programme elements being identified as attraction qualities, and the communication, alliance management and business development aspects being regarded as retention qualities.

Co6: Alliance Reward System (What Does Your Compensation Plan Look Like?)

This point is very closely related to Co5 above. Only after they have decided the important aspects to measure do best practice companies embed the appropriate behaviours for those key metrics. Always remember that the grandest partnering schemes and strategies need to be implemented at the operational level. At this most basic level, it has never been truer that 'What gets measured gets done.' It is no use if the executive teams of either partner talk a good game of alliance inter-operation, and then reward direct sales and confrontational behaviour.

Regardless of what alliance balanced matrix set is employed (see the section 'Co5: Key Metrics' above), it is essential that organisations suitably reward good collaborative behaviour, for it is this behaviour they are seeking to achieve in any alliance or partnering situation. The high-tech business sector has probably devoted the most effort to exploring and understanding the impact of compensation plans on alliance performance. From a research involving discussions with a range of clients, Alliance Best Practice has concluded that the following issues are critical in considering the context of compensation plans:

- developing and documenting the 'alliance mission';
- understanding the link between direct and indirect sales and how positive discrimination is exercised towards indirect sales;
- looking closely at the characteristics that make for an effective incentive programme with a range of potential partners, from strategic to preferred to alliance to re-seller;
- avoiding the common pitfalls and barriers that afflict many organisations when they attempt to implement a compensation plan;
- encouraging a cross-functional compensation philosophy.

In considering a well-balanced compensation programme, a number of stakeholder groups need to be considered:

- **The individuals themselves** – The alliance managers themselves need to be considered in terms of:
  - the quotas they carry;
  - their direct and/or indirect contributions to objectives split between commercial and non-business opportunities;
  - their career development objectives;
  - the degree of professional competency development they or their organisations have instigated.
- **Alliance teams** – These need to be considered in terms of:
  - the project or programme campaign milestones;
  - the ability to innovate;
  - the balancing of workloads and competencies within the team;
  - team unity.
- **Functions, divisions and companies** – These need to be considered in terms of:
  - top- and bottom-line objectives;
  - group/functional competency development;
  - corporate contribution;

- group/company efficiency and effectiveness.
- **The alliance** – The alliance as a whole needs to be considered in terms of:
  - operational alliance objectives;
  - partner reputation and brand;
  - alliance inhalation;
  - competitive differentiation.

Any compensation plan should have the following key characteristics:

- It should provide competitive total pay opportunities that help to attract and retain quality individuals.
- It should promote a sense of urgency in the individuals to achieve their desired goals within the current planning timeframe.
- It should establish a direct link between business results, individual performance and remuneration.
- It should be easy to understand and communicate.
- It should be responsive to the changing needs of a company in the marketplace.

There are also a number of other considerations to be borne in mind when developing an alliance compensation plan, including the following:

- How can programme funding balance cash flow responsibility with competitive pay levels in the marketplace?
- Internally, is the plan affordable and realistic (for example, does it incite unrealistic expectations)?
- What are the defined points at, above and below target expectations?
- Externally, are the costs aligned with the market:
  - as a percentage of sales or profitability?
  - relative to the size of the organisation?
- Going forward, are costs predictable in terms of:
  - the impact of hires and replacement hires?
  - sensitivity to changing performance expectations?
- Are positions that have direct influence over the close of business eligible to participate?
- What are the required sales roles, including:
  - management?
  - support positions?
- Which roles have the greatest impact in sales results?
- What is the desired level of coverage?
- What is the role of channel management in terms of:
  - coaching?
  - closing?
- How can performance measures support the desired business results and behaviours of the channel organisation?
- What are the critical performance metrics and operational metrics in terms of:
  - speed and time to objective?
  - customer service satisfaction?
  - territory capture/expansion?

- competency and capacity expansion/organisational learning?
- cost reduction?
- risk management?
- What is the balance between progress indicators and the performance matrix?
- How do measures differ by role for:
  - management?
  - individual contributors?
- How can performance measures support the desired business results and behaviours of the channel organisation?
- What does target performance represent in terms of:
  - budgeted expectations?
  - stretch performance?
  - growth over prior performance?
- How is the range of performance defined for factors such as:
  - minimum expectations?
  - outstanding performance?
- What is the probability of achievement based on:
  - historical performance?
  - territory potential?
  - incumbency?
- How can you ensure that the award structure is simple to communicate and objective in determining performance?
- What type of plan is most appropriate:
  - commission?
  - bonuses?
  - a combination of these?
- If a commission structure is used, how is it designed:
  - flat?
  - incremental?
  - retroactive?
  - decelerated?
- If a bonus structure is used, how is it designed:
  - as a percentage of the goal?
  - in binary terms (for example, hit or miss)?
- How can you make the award structure simple to communicate and objective in determining performance?
- How should incentives be communicated:
  - as a percentage of base salary?
  - as a flat financial amount?
  - as a role-specific commission rate?
  - as an individualised commission rate?
- How should the payout curve be designed:
  - as the slope of the curve below, at and above target?
  - based on predictability of performance?
- Should a minimum level of performance be required prior to payout based on group or individual performance?
- Should there be a cap on maximum earnings?

- Should payouts balance an individual's motivation?
- At what point(s) during the sales process does it make sense to deliver incentives:
  - driven by responsibilities (pre- and post-close)?
  - reflecting role influences?
- Is the plan intended to provide some aspect of retention:
  - for the position?
  - for the relationship?
- How are financial constraints balanced with plan motivation in terms of:
  - paying sooner versus later?
  - handling multi-year deals?
- How can the company accurately track and report performance?
- What ability does the company have to track performance on a regular and credible basis?
- Is each measure trackable and relevant at different intervals:
  - monthly?
  - quarterly?
  - annually?
- At how many points in time are incentives earned through the sales process:
  - upon signing?
  - upon booking?
  - upon shipment?
  - upon collections?
- How can you clearly define the 'rules of the game' to foster programme credibility and management trust?
- How comfortable is the company with its goal setting process? Is it:
  - top-down?
  - bottom-up?
  - collaborative?
- How should drawers be used: recoverable or non-recoverable?
- What is the preferred sales crediting method:
  - double?
  - split?
  - at management's discretion?
- What are the plan's provisions for:
  - new hires?
  - terminations?
  - charge-backs?
  - windfalls?
- How can you effectively execute the plan's implementation to ensure success?
- What are the 'stories' about:
  - key business themes?
  - the rationale behind the plan?
  - an overview of how the plan works?
- Initially, what vehicle should be used:
  - group presentations?
  - one-to-one conversations?
  - programme documentation?

- How will ongoing communication occur:
  - management briefings?
  - incentive calculators?
  - individual performance reporting?

There are several pitfalls and barriers to success. A summary of these is as follows;

- Several factors lead to the successful execution of an alliance strategy.
- The relationship mission must be affiliated.
- A set of mutually agreed alliance objectives must be established that are measurable, time-bound and definitively linked to core organisational goals and objectives.
- There must be clear executive management support and commitment to the relationship mission.
- Cross-functional resources must be trained and deployed in support of the relationship mission.
- Compensation must be aligned with the alliance objectives.
- Key alliance management personnel must be retained to ensure continuity and strategy execution.

The lack of any one factor in this list can derail a well-planned strategy. A poorly defined relationship mission will not provide sufficient direction for tactical decisions:

- Unclear alliance objectives allow for multiple interpretations of overall success. This impairs the ability to implement a meaningful incentive programme.
- A lack of executive ownership and support will dampen the sense of urgency and accountability.
- A silo approach to execution or a lack of cross-functional resources will create process bottlenecks and reduce influence over strategy execution.
- Misaligned compensation plans will send conflicting messages to those in the organisation.
- Turnover of key alliance manager personnel will put timelines at risk.

Co8: Commercial Benefit (How Much is Your Alliance Relationship Really Costing You?)

Most organisations have no idea how much their alliance relationships cost. However, best practice companies are now making strenuous efforts to allocate commercial value to some non-financial factors. The reason they are doing this is to gain a better understanding of the full value of their relationships using the only commonly available measure – cash revenue!

Many are now looking actively at this area to identify first-line costs such as: the cost of the staff employed by both sides to manage the relationship, the joint marketing funds available to both organisations to achieve common goals, and the direct costs of interaction (for example, buildings, R&D and training). However, leading-edge organisations are now going one step further and identifying the second-line 'add-on' costs of such aspects as: the time of line managers taken up by alliance initiatives, the opportunity costs of not pursuing suitable initiatives or pursuing them ineffectively, and the costs of knowledge 'leakage' to a partner.

It may appear simplistic to suggest that in a well-managed strategic alliance relationship individuals should bear a clear understanding of both the costs and benefits in mind at all times. However, our experience shows that this is by no means always the case. First of all, there is the problem of the 'stars in their eyes' alliance collaboration – a scenario where a relatively smaller or less well-known partner will actively seek a collaborative relationship with a larger partner simply because it is large and perceived to be exceptional in a particular area. Many organisations have racked up huge costs seemingly without reviewing the costs incurred simply to secure a strategic alliance relationship with these types of organisations. When challenged about this, many are forced to admit that the cost of acquiring such a partner has become completely prohibitive, and the value created by the alliance relationship is a tiny fraction of the costs incurred in securing it.

When considering costs, most organisations these days are prepared to concede that there are definite and obvious costs in alliance relationships. However, many of them only consider the first-line or primary costs involved. They fail to take into account the second-line or add-on costs. For example, first-line or direct costs could include the salary and/or bonus structure of the relationship manager in the alliance relationship, or they could include the amount of marketing budget allocated to the relationship (sometimes shared with the partner). However, the add-on costs which are hidden in the overall context of the relationship are those demands in terms of time and/or budget which the alliance relationship places on both organisations in order to develop the products or processes or to incorporate relationship messages into already established marketing communications. In our assessment, the second-line costs involved in such scenarios can outweigh the first-line costs by as much as 300–400%.

In considering the commercial benefits, likewise many organisations only take into account direct, obvious or primary benefits such as extra revenue earned or extra market share secured. They do not consider such things as extra knowledge gained, extra intellectual property rights secured or the knowledge of certain new sectors or access to clients which were previously beyond their capabilities. In our opinion, this is a mistake because a financial value should be allocated to such relatively intangible considerations. Failure to do this means that one or both/all of the partners involved in the balancing equation will feel 'short-changed' by the other partner(s) for providing value which is not being recognised in commercial terms.

In our opinion, the only successful solution to such a situation is for all parties to the alliance relationship to agree on a commercial value to be allocated to all contributions or all demands for resources in the relationship, and to construct an integrated 'give to get' profit and loss sheet for the alliance relationship so that at any time each partner can see what it is giving and what it is getting back in return. While it would be unreasonable to suppose that such a 'give to get' equation can be balanced at all times, it is significantly damaging if it is out of kilter over a considerable period. If one of the partners feels that it is giving considerably more than it is getting, or at least it is not getting, what it was promised from the alliance relationship, this will very soon lead to feelings of disillusionment, lack of trust, a shutdown in communication and a tendency to be uncooperative. Such behaviours will very quickly damage the overall relationship, producing a self-fulfilling prophecy as the commercial value of the relationship spirals down into nothingness.

Because of the delicacy of this balance, many organisations have taken to actively developing models which predict their desire for a cost payback. A generic description of these is considered in the subsection on 'Expected Cost/Value Ratio' below).

Co9: Process for Negotiation

Negotiating an alliance is not the same as negotiating other commercial deals.

It could be argued that it would be more appropriate to cover good negotiating practice in Chapter 10 on 'The Cultural Dimension', but the ABP methodology deals with it as a Commercial factor because it has such a powerful impact on the value of the deals that are agreed.

Typically, when negotiating a deal both parties take an adversarial position and believe that for either of them to win, the other must 'lose a little'. However, in true collaborative relationships both partners understand that they are not looking to strengthen their personal position per se, but rather trying to strengthen the value and effectiveness of the relationship.

This leads to some interesting insights into what constitutes good negotiating practice in alliance relationships. This unusual type of negotiating has come to be called 'co-collaborative' negotiating, to emphasise the aspect of understanding and strengthening partners' commercial positions and the role such a view plays in forming outstanding alliances.

Co10: Expected Cost / Value Ratio

The key word in this phrase is 'expected' – this assumes that organisations which enter into strategic alliances already have a solid and robust understanding of the commercial costs and benefits or value they are receiving from a particular relationship. In addition, they will also have a ratio or a factor they expect to receive from the relationship. This factor could be 10:1 or 100:1, but whatever the case, it represents the financial return they will receive from the relationship as compared with the investment in terms of time or other resources such as staff or marketing budget. Indeed, many organisations are now beginning to develop expected cost/value ratios in sync with their strategic alliance 'tiering' policies (see Figure 7.5).

As discussed above, best practice companies are increasingly looking in more detail and with more exactitude at the twin elements of commercial cost and commercial benefit. This allows them to develop cogent views about the cost/value ratio of selected relationships or alliance programmes. However, this CSF goes somewhat deeper than this simple observation.

Increasingly, best practice companies are conducting their own internal research to identify similar classes or families of alliances which can be compared directly. When they do so, they discover that the best indicator of success is the expected cost/income ratio.

If relationships are not meeting the standards established for good alliance performance, then they are usually quickly dissolved to save scarce collaborative resources that can be used for other and better-performing relationships.

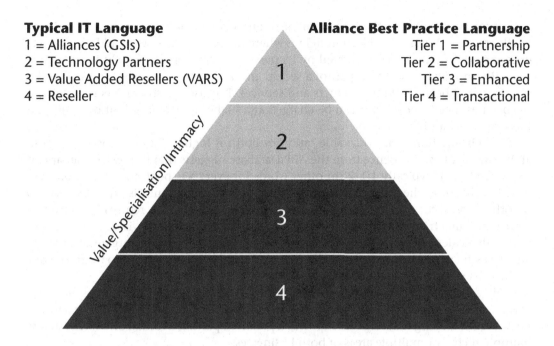

Typical IT Language
1 = Alliances (GSIs)
2 = Technology Partners
3 = Value Added Resellers (VARS)
4 = Reseller

Alliance Best Practice Language
Tier 1 = Partnership
Tier 2 = Collaborative
Tier 3 = Enhanced
Tier 4 = Transactional

Figure 7.5 Example of a partner segmentation pyramid for high-tech industry
Source: Based on original research conducted by Vantage Partners, LLC.

Organisations recognise that as the degree of business intimacy increases between themselves and their partners, the value (or indeed, the value in the cost/value ratio) should increase. Many are now beginning to explore the concept of establishing the cost/income ratio as a precursor for a partner's entry into certain categories of strategic partnership.

Figure 7.5 shows a generic example of this, where the organisation has a large number of reseller partners. Although it uses the term 'partners' to describe these organisations, in truth a more accurate term is 'reseller organisations'. There is very little business intimacy in this relationship, neither side feels constrained to share any particularly sensitive information, and both are will aware of what it is seeking from its partner.

Typically, such relationships are relatively disloyal, because if the resellers could find the same products and services for a cheaper price, or better products and services at the same price, then they would sell those instead. Increasingly in today's 'global village', this is becoming a significant headache for Western companies because while Indian suppliers have been pre-eminent over the past few years, next year they could be replaced by Chinese suppliers which may significantly undercut their Indian rivals.

In such a relationship, the expected cost/value ratio is relatively low. This is because the margin that either side can charge for the resale of its products or services is rather limited. For this reason, many organisations are seeking to attract their partners into full alliance relationships, as identified and illustrated Figure 7.5. The typical characteristic of such a relationship is that there is now a higher degree of business intimacy. This intimacy is evidenced by a higher degree of communication between the organisations and greater trust through the sharing of sensitive and potentially competitive information.

A typical scenario for the development of an alliance relationship, as opposed to a reseller relationship, in the telecoms field is where the reseller chooses to add its products or services to the offerings generated by its partner to develop a new solution which is generally specific to a sector or part of a sector, and which depends for its success on the specific use of both partners' products and services. Because the solution is now solving the business need, generally it can be charged at a higher rate. Notice that both sides in this case enjoy a higher margin.

In such situations, the cost/value ratio (for both) is higher than the cost/value ratio at the supplier level. Evidence from the ABP Database suggests that the cost/value ratio at the resale level is typically 1:1–2 (in other words for every $1 spent, the reseller receives $1–2 in return). At the alliance level, the degree of cost/value return is typically 1:10–20 (in other words, for every $1 spent, the reseller receives $10–20 in return). Because this return is so much greater and because the success of such a solution is so much greater (generally evidenced by the fact that it may be unique in this sector), organisations that are successful in one or two isolated alliance relationships generally tend to want to move to the next stage: full collaboration.

Full collaboration occurs when both parties have recognised the success of pilot programmes in particular markets, niches or technologies and now want to go to the next stage of making that relationship with a preferred partner a formal one spread across multiple niches or multiple areas of both businesses.

Clearly, neither organisation (no matter how big) can have an unlimited and endless supply of preferred alliance partners. Indeed, the very term 'preferred' suggests some degree of preferential treatment or some degree of selectivity in choosing the partner. These partners tend to be those organisations that have committed their business strategy wholly to their partner's products or services. Their future is intimately bound up with the strategic success of their partner. Consequently, they receive a far higher degree of business value (typically 20–80:1).

Full partnership is the highest level of alliance possible. At this stage, the organisations enter a formal joint venture relationship and seek to systematise and structure their alliance efforts in a far more formal manner.

Most organisations will have no more than half a dozen truly strategic alliances (apparently more or less regardless of size). However, these strategic alliance relationships will deliver payback levels of a quite staggering scope and scale (in some cases, as high as 200–300:1).

8 *The Technical Dimension*

T11: Valuation of Assets

It is important for both partners to feel they are receiving equal and reciprocal amounts of value in any balanced collaboration. Consequently, many leading-edge organisations are now beginning to attribute a monetary value to the assets in the relationship. As mentioned in Chapter 1, this usually happens as a two-stage process. The first stage identifies and quantifies the hard assets (for example, marketing funds, R&D facilities, personnel and so on), and in the second stage the parties usually progress to include such aspects as intellectual property rights, client mindshare and knowledge transfer. This process is extremely important as it identifies any actual or perceived differences in value provision in the relationship. Without this process, deep-seated but unspoken disquiet can ferment into active discouragement and sabotage.

Most partnering organisations understand the need to value the assets generated as a result of the relationship. Note that this is not merely an observation of the 'balance of trade' between both/all organisations (that is, one organisation sells good and services to the other while at the same time buying goods and services from the other); rather, the assets generated as a result of the combination of both/all organisations' collaboration originate from the particular and specific capabilities and benefits each organisation brings to the alliance.

These assets may be tangible or intangible. For example, it maybe that in a high-tech collaboration both organisations develop a specific piece of software or hardware (or combination of both) which produces a product that can be sold on the market. This is, or should be, recognised as an asset of the relationship. An example of an intangible asset might be the access to a market or markets both companies enjoy as a result of the strategic alliance relationship, or it could be some further more nebulous aspect that one or either partner views as important (for example, intellectual property rights).

It is interesting to observe what both parties regard as assets in the relationship. In general, in the Western world most organisations seem to value commercial assets most highly, and tend not to consider any other forms of assets generated as a result of the relationship. However, this is not the case in the Far East, where access to knowledge and learning is seen as the principal advantage of entering into a strategic alliance relationship. The Asian mindset appears to be that commercial advantage flows as a result.

The reason why valuing the relationship's assets is important is that it forms a basis for development/investment decisions by senior management to either expand the relationship or to retrench. Without clear knowledge of the value currently being created by the relationship, it would prove extremely difficult to convince senior management to invest further in the structure. The difficulty, of course, lies in the ways organisations value some of these tangible and intangible aspects of the relationship.

It is obviously not the case that in every strategic alliance relationship both/all parties are in perfect alignment and balance at all times with regard to their development and enjoyment of the assets generated from the relationship. Without doubt, all alliance relationship go through a period of dynamic imbalance in which one of the parties is currently either contributing more or receiving more from the alliance relationship in its view, or indeed in that of its partner(s). However, if this imbalance is left to exist for too long, it becomes a damaging disturbance. One party or the other(s) will determine that it has been contributing far more than its partners for an unacceptably long period and will become disillusioned with the 'give to get' nature of the relationship. In such a situation dissatisfaction sets in quickly, and inevitably leads to a rapid downward spiral of reduced value on all sides.

The development of a common, joint and shared process for valuing the assets developed as a result of the relationship is a key defensive measure in this area. If both/ all sides can agree on a process and methodology (however simple) to value those aspects of the relationship which are valuable either to each other or to the market or to the end consumer, then a reasonably accurate account can be taken of the balance of value enjoyed by both/all sides. The usual problem is that there is no commonly agreed and accepted procedure to value these specific assets. This issue strikes to the heart of strategic alliance relationships, because most individuals and/or organisations enter into a strategic alliance because of their desire to realise differing (if not entirely different) aspects of value. For example, one organisation may have excellent access to customers but no new products to sell them, while their partner may have a very good set of new, innovative products but lack a large and captive customer database to which to sell them. In such a situation, what both parties regard as value, or an asset, differs greatly. One regards access to customers as the chief asset of the relationship, while the other regards the new product or service as the main element of value. Given the diversity of strategic alliance relationships (particularly international ones), it is not surprising that this area gives rise to practical difficulties. Another aspect of the difficulties created is the comparison of tangible and intangible value. For example, in the example quoted above it may be quite straightforward to value the product developed with reference to the time it has taken to bring it to market, the intellectual property rights involved in its construction, the cost of sales, and so on. But how does one compare such a tangible asset to the substantial, albeit intangible, nature of the ease and access to customers granted by the other partner?

The answer appears to be (from observation of many thousands of strategic alliance relationships) that most organisations break the assets down into the only common form of comparison available – money! Those organisations that are currently actively developing in this area seem to agree that the only sensible common denominator is to put a cash value on the element being considered. Sometimes this is extremely difficult, but the effort is usually extremely worthwhile since it allows both sides to clearly understand not just the value to the relationship of that particular asset, but the value a particular partner places on it. The resulting discussion regarding relative perceptions of value is usually extremely proactive, heated and valuable.

Case Study 9: Rover and Honda

In the mid- to late 1990s the Rover Motor Company in the UK was approached by Honda from Japan with a view to establishing a strategic alliance relationship. Rover was, not surprisingly, a little suspicious of the approach from what it regarded as a key competitor. However, since the approach seemed genuine and was supported by a significant degree of senior executive attention, some senior Rover executives agreed to meet with their Honda counterparts. During the meeting, Rover posed the question that lies at the heart of the starting process of any strategic alliance relationship: 'What do you offer, and what do you expect from us?'

Honda's reply was: 'We offer access to a breakthrough new technology [the extremely valuable Honda VTEC engine], and we require access to European markets.'

This answer was logical, reasonable and believable, and as a result Rover and Honda signed a three-year strategic alliance deal in which Honda would provide the Honda VTEC engines which would be installed in a defined range of Rover motor cars (initially the Rover 75, but later also the Rover 25).

All appeared to be going well, and both sides implemented various aspects of best practice into the relationship. For example:

- They regularly visited each other's workplaces and maintained contact with customers.
- There was a high degree of senior executive involvement and interaction.
- They documented what each side expected from the relationship.
- They conducted a formal annual review of the alliance relationship.

However, many commentators observed a curious fact: Rover sent relatively small groups of executives to Japan to meet with Honda (because air flights were expensive), and when they arrived they were accompanied everywhere by English-speaking Japanese translators provided by Honda. In fact, there was nowhere a senior executive could go where he was unaccompanied by a translator. On the other hand, when Honda sent representatives to the UK and Europe they sent huge teams of people – not just senior executives, but shopfloor mechanics, foremen, distributors, customers, technicians, R&D specialists and so on. And when they landed in Europe they exploded onto the Rover distribution network with a very pointed and voracious desire for information of any and all kinds about how Rover distributed its cars, both in the UK and Europe.

At the review meeting at the end of the first year both sides professed themselves satisfied with the relationship and agreed to continue with it into the next year. During the course of the second year, sales of Rover cars, not surprisingly, increased since they now had a breakthrough piece of technology under the bonnet. Consequently, at the review meeting at the end of the second year both sides again expressed themselves completely satisfied.

Imagine Rover's surprise, therefore, when at the end of the third year, having sold even more cars in year three than in years one and two put together, Honda suddenly announced that it wanted to end the strategic alliance relationship. The Rover executives were dumfounded. Why would Honda want to exit a situation in which it was clearly earning a great deal of money through access to new markets? The answer, of course, was that the value Honda placed on something in the relationship differed from Rover's valuation. The reason Honda entered into the relationship in the first place was its desire

> to understand how to distribute cars in the UK and Europe. Having achieved that in the three-year timeframe, Honda now believed that it didn't need Rover any more and could take this on itself.

What does this single example tell us about the problem of valuing assets on both/ all sides of the relationship? In essence, it points to the fact that the mindset in the Asia-Pacific region tends to favour knowledge acquisition over immediate commercial advantage. It also points to the fact that the Asian definition of 'lengthy' or 'strategic' is usually far longer than that of the average Western counterpart.

It also says something quite interesting about the creation of value. One side, Rover, saw commercial value and sales as the only objectives of the relationship and the only assets the relationship could deliver. The other, Honda, had at least two elements to its strategy, and viewed knowledge acquisition as the primary asset of value to be gained from the relationship.

Case Study 9 is an interesting one: it teaches us to treat with extreme care the perspective(s) of our partner(s), particularly in co-opetition situations (ones where one or more partners are not only collaborating, but also competing). It is unlikely that in a co-opetition scenario a partner will always reveal to you the true and full extent of its ambitions regarding the relationship and what it views as valuable in it. However, partners in such a situation should seriously consider some form of risk analysis and/or risk mitigation (see the sections on common success factors S22 and S23 in the Strategic Dimension chapter below).

Originally, the assets that were valued in most alliance relationships (particularly in Western Europe) were commercial ones, and these would typically be tangible assets (for example, new services). However, over the last three to five years organisations have increasingly come to recognise the value of innovation and of the ability of other partners to create innovation within their own organisations through the interaction of a different mindset and/or organisational culture.

Such innovation or exponential breakthroughs can be extremely valuable. This is well illustrated by organisations in the fast-moving consumer goods sector like Procter & Gamble, Unilever and Reckitt Benckiser which now recognise that the majority of their gross turnover comes from products which have been launched within the last five years. Consequently, this focus is placing an inordinate strain on their R&D functions. The answer for many of them has been to proactively seek alliance relationships with other organisations, even those in their own business sector. The value they generate from such an approach can sometimes be considerable, particularly bearing in mind that the cost of developing products to launch to market can be very high.

Procter & Gamble, for example, displays on its website quite specific details of some of the products and services it has been trying to launch over the last ten years but which have unfortunately failed their R&D process. It has done this is to try to attract creative minds or other organisations which can take a nearly successful product (meaning that it failed the R&D process late in its product lifecycle) in one business sector and transform it (with the addition of their own product/knowledge/services) into a breakthrough successful product in another area.

Procter & Gamble recognises that the pressure to be innovative within an organisation is producing extreme strains on the creative bandwidth of its internal staff. It recognises, for example, that in any brainstorming session involving just Procter & Gamble people, the boundaries of the discussion will be dictated by the context, culture and operating methodologies of Procter & Gamble itself. It is seeking to achieve a breakthrough using existing nearly successful products allied to the creative thinking of an entirely different mindset from outside the organisation (an external alliance).

An example of the success of this approach can be seen in the development of the Procter & Gamble and Hoover hard floor cleaning machine in the United States.

In this case Procter & Gamble announced on its website that it had developed an extremely effective cleaning agent that was very caustic, extremely powerful and seemed to work well on hard surfaces. It was approached by Hoover, which notified Procter & Gamble that it was facing market share erosion from the fact that many householders in the United States were turning to installing hard floor coverings rather than carpets in their homes.

This resonated with Procter & Gamble, which had also detected this market trend. Both sides agreed to a non-binding series of brainstorming meetings in which they explored the idea of bringing together Hoover's mechanical cleaning technology and Procter & Gamble's deep understanding of fluid cleaning agents.

The result was a hard floor polishing machine utilising the best of Hoover's mechanical engineering excellence gained over the last hundred years and Procter & Gamble's outstanding chemical cleaning knowledge developed as a core competence of the company from its earliest days.

The results were outstanding sales of the new polishing machine, and both organisations leveraged a nearly successful product in their own sector into an outstandingly successful product/service combination in another sector. Note also that this combination satisfied a market need which both organisations had observed.

In the future it appears likely that many organisations will seek to proactively engineer such collaborations and partnerships, rather than simply observing them when they happen by chance. This will necessarily increase the stresses and strains on the relationships formed, particularly those that are formed within a business sector (co-opetition).

T12: Partner Company Market Position

Many partnering organisations do not take enough time to critically examine the current and future market positioning of their prospective partners. They take the view (sometimes erroneously) that what has gone before will continue into the future.

However, this is very often not the case, and all organisations considering strategic alliance relationships need to develop a clear and sophisticated understanding of both their own an their prospective partners' market positions. This is usually generated by extensive and deep market research. This type of market research is very common and very detailed in the pharmaceuticals/biotech business sector, but less common, or at least less detailed, in the high-tech business sector. So, for example, it is not unusual for organisations in the pharmaceutical/bio-tech sector to conduct due diligence exercises of strategic alliances which can take anything from nine months to two years, depending on the importance and/or complexity of the relationships being considered. In conducting such due diligence, a high degree of importance is afforded to the market position of the partner(s). In the high-tech business sector, such a degree of attention to detail and depth of analysis is unusual. This is principally because the most common cycle of business planning in this fast-moving sector is 90 days (that is, one quarter). Consequently, organisations entering into partnerships in the high-tech sector do not have the luxury of the relatively slower-moving and more static characteristics of the pharmaceutical/bio-tech market place.

However, developing an understanding of prospective partners' positions is equally important in the high-tech sector. Conflict arises when each partner wants to only partner with those collaborators which have a pre-eminent or leading position in a defined market sector, and do not wish to partner with any organisation which does not enjoy such a leading position. This necessarily leads to tension, since it is unlikely that both partners will enjoy a naturally pre-eminent position in the market sectors where they wish to partner.

An example may help to make this clearer. A global consultant/systems integration business wishes to partner with a software company to exploit the logistics business sector. In doing so, it looks around for the software company which has the largest market share in that sector. It wants the collaboration because of its relative under-exploitation of that particular sector. However, let's consider the point of view of the partner it approaches. The software company already has a market presence in this sector, and is not looking to partner with organisations that do not already have such a presence; rather, it wishes to partner with a consultant systems integrator which has an equally strong position in this business sector. The dynamics of this decision are further complicated by the fact that both organisations may be truly global players, which means that they have differing positions with regard to differing market sectors or different geographies around the world. Another complication is that both sides recognise the inappropriateness in business risk terms of placing all their eggs in one basket by committing solely and absolutely to a particular partnership. What results is an extremely complex and fluid interaction of multiple alliance relationships around the world, some of which may be exclusive, and others not. The fundamental cause of this dynamism is, of course (as it very often is!), money. There is no doubt that in a relationship where both partners commit absolutely and solely with a high degree of exclusion to a partnership, the amount of money generated is higher as a result of the trust generated and the absolute commitment of both sides to making the partnership work. However, in a fluid situation where both partners have multiple instances of contact around the world, such a perfect scenario is not always possible.

A consideration of a prospective partner's market position, either sector-by-sector or market-by-market or geography-by-geography, is incredibly important because it helps to define the structure and content of the strategic alliance relationship as a whole. So, for an example, in a relationship between, Logica and Oracle, both sides recognise that they don't compete in each other's business spaces – Logica doesn't write software, and Oracle doesn't conduct enterprise-wide systems integration (for the purposes of this example, let's ignore the fact that Oracle does have a separate consulting arm which carries out systems integration work). However, both parties recognise that there are other prospective partners out there for both of them which could equally give them access to other markets, and they also realise that they have a multiplicity of differences country-by-country in terms of the nature, scope, depth and success of the instances of that strategic alliance relationship.

The result is an extremely delicate and confusing balancing act conducted by both sides on an ongoing basis, each seeking to understand whether the value gained from its partner supplying an introduction into market sectors where the partner is stronger is greater than the value of introducing the partner into sectors where it doesn't have a pre-eminent position. Once again we are at the crux of a meaningful strategic collaboration – the 'give to get'.

Most organisations at the corporate strategic alliance planning level have some form of large 'maps' pinned to their walls which display each partner and its relative market position country-by-country and sector-by-sector across the world. Sometimes these documents are called 'heat maps' because they show the relative degree of 'heat' generated by the partnerships, usually using a red/amber/green coloration scale.

In the most successful cases, taking into account the pluses and minuses of each individual aspect of the relationship, the overall outcome is a net plus situation for that organisation. Such a partner mapping process, although simple in intent, can become extremely complex, particularly when one bears in mind the fact that the day-to-day commercial decisions made by these large organisations is generally undertaken at strategic business unit or country business unit level, which means that the corporate plan is often in direct conflict with the local country plan, even within the same organisation.

Many corporate alliance departments spend an inordinate amount of time trying to resolve these very real internal conflicts, which are extremely damaging. The better and/ or more leading-edge companies have recognised that in their discussions and debates with major global players, they need to be able to share the existence of such a map and discuss it openly with their prospective partners. In such a situation, the map will only show the interaction between the host company and that particular prospective partner, with the rest showing blank areas which represent other competitors.

However, the very fact that the host company can reveal the map and show the relative degree of its global coverage to the prospective partner can be reassuring and foster the trust required for it to reciprocate. The resulting discussions can be extremely valuable, because both organisations can now discuss specific countries, or indeed specific market sectors (or a combination of both), which will provide value to both organisations because of the agreed degree of prioritisation of those opportunities.

The alternative scenario is for organisations to adopt a strategy of independence, ready to partner with anyone and showing no favouritism. Such a strategy has extreme dangers, typically revolving around the erosion of the organisation's market share, which can be nibbled away by commitment to specific partnerships in small but significant sectors. A good example of the dangers of an independent approach is a situation that existed between Capgemini (a global consulting systems integrator) and SAP (a global software company) in summer 2005. In this case Capgemini approached SAP to discuss the partnering opportunities in North America. SAP expressed its delight at the prospect of working with Capgemini, and asked what degree of commitment or specificity Capgemini would allocate to various market sectors. Capgemini responded with the answer it had successfully used with customers and clients over the previous 20 years, which was that Capgemini was an independent systems integrator and would work with any software company, with only the client's best interests at heart. SAP applauded Capgemini for its approach and confirmed that it would be happy to work with Capgemini anywhere on the North American continent except with power and utilities organisations that had an annual turnover of $1–5 billion.

When Capgemini expressed surprise that it was being excluded from those companies and asked why, SAP was able to answer: 'Because those are the organisations where we have agreed to partner with Deloitte.' When this piece of market intelligence was communicated back to Patrick Nicolet, the Global Head of Sales and Alliances for Capgemini, in itself it presented a particular challenge for the Capgemini board. However, in Nicolet's mind it reflected a disturbing trend which he was picking up from multiple alliance managers all around the world.

It appeared that other consultant systems integrators were nibbling away at Capgemini's market share among global software companies by proactively attacking specific market sectors and/or countries through the use of focused and dedicated strategic alliance relationships. In itself, the amount of business Deloitte (a competing global systems integrator) would be able to achieve in North America from the power and utilities companies with turnovers of $1–5 billion was relatively low. However, when one added together the business Deloitte would take from Capgemini in North America in that particular sector and the business Accenture would take from Capgemini in the UK in the area of financial services in the SME sector, along with the specific business Aeonis would take from Capgemini in Italy, the total mounted up.

The situation generated an extremely passionate and involved discussion at executive board level about the distinguishing characteristics between 'independence' and 'agnosticism' in the systems integration field. The result was that Capgemini investigated its customers' perspective on the software it employed in its solutions and discovered a startling fact: in many cases customers did not have a preference for one piece of software over another (even when they already had that software embedded into their existing architecture). Rather, they were looking to Capgemini for advice about what elements of the solution to provide to solve a particular problem. In other words, the clients were asking Capgemini to 'climb off the fence' and commit to the best combination of hardware, software and its own systems integration advice to solve business problems – they were not looking for Capgemini to remain agnostic and leave such decisions to the clients.

Such a model was prevalent in the early to mid-1990s, but moving into the twenty-first century, Capgemini recognised that clients no longer wanted to have to make technical decisions; they would prefer those decisions to be made by an independent and extremely technically competent business adviser/systems integrator. The consequence of this wide-ranging discussion and subsequent research was twofold:

1. Capgemini invested in a new model for interaction with its customers, 'The Collaborative Business Experience', at the heart of which was a frank acknowledgement that to solve its customers' business problems, Capgemini needed to ally with market-leading companies around the world. In deciding which companies to seek alliances with and which technologies to employ, Capgemini would interact very closely with customers to seek their advice, but at the end of the day it would be Capgemini's decision which elements to combine to satisfy customers' needs.

2. Capgemini investigated a new technology model originally described as the 'Services Orientated Enterprise', underpinned and supported by a services-orientated architecture and a services-orientated infrastructure. Subsequently, the entire concept has increasingly become known as the Services Orientated Architecture (SOA).

The concept behind this thinking is that customers should not have to choose which technology to employ; in fact, customers would not even know which technologies were being employed. They would simply draw on the technologies necessary as and when required, and their exploitation (usually on a 'pay per use' basis) of these technologies, services and/or software would co-ordinated by their trusted adviser/systems integrator – in this case, Capgemini. The SOA model now permeates most, if not all, aspects of Capgemini's thinking, particularly with regard to its strategic alliance relationships; hence, one of the key questions Capgemini now asks prospective partners at multiple levels is: 'What is your stance on services-orientated architecture, and what evidence can you give us that you have industry-qualifying services-orientated architecture components?'

This services-orientated architecture focus also results in Capgemini's active support of industry initiatives supporting business-to-business interoperability (for example, Capgemini's support of the Open Group in managing open source technologies.[1]

The future in this area appears relatively clear, but its implications will have a substantial impact on global companies. The indications are quite clear that organisations earn considerably in cost/value terms from relationships where there is a high degree of commitment than those where there is agnosticism. This places extreme pressures on organisations to choose with great care the organisations with which they partner in a dedicated manner. This in turn means that to be successful in this area, organisations will need a fundamental understanding of the market positions of both themselves and their partner(s).

The implications of such strategies are well explored in the 2006 book *Dealing with Darwin* by Geoffrey Moore.[2] In it, Moore documented not only the lessons nature teaches us with regard to understanding our prime purposes and the core of our being and developing over a considerable period capabilities to enhance that core competence, but also a model of successful collaboration based around allying our own core competence to another's 'context competence'.

Context competence is the competence necessary to enable you to do what you do as an organisation extremely well (core competence). Moore suggests that the best international strategic collaborations are those in which organisations link their own core competence to another organisation's core competence, where the link represents context competence for both.

The practical implications of this model can currently be observed in a worldwide trend towards increasing organisational specialisation and a focus on the organisation's core competence. In such scenarios, understanding the market positions of your own organization and that of your partner(s) is essential.

T13: Host Company Market Position

Just as a clear understanding of the market position of your partner(s) is critical (CSF T12), it is also crucial that your organisation understand its own market position. Although this

---

1   See www.OpenGroup.org.

2   Geoffrey Moore, *Dealing with Darwin: How Great Companies Innovate at Every Phase of Their Evolution*, Mankato, MN: Capstone, 2006. Moore is perhaps better known for his earlier seminal work on new product adoption in the high-tech space, *Crossing the Chasm: Marketing and Selling Technology Products to Mainstream Customers*, Mankato, MN: Capstone, 1991, and his subsequent work concerning developing value from this adoption, *Inside the Tornado: Strategies for Developing, Leveraging, and Surviving Hypergrowth Markets*, New York: HarperBusiness, 1995.

topic verges closely on business strategy and analysis, it still has extreme relevance in the area of strategic alliances.

It is remarkable how few large organisations can express with absolute clarity their market position in a given geography with reference to a given technology, service or product set. The best organisations create communication programmes for their alliance operatives so that this message can be communicated with clarity to all partners in a consistent manner. This CSF is closely linked to CSF O43, 'Communication'.

T14: Market Fit of Proposed Solution

Having decided on the relative market positions of both organisations considering collaboration, another factor must be borne in mind: the market fit of the proposed solution generated as a result of the collaboration. In some cases the solution will simply be an offering that matches the collaboration's offering. However, in the best scenarios a solution developed from two radically different organisations with a clear understanding of both their own business core competences and their own market positionings should result in a breakthrough product or service which will rapidly gain acceptance and increase market share.

It is important to understand the market fit of the proposed solution because different market fits will obviously require different approaches to ensure success. This in itself will have significant implications for matters touched on elsewhere in this book regarding the value both sides identify and acknowledge in the relationship.

So, for example, if Intel considers a strategic alliance relationship with Capgemini using Services Orientated Architecture as a co-defining offering to market, both organisations have a radically different understanding and expectation of the market fit of such a solution.

In Capgemini's case, it is using the strategic alliance relationship to drive market adoption of the SOA model and to persuade Intel to adopt the solution at the very earliest opportunity (for example, the hugely successful long-running 'Intel Inside' market adoption campaign run by Intel from 1994 to the present day). Intel's intention in this case is to ensure in any services-orientated solution the customer will request the involvement of Intel as one of the constituents because of the customer's understanding that flexible and responsive IT architectures need Intel at their heart. Now consider Capgemini's requirements from the SOA. Its intention is not so much to establish the market, but to ride the wave of market adoption in generating significant revenue from SOA assignments. In its case what it is seeking to do is leverage the market-creating potential and activities of Intel to generate significant opportunities for itself at the leading edge of SOA assignments.

Clearly, both organisations have differing perspectives on the market fit of the agreed solution, even though they both agree fundamentally what the product/service is (the SOA concept).

In practice, most organisations do not appear to have a formal – or indeed, even an informal – process for understanding and exploring this critical dimension of strategic alliance relationships. Most appear to rely on a crude categorisation of strategic alliances within these contexts:

- Is it a research and development project and/or service in which it is a new offering to the marketplace? If so, we will use our existing R&D and demand-generation techniques to ensure adoption.
- Is it a breakthrough value proposition generated as a result of a combination of two completely different mindset organisations, and how will that affect our decision about the sectors where we choose to market it (for example, new product new sector, new product existing sector, existing product new sector, existing product existing sector)?
- Is the product or service an enhancement of an already existing product or service which may or may not have become 'tired' over the last three to five years, and consequently, is our market adoption strategy already set, with our channels to market and routes to market clearly identified?
- Does the product or service span multiple parts of the product lifecycle? If so, what are the implications for us, and for our partner(s)?

In the future, it is likely that many organisations will begin to take the question of the positioning of a new product or service far more seriously. Indeed, there is a great deal of evidence that organisations are already beginning to invest significant amounts of money in developing such a joint understanding.

For example, in an alliance relationship between SAP and Siemens Communications, both parties agreed to run a quite separate market adoption workshop as part of their overall global strategic alliance relationship. In that case each company nominated 13 people to attend a three-day workshop co-ordinated by external facilitators who had been flown 6,000 miles to Walldorf in Germany (SAP's global headquarters) to conduct it. The purpose of the exercise was to generate at least three products and/or services (on paper) which could be presented to the senior executive teams of both organisations. The new solutions had to satisfy the following criteria:

- The proposed new service/product/solution would need to be able to be developed within 12 months and available for market launch within 15 months.
- The combination of three solutions would have to bridge at least three different types of market positioning (new and innovative/breakthrough, building on an existing market position, refreshing an ailing product/service line).
- The combined development costs from both organisations of the new product or service were not to exceed €500,000, and the forecast revenues within the first three years of sales of the new solution needed to be more than €5 million.

The exercise cost both organisations many thousands of euros, but both professed themselves inordinately satisfied with the outcome (five products that satisfied all the criteria). Although the workshop was professionally facilitated, there was no introduction of any external marketing knowledge or intelligence, and the insights generated by the team resulted from knowledge already contained within both organisations. The composition of both teams was complex, requiring, as it did, a degree of marketing/sales/alliance/technical/financial capability.

At the time of writing, considerable attention in business circles is being devoted to the twin challenges of innovation and sustainability. While these two business imperatives are sometimes regarded as mutually exclusive, the better-performing organisations see them merely as different points on the same value-added circular continuum. In other words, the more forward-thinking organisations are looking at continuous innovation as a way of sustaining market share and positioning. More and more organisations are turning to strategic alliances and collaborations in their efforts to ensure this freshness in innovation thinking.

Increasingly, alliances are being viewed as 'engines of innovation' in this equation. See, for example, work conducted by Robert Porter Lynch of the Warren Company (www. warrenco.co) in facilitating the interaction between non-competing (and sometimes competing) organisations with a view to leveraging one's core with the other's non-core or contextual competencies.[3]

The genesis of this thinking can be traced back to the seminal work by Adrian J. Slywotzky entitled *Value Migration*,[4] in which he gives a satisfactory and compelling explanation of why certain organisations seem to thrive in a given market sector with given environmental factors, while other more advantageously placed organisations do not succeed to the same degree. For example, the book contrasts the relative gain in market share of Microsoft with that of DEC in the early to mid-1990s. Slywotzky argues compellingly that the best organisations have a high degree of focus on their customers' shifting perceptions of the value of the products and services provided, and the best organisations have an extremely subtle, sensitive and sophisticated understanding of the degree and implication of that knowledge.

While Slywotzky substantiated his original findings with reference to individual companies, his later work has explored the impact strategic alliances have on organisations' ability to launch more sophisticated and customer-friendly products and services.[5]

T15: Product Fit with Partners' Offerings

The issue of the output of the strategic alliance relationship being complementary to the offerings of both partners is extremely important, particularly when one considers the downsides if this is not the case.

Consider, for example, a strategic alliance where the relationship aims to develop and deliver a product which is already in existence in one or either of the partner's product/service portfolios. Such situations are not uncommon, particularly in the pharmaceutical/bio-tech sector, and the complexities and internal stresses and strains on both organisations can be considerable if, for example, Company A is a bio-tech organisation with 10–15 staff who have developed an extremely promising compound and Company B is a large multinational pharmaceutical company with extensive distribution capabilities worldwide). Company B approaches Company A to engage in a strategic alliance relationship to develop Company A's compound to take it to market as a fully regulated drug. The approach is welcomed by Company A since it accepts that it does not have access to the financial capital or market expertise required to steer its nascent

---

3   See Robert Porter Lynch 'Alliances as Engines of Innovation,' available from www.warrenco.com.

4   Adrian J. Slywotzky, *Value Migration: How to Think Several Moves Ahead of the Competition*, Boston, MA: Harvard Business School Press, 1996.

5   Adrian Slywotzky and Karl Weber, *Demand: Creating What People Love Before They Know They Want It*, New York: Oliver Wyman, 2011.

compound to market successfully. The relationship is equally satisfactory for Company B since the compound in question is not part of its existing portfolio of offerings to market.

Now consider what happens after the formation of the strategic alliance relationship with the formal signing of an agreement on both sides. Imagine you are the alliance manager of Company B and you have an extremely warm and effective relationship based on personal chemistry with all the representatives of Company A. Company A has no problems with the idea that the new compound will clash with an existing compound or service offering it already has on its stocks – because it doesn't have any! However, in Company B's case it could well be that a compound it is considering developing will compete directly with the new one, or it may have a new strategic alliance relationship in mind which could directly compete with the new compound.

How do you, as alliance manager for Company B, deal with the internal stresses and strains of knowing that the output of your strategic alliance relationship with Company A is under direct threat from an internally developed compound or product from your own company?

How do you manage the governance issues and the regulatory issues, and how do you ensure that you and your team do not inadvertently allow market-influencing intelligence to leak to your partner, Company A?

The potential for such scenarios is widely recognised in the pharmaceutical and bio-tech sector, and extensive internal governance models have been developed to deal with them. However, the root of the problem remains, and is still a major stumbling block for many strategic alliance relationships.

However, let's consider the problem from another perspective – the high-tech sector. Why is it that Cisco (for example) is extremely successful in its strategic alliance relationships with systems integration businesses, whereas Oracle and SAP (for example) are relatively less so? Could the answer lie in the fact that Cisco has no systems integration consulting business as part of its overall make-up? In other words, there is absolutely no cross-over in the output of the alliance relationship, or indeed in the intention of the strategic alliance relationship, which conflicts with a global systems integrator such as Accenture, Capgemini, Deloitte, HP or IBM. However, in the case of SAP and Oracle, both run substantial and successful consulting businesses, each using their own software. In such a case there is a clear overlap of intention between SAP and Accenture or Oracle and Deloitte which makes the negotiation of a strategic alliance relationship all the more difficult.

In this case, the adoption of internal 'Chinese walls' of governance is an absolute necessity, and the skill and ability of Oracle or SAP in convincing their systems integration partners that these internal governance models are effective is paramount in establishing the effectiveness of the external relationship.

Perhaps the past master of establishing these internal governance models is IBM, because, as one IBM insider phrased it: 'IBM competes with everybody!' His point is well made, since IBM not only has a hardware business, but also substantial software business and an extensive and global systems integration business. So whenever IBM collaborates with either another hardware provider, a software provider or a systems integrator, it needs to be able to convince the partner that its internal governance rules are sufficiently robust that the external alliance relationship will be allowed to flourish and will not be endangered by inappropriate transmission of confidential or sensitive information to other parts of IBM.

It is not surprising, therefore, that IBM has had to pay considerable attention and devote a great deal amount of time and money to developing these internal procedures and processes, and has also had to inculcate the degree of mature individual morality necessary to allow such systems to work efficiently. Every year, all IBM employees are required to sign an ethics document to indicate that they understand the how they should be operating both internally and externally, and also the guidelines and rules which will guide them in their effective fulfilment of their roles. IBM takes any breach of these ethical contracts very seriously.

The reason why a consideration of one's product or service fit with a partner's offerings is so important is that if there is any degree of overlap or confusion, it will have a significant impact on the effectiveness and efficiency of the relationship in question.

With the increased specialisation and sophistication of strategic alliance relationships, it seems likely that this area will continue to increase in importance and risk. It also seems likely that many organisations will begin to give detailed consideration to internal stresses and strains like those organisations such as IBM or many of the larger pharmaceutical organisations have already faced over the last ten to fifteen years.

Originally, the tactics and methodologies employed by such large organisations were very much based around the concept of using non-communicating silos of knowledge. However, the new, more flexible, model of strategic alliances – requiring as it does the inter-operation of multiple functions within organisations – militates against such a simplistic model, and it appears that more effort will need to be devoted to research in this area, not only to establish suitable, simple, effective and monitorable internal systems, but also to ensure training and active auditing for senior members of staff in applying such complex sets of rules.

In addition, the commercial implications of inappropriate and sensitive information being leaked regarding competing products and/or services could in itself drive a high degree of business focus. It seems clear that consideration of this common success factor is intimately linked to two other common success factors – S22, 'Tactical and strategic risk', and S23, 'Risk sharing' – and also has an impact on O45, 'Memorandum of understanding and principles or alliance charter', O50, Internal alignment', and O48, 'Business-to-business operational alignment'.

T16: Identified Mutual Needs in the Relationship

In the best strategic alliance relationships there are clear mutual needs both sides share, and it is these which generate a high degree of both progression towards a common goal and cost-effective achievement of certain strategic ambitions (because both sides desire the outcome regardless of interaction with the other, so the help and support the other can give simply allows the organisation to share the cost of achieving that strategic objective – which is an excellent result for both sides).

The difficulty stems from the nature of the identification of the *mutual* needs in any relationship. There are many strategic alliance relationships where there are complementary needs in which one or the other partner desires an outcome which complements the desired outcome of the other. However, in the best possible situation the outcomes are in fact the same. Although uncommon, such situations are not unheard of, and generally revolve around some business strategy which both sides can agree is an overwhelming concern of theirs. For example, a joint identical desire to grow market share in a particular sector could well represent a mutual need for both partners, and the launch of a completely new product or service could also represent a mutual need that both sides share.

The reason this area is important is because if the area is a genuine mutual need, it means that both sides had the need in the first place, so they would be expending their organisation's resources and efforts to achieve this objective anyway. Therefore, the involvement of another party to help them achieve such a goal can add substantial value.

Unfortunately, not many organisations are successful in identifying mutual needs – they do not consider spending time, energy and effort on identifying them to be a high priority. In many cases organisations have already identified a need which they are looking for a relationship to satisfy, so they are not particularly interested in expanding the scope or type of need to accommodate or adapt to satisfy their partner's desires. However, leading-edge organisations that do make this effort have conducted some mutual workshops where they have exchanged relatively sensitive information (usually under the defensive auspices of non-disclosure agreements) to allow both sides to understand where each is going in strategic terms (there is an obvious link here to S26, 'Business-to-business strategic alignment'). In conducting the exercise, both organisations are faced with and forced to identify and confront the nature of their core strategic intentions and to recognise why certain outcomes are overwhelming needs.

In many situations both sides can usually develop a set of high-level strategic intentions or objectives which can genuinely be said to not just be complementary, but similar. The skill and/or trick involved is to deconstruct these high-level generic statements into specific statements of action as they apply to particular market sectors, segments, product and/or service lines or technologies in a way that entirely reflects and mirrors the partner's requirements. By its nature, such a deep discussion of data that is of such importance to either side tends not to happen at the beginning of strategic alliance relationships when business-to-business trust is being developed, but rather occurs on an ongoing basis, usually at the annual review, when both sides have an already existing degree of trust in place and are looking to develop their understanding of the strategic intent of the relationship further with reference to their mutual needs.

The best partnering organisations are beginning to recognise that the value of a detailed and formalised understanding of mutual needs in an alliance relationship more than outweighs the time invested in developing such a perspective. Further, leading-edge collaborators are documenting such understandings so that there is an empowering element in the overarching vision of the relationship (see CSF S30, 'Common vision').

It appears likely that recognition by both/all sides of the leverageable power of mutual needs in terms of cost-effectiveness and strategic impact will drive the adoption of processes to identify agreed common needs much earlier in strategic alliance relationships. This will place increased demands on the infrastructure of governance adopted by the parties, which will in turn drive a greater need for standardised and robust strategic alliance governance models. It will also lead to greater emphasis on the adoption of mature and ethical moral codes of behaviour by alliance managers of all types and at all levels of seniority, and this will be an area which many organisations will actively seek to audit through their existing formal processes.

T17: Process for Joint Problem Solving

Joint problem solving in this context does not just involve assembling a team from one organisation or the other, it entails constructing a multicultural, multifunctional team of representatives from both/all sides of the collaboration. Such a process is not merely window-dressing, but is a prerequisite for effective strategic alliances. The reason there is a need for joint problem solving is that both/all parties in a strategic alliance relationship need to feel they are intimately involved in solving the alliance's problems. The last thing they need to feel is that partners are taking problems away and solving them without their active involvement. Such an impression would undoubtedly create short-term stresses and strains, and if left unaddressed, would very quickly undermine morale. This area is important because:

- It is a prerequisite for the effective interaction of all aspects of the alliance relationship, since most alliance problems do not exist in isolation and so are not amenable to being solved by one party alone. They need to be resolved with reference to both/all parties to the alliance.
- There is clearly documented evidence that team-based solutions are far more effective than individual-based solutions, so team problem solving is very much favoured because of the wealth of alternative perspectives that can be brought to bear on problems. Joint problem solving is cost-effective, and benefits from the creativity brought to bear by interactions between different mindsets, different cultures, and different perspectives and points of view.

In essence, joint problem solving means that you arrive at better solutions more quickly.

Many organisations fall into the trap of dealing with certain types of problems (for example, technical, sales, marketing or operations) among their own staff, and only sharing them with their partners at points where they are affecting the process of alliance management. This is not problem solving, it is problem sharing, and it is less effective than open and active mutual notification of problems at all times.

Many organisations are now exploring the use of collaborative technologies for joint problem solving. Some are constructing relationship or alliance 'virtual rooms' where contributors from both/all sides are actively encouraged to lodge documents, discussions, thoughts and issues in an interactive newsgroups or discussion forums. The use of technology in such a way has been extremely efficient in allowing interaction among multiple organisations.

Leading-edge organisations are now actively exploring existing psychometric tools, techniques and methodologies to identify inter-organisational models of operation which can be used to improve the effectiveness of joint team problem solving in alliances. (See, for example, the research work being conducted by Alliance Best Practice Ltd into the combination of Myers-Briggs and Belbin to develop an alliance manager assessment tool[6] and inter-organisational collaboration model. See also the identity compass tool from Di Tunney – The Best Organisation, www.thebestorganisation.org).[7]

---

6   Further information on the Alliance Manager Assessment Tool is available from the Alliance Best Practice website at www.alliancebestpractice.com.

7   Further information on the Identity Compass can be found at www.identitycompass.com.

T18: Shared control

This CSF is intimately connected to T17, 'Process for joint problem solving', and T19, 'Partner accountability'). The essence of this factor is that for a relationship to be effective, control must be exercised as far as possible to allow both/all sides to feel that they have sufficient sense of ownership of the direction, planning, construction and outputs of the strategic alliance.

You only have to consider the alternative to understand how important this aspect can be. For example, you could argue that a relationship between a fast-food restaurant chain and a prospective franchisee could be regarded as a strategic alliance relationship because the chain provides the infrastructure of location, brand, products and operating procedures, and the prospective franchisee contributes an investment in terms of finances, but also personal energy and commitment. However, understanding such a relationship as a strategic alliance relationship fails when you consider one critical issue: in this scenario there is no shared control. The franchisee is told exactly what foods he can sell, in what combinations and in what amounts. He is told exactly how to conduct his business, to the extent of how often to wash the tables and floors, and is given very little control over any aspects of the day-to-day operations of his restaurant. You can understand that it's extremely important from the chain's point of view that there's a consistency of 'look and feel' between its restaurant in Florida and its restaurant in Alaska (or indeed between its restaurant in Chicago and the one in Tokyo if it's a global chain), but it means that the degree of control is inordinately skewed towards the chain rather than the franchisee. In the terms identified in this book, such a relationship is not a strategic alliance.

An associated but slightly different perspective should be identified that is not conducive to strategic alliance relationships: where control is handed backwards and forwards between the parties depending on the nature or stage of the relationship and/or the problems it's experiencing at a certain points in time. Again, this is not shared control – this is selectively delegated control from time to time – and once again the impact of such an approach is detrimental to the spirit and essence of a strategic alliance relationship.

The reason why shared control is important lies in the knock-on effect it has on so many other areas, such as trust, commitment and resource allocation. If either/all of the partners feel that they do not have sufficient control over the relationship, their degree of commitment to it is likely to be much less, and this will be reflected in the time, energy, effort and resources it allocates to the relationship.

The dilemma for most organisations and individuals at a personal level is that in most strategic alliance relationships there is no individual, nor indeed any single organisation, that exercises overall control of the relationship; by its very nature, control is shared and allocated among the various parties. Understanding such a complex business model is difficult for many organisations and individuals.

Most organisations have some form of internal governance documentation which indicates where and how control will be exercised. At present, these tend to be relatively simplistic and focus on scripted procedures. The better known and understood the procedure, the greater the applicability of the script (for example, a strategic pharmaceutical alliance relationship in which one party has a compound and the other party has a distribution network is much clearer than a high-tech or financial services strategic alliance relationship in which the intentions of both parties are much less clear).

Unfortunately, documenting internal procedures doesn't help to guide the individuals who need to execute those procedures with the correct behaviours, mannerisms and mindsets, and organisations are increasingly turning to providing more training, coupled with more detailed examination of the behaviours necessary in the highly flexible world of strategic alliance control sharing.

It seems inevitable in the future, as organisations recognise that they have passed through Stage I in the alliance maturity spectrum, recognising the need for shared control and the documentation procedures and processes required to exercise it, that they will turn their attention to providing more focused training to educate alliance managers at all seniority levels about effective collaboration. Such training will be very cost-ineffective if the individuals' personality profiles mean that they find such a mindset almost impossible to achieve. Consequently, many organisations will look to develop personality profile testing systems that can assess collaborative executives at all levels before placing them on training courses.

T19: Partner Accountability

It is extremely important in strategic alliance relationships for both/all partners to be very clear about the aspects for which they hold their partner(s) accountable. Such accountability can be documented in various types of documents.

Generally, this accountability is formally expressed in a legally binding contract signed by the parties. However, there is a good case for suggesting that the documentation of an MOUP or charter is useful in this context. Within the MOUP, which is not a legally binding document, both parties will clarify those points for which each partner will be accountable.

Partner accountability is incredibly important, because you need to be able to hold your partner answerable to certain previously defined terms of operation so that as the situation that prompted the formation of this strategic alliance in the first place changes, both/all sides of the alliance relationship continue to comply with these parameters. Without this, anarchy will reign in the relationship as both/all sides are left to decide what they are and are not accountable for. Bearing in mind the extremely dynamic and fluid nature of many strategic alliance relationships and the speed of change, both in managerial teams and also in the direction of many relationships, it is even more essential that these accountabilities be formally documented at an early stage and only changed in a previously agreed and scripted manner – usually with the consent of both/all sides.

The best organisations recognise the need to document in formally binding agreements the accountabilities of each/all parties to an alliance agreement. This can be done either in a contract, if the relationship is a formal one, and/or in a charter or MOUP if the aim is speed or, at an early stage, simply to set expectations.

In either case, simplicity of language and clarity of expression will be important in identifying what each party expects of the other(s) in the relationship. In addition, some form of accountability change process needs to be clearly documented – usually a process which has the openly acknowledged commitment of all parties to the strategic alliance relationship.

9 *The Strategic Dimension*

Clearly, defining the strategic aspects and implications of important alliances is essential, both to establish them as truly strategic, but also to provide a framework enabling the parties to understand the future implications of the relationship.

By their nature, strategic alliances are not tactical or temporary in nature, so they need to feature some aspects of longevity and sustainability to qualify as such. Unfortunately, all too often strategic alliances are characterised and defined in organisations according to the amount of money (revenue or cost savings) associated with them. This is an erroneous, misleading and dangerous mistake.

The vast majority of strategic alliances are, coincidentally, extremely valuable relationships. However, the converse does not always apply. The fact that a relationship is extremely valuable and generates revenue does not necessarily make it a strategic alliance relationship, and the implications of treating it as such can be quite damaging.

Take, for example, the example of two major high-tech European organisations. Company A was a large telecommunications organisation whose strategy was to move from being products-focused to services-focused, as reflected in its concentration on the information and communications technology marketplace rather than simply the telecommunications sector. Company B was an extremely successful global personal computer and server manufacturer which had a substantial operation in Europe, the Middle East and Africa. Because the amount of business each company conducted with the other was significant (indeed, sometimes very large), Company A regarded the relationship as a strategic alliance, therefore treating it in a similar manner to its other strategic alliances. This meant that it appointed a fully dedicated partnership director to the relationship and sought to instigate connections with Company B at multiple levels up and down the hierarchical chain of command. In addition, it wanted to run joint work sessions with Company B to develop new products and services both organisations could take to market together in order to support a common vision of their strategic alliance relationship.

Company A was somewhat surprised at the lack of enthusiasm from Company B. It wasn't that it refused its overtures, but rather there was a degree of indifference. This puzzled Company A, as it clearly saw the relationship in strategic terms and was confused why Company B wouldn't want to talk about the future in terms of such matters as vision, strategic direction, market intentions and growth opportunities. After an expensive, time-consuming and fruitless nine months of trying to engage with Company B, Company A finally confronted the Company B's senior executives with the fundamental question: 'Why don't you want to be a strategic alliance partner?' The reply from company B was insightful, and had a significant impact on Company A's future attitude to strategic alliance relationships. In essence, the answer was: 'We don't want to have a strategic alliance relationship with you, we just want to sell you lots of PCs and servers!'

Once Company A understood that the relationship between the two organisations was essentially one of buyer and seller or customer and supplier, it became relatively easy for both companies to organise themselves in the most appropriate way to facilitate such a relatively simple relationship. There was obviously no need for deep and wide-ranging research-based meetings at which one or both organisations explored the future direction and strategic intentions of the other. There was simply a need to make the transactions involved in the relationship as efficient as possible.

Clearly, in this situation both organisations were at a transactional level of business intimacy, and at least one had absolutely no intention or desire of growing the relationship further. Any attempt by Company A to do so was viewed by Company B with a high degree of frustration. However, Company B was reluctant to inform Company A about this because it wanted to continue conducting a great deal of business with Company A. In the words of one senior executive:

> We didn't want to offend them by not returning their phone calls or not attending their meetings because we wanted them as a good customer, but the things that they were asking us to do were frankly immaterial or at best extremely peripheral for us. So we saw it simply as a waste of time!

It is clear, then, that this dimension of strategy is crucial, both in defining a relationship as a truly strategic alliance or collaboration, but also in identifying those aspects of strategic inter-operation which will drive the relationship forward and establish a more wide-ranging agenda than simply a transactional alliance relationship.

S20: Shared Objectives

In the majority of strategic alliance relationships there will obviously be some strategic objectives which are identified by one or all parties. Very often these objectives are specific to one organisation or the other, and in the better-performing alliance relationships these specific objectives are shared between both/all of the parties. However, the most powerful scenario is one where both parties have a common set of strategic objectives. Indeed, such a sharing of important strategic focus and direction can be an overwhelming enabler of success.

Take, for example, the situation in which Unisys Corporation found itself in the early 1990s. Unisys at that time was predominantly an electronic software and products company based in Philadelphia. It was operating in more than a hundred countries with more than 39,000 employees worldwide, and its revenue was in excess of $5 billion per year. Unisys's strategic intention was to become not just a business products company, but a business solutions and services company, and to that end it had spent some of the early 1990s developing its consulting and advisory capabilities. In 1994 Unisys was faced with a significant opportunity. It had developed a very sophisticated range of IT data servers (the ES7000 range). These servers had a unique value proposition:

- They had an extremely competitive price/performance advantage over their competitors.
- They allowed IT users to simplify their mainframe environments (data centres).

- The entire range had a flexible design which could adapt to changing business requirements.

However, Unisys did not have any alliances with leading application providers or their system integrator partners, and as a result was finding it incredibly difficult to break into the data centre market, at that time dominated by IBM, ICL, DEC and others.

Unisys established a dedicated and highly focused revenue-driven team to take the ES7000 range to market. The team's task was to develop business in partnership with independent software vendors (ISVs) as well as systems integrators (SIs). The team began life as a very small group of experienced marketing and sales managers, all with significant channel and partner experience. Critically, they had 100% support form senior management.

The team developed a relationship charter designed to encapsulate all it was trying to achieve with its product in the marketplace. The charter had two essential elements:

- Establish the ES7000 range as the industry standard high performance platform for leading ISVs and SIs.
- Build a foundation for a strategic ISV partnership programme, starting with five new ISVs and growing as success increases.

In its review of the partners available (Co2, 'Due diligence'), Unisys quickly identified a number of significant software providers that could help it break into the data centre market. Key among these was Microsoft. What made Microsoft so appealing was the fact that it too had a strategic intention to break into the data centre business sector and had two significant products it felt would achieve this goal: Microsoft Windows 2000 Data Centre and Microsoft SQL Server.

What both organisations discovered as a result of exploring this strategic alliance was that Unisys had an extremely efficient and small-footprint data server which was powerful enough and whose architecture enabled software to use more than one processor at a time (some of the ES7000 range used as many as eight processors in parallel), and Microsoft was experiencing increasing demand from customers with databases that were growing so large that they needed multiple-processor servers to deal with them – hence, the best of both possible worlds for both parties.

What made the relationship so powerful, however, was the fact that both organisations had a very clear strategic direction and intent: to become significant players in the data centre business sector. This shared set of strategic objectives allowed them to benefit from the other's actions, since they had such an impact on this area. For example:

- Each organisation was able to leverage the marketing funds allocated by the other to exploit new opportunities.
- Each organisation was able to tailor its offerings to work at the optimum level with the other's products.
- Both organisations were able to combine their individual offerings to be more attractive to the third partners necessary in this triangle – global consultant systems integrators.

The organisations were subsequently able to introduce their partner to other very important partners, each secure in the knowledge that they were doing so to execute a business strategy to which both were deeply committed. As a result, the elements of business development, marketing, alliance management, sales, R&D, manufacturing and many others were significantly enhanced in cost/value terms because of the sharing aspect of the relationship. Indeed, the partners enlisted to work on this initiative (and who were very happy to be involved) read like a 'Who's Who' of the global systems integration software businesses: SAS, SAP, PeopleSoft, JD Edwards, Accenture, Avanade, Capgemini, BearingPoint, Atos Origin, Siebel, EDS, Cedar, CSC and BusinessObjects.

In identifying the success factors in what was an outstandingly successful global strategic alliance relationship, Mike Pregler, the Marketing Director of Unisys, identified a number of specific keys to success. The first was strategic alignment through a common set of shared objectives (establishing a foothold in and later dominating the data centre market). This objective was absolutely critical to the business strategies of Unisys and Microsoft, and later the other organisations identified in the extended partner eco-system identified above.

The second key to success was demonstrating value. By 'demonstrating value', Mike was clear that this meant selling some value to your partner as well as the end consumer. In Mike's words:

You had to sell the relationship as much as the product! It was a matter of leveraging your resources and finding areas to add extra value. It was good at the start because we only had Microsoft to deal with, but it got even better as each new partner joined the relationship because they brought with them extra areas of expertise that we could use to add even extra value.

The next key to success Mike focused on was attitude – in particular the attitude of all the partners involved:

We didn't expect our partners to sell or recommend our product, either exclusively or specifically. We understood that we had to sell to them the idea that they should recommend our ES7000 range as part of the overall solution. We did that through building trust in the relationships with key influences and thought leaders, and pre-eminent in our ability to do that was demonstrating a very closely aligned strategic direction through sharing our commonly and openly stated strategic objectives.

The final aspect Mike highlighted in summarising the relationship was the timescales involved in such a significant undertaking. The initial thinking regarding the relationship occurred in 1998–9, but the programme was actually instigated in 2001, when relationships were established with targeted partners. During that period the number of ISVs grew from one to nine, and the number of system integrators from two to seven. In addition, Unisys hired and staffed specific business-to-business development teams. In 2002 the main objective was to fill the pipeline with business. The focus during this period was on sales engagement training and refining the go-to-market plans. Critical to refining the go-to-market plans was the development of solution statistics backed by clear value propositions. It was 2003 before Unisys was able to execute on the relationship and drive deals and field engagement with its ISV and SI partners. During that year it was able to promote its solutions to the target markets. The entire programme took three years to come to fruition.

It is not possible in all cases to identify specific shared objectives. Sometimes the objectives of one or more organisations run somewhat counter to the identified objectives of the other(s). However, when one or more organisations can identify such shared objectives there is no doubt that it leads to rapid acceleration of alliance success and adds greatly to the chances of alliance longevity beyond the three- to five-year horizon normally associated with such relationships.

In a world increasingly dominated by flexible, interactive, fluid collaborative relationships we are already beginning to see the emergence of consortiums focused specifically on a target market segment or business problem as a way of generating such a common set of shared strategic objectives.

For instance, a range of smaller telecommunications companies in Europe have banded together to compete with the larger providers. The Open Group has a clear and distinct focus on services-orientated architecture solutions. Exel developed the Global Logistics Alliance as a way of articulating end-to-end value to its customers.[1] In 2006, six leading technology companies created the Smart Energy Alliance to help utilities to turn their transmission and distribution challenges into opportunities.[2] In this case, the partners were so attuned in their strategic objectives that they were able to identify a joint mission and mission statement: to 'deliver business and technology solutions for power distribution operations with unmatched levels of functionality, performance, inter-operability and ease of deployment'.

The vision of the Smart Energy Alliance is to combine services, technologies and industry leadership to give utilities companies a competitive edge that enables them to serve customers more reliably and cost-effectively than ever before. The Smart Energy Alliance 'helps clients go from today's distribution roadmap to tomorrow's reality'. The alliance's six founding members are Capgemini, Cisco, GE Energy, Hewlett-Packard, Intel and Oracle.

S21: Relationship Scope

Although relationship scope may seem a simplistic aspect of strategic alliances, it is our experience that this single factor is one of the most abused and misunderstood of the 52 common success factors. An inadequate articulation of relationship scope can be found almost universally in under-performing, confused, and contentious alliance relationships.

In the better- or best-performing relationships there is clear evidence that in the majority of cases there is an extremely clear and well-articulated scope statement for the relationship. This is almost always documented in an auditable fashion. The importance of having a clear scope definition cannot be underestimated: it provides the boundaries for a cohesive framework within the relationship.

This is extremely important in today's modern commercial environment, where the flexibility and fluidity of collaborative relationships leads partners into a variety of areas of operation and gives multiple access points to differing business sectors, technologies and/or customers. It is crucial that all contributing parties understand the 'universe' in which they are all operating, especially since in many cases the partners will be both

---

1   See www.globalalliancelogistics.com.

2   See www.smart-energy-alliance.com.

collaborating and competing in various aspects of their operations at the same time (such relationships, known as co-opetition, were discussed in Chapters 7 and 8). A simple, robust and understandable scope statement will go a long way to helping organisations identify with clarity the boundaries of their interaction when faced with potentially valuable collaboration opportunities. The scope statement forms the bedrock for much that will follow in terms of relationship governance.

Surprisingly, many organisations fail to develop scope statements for their alliance relationships. They seem to believe that the assumptions they have made about where and how these relationships will be conducted are quite clear to their partners. Unfortunately, the partners may have made assumptions too, but the problem is that they may have made different ones. Nowhere is the saying 'if it isn't written down, it doesn't exist' more applicable.

In the best relationships a scope statement is usually identified in the memorandum of understanding and principles or relationship charter. It may focus on individual contracts or individual sub-agreements which are specific to a particular sector, geography, technology or business solution, but at least it identifies the scope of the arrangement between the organisations which are parties to the strategic alliance. For example, a scope statement could cover a relationship between a global systems integrator and a large software company in which both organisations agree to draw on the other's competencies in a specific business sector (for example, logistics, fast-moving consumer goods, financial services or manufacturing) or it could be that the partners decide to focus on a defined number of geographic locations (France, Germany, Italy, UK, Netherlands and so on) or on newly growing economies (India, China, Singapore, Malaysia, Australasia and so on). Alternatively, the organisations might choose to focus their energies on a specific business problem (customer relations management, compliance, risk management, knowledge sharing, data analytics or route to market planning).

In the future it will become increasingly important for organisations to draw up clear and unambiguous scope statements, for number of reasons:

- Every organisation in flexible collaborations needs to understand the target areas for the collaboration and what does and doesn't fall within its scope;
- The requirements of the Sarbanes-Oxley Act in the USA, the Basel II and Basel III accords and the fallout from the Enron scandal demand documented clarification of the purposes, intents and scopes of strategic alliance relationships.
- The increasing sophistication of the strategic alliance marketplace means that larger organisations will have a variety of partners in multiple market sectors, and they will need to have clear scope statements to understand how the collaboration sets interact.
- The increasing number of mergers and acquisitions makes greater clarity about scope essential. When Hewlett-Packard bought EDS some years ago, IBM received a boost in alliance revenue from partners which had previously partnered with HP. The reason for this was explained by a high-ranking Tata Consultancy Services executive:

Until now we have partnered with HP because they don't have a systems integration or consultancy business. That's why we don't do much with IBM, because they do have that capability and there is the danger of a conflict of interest. However, now that HP have bought EDS they suddenly have a part of their business which competes with us directly (outsourcing), so we need to review our global strategic alliance relationship with them. As a result, we have concluded that IBM is better at establishing internal 'firewalls' or governance models, so we will be doing more business in the future with them.

- The increasing complexity of business solutions (particularly in the IT sector) makes the inter-operation of multiple alliances a necessity. Solutions such as 'cloud computing', 'advanced transformational outsourcing' and 'software as a service' are creating new business battlefields where the scope of collaborative relationships is key. One example will suffice to illustrate this point (although many more exist): the collaboration between VMware, Cisco and EMC to offer 'virtual data centres' spawned a rush of similar alliance groups to compete with them, including Microsoft, Oracle, SAP, IBM, HP, Accenture, Capgemini and Alcatel-Lucent.

S22: Tactical and Strategic Risk

It is surprising how many experienced alliance professionals refuse to accept the existence of risk in alliance relationships. Those who do accept that it exists are generally pitifully inept in their understanding of the risk factors in strategic alliance relationships and how to deal with them.

It is, of course, axiomatic that every business relationship carries some degree of risk, whatever its nature. But the highly leverageable ability of strategic alliance relationships to generate outstanding returns and investment means that business professionals in the twenty-first century need to be clear that 'The greater the return, the greater the risk.' This risk/return ratio seems to apply in just about every other business context, and there's no reason why strategic alliances should be any different.

The particular risk implicit in strategic alliance relationships stems from the fact that most of the time no single partner can exercise absolute control over the relationship, leading to a lack of overall control. This risk can be categorised into two broad areas: tactical and strategic.

Tactical risk includes such aspects as the commercial risk of allying with a particular partner to secure a particular business deal or opportunity, only to find that the target customer or client chooses another combination of partners because it is dissatisfied with your chosen partner. It is unlikely in such a situation that your partner will be totally open with you about the nature of its damaged relationships with prospective clients that may impede the chances of success in your collaboration. In fact, in many cases an organisation which has a difficult relationship with a prospective target customer may well welcome you as a partner to serve as a 'white knight', able to alleviate the bad impression they have already created through your own relatively good reputation in the client's mind. However, tactical risk is not limited to simply dealing with success or failure; it can also have implications in areas such as R&D, cost control, quality and customer satisfaction.

Strategic risk can sometimes be far more subtle, but can also be wide-ranging and more impactful. So, for instance, if you have signed a contract for a strategic alliance relationship with a particular player in a market sector and have committed to a given period (for example, five years), then a new and more innovative and aggressive potential partner comes onto the scene, you are faced with a difficult decision. Do you break your existing strategic alliance relationship with your existing partner to court the new one, or do you stay with your existing partner and simply accept that you are partnering with the second best in the sector.

This long-term risk leads a large number of organisations into the flawed strategy of non-specialisation: they decide not to choose a preferred partner in a particular area because they believe that there will always be a new partner somewhere on the horizon at some time that could do a better job. The problem with this strategy is that the amount of commercial return that the organisation enjoys through not committing absolutely to a small range of partners far outweighs the potential commercial value it might achieve if another player entered the marketplace.

Organisations that deal with strategic alliance risk in a mature and sophisticated manner recognise the nature of the problem, and 'time box' their strategic alliances so that they are able to review the business landscape at defined intervals. These intervals can be as relatively short as three to five years in the high-tech sector or as long as ten to fifteen years in the pharmaceutical or defence sectors. In either case, the strategy is the same: the organisations perform a risk assessment as part of the due diligence process of choosing and committing to a new partner in a strategic alliance relationship.

In establishing the boundaries of this risk assessment, organisations take into account a multitude of different factors. These could be commercial factors ('What are the chances of commercial success with a particular partner, both tactically and strategically?), operational factors ('Can we work together successfully with this partner at relatively low risk?) or marketing factors ('Can we trust this partner with our brand association?').

Having performed some form of risk assessment at the beginning of an alliance, leading-edge organisations typically maintain an ongoing risk register, which can be as simple as a two- or three-page document identifying the elements of risk that have been observed by both/all organisations. In this way, the organisations forming the alliance are able to discuss openly the risk elements as they arise during the course of the relationship, secure in the knowledge that they are documented and there are procedural rules about how such risks should be dealt with. Such an approach, reflecting a degree of openness, trust and commitment on both/all sides goes a long way towards reassuring all parties that their interests will be as secure as possible, both in the short term (tactical) and in the long term (strategic).

This area more than any other will be significantly affected by the increasing number of multinational or global governance bodies that are tracking managerial control of their business alliances. Internal and external auditing bodies are already approaching many organisations' alliance functions and asking to see full documentation, not only of the risk registers with regard to the organisations' external partners, but also the processes, procedures and protocols the organisations are using to control these risks. This trend can only accelerate and increase the need for a higher degree of professionalism in this area. At the very least, organisations will be required to maintain accurate documentation and demonstrate accountability and the ability to execute their risk oversight programmes.

S23: Risk Sharing

In the best strategic alliance relationships all parties seek to share any identified risks. Obviously, some risks will be specific to one partner or another, but the more sophisticated alliance organisations of the twenty-first century recognise that shared risk brings shared rewards, and that risk sharing is a fundamental platform on which organisational business-to-business trust can be built, since it is a powerful indicator of having 'skin in the game'.

Risk sharing is important because it satisfies so many different dimensions in strategic alliance relationships. For example:

- It increases the business-to-business trust so crucial for the day-to-day operation of even the simplest strategic alliance relationships.
- It mitigates the overall risk to individual organisations by sharing the risks identified between multiple players. This is an extremely important and desirable consideration, particularly in light of legislative frameworks such as the Sarbanes-Oxley Act, Basel II and Basel III.
- Risk sharing can also be useful as a screening condition to ensure that any party wishing to enter an alliance appreciates the pros and cons of the relationship and is fully committed to it.

Most organisations maintain a risk register (see S22, 'Tactical and strategic risk', above) that sets out how risks will be shared. The most obvious parameter to use in allocating risk shares is commercial return: the contribution of exposure in percentage terms is used as a guide to the percentage of enjoyment of the benefits the partners can expect from a given set of initiatives.

A good example is the relationship initiated by BASF's agricultural products division when it closed its research and development function located in North America in 1999. At the time of the closure BASF was left with a number of potentially lucrative compounds which could be taken to market, but no resources in its now limited R&D function to enable it to progress the compounds through the regulatory protocols required to bring them to market. In this situation, one creative individual found a surprisingly elegant solution.

At the time, Paul Leonard was a product manager at BASF and was facing the prospect of simply dumping a number of seemingly highly promising compounds. Rather than do so, he approached a range of contract research organisations (CROs) and offered them a creative and innovative strategic alliance deal: the CROs would do all that was necessary to take the compounds through regulatory approval at no fee to BASF, and in return BASF would agree to recompense the CROs through a series of royalties contracts for the products sold. The amount of money the CROs could reasonably expect from these sales was greater than the simple 'fee for service' they would receive as outsourced research organisations.

A number of CROs showed interest, and as a result, during 1999 and 2000 the CROs were offered a range of compounds at various stages of progress through the research cycle and conducted their own very expensive due diligence to reassure themselves that these products represented genuine opportunities rather than just 'dud products' BASF was trying to get rid of.

Critical to the success of these relationships was the common understanding of the shared risk/reward model, which was documented in an extremely detailed and painstaking manner. As Leonard put it himself:

> It took us a lot of hard work and patient negotiating to come up with a form of words which accurately reflected the degree of risk that both sides were taking on board. Obviously, the contract research organisations felt that they were burdened with all the risk because BASF

was paying them nothing to begin with, so if the product didn't make it through regulatory authority, they would receive nothing but would have incurred significant costs.

On the other hand, BASF felt that they were involving themselves in (to some people's minds) an unacceptable degree of risk because they were associating themselves with a compound that could turn into a potential product whilst they had no direct control over the manner in which the compound was researched, tested, validated and taken through regulatory authority. The image that we came up with to describe such a relationship was that of a pilot/co-pilot in an airplane. The CRO would be the pilot, in that they would take all the necessary operational actions, but we at BASF would be the co-pilot, in that we would guide and advise the pilot during the course of the journey.

The results were a resounding success. Bearing in mind that the products these CROs were taking on board were due to be discontinued and therefore had no value, and indeed that this discontinuance would actually cost BASF money in terms of the wasted effort and resources already expended, the revenue so far generated for BASF runs into many millions of euros, while the CROs have increased the amount of revenue they have received from BASF to levels they could not have expected from a CRO relationship which did not include an element of risk sharing.

This relationship model has been so successful that some of the CROs are now seeking to apply it to alliances with other agricultural product companies, although this is proving problematic because of mutual non-disclosure agreements between BASF and the CROs.

Note that the factors Leonard alluded to in his estimation above of what made for success were aspects such as clear documentation of the 'rules of the game', not just through binding contracts (although these were extremely extensive), but also through the publication of a series of operating procedures which specified not only what was to be done, but how it was to be done and the behaviour of all parties to the relationship.

It seems clear that shared risk reward models such as this provide a tangible evidentiary benchmark of the new supply chain model of 'value added supplier'. Many leading-edge supplier organisations are now actively seeking such alliances as a way of proving that are looking for more intimate business relationships than simply that of transactional supplier. Indeed, many of them are now beginning to use the phrase 'smartsourcing' to describe this new type of relationship. Smartsourcing is applicable where a customer does not want to outsource the provision of a product or service because its too important, but neither does it want to insource the provision because it lacks the capability to do so efficiently. Therefore, it chooses to smartsource by entering into a strategic alliance with a world-class provider of the products or services, offering guidance and advice, and possibly sharing extremely sensitive data, for instance regarding customers, operations and customer market segments.

For a more detailed examination of insourcing, outsourcing and smartsourcing, see Chapter 13.

S24: Exit Strategies

Exit strategies involve one or more of the organisations forming an alliance clearly articulating at the beginning of the relationship how it can be dissolved if a specified set of factors occurs. Agreeing such conditions is extremely important in ensuring that a strategic alliance does not spiral down into something less valuable and ultimately very damaging through the application of outmoded or outdated conditions and protocols to a novel situation. Exit strategies are extremely important because they allow organisations to disengage from each other elegantly when appropriate, without leading to undue acrimony or even costly legal actions.

Organisations typically tend to brainstorm the conditions which would allow one or other of the parties to invoke the exit strategy. This doesn't necessarily mean that the relationship will actually be terminated, but it does mean that the partners can invoke the process to explore problems as they arise without the fear that they are inevitably degenerating towards legal action. The provision of mediation or alternative dispute resolution (ADR) can be helpful in facilitating debate and discussion of these issues. A number of high-profile legal cases at the turn of the twenty-first century have made it abundantly clear that the overworked and overburdened nature of the legal mechanisms in the Western world (particularly in Western Europe) mean that ADR is now being seen as a necessary addition to any significant contract, and if organisations go to court without having thoroughly and thoughtfully explored mediation or ADR, they are likely to be instructed to do so, usually with numerous additional costs attached.

Most organisations document this area by identifying triggering conditions that can be articulated in a reasonably succinct and simple manner. For example:

- if one of the partners changes its fundamental business strategy, leading to a change of focus for the alliance relationship;
- if one of the partners changes its senior management team and accompanying strategic direction.

A good example where an exit strategy would have saved alliance partners a considerable amount of money (along with fending off the prospect of ruin) is that of Ford and Firestone. The two companies established an extremely valuable mutually beneficial strategic alliance in the early 1990s whereby Ford agreed not to research and develop motor car tyres and Firestone agreed not to build cars, and both organisations agreed that they would focus on what they were best at. As a result, Firestone's R&D function was able to develop advanced tyre compounds and structures which were used on the Ford range of motor cars. Indeed, Ford even paid for and contributed to the Firestone research initiatives for the benefit of both parties. In return, Firestone regarded Ford as its preeminent customer and agreed to a period of delay before it would actively and publicly market the newly developed breakthrough sets of tyres and compounds initially available exclusively to Ford, giving it a period of market leadership.

Everything went well with the relationship for quite a while, based as it was on a clear understanding of what each party was doing, their relative strengths and weaknesses, and the strategic intent and direction of the relationship, which was to develop the best motor car tyres possible to enhance the customer experience of purchasing Ford motor vehicles.

However, at a certain point Ford faced a difficult business scenario that had nothing to do with the strategic relationship itself: globalisation meant that a number of other motor car manufacturers were now able to sourcing their motor car tyres at a lower cost per unit. The new Ford management team approached Firestone and demanded it reduce the cost of its tyres.

If an exit strategy had been drawn up, at this point either or both parties could have invoked it, since the strategic purpose of the alliance relationship was clearly being challenged: it was no longer provision of the best-quality tyres that was required, but rather the cheapest.

Although Firestone protested loud and long at the change in the relationship, it was in no position to refuse Ford's demands since at the time Ford was by far its major customer, so it agreed to cut its prices. However, the inevitable corollary came into play: 'The cheaper the tyres, the lower the quality.' Ford installed the new cheaper and lower-quality tyres on some of its high-performance SUVs. The result is exemplified by a standing joke at the time which renamed the Ford Explorer the 'Ford Exploder'.

However, senior management at Ford and Firestone didn't find this funny. The implications had wide-ranging and extremely damaging fall-out for both organisations. Individual customers took out private class actions against Ford and Firestone, both individually and collectively, that cost the companies many hundreds and millions of dollars to defend or settle out of court. There was also an immediate and enduring impact on both organisations' share prices, which dropped significantly. And finally, the long-term impact on both organisations' brand value was astronomical – so large, in fact, that at one point it threatened to close down both companies.

If either company had included a simple clause in their strategic alliance agreement which allowed them to understand that they could walk away from the previous arrangement in an elegant manner and renegotiate separately, it would have gone a long way towards obviating the extremely damaging consequences of persisting with a strategic alliance relationship in a changed set of circumstances which made such a relationship inappropriate.

Unfortunately, in this area many people and/or organisations mistakenly compare an exit strategy in a business-to-business relationship with a prenuptial arrangement in a marriage relationship. Mistakenly, they voice the opinion that including a condition which specifically conceives of the idea of failure does nothing to enhance or build trust at such an early stage. Such a comparison is erroneous, and leads to flawed thinking. In our experience, it is essential to draw up a robust set of exit conditions and the manner and means and protocols by which all partners can invoke them. Such a simple articulation at the beginning of a relationship is fundamental to the ability to disengage quickly, elegantly and in a cost-effective manner while leaving the parties free to choose to partner with each other again at some time in the future. It seems inevitable to us that the rapid increase in alliance relationships of all kinds will lead to a situation where allowing for disengagement in this manner will be a key competitive business factor, encouraging better-performing organisations to construct more flexible combinations of partners to satisfy identified business needs.

S25: Senior Executive Support

In the context of strategic alliances, 'senior executive support' refers to senior individuals on both/all sides of the relationship actively supporting the relationship itself, rather than their own organisation's narrow proprietary needs from the relationship. This support is crucial in establishing a degree of commitment from all partners in the alliance relationship. Some experienced alliance practitioners rank senior executive support as equally important to business-to-business trust (Cu31: see Chapter 10).

There is no doubt that in the best-performing strategic alliance relationships we have seen there is a very high degree of inter-personal 'chemistry' in terms of understanding, respect for and interest in each other's particular point of view, and it is this senior executive chemistry and active support in both/all organisations which enables so many potential barriers and bars to be 'facilitated away'.

There is nothing more tangibly obvious to the alliance teams on both/all sides of a relationship than seeing their very senior executives getting on well. The relationship will not necessarily survive and thrive simply because significant senior executives have a good relationship, but if they make public pronouncements about the intentions of the alliance relationship itself, this conveys powerful messages, not only to the organisations in the relationship, but also the industry analysts employed to test public perception of the robustness and commitment of the relationship.

We should clarify, however, that in discussing the issue of senior executive support we do not simply mean the obvious photo-opportunities available when extremely important and influential brands combine for a common purpose. Such opportunities are worthwhile, and can add value to the relationship by influencing public perception, but what we mean by senior executive support is far more significant: the active, regular and ongoing commitment of the executives to commit time to understanding and contributing to the success of the relationship.

Most organisations which have recognised the importance of this area appoint a relationship executive sponsor. In many cases this executive sponsor does not have (or does not necessarily need to have) specific technical, marketing or product knowledge associated with the products or services to be marketed by the relationship. Rather, the role of the senior executive sponsor is to break log jams in each partner's organisation by throwing his weight behind the propositions and suggestions of the alliance teams further down the hierarchy.

Most organisations that appoint a senior executive sponsor also appoint some form of governance committee or joint steering group or procedure (sometimes called an executive summit) where the executive can contribute to the agenda in advance. These events normally take place at least once a year (sometimes as often as twice a year), and their purpose is to drive the strategic agenda of the relationship in such a way that it ties into and engages fully with the operational agenda. Such high-profile meetings can be extremely beneficial to the relationship overall.

A good example of this would be the case of a newly appointed chief operating officer in a global fast-moving consumer goods company which had a range of business relationships (as many as 15,000 around the world). The majority of these were simply customer–supplier relationships, but a significant minority (50–150) were generally regarded as strategic alliance relationships, or at least on the way to developing into them. The officer set himself the daunting task of developing each of these strategic alliance relationships to secure a higher degree of interaction, purposefulness and commitment from the partners, and the simple expedient he used to bring this about was to announce that he would personally attend the next executive review of each of the selected top 25 global relationships.

The effect was immediate and predictable. The organisation's partners immediately felt the need to reciprocate by sending suitably senior representatives to the meeting (not in all cases a chief operating officer, but often a senior vice president of either sales, marketing, R&D, technology or customer relationship management. Before the first of these structured meetings, the officer called a together the entire team involved with a particular strategic alliance relationship which was due to be reviewed in four weeks time. The team comprised five individuals in various functions within the organisation. The officer's brief was very simple and very clear.

He asked them to suspend whatever it was they were doing in operational terms on the relationship for the next four days, and instead to develop a range of structured briefing documents for him, 'so that when I go into this meeting with Company B, I will know more about their day-to-day operations than whoever they send as the senior executive responsible for the relationship'.

The team dutifully complied with these requirements and spend four solid days (a total of 20 man-days) articulating, tracking, monitoring, documenting and briefing the officer on every aspect of the relationship's operation.

In contrast, the senior executive dispatched by the partnering organisation was simply briefed in the limousine hired to take him from the airport to the meeting location. This consisted of a few hurried conversations over the course of some 40 minutes, along with some key requirements the alliance manager suggested the organisation wanted to achieve from the meeting.

During the four-hour meeting the officer regularly embarrassed all the partner organisation's representatives, but in particular the senior executive allocated to sponsor the relationship, by making it perfectly obvious that the senior executive had little, if any, grasp of the substantial issues both organisations wished to discuss.

The result was an impromptu meeting in the car park of the host organisation, at which the senior executive from the partnering organisation lined up his alliance team and made it plain in no uncertain terms that he would never again be embarrassed in such a way by having so little information. He demanded to be equally well briefed for any future event as the officer of the host organisation.

The result of this exercise was that the senior alliance managers from both organisations got together and realised very quickly that they could not allow such a meeting to happen again. They had to share not just information, but also expectations on both sides to ensure that their senior executives would never be embarrassed personally in such a monumental way again.

The result was a series of meaningful action points generated by the teams at multiple levels on both sides to enhance, reinforce and make far more effective the communication between them. The next senior executive meeting held six months later was a far more vibrant affair which moved at a significantly faster pace than the previous one. Neither side was willing to appear unprepared, so they both discussed some very meaningful issues over a very short period that in turn generated a virtuous circle in which both sides recognised that they got more done by being well prepared and therefore committed a new 'governance/behavioural rule': that for all future summits, both parties would allocate a minimum of five days' preparation time, with open disclosure of documentation to allow the meeting to move ahead more quickly and more powerfully.

Although this example is a rather extreme one, and the strategy employed by the officer was extremely brutal (and could have had catastrophic consequences), it does illustrate a fundamental point about senior executive support: executives often lay their creditability, ego, face and reputation on the line in any strategic alliance effort. Anything which threatens these or anything which enhances them is regarded at a personal level as an extremely good or bad thing respectively, and any process which can enhance them is to be seen as beneficial.

Senior executives from many leading-edge collaborative organisations are now actively seeking other similarly minded collaborative individuals with whom they can work effectively. Prime Minister Margaret Thatcher once famously said of Mikhail Gorbachev, then leader of the USSR: 'I like Mr. Gorbachev. We can do business together.' What she meant by this was not that his intentions, strategies or objectives were entirely in sync with her own, but that he acted in a manner which allowed her to engage with him on the basis of some known behavioural rules.

Similarly, chief executives and senior executives of large multinational organisations are now constantly on the lookout for individuals in other organisations with whom they can develop a strong personal chemistry that enables them to work together efficiently. Often this is not evidenced in the glare and bright lights of media announcements, but rather in effective behind-the-scenes inter-operations at a meaningful level between two organisations committed to becoming 'zippered' – meaning that they interlace with each other at multiple contact points in both organisations, not just at the strategic level, but also the managerial and operational levels.

S26: Business-to-business Strategic Alignment

Business-to-business strategic alignment is the degree of compatibility and synergy between organisations which allows them to drive forward towards a common strategic goal. This area represents the broad canvas within which the strategic alliance relationship exists. It could be, for example, that one organisation's strategic objective/directional path leads it to want to exploit emerging markets (for example, in India or China). Its partnering organisation may have a similar broad strategic intention, in which case the organisations are said to be in strategic alignment. However, if one organisation wishes to exploit emerging markets while the other wishes to consolidate its position in mature markets (for example, in Western Europe), then there is a much lower degree of top-level business-to-business strategic alignment. This does not necessarily mean that the alliance relationship itself cannot be a success. However, it does mean that the alliance cannot benefit from a high degree of organisational enthusiasm for the organisations' strategic direction. This factor is important because of the energy and resources partner organisations can contribute to achieving each other's aims.

Imagine the US space shuttle taking off for a manned excursion to the Moon. The space shuttle sits on top of huge booster rockets, each of which can be seen as a partnership the shuttle has entered into to achieve its long-term objectives. On blast-off, all partners have a clear objective: to reach their target – the Moon. Their combined energy allows them to achieve this, whereas each one in isolation could not. (We shouldn't stretch this analogy too far, however, since obviously in this metaphor the booster rockets have a relatively limited time value: once they have enabled the shuttle to escape the pull of the earth's gravity they are discarded into space – in a typical strategic alliance relationship, this is not the intention!)

Quite simply, organisations achieve business-to-business strategic alignment by sharing their observations and understanding of the strategic direction of their own company, their partner(s) and the market in the areas that impinge on the strategic alliance relationship. Such an interaction and discourse obviously relies on a high degree of business-to-business trust and a willingness to share quite sensitive business knowledge.

Here we see the 'chicken and egg' nature of a successful strategic alliance relationship: the relationship is successful because meaningful and intimate detailed strategic knowledge is being shared between the partners; but the information is being shared because the relationship is successful and viewed as strategic. This key catalytic element of business-to-business trust (Cu31) will be considered in more detail in Chapter 10.

S27: Fit with Strategic Business Path

This area is particularly associated with CSF S26, 'Business-to-business strategic alignment'. It concerns how a particular strategic alliance relationship fits the strategic aims of the partner organisations and their attitudes towards each other.

Except for the smallest organisations, most sophisticated collaborative companies are now using combinations of partners to achieve their strategic ends. Consequently, they have usually a high-level strategic roadmap or wallchart which identifies which sectors they are targeting and which partners they wish to work with in each sector. They often need to have conversations with partners to articulate the roles each will play in their strategic roadmap. While they can't always share every detail of the roadmap, since that would entail sharing sensitive competitive information, they can at least show where each partner fits on that roadmap.

Obviously, if a partner's role of the roadmap is too small then it will have little or no enthusiasm to engage in collaboration, whereas if its involvement is too large, it will see this as an open invitation to engage in power broking negotiations, and will also question the desirability of being so intimately linked to a single partner. Figure 9.1 shows an example of such a situation.

S28: Multiple Relationships with the Same Partner(s)

This CSF relates to the number of instances of specific interaction between strategic partners. There is clear evidence that the number of instances of a strategic relationship between any two partners is directly proportional to the success of the instances: in other words, the more aspects of the relationship there are, the more successful each individual aspect will be. The reason for this appears to be that each partner develops a comprehensive understanding of the operating procedures, protocols, cultures and behaviours of the other, and is thus able to develop a more balanced point perspective on the context of its own interactions. This leads to a higher degree of balance on both sides and a more well-judged perspective of the intentions of each party. Also, there is a natural amplifying effect, whereby one successful interaction positively affects the rest. (Note that the reverse also appears to be true: that in a situation with a number of interactions, a bad interaction can have a significant harmful knock-on effect on the entire relationship.)

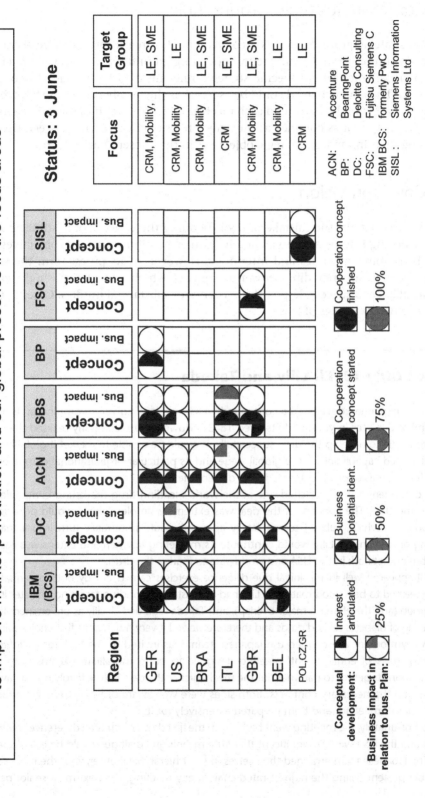

Figure 9.1 Professional Services strategic consultancy partnerships

S29: Common Strategic Ground Rules

'Common strategic ground rules' is a convenient shorthand for the more accurate but unwieldy 'common strategic and tactical operating ground rules'. This CSF covers those aspects of an alliance where specific strategic rules need to be in place to govern the relationship. The issues covered could be as banal as the number of times staff will meet, the types of staff who should attend each meeting or the geographies that will be involved in the relationship, or as complex as the agreed rules of engagement between the parties in pursuing their individual strategic objectives in the chosen market sectors.

S30: Common Vision

Many executives make the mistake of pooh-poohing the concept of a 'strategic alliance vision', believing it to be akin to a combination of mission statement, objectives, goals, targets, behaviours, attitudes and intentions. However, in its purest form the strategic alliance vision is an incredibly powerful concept which can almost single-handedly drive the alliance to success despite the existence of substantial hurdles. Cases Studies 10 and 11 give two examples of this.

Case Study 10: Eli Lilly and Takeda

Takeda in Japan had developed a compound which was looking very promising in its ability to combat diabetes in young adults aged 18–32. However, the company realised that even if it were able to develop the drug successfully, it would be unable to market it globally since it had limited capabilities on the global stage and its particular organisational competencies were in the areas of product research and development.

Consequently, it approached one of the world's leading drug marketing companies, Eli Lilly in the USA. The concept of the deal was extremely simple: Takeda would provide the compound – which, subject to regulatory approval, could potentially turn into a market-leading drug – and Eli Lilly would contribute its marketing acumen and extensive sales and distribution network in the USA and worldwide to market the drug.

All appeared well in the initial due diligence exercises carried out by both organisations. There seemed to be a good match: Eli Lilly had no existing major drug targeting diabetes in this age group (and therefore no major overlap), and Takeda regarded Eli Lilly as pre-eminent in the marketing of diabetes-related drugs and therefore viewed it very much as its first-choice partner.

A key moment arose when the Japanese team was invited to the USA for an intensive four-day 'rules of engagement' meeting designed to bring the alliance teams from both organisations together to hammer out the mechanics of the deal before involving the lawyers to draw up the necessary contracts. Both sides were well aware of the extremely important nature of this meeting, and both prepared extensively for it.

Unfortunately, the meeting went badly from the first day. The cultural differences between Japan and the USA were so significant that little meaningful dialogue could be established.

The Japanese team arranged themselves in strict hierarchical order, with the most senior member present taking the highest-rated chair at any meeting, the next most senior person taking a position immediately to his left-hand side, and so on throughout the team.

Furthermore, in the course of the discussions no person from the Japanese team could speak unless his immediate superior had spoken first. The American team found this manner of negotiating extremely cumbersome, if not impossible, since some of the technical knowledge it needed to form the basis of its predictive structures was only available from the more junior Japanese team members. In addition, very few of the Japanese team spoke any English and none of the American team spoke any Japanese, so a lot of the dialogue was conducted through interpreters.

The relationship appeared doomed to failure, but after three days of extremely arduous yet fruitless negotiations, the senior member of the Japanese team and the senior member of the American team both happened to bump into each other at the water fountain during a break in negotiations. Both had their personal interpreters with them, and to break the tension, the American team member asked the Japanese team member why he was interested or involved in this particular compound to combat diabetes.

The answer was given quietly, with sadness and reflection: 'My brother has a nephew who is only 17 years old and has recently been diagnosed with diabetes.'

There was a shocked moment of silence before the American team member said: 'My uncle died of diabetes when he was 21. I was very young at the time, and it had a powerful and dramatic impact on me.'

Neither man said another word, but they looked at each other and both strode purposefully back into the conference room being used for the negotiations. When the teams had reconvened, the American lead invited the Japanese lead negotiator to join him at the top of the table.

They both looked down the long conference table, populated as it was by the Americans on one side and the Japanese on the other, and both said through their translators: 'It is wrong that people die at such an early age of diabetes. We are privileged to have the opportunity to stop that happening, and we are in danger of disgracing that responsibility by allowing our personal agendas and cultures to get in the way of the greater good. Can we both strive equally with all possible determination so that when we leave this room, either with or without a deal hammered out, we can honestly say that we didn't let down all those people who might be relying on us?'

The impact was, of course, electric, and very quickly the organisational and cultural barriers preventing open dialogue broke down in the face of such an overwhelming visionary statement.

Within 30 minutes the team had scribbled on a whiteboard, 'Our vision is to eradicate diabetes from young adults between the ages of 18 and 32.' The vision established in that conference room was so powerful that it sustained the relationship through the very serious trials and tribulations that were to follow.

There were, for example, significant difficulties with the Food and Drug Administration in the USA. There were also serious problems manufacturing the compound. However, nothing seemed to get in the way of the combined purpose and desire of both teams to make this global change.

As a result, the product developed from the Eli Lilly–Takeda strategic alliance relationship is now one of the most effective anti-diabetes drugs on the market. It is also one of the most commercially successful ever launched, and one of the fastest ever drug launches in the FDA's history.

The team members from both organisations have such a strong bond and sense of mutual purpose that they regularly communicate outside the project team and hold social events together.

In Case Study 10, a passionate and powerful shared vision important to both parties energised the combined partnership team. Case Study 11 describes a similar example in which slightly different strategic objectives were combined to create a powerful joint vision moving forward.

Case Study 11: North Yorkshire Fire Brigade and McCain Corporation

At the beginning of 1992 it was unthinkable for any advertising to be displayed on the fire engines of the UK Fire and Rescue Service. However, Brigade Commander Eric Black was searching for a way to solve a very difficult and literally life-threatening problem.

Black was the most senior fire officer in charge of Yorkshire, one of the largest counties in the UK, and in that county people commonly used home-made deep-fat fryers consisting of a large saucepan filled with cooking oil heated to a very high temperature which then had peeled and chopped potatoes dropped into it. The result, if successful, was that peculiar English delicacy known as chips, referred to in the USA and other parts of the world as 'French fries'.

The problem for Black was that the open nature of these pans and the extremely high temperatures they created on the gas and electric rings of home cookers made for an extremely dangerous combination, and incidents of 'chip pan fires' were among the commonest contributors to deaths connected with home fires attended by the Yorkshire Fire Brigade in 1993 – there were 54 of them. Black was racking his brain as to how to persuade householders to stop using such a primitive and dangerous means of producing this domestic comestible.

What he came up with was both revolutionary and novel. He approached a company called McCain, which at that time was just launching a new product known as the 'oven chip', which as the name suggests could be cooked in the oven – a far safer procedure than using a chip pan.

Black offered McCain advertising space on the sides of all the fire engines in Yorkshire. McCain in return offered to pay for this advertising, and Black used these funds to pay for an Education Officer known as 'Mr Chippy' who would tour the schools and colleges of Yorkshire extolling the virtues of safe home cooking, with a particular focus on home chip pans and McCain oven chips.

The results were both dramatic and satisfying for both organisations. McCain's market share of the oven chip market rocketed during 1994–8, based on the massive surge in popularity of its product in Yorkshire. In addition, the number of deaths from chip pan fires reduced dramatically over a three-year period, from 54 to three.

In this case, the strong desire of one individual to stop what he saw as a needless and senseless series of preventable deaths coincided with the not unreasonable desire (albeit less altruistic) of a major organisation to break into a profitable market sector with a new product.

In retrospect, this combination appears natural and reasonable (particularly given the results). But consider for a moment the words of Eric Black as he explains some of the practical problems involved in such an enterprise.

'We had a hell of a time getting it through the National Fire Brigade executive structure. Many fellow officers thought that I was "selling out" commercially and disgracing the proud heritage which the fire brigade had had for many hundreds of years in the United Kingdom. I tried many arguments and had many passionate discussions, even rows, with many of them, but it kept coming back to the same fact: that I genuinely thought that if I did it I might save some lives, and when you put it like that, it's difficult to allow the cosmetic aspects of the look and feel of a piece of tin (which is what a fire engine is, really) with people's lives. Eventually, we were successful, and I count it as one of the greatest successes of my stewardship as a Chief Fire Officer of the North Yorkshire Fire Brigade.'

In this case, one man's passionate vision was enough to drive the relationship and to establish a whole new model of public/private sector initiatives. Today such collaborations are commonplace, but very few of them have such spectacular results in terms of saving human lives as this relationship.

10 *The Cultural Dimension*

Cu31: Business-to-business Trust

Trust is probably the most frequently cited and most easily identified of the cultural CSFs. Partnerships can endure virtually any stresses and strains if there is a high degree of business-to-business trust. In the Alliance Best Practice lexicon, trust is described as a 'high impacter'. This means that it has a substantial and significant impact on relationships (for good or ill), but that it usually takes time to develop. However, although it has a high impact, it is notoriously difficult to develop and improve. Trust is not an element that can be turned on and off at will. It is usually created when one partner makes an extra effort for the benefit of the relationship. A good example of this is the strategic alliance relationship between GSK Healthcare and Cardinal Health described in Case Study 12.

Case Study 12: GSK Healthcare and Cardinal Health

One of the products GSK Healthcare markets is a transparent nicotine patch call NiQuitin. The patches themselves are packaged by one of GSK's crucial partners, Cardinal Health. One of the seminal points in the relationship (according to both sides) was when, at an early stage, GSK contacted Cardinal Health one Friday morning and requested an emergency shipment to be packaged and sent out within three to four days. Unfortunately, GSK's central office hadn't appreciated that this was a bank holiday weekend in the UK and all Cardinal Health's staff were due to take the Monday off. Many of Cardinal Health's staff had already made plans to spend time with their families. However, knowing how important this shipment might be to the future relationship between both parties, Cardinal Health's Director of Strategic Relationships contacted the Director of Production and pleaded for the shipment to be manufactured, packaged and dispatched by the GSK's deadline of 5 p.m. on the Monday. Because he was convinced that the shipment was crucial, the Production Director moved heaven and earth to put together a skeleton staff who would be prepared to work over the bank holiday weekend, and the shipment was sent out on time.

There are a number of aspects to this event which are interesting in terms of the growth of the relationship between GSK and Cardinal Health. First of all, the shipment of the nicotine patches within a three-days was above and beyond the service level agreement agreed by both parties, which specified a five-day turnaround, so Cardinal Health was contributing something it wasn't legally obliged to do.

Secondly, Cardinal Health was paid nothing extra for accelerating the shipment in such an ambitious manner, it was simply paid the same amount as if the shipment had gone out in five days.

Notice also the line of trust that had to be constructed and employed to achieve the outcome. The Production Director had to trust the Relationship Director when he said that this particular shipment was crucial to the relationship (there had been many times in the past when customers had asked for a rush order).

The chain of trust doesn't stop there: the individuals the Production Director approached to work over the weekend to get the shipment out on time also had to trust the Production Director when he said that it was of critical importance to the future of the organisation.

The outcome was that the degree of trust and mutual respect between the two organisations was significantly enhanced, and subsequent interviews showed that many of the key players in the relationship identified this particular event as a key enabler in moving to the next degree of intimacy required to make a success of the strategic relationship.

There is a fundamental difference between person-to-person trust and business-to-business trust, but one is usually built on the other. For example, in interviews many alliance personnel stated they trusted their partner organisations because of the specific actions of a number of key individuals who exhibited personal integrity, honesty and high standards, leading to sense that they could trust them in the relationship.

However, in Alliance Best Practice's terms, it is business-to-business trust we are seeking, rather than personal trust, because personal trust is at best a transitory advantage. If a particular individual involved in a relationship moves on or is replaced for any reason, then if trust is based on personalities, it will be lost and will need to be rebuilt.

The problem is that many organisations do not have simple and robust trust-building models. The issue of trust is often connected to the issues of control and accountability, and is crucial in underpinning both. Earlier passages in this book have highlighted the importance of the issue of control, since in a fluid and well-balanced strategic alliance relationship no side, or no individual, ever has full independent control. To deal with such ambiguity, clarity concerning partner accountability is required. Control over a relationship, and sometimes accountability within it, often changes quite markedly during its life cycle, and trust is required for one side to grant control and accountability to the other.

In talking to a very wide range of alliance executives, many were quite unsure as to how to achieve this ephemeral advantage called 'trust'. However, virtually all of them said: 'We know it when we see it.'

Bear in mind in your alliance relationships that trust is not the same as liking someone. There is an excellent example of a global strategic alliance relationship which is perfectly fluid and has some well-defined rules as the basis of the relationship, along with equally well-defined penalties for breaking them – indeed, there is a high degree of trust in the relationship. However, I don't believe that you could claim that any or all the partners 'like' each other, since the example I'm thinking of is the Mafia!

Among a number of elements we at Alliance Best Practice have observed when our clients are looking to develop trust in strategic alliance relationships, four important aspects stand out:

1. Trust involves obligations – both making and keeping them – towards your partner(s).
2. Trust is closely connected to integrity, or to put it another way, it is extremely difficult to trust any individual or organisation that acts dishonestly or operates according to a hidden agenda. Generally, one openly dishonest or untrustworthy act will be sufficient to destroy trust for a long time. One deliberate lie will ruin any particular individual's standing as a person worthy of trust. One piece of misinformation or 'spin' will do the same for an organisation. Lies and dishonesty are totally incompatible with trustworthiness.
3. Openness is essential. It is not impossible to trust someone who is secretive, but it takes much more faith to do so. Secrecy implies that whatever is being hidden is been concealed for a purpose that itself may not be honest or acceptable, or else why is it being hidden?
4. Although not associated in the same way as the three points above, the question of leadership appears to be instrumental in establishing trust in relationships, particularly at a personal level. Leaders who are trusted by their own workforce and who can transfer that degree of trustworthiness to their partners' teams seems to inspire a high degree of loyalty, openness and a 'no blame' culture within the relationships they are associated with. These activities, more than anything else, help to develop a strong sense of trustworthiness.

Another excellent example of trust being used as a key driver or motivator in a strategic alliance relationship was demonstrated in the relationship between Rolls-Royce and TNT Express, as discussed in Case Study 13.

Case Study 13: Rolls-Royce and TNT Express

Rolls-Royce is a large engine manufacturer based in the UK. It typically produces large engines in three main areas: marine, defence and aerospace. TNT Express was at the time (2002) a road transport and logistics company.

   The background to the situation was that the Global Director of Global Physical Logistics for Rolls-Royce, Dr Ian Shellard, was looking to put together a collaboration between a number of Rolls-Royce's strategic suppliers. Shellard recognised that to be efficient and effective in the maintenance of large aero engines worldwide, he needed an intricate and complex combination of different types of partners. These partners would need to reflect various functions performed in the physical act of moving both large and small parts around the world that were necessary in the maintenance of Rolls-Royce engines.

   Shellard named this innovative relationship model 'The Starfish Alliance', because the heart and brain of the alliance was at the centre (Rolls-Royce), and there were five important legs to the relationship representing the functions necessary for success: (1) road transport, (2) freight forwarding, (3) warehousing, (4) inbound/outbound logistics and (5) packaging. Just like the starfish that inspired the idea, the whole could survive for a time if it lost one of its 'legs', because the other four had sufficient resources to support it.

   Shellard called together eight potential road transport key partners, and began the meeting by outlining Rolls-Royce's requirements of the single successful partner that would be chosen. It needed to have global reach and coverage in its road transport capability, and it needed to be able to offer an end-to-end fourth-party logistics capability.

There was a palpable and awkward silence while the senior executives from the road transport organisations tried to assess the implications of Rolls-Royce's requirements for them. Finally, the Managing Director of TNT Express spoke up: 'We would very much like to take part in this initiative and be the chosen strategic partner for the road transport leg of The Starfish Alliance. You require that the successful partner will need to have end-to-end coverage and global reach. There is only one problem there. We currently, in TNT Express, have neither of those things. However, if you were to choose us, we would commit to developing that capability as part of the partnership.'

Although there were a number of other reasons why TNT Express was eventually chosen as the successful partner for The Starfish Alliance, Shellard later identified that moment as when he knew that he could work very well with that individual managing director on a personal level. The managing director had been open and honest enough to explain in front of a room full of his competitors the two significant weaknesses in his own organisation, but then he had also expressed the desire to work with Rolls-Royce on an ongoing basis to develop those competencies.

This degree of openness and honesty from TNT Express persuaded Shellard to include them among the selection criteria. Although TNT Express scored less well on the number of trucks and sheds it had available, its road transport function was regarded as highly effective and a good choice because of its desire to improve to meet Rolls-Royce's needs. Notice once again that even though the trust required was organisation-to-organisation, the trust itself was actually developed person-to-person.

Cu32: Collaborative Corporate Mindset

The collaborative corporate mindset concerns an organisation's desire to enter a partnership coupled with that organisation's degree of the maturity in thinking about partnering. Some organisations appear to be 'alliance-friendly', while others are definitely not built for collaboration. An example of an organisation which was very definitely not alliance-friendly was CSC, a large US systems integration business operating in Europe, as described in Case Study 14.

Case Study 14: British Telecom and CSC Corporation

CSC had just secured a major partnership with British Telecom. As a result, BT had allocated a full-time partnership director to the relationship (see Cu34, 'Dedicated alliance managers', below), but CSC failed to do so.

When questioned as to why this was the case, CSC was very forthright. Its President of Operations in Europe stated: 'We are all about doing deals. We don't want to collaborate with anybody; we just want to win business!'

The unfortunate consequence of this attitude and behaviour, which was endemic in the organisation in Europe, the Middle East and Africa, was that despite some good opportunities being available to both parties to secure extra business and, despite the fact that both had been successful in securing two or three very large bids in the outsourcing arena, within three years the relationship had deteriorated to the point where BT no longer bothered to dedicate resources to it. This was as a direct consequence of CSC's attitude to collaboration.

In our work we have identified three distinct stages of alliance maturity among organisations:

1. **Opportunistic** – This stage is typified by organisations (like CSC in Case Study 14) that see alliances and collaborations simply as ways to win deals that are either too large or too complex for them to win alone.
2. **Systematic** – In this stage, organisations have woken up to the fact that a large number of the deals they have won have been gained by working with external partners. Now a considerable amount of business is locked up in the relationships they have with these other organisations, so they start to devote time, energy and effort into systematising their alliance efforts.
3. **Endemic** – In this stage, organisations have realised that partnering is not something conducted by one particular department or function within the organisation; it is a mindset and a way of life, and looking for collaboration and leverage opportunities in all aspects of daily working life generates massive benefits for the organisation. Organisations in this stage typically embed collaborative thinking in their appraisal and remuneration systems.

Some organisations just don't want to collaborate; they would rather be acquisitive. A good example of this is a conversation Alliance Best Practice had with a large European systems integrator, whose representative said:

Although we pay lip service to the idea of collaboration and partnering, really we are just looking to affect a 'kiss to kill' strategy. In other words, if the organisation we partner with is good and could be seen as a threat, then we look to establish an alliance relationship with them to help us understand them better, and either buy them or understand how to compete with them more effectively. Our executives don't want to partner, they want to punish!

What happens when two organisations with vastly different levels of understanding regarding collaboration try to work together? It appears to us that one ends up having to teach the other how to form this thing called 'a collaborative alliance', and that real commercial progress is therefore necessarily slowed down. This issue more than any other seems to lie at the heart of the difficulty of very small organisations partnering with very large ones.

Note also that this question of organisational understanding of partnering is distinct from individuals' understanding of it. There are any number of examples we could cite of particular charismatic and visionary leaders in organisations (of whatever size) who clearly understood the potential for and the power of collaboration. In certain cases these leaders actually managed to find another individual at a similar level in a prospective partner's organisation who had similar views, so a powerful personal rapport developed very quickly that led to a significant strategic alliance being announced. However, as soon as the two individuals left the room, the executive teams of the two organisations had extreme difficulty putting together a partnering process which would accommodate the leaders' intentions. In almost all these situations their relationship was doomed from the very first day.

Case Study 15: Siebel CRM Systems Inc.

A good example of an individual having a particular attitude to partnering which did produce appropriate organisational beliefs and principles was that of Tom Siebel, founder of the Siebel IT software organisation. From the very first day, Tom Siebel set the collaborative corporate mindset in his company when he inaugurated systems which enforced the principles that Siebel would never use consultants, and that it would always collaborate with other consultancies to deliver its software solutions.

Even when Siebel grew to the point where it needed internal consultant resources to teach other systems integrators how best to best to deploy its solutions, Tom Siebel steadfastly refused to call them 'consultants', insisting on calling them 'product experts'.

It was this attitude and belief more than any other that allowed his organisation to collaborate effectively with large and small systems integrators in a way that firms like SAP and Oracle often find difficult because both of them maintain a sizeable and commercially viable consultant division within their own organisations.

There appear to be relatively few companies that have a naturally collaborative corporate mindset. This is possibly because collaboration is not usually seen as a 'sexy' management style. Seeing the middle way, taking account of one's partners' desires and making concessions before one's partner does are not characteristics which readily come to mind when thinking about successful CEOs on Wall Street. The corporate environment in the West generally tends to promote hungry and avaricious killers, not collaborators.

Somewhat surprisingly, therefore, the global systems and outsourcing organisation Accenture, although not noted for being a 'soft', appears to be a company with a strong collaborative mindset. This stems in part from the company's traditional practice when inducting new employees, based on the induction procedure for US marines. New employees are taken to a certain location (usually Chicago) and are given a three- or four-week induction programme designed to establish and overlay an Accenture-specific culture on top of the national characteristics or natural preferences of the individuals concerned. This approach allows Accenture to put together people from a variety of geographic locations and ensure that each one will be able to operate efficiently and effectively within Accenture's corporate culture.

Such an approach recognises that inter-operability between individuals and collaboration in teams at the national and international level is the only way for a global organisation like Accenture to deal with globalisation. The model is particularly successful at establishing multicultural teams and giving them simple and robust rules on which to rely when they are collaborating across different functional areas in their organisation, be they technical, procedural or geographic. This bedrock understanding allows Accenture personnel to explain the organisation's culture very clearly to prospective partners, thus achieving high scores in the critical success factors shown in Table 10.1.

Table 10.1   Example of a 'lite' CSF model

Commercial	Technical	Strategic	Cultural	Operational
Co1: Business value proposition	T12: Partner company market position	S25: Senior executive support	Cu32: Collaborative corporate mindset	O39: Alliance processes
Co2: Due diligence	T13: Host company market position	S30: Common vision	Cu37: Other cultural issues	O40: Speed of progress so far
Co8: Commercial benefit	T14: Market fit of proposed solution		Cu38: Business-to-business cultural alignment	O41: Distance from revenue
Co10: Expected cost/value ratio	T15: Product fit with partners' offerings			O43: Communication
	T19: Partner accountability			

Cu33: Collaboration Skills

Given that alliance managers are asked to perform the act of collaboration so often, it's somewhat surprising that in our extensive research we have found so little formal training in how to collaborate.

Individual collaboration skills are the counterpoint to Cu32, 'Collaborative corporate mindset'. Although the organisation may have a strong desire to be collaborative and may have a good collaborative mindset, it will be at the individual level that those aspirations will be put to the test. Cu33 refers specifically to the ability of individuals to collaborate effectively, both within their own organisation but also with their partners' organisations.

But what exactly does 'collaboration' mean, and what do collaboration skills entail? We have received a range of answers to these questions. Many seem to focus on interpersonal skills, communication (both internal and external), there being no surprises, seeing the situation from the partner's perspective and co-collaborative negotiation.

Despite extensive research on this subject, Alliance Best Practice has been unable to find a defined collaboration skills training course. Rather, organisations seem to focus on elements of personal development in areas such as interpersonal skills, communication, negotiation, self-awareness and empathy, and regard these as sufficient training for alliance executives.

Indeed, there are some senior executives who question whether there is such a thing as 'collaboration' at all, let alone whether it can be taught. Many executives put forward the reasonable view that collaboration is really just another aspect of commonsense business.

There are currently over 180,000 entries in the ABP Database of instances of alliance best practice in action. One of the specific areas of data we capture is that of collaboration skills. When we have asked alliance executives whether they had ever taken part in or received any formal collaboration skill training, less than 6% of all those we have interviewed over the last ten years have ever had any formal training at all with regard to alliances, and of those more than 50% have restricted collaboration training to specific aspects such as negotiation or communication.

Cu34: Dedicated Alliance Managers

There is absolutely no doubt from the Database that having dedicated managers for strategic alliance relationships improves the chances of success enormously. However, there is a damaging and disturbing 'Catch-22' scenario here: many senior executives will not appoint a dedicated resource to a relationship until that relationship has reached a certain level of activity or value. The dilemma is that the relationship will never reach that level of activity or value until a dedicated resource is devoted to it to actually manage the actions required. This is encapsulated in the phrase, 'Alliances don't manage themselves – they need to be managed.'

The problem for many senior executives appears to be that they have no clear idea of the range of tasks and activities that alliance managers need to perform, and they obviously believe that the work of an alliance manager is predominantly that of signing the deal, and once this has been done, as long as the partner's representatives can be sufficiently wined and dined, then the relationship will be a healthy one.

Nothing could be further from the truth. In any reasonably significant alliance relationship there is a large amount of work for the dedicated alliance manager to do in terms of aligning internal and external resources, communicating the needs and aspirations of the relationship to a wide range of internal and external stakeholders, developing and scoping an appropriate action plan to develop the relationship as well as the products and services to be delivered by it, and once the action plan is developed, a great deal of day-to-day activity is involved in managing (some might even say project managing) the relationship to a successful conclusion.

If more senior executives had a better understanding of this aspect of alliance management, it is likely that they would have fewer reservations in dedicating resources to their important relationships (at least for a finite period of, for example, 90 or 180 days). If they did so, they would usually see an exponential increase in the success of those relationships.

The converse is also true, in that Alliance Best Practice has observed a number of individuals who have been given the title of Strategic Alliance Manager, but instead of being allowed to focus their efforts on a truly large and strategic (important and complex) relationship, they have been forced to divide their time and efforts to run more than one alliance relationship (sometimes as many as seven or eight). This leads to painful self-fulfilling under-performing scenarios, which usually go as follows. Because the individuals don't have enough time to spend strategising, visioning and planning the relationship, they spend all their time firefighting. Because they spend all their time firefighting, the relationships constantly lack any long-term planning, which leaves them at a tactical rather than at a strategic level.

An example may help to make this clearer. Alliance Best Practice was called in to help explain why a particular strategic alliance relationship was not performing as satisfactorily as either party would like. The relationship in question was between a small software company currently based in the UK and USA, and a large global systems integrator. The scenario was that the managing director of the software company had just about reached his wits end. He had been trying for three years to get the systems integrator to regard his company and his software offerings as strategic. He argued (with some degree of justification) that his company's software would give the systems integrator a critical ability to effect IT migrations much more quickly and easily than would otherwise be the case, so the systems integrator would generate a competitive advantage over its competitors by using his software. The problem was that the systems integrator had many similar software companies knocking on its door asking to be regarded as a special case, so it had appointed just one partnership director to deal with all these companies.

Alliance Best Practice argued that if the systems integrator devoted a dedicated resource to the relationship with the small software company for a limited period of 90 days, then the amount of business generated would either prove once and for all the business case for partnering with this particular software company, or prove that it would not work.

So convinced was the systems integrator's managing director that he funded the appointment of a partnership manager to deal with the partner organisation for the 90-day period. When this partnership manager was appointed, Alliance Best Practice was able to give him a complete project plan for the 90 days which would effectively develop the relationship and the propositions both parties would take to market. The make-or-break factor involved in the ultimate decision would be how many sales the new relationship had developed by the end of the period.

Over the preceding twelve months only three joint go-to-market sales had been achieved by both parties working together. However, investment in dedicated resources by both parties that had adequate tools and a specific list of activities to perform meant they were able to generate over 30 business prospects in the trial period. When both parties reviewed the scenario at the end of the 90 days, they each unequivocally confirmed the appointment of full-time dedicated alliance managers for the relationship.

The coda to this case example is that over the previous three years the amount of income generated had never exceeded £3.5 million per annum. In the year following the appointment of the dedicated alliance managers, the joint revenue generated by the relationship was £17.5 million.

Cu35: Alliance Centre of Excellence

Since it is not a strictly a cultural point, this element could have allocated to another category, but its existence or absence often indicate the level of maturity of the collaborative corporate mindset of an organisation. Typically, an alliance centre of excellence makes an appearance in organisations in Stage II (systematic). The reasons why organisations develop alliance centres of excellence are typically as follows:

- **Risk** – Organisations are uneasy if multi-million-dollar accounts or relationships are heavily dependent on a particular individual. What if that individual leaves? The impact can be considerable. To counter this, organisations look to develop alliance centres of excellence that can serve as a co-ordination and audit point in their major relationships.
- **Consistency** – Organisations want to see a greater degree of consistency in the success of their relationships across the board, not just in one or two isolated examples. A central unit helps to facilitate this.
- **Best practice** – Organisations want to repeat successful strategies and plans in situations across the company.
- **Knowledge sharing** – Companies want good ideas to be shared around effectively.
- **Conduit for external benchmarking** – Centres of excellence are typically the key interface to worldwide best practices.
- **Internal coaching** – Alliance professionals from centres of excellence have a valuable role to play in coaching field staff in how to partner effectively.

The constituent features of an alliance centre of excellence are a back office and a front office. The back office runs the governance elements, and the front office runs the innovation and new product/service development elements.

It is an interesting question whether an alliance centre of excellence is the same thing as an alliance programme office. In our view, the two are not identical. An alliance centre of excellence, while it may perform the function of an alliance programme office, also provides the function of a knowledge exchange or knowledge transfer point within the organisation, and also a conduit whereby external best practice knowledge can be channelled to the rest of the organisation.

It is conceivable that as many partnering organisations mature, they will establish an alliance centre of excellence at Stage II (systematic), then later, at Stage III (endemic), divide the functions of that centre of excellence between individual business units. In fact, this was exactly what happened within the Starbucks organisation, where alliance centres of excellence were established in various parts of the organisation, depending on their role or culture (for example, production, R&D, sales, marketing or franchisee management). However, Starbucks recognised that these centres of excellence were being regarded as 'ivory towers', and that if it was to truly embed alliance thinking and alliance practices and principles into its organisation, it needed to break apart such isolated towers and embed the thinking rather more deeply into individual business units on a day-to-day basis.

Table 10.2 shows examples of the tasks undertaken by alliance centres of excellence.

Table 10.2 Examples of alliance centre of excellence tasks

Front office	Back office
Design and develop alliance campaign management and training programmes	Manage all global contracts relating to alliances
Develop global alliances marketing plan	Advise regional alliance managers on country-specific contracts and maintain a database of these
Develop alliance/sales tools, methodologies, policies and so on	
Web management (partner portal)	Manage the accounts receivable and payable and track individual alliance effectiveness to a predefined cost/income ratio
Events co-ordination, including global communication plans and analysts' briefings	
Manage partner portfolio	Manage the cash in/out and manage the alliance funding and its redistribution
	Support the regions in all administrative activities that can be de-localised

Cu36: Joint Decision Making Process

It is important that the decision making processes of both organisations are aligned. It is even more important that the manner in which decisions are to be made in alliances is clear from the outset. These issues are usually covered in alliance manuals in sections on alliance governance. However, be aware that simply because such issues are covered in the alliance governance section does not mean that they will not have a significant impact on the commercial value of the relationships you will establish.

For example, a large and global consultancy business established a strategic alliance relationship with a telecommunications company based in Europe. The consultancy was organised around a command and control model, which meant that its decisions were made quickly and usually enforced in a hierarchical manner. The telecommunications company, on the other hand, had traditionally operated a consensus model of making decisions.

This meant that at key points in the relationship, the consultancy assumed that a decision had been made to take a certain course of action. In the particular example Alliance Best Practice observed, this was a decision to travel to Redmond in the USA to discuss with Microsoft the development of a new service offering based on Microsoft software.

The consulting business had six consultants in a departure lounge at Heathrow airport ready to leave three days after the decision had been made, and was surprised when the telecommunications company didn't send a similar number of individuals to accompany them on the same trip. On their return, they discovered that the members of the alliance team from the telecommunications company had regarded the first decision as merely a 'green light' to begin the decision making process: 'We thought you guys understood that when we said that we wanted to do this thing, we now had to get the active support of a wide range of interconnected senior executives in our organisation. We have to get their consensus first before we can move ahead.'

This example illustrates problems that resemble those that face any partners which have fundamentally different decision making processes. In this case, these problems became so acute that the relationship was suspended after a fairly short period.

Be aware when you are developing your strategic alliance relationships that you should talk openly about how your own organisation makes decisions, but also be sure you understand your partner organisation's decision making process, in particular the pace of decision makings and what it involves. This is very often linked to CSF O52, 'Issue escalation' (see Chapter 11).

Cu37: Other Cultural Issues

There will always be some organisational cultural issues which will impede alliance success. Typical examples include organisational arrogance based on either size, technical ability, quality or experience with certain situations, or perhaps aspects of an organisation's culture which the partner either doesn't fully understand or doesn't even know exist.

In the section on 'Cultural Direction' in Chapter 7, we discussed the cultural alignment issues that arose between Air France and Delta Airlines when they entered the SkyTeam strategic alliance. These required skilled and expert intervention from organisational behaviourists to enable both parties to resolve their emotional and cultural differences and move on.

Cu38: Business-to-Business Cultural Alignment

An increasing number of organisations now recognise the need for good cultural alignment with their partners. To respond to this, they are either beginning to develop cultural alignment models of their own, or are using some of the wide variety of resources that are commercially available.

It should be pointed out of course that the objective of effective business-to-business cultural alignment is not to subsume the organisational culture of one partner in preference to the other; but rather to combine the best aspects of both for the betterment of the alliance.

11 *The Operational Dimension*

O39: Alliance Processes

An alliance process is any combination of inter-related collaborative activities performed in a logical fashion that allows organisations to achieve known and desired partnership outcomes. The proceduralisation of alliance activities into formal processes which could be written down and measured was pioneered in the USA in the 1980s and 1990s. This approach was far more common the USA than in Europe, for example, throughout the last decade of the twentieth century.[1] It is only relatively recently that Europe has caught up in formalising collaboration as a process-based activity. (See the outputs of the third State of Alliances Report from Ard-Pieter de Man and Geert Duysters sponsored by Maastricht University.[2])

The existence of a defined alliance process and the effective execution of that process in practice is one of the most influential common success factors in the ABP Database. Its existence alone is a reliable predictor of alliance success and indicator of alliance corporate maturity. Alliance processes are normally associated with partnering maturity Stage II organisations which are entering the systematic mode and need to track that their alliances are being managed consistently.[3] Organisations that are at maturity Stage I (opportunistic) generally tend not to have any defined alliance processes.

Originally, alliances and collaborations were flexible, transient transactions which had little need for defined processes. It is only recently that more attention has been devoted to this area because of the growth in alliances and their use as business development engines. This makes sense in corporate terms for the following reasons.

There are generally acknowledged to be three distinct growth strategies that companies employ: build, buy or ally. This growth model has been consistently taught in MBA business schools for the past 20 years. Essentially, it means that firms can either adopt an organic growth strategy (the 'build' model), in which they use their own internal resources to make products and services and sell them using their own salesmen, or they can use mergers and acquisitions to accelerating growth (the 'buy' model), or they can use other organisations' resources through collaboration to grow the business (the 'ally' model).

If firms choose the 'ally' model, then it is logical to ask what the 'ally' or alliance process is, because both of the other models have their own clearly defined processes

---

1   See, for example, http://www.duysters.com/downloads%20presentations/ASAPpresentation02.pdf.

2   http://www.duysters.com/Downloads%20managerial/ASAP%20survey.pdf.

3   See Alliance Maturity Model.

supporting them. Indeed, internal and external auditing organisations will look closely at the execution of these key corporate strategies when conducting their reviews. In addition, sales managers will insist that employees follow a pre-defined process for corporate sales (particularly large sales), as it enables them to understand progress in the sales process (the pipeline) and expected outcomes (forecasts).

However, our research suggests that the existence of alliance processes in organisations at Stage I is not common, and that many organisations rely entirely on the efforts of individual alliance champions to research, instigate, launch and manage alliance relationships.

Typically large organisations at Stage II will have a wide range of inter-related alliance processes, and the complex task of matching these varied procedures is one of the reasons why large, enterprise-wide strategic alliances take so long to get off the ground, because both/all parties need to match their 'competing' alliance processes.

There is a surprising lack of defined alliance processes in the ABP Database (87% of the organisations admitted to having no formal alliance processes at all). This might be because alliance management as a specific area of study is of relatively recent origin.

Typically smaller partner companies will agree to use the larger partner's alliance process because: (a) they don't have one of their own, and (b) they are happy to defer to the larger company because they assume (sometime erroneously!) that the larger company has a wide range of suitable processes that it can 'pull off the shelf' and apply immediately. There is also no doubt that there is an element here that reflects the relevant power positions of the organisations. The larger may take the view that 'We are the bigger company with more power in the relationship, so we will impose our own processes.'

Alliance processes will typically differ from sector to sector depending on the business being conducted by the alliance and the purpose of the individual process (see Figure 11.1 for a generic explanation).

EXPLANATION OF FIGURE 11.1

The ABP Framework originated in a piece of research which looked specifically at the question, 'What works in strategic alliance relationships?' – in other words, what activities, behaviours, approaches, methodologies, measuring systems and so on contribute to alliance success, as defined by both/all parties to a relationship? The result was a discovery that alliance success is founded on the appropriate combination of alliance best practices and processes into an alliance best practice framework.

ABP defines an alliance best practice framework as: 'a collection of: processes, tools, training, and other support materials which make achieving alliance success much more likely than it otherwise might have been'.

ABP defines 'alliance success' as: 'the realisation of desirable outcomes at an advantageous rate of cost/value exchange'.

ABP believes that the appropriate use of a suitable alliance framework will greatly enhance an organisation's chances of success in its partnerships. This view is supported by a 'logic trail' underpinning alliance frameworks and their usefulness:

1. Appropriate activities and behaviours in a given alliance situation will lead to desirable outcomes. This is encapsulated in the phrase, 'Do the right things, and you will get the right results.'

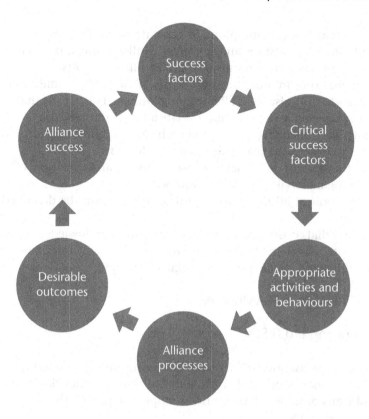

Figure 11.1 Alliance processes

2. Desirable outcomes can be defined as the output of successful alliance relationships. Examples include: cost effective revenue generation, business growth, new products and services, entry into new markets, cost reductions, quality improvements and so on.
3. The greater the number of desirable outcomes generated from an alliance relationship, the greater the value to the partners.
4. Some desirable outcomes are known in advance (from research and experience) to contribute powerfully to alliance success. These are known as success factors.
5. A number of these success factors have been observed to recur in successful alliance relationships, leading ABP to regard them as statistically relevant. These are known as common success factors.
6. Common success factors can be either causes or effects of other success factors in the framework.
7. The combination of some common success factors was observed to produce a higher rate of desirable outcomes at a lower unit cost. ABP designated these combinations as 'best practices'.
8. A series of pre-planned activities known to produce desirable outcomes and performed in the right order is known as an alliance process.
9. There are multiple alliance processes in an alliance framework (See 'Examples of Alliance Frameworks' below).

10. Two factors that help organisations to generate desirable outcomes using alliance frameworks are relationships and resources. Utilising the appropriate amount and quality of these two factors results in superior alliance results.

11. Many organisations are now turning to the '3F Model' – Frameworks, Forum and Facilitation – to optimise their alliance programmes. This means that:
   - first, they develop and utilise appropriate alliance frameworks;
   - secondly, they encourage executives with responsibility for partnering to gather together to discuss the materials in alliance forums;
   - finally, they invest in either internal or external facilitation of relationships utilising the materials and skills developed.

12. The combination of all the factors mentioned above can be described as 'alliance best practices'.

13. Organisations that consciously seek to use accumulated knowledge, tools, procedures, templates and behaviours that have been proven to deliver desirable outcomes are said to be following an 'alliance best practice' strategy.

EXAMPLES OF ALLIANCE FRAMEWORKS

Partnership Sourcing Ltd (PSL)

PSL is a UK-based organisation which offers partnering advice, training and consultancy. It has an alliance framework called CRAFT: Collaborative Relationship, Assessment, Fulfilment and Transformation. It comprises multiple practical guides, tools and workshop applications created by PSL.

The CRAFT framework consists of eight distinct stages:

1. Awareness
2. Knowledge
3. Internal Assessment
4. Partner Selection
5. Working Together
6. Value Creation
7. Staying Together
8. Exit Strategy.[4]

The Partnering Initiative (TPI)

The Partnering Initiative, was initiated in 2003 as an alliance between the International Business Leaders Forum and the University of Cambridge Programme for Industry, and became an independent not-for-profit organisation in 2013. Founded on the passionate belief that only through collaboration can we tackle the biggest challenges of both business and societal sustainability, TPI works with business, international NGOs, the UN system, governments and donors to drive effective cross-sector partnerships for sustainable development. TPI works through:

---

4   See www.instituteforcollaborativeworking.com/pdfs/CRAFT%20Overview%20_summary.pdf (accessed 8 April 2014).

- advocating for partnerships in international and national policy discussions;
- developing in-country partnership action hubs to systematically engage stakeholders and drive innovative collaboration;
- directly brokering and supporting partnerships to create innovation and deliver impact;
- helping organisations to develop partnering strategies and undergo the organisational change and capacity building required to be effective as partners;
- developing professional partnering competencies through training, tools and guidebooks.

The TPI Partnering Framework is based around the Partnership Framework shown in Figure 11.2.

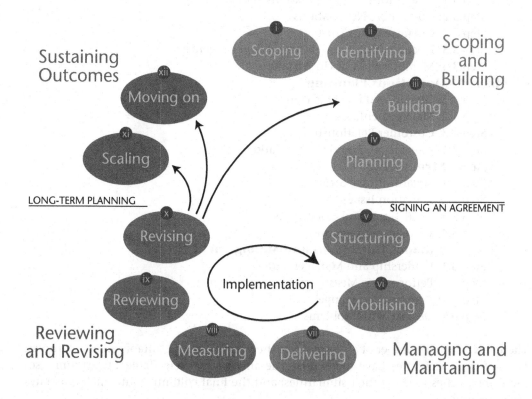

Figure 11.2 The TPI Partnering Framework
Source: Copyright © 2009 The Partnering Initiative. http://thepartneringinitiative.org/.

The Association of Strategic Alliance Professionals

ASAP has its own framework based on original work by Robert Porter Lynch of the Warren Company.[5] Its framework is divided into six phases:

---

5   www.warrenco.com.

- **Phase 1 – Strategy**
  - Step 1.1: Key Strategic Questions
  - Step 1.2: Strategic Drivers and Value Migration
  - Step 1.3: Value Added Proposition
  - Step 1.4: Stratagems
- **Phase 2 – Alliance Analytics**
  - Step 2.1: Candidate Research and Due Diligence
  - Step 2.2: Risk Evaluation and Business Model
  - Step 2.3: Strategic Return on Investment
  - Step 2.4: The Strategic Spectrum
- **Phase 3 – Negotiations**
  - Step 3.1: Champions and Negotiations Teambuilding
  - Step 3.2: Co-creative Negotiations
  - Step 3.3: Chemistry and Trust
  - Step 3.3: Documentation and Detailed Due Diligence
  - Step 3.4: Memorandum of Understanding
- **Phase 4 – Operations Planning**
  - Step 4.1: Operational Business Plan
  - Step 4.2: Management Issues
  - Step 4.3: Customer Relationships
  - Step 4.4: Integration, Empowerment and Control
- **Phase 5 – Structuring**
  - Step 5.1: Organizational Structure
  - Step 5.2: Valuation Issues
  - Step 5.3: Legal Terms and Conditions
  - Step 5.4: The Closing/Opening
- **Phase 6 – Alliance Operations and Management**
  - Step 6.1: Leadership and Management
  - Step 6.2: Performance Measurement
  - Step 6.3: Adapting to Change
  - Step 6.4: Dealing with Problems.

There have been a number of attempts over the years to draft a suitable alliance process. Most of these examples have focused on the alliance lifecycle. Table 11.1 summarises these approaches to show their similarities, and the final column, 'Outcome', illustrates a generic process.

Note: The dates given for each author refer to multiple reference works rather than a single book or article reference alone. The year chosen is when the author first published references to a codified alliance process and are indicative only.

Table 11.1 Alliance processes developed over the years

Pekar (1994)	De Man (2000)	Dusters (2004)	Porter Lynch (2001)	Harbison (1998)	De Man (2004)	Yoshino (1995)	Ring (1994)	Outcome
Strategy development	Context	Organisation strategy	Strategy	Defining strategy and objectives	Business strategy	Rethinking the business	Negotiation	Business strategy
Partner assessment	Content	Alliance strategy	Analytics	Screening for partners	Network strategy	Crafting an alliance strategy	Commitment	Alliance strategy
Contract negotiation	Partner selection	Partner selection (including negotiations)	Negotiations	Assessing tradeables and leverage	(Network structure)	Structuring alliances	Execution	Partner selection
Operation	(Content)	Implementation and operation (including operational planning)	Operations planning and integration	Defining opportunities	Partner selection	Managing alliances	Re-evaluation	Negotiation
(Operation II)	Management	Management and evaluation	Structuring	Assessing impact on stakeholders	(Network structure)	Evaluating alliances		Operational planning
	Upgrading		Operations planning and integration	Assessing bargaining power	Implementation			Implementation
			Management	Planning integration (based on activities)	Management			Evaluation
				Implementing	Change			Renewal

What is striking about the summary in Table 11.1 is the similarity in approaches of all the major authors in this area.

Table 11.2 shows an agenda for an IBM sub-process usually utilised in the operational planning phase, called 'Alliance to Win'. This would normally be a two- or three-day workshop which IBM would facilitate with its chosen partner and a group of internal IBM executives essential to the success of the relationship (for example, sales, marketing, technology, business unit lead).

Table 11.2   Example of the 'Alliance to Win' process practised by IBM

Day 1		Day 2	

8.30 a.m.	Opening:
	• Objectives and Agenda
	• Alliance Status
	    IBM: Presenter X
	    Partner: Presenter X
		8.30 a.m.
		
		9.00 a.m.
			Opening Discussion
			
			Go-to-market Planning:
			• Sales Engagement Model
			• Target Geographies and Accounts
			• First Draft of Business Case

9.00 a.m.	Introductory Presentations: • Partner: Presenter X • IBM: Presenter X	Noon	Working Lunch
10.00 a.m.	Solution Definition and Stack	1.00 p.m.	Action Planning, for example: • Business Plan and Governance • Solution and Services Plan
Noon	Working Lunch		• Sales Execution • Marketing and Sales Enablement
12.30 p.m.	Solution Definition and Stack (cont.)	5.00 p.m.	Close Meeting – End of Day 2
1.30 p.m.	Agreement on Customer Analysis and Market Characteristics		
2.30 p.m.	Competitive Analysis Solution – Web (optional)		
4.00 p.m.	Revenue Modelling and Agreement on Vision and Objectives		
6.00 p.m.	End of Day 1 – Team Dinner		

Alliance processes are important for the following reasons:

- They allow you to track progress and know what the next steps, are thus saving time and money and avoiding confusion.
- They allow both/all sides to have a common view of the stage they are at in the alliance lifecycle, improving the degree of alignment of expectations.
- They allow alliance senior management to compare progress on multiple alliances concurrently, and to understand why some are making progress while others are not.
- They allow organisations to provide appropriate funding to alliance initiatives by establishing various checkpoints as 'gated progress points', progression beyond

which is subject to checks and monitoring and usually requires evidence of previous deliverables before proceeding.

Table 11.3 shows how alliance processes are connected to the other CSFs.

Table 11.3   Connections between O39 (Alliance processes) and the other CSFs

Directly connected	Indirectly connected
O40: Speed of progress so far	Co4: Alliance audit/healthcheck
O41: Distance from revenue	S26: Business-to-business strategic alignment
O43: Communication	S28: Multiple relationships with
O44: Quality review	same partner(s)
O46: Relationship change management	S29: Common strategic ground rules
O48: Business-to-business	Cu31: Business-to-business trust
operational alignment	Cu32: Collaborative corporate mindset
O50: Internal alignment	Cu36: Joint decision making process
O51: Relationship development plan	

These can to be any reasonably structured series of activities which accomplish the determined alliance goals, for example:

- the IBM developer relations alliance process;
- the ASAP best practice alliance framework;
- the Partnering Initiative partnering framework;
- the PSL CRAFT methodology.

For a more detailed description of all these processes, see Appendix 6 'Useful Additional Resources'.

The following points are important to remember when you are considering alliance processes:

- Any alliance process or processes (good or bad) will improve alliance performance if both/all parties to the relationship follow them in a reasonably consistent fashion. In particular, they will have an important (that is, direct) impact on the associated CSFs O40 (Speed of progress so far), O41 (Distance from revenue), O43 (Communication), O44 (Quality review), O46 (Relationship change management), O48 (Business-to-business operational alignment), O50 (Internal alignment) and O51 (Relationship development plan). It will have a less important though still discernible (that is, indirect) impact on CSFs Co4 (Alliance audit/healthcheck), S26 (Business-to-business strategic alignment), S28 (Multiple relationships with same partner(s), S29 (Common strategic ground rules), Cu31 (Business-to-business trust), Cu32 (Collaborative corporate mindset) and Cu36 (Joint decision making process).
- The existence of an alliance process will almost always lead to better alliance results.
- The existence of one or more codified alliance processes is an indication that the organisation in question is at maturity Stage II (systematic).

- An alliance process is a fundamental underpinning for alliance skills training and job descriptions.
- An alliance end-to-end process or collection of integrated alliance processes can be described as an alliance framework.
- A good alliance framework should closely match the stages of alliance development in the organisation concerned.
- The importance of the alliance common success factors change as the stages in the alliance lifecycle change.

If your organisation does not have any discernible alliance processes, then it would benefit both you and your organisation to develop them immediately. This can be done easily by using the generic examples quoted in this book in Appendix 6: Useful Additional Resources.

O40: Speed of Progress so Far

Speed of progress so far tends to be an effect rather than a cause. Nevertheless, it was cited by many respondents in our research as an important success factor in strategic alliances. The reason was that if people could see discernible progress in the relationship, and if that progress was seen to be at a pace which was considered rapid, it was assumed that this was generating a degree of competitive business advantage to both/all sides involved in the relationship.

The pace at which an alliance moves through the various stages of the alliance lifecycle is heavily dependent on the existence or otherwise of a number of other key factors

However, speed of progress so far deserves attention because by focusing on it you can observe the results of the underlying causes of success or failure. As such, it is a great early indicator that something is amiss, in a similar way to if I find I have a temperature of 40°C and I know that the norm is 37°C, then I can conclude that maybe there is something wrong with me.

The problem for most organisations is understanding what would represent a 'normal' or 'standard' pace of progress for the relationship in question, given the industry, current stage of the relationship in the lifecycle, the alliance maturity stage of the organisation(s) concerned, the prime purpose of the relationship and so on. For example, the ABP Database suggests that for relationships between European and American organisations in the high-tech sector, the time from pre-formation to the end of a relationship is typically five years, with each stage (pre-formation, formation, maturity, extension and decline/renewal) taking roughly one year, and that the average value generated by the relationship per year in that cycle is £2 million–20 million gross revenue.

Returning to Case Study 8 in Chapter 7, we can see how the relationship between Siemens and PwC in Germany in 2003 was not making structured progress towards its goals (the pace of progress was not rapid). However, the lack of a suitable MOUP or planning document prevented both sides from accurately assessing the pace of progress, thus time was spent on inconclusive and ultimately futile meetings talking about progress rather than measuring and identifying the reasons for the lack of it. The results were ultimately fatal, not just for the relationship, but also for the two alliance managers concerned.

O41: Distance from Revenue

The planned or anticipated distance from revenue compared to the actual distance from revenue is a significant factor in a successful relationship. In some instances (for example, in the software industry) the distance may be very short (less than 90 days); in others it can be disproportionately long (in the pharmaceutical sector, five to seven years). Whatever the empirical distance from revenue, it is important that both/all parties have a clear understanding and genuine acknowledgement of what it is; if clarity is not achieved on this particular success factor, then the chances are that at least one if not both/all the senior executive teams responsible for the provision of resources and budget will quickly become disillusioned and there will be a consequent reduction in attention, support and budget for the relationship.

This factor is most often closely related to CSF O40, 'Speed of progress so far', and it is also an effect, not a cause. The factors that affect distance from revenue obviously relate to planning: for example, developing a suitable business value proposition, developing a go-to-market model, and understanding the range, depth and sophistication of S26, 'Business-to-business strategic alignment'. All of these have a great influence on when suitable revenue returns can be expected. In the best relationships, the timing of this return is clearly articulated in the relationship project plan.

This factor deserves attention because by focusing on it you can deduce the lack of existence of other common success factors. For example, if you find that an alliance relationship that you have responsibility for is not making the progress you (or your partner, or both/all of you) expected, then it is a fair indication that something is lacking, and a good first place to look is the governance model in general. Are the expectations of both sides articulated clearly? Is there a clear and unambiguous documentation of partner accountability (what we expect both/all partners to do to achieve success in this relationship)? More often than not, disappointing results here point to a lack of governance or a lack of focus on the governance model on which commercial progress is reliant.

By utilising the framework in this way, the alliance executive is acting rather like a general practitioner, diagnosing underlying problems by noticing symptoms of malaise.

O42: Formal Joint Business Plan

In most strategic alliances (or alliances of any reasonable size) there should be a formal business plan for the relationship. This is easier to appreciate if one recognises that the relationship is possibly anticipated to earn both/all parties many hundreds of thousands (or even millions) of pounds. Clearly, if you were an entrepreneur with a business worth more than £1 million, it is almost inconceivable that you would not have a formal business plan, yet it is surprising how many relationships ABP has observed where the partners do not take the time and trouble to articulate a formal business plan for the relationship.

Typically, there may be a business forecast that anticipates the gross revenue, cost savings, quality increase or similar factors, but this is only half the equation. The other side – resources, costs of the relationship, dedicated management time and so on – seems to be largely ignored. It is almost as if, having decided that there will be a relationship, one or both/all parties regard the announcement itself as sufficient to drive revenue.

This is clearly erroneous, and leads to a simple insight: relationships do not manage themselves; they need to be managed actively in order to realise the anticipated value.

A good formal business plan for a relationship will therefore not only forecast the anticipated value to be gained from the relationship, but also the anticipated costs of managing the relationship and realising its value.

When a business plan does exist, typically there will be a different version depending on which partner one is talking to. Obviously, to be effective the business plan should be a *joint* business plan, committed to by both/all partners in the relationship. In the high-tech business sector this plan is most often called a 'joint account plan', and serves the same purpose. There are some excellent templates in existence to help alliance managers produce such a joint account plan – see, for example, the CHAMP (Channel and Alliance Management Process) model.[6]

In the pharmaceutical and biotech business sector the formal business plan is likely to be called the 'joint project plan', as in this case the purpose is usually to take a compound or new discovery through a closely regulated process towards eventual consumption.

There is a strong link in the ABP Database between CSF O42 and O45, 'Memorandum of understanding and principles or alliance charter', and there may be a slight overlap in terms of business objectives and anticipated results. But do remember that the two are *not* the same, either in purpose or output. The MOUP is designed to articulate the high-level or strategic intentions of the relationship by focusing on such things as vision, key stakeholders, business value proposition(s), scope and the governance model, while the business plan clearly looks at such things as revenue, costs, resources, activities, milestones, objectives and anticipated results.

In those relationships that have a formal business plan in the ABP Database, we noticed that the corresponding CSF scores were significantly higher (73% on average). This seems to suggest that the existence or otherwise of a formal business plan in strategic alliances is a good indicator of potential commercial success. Obviously, when one thinks about it, this observation is entirely logical since it suggests that relationships with a formal business plan are those in which the participants have taken the time and effort to articulate 'what success looks like' in commercial terms, and have taken steps to ensure that such outcomes are realised. In addition, this CSF was very often was misconstrued. For example, in the high-tech sector many alliance professionals who claimed to have formal business plans in fact had forecasts for new business rather than a balanced plan showing both investment and revenue returns. This was the case in 38% of the relationships examined. The existence of a well-defined and formal business plan appeared in a relative minority of those relationships examined (22%).

There are a number of things to remember about a formal business plan:

- To be most effective, a formal business plan should include both revenue *and* cost estimates.
- The best formal business plans are joint plans which have been developed by both/all parties to the relationship.
- A well-crafted joint business plan is a strong indicator of potential commercial success.

---

6   http://www.dezwarte.com/pages/champ.html.

O43: Communication

Communication is generally acknowledged by even the most poorly performing collaborating companies to be a key factor in strategic alliances – and so it is. However, the better-prepared organisations know exactly what they mean by the general term 'communication'. In some respects communication is very similar to CSF 'Cu31, 'Business-to-business trust', since both can be regarded as the 'oil in the machine' of the relationship which help to prevent relationship frictions leading to conflict.

In the vast majority of cases in the ABP Database (98%) broadly three levels of key stakeholders are represented (see also S25, 'Senior executive support'): strategic, managerial and operational. It is the effective interaction and communication between these three levels on both/all sides that ABP defines as effective communication.

Communication can be defined as internal or external. 'Internal communication' usually refers to communication which takes place inside the relationship at various levels, whereas 'external communication' is directed at key stakeholders outside the relationship. Internal key stakeholders often comprise senior executives from marketing, sales, operations, technology, R&D, finance, procurement and so on. External key stakeholders can be industry analysts, consumers, other partners in the same business sector and so on.

The primary purpose of internal communication could be said to be the development of consensus – in other words, the development of a situation in which both/all parties to the relationship at the three levels identified regard the relationship in the same way. It is through this common understanding that common goals and purposes can be constructed, and at the highest level, common business strategies can be pursued.

The most common purpose of external communication is to extol the virtue of the relationship to industry analysts and consumers alike while at the same time striving not to offend other potential partners of both/all parties to the relationship. Although this balancing act is sometimes hard to achieve, there is clear evidence that when it is conducted effectively, market acceptance and relationship value rise proportionately.[7]

There are many examples of good alliance communication available to alliance managers, particularly in the high-tech sector. Copies of most can be found in the reception areas of the major offices of the organisations concerned, and many examples are co-branded with both/all partners' logos and identities.

Another good indicator of communication success is the annual Association of Strategic Alliance Professionals awards for best collaborative relationship in a range of categories.[8] A recent innovation in this era of Web 2.0 technology is the development of virtual team rooms by many organisations to improve connections between alliance participants. Typically, these are document storage areas which hold such things as project plans, common planning documents, key stakeholder contact information, and relationship governance and enforcement documents. As a result of the worldwide recession which began in 2008 and at the time of writing is still continuing, many organisations favour this and other types of virtual communication rather than the more costly face-to-face communication. A relatively new and development is partner relationship management (PRM) systems. There are relatively few of these available to alliance managers, and those

---

7   See, for example, the Booz Allen Hamilton research conducted by Peter Pekar Jr and John Harbison into the Media and Entertainment industry in the period 1996–2006.

8   A list of the previous winners of these awards can be found at www.strategic-alliances.org.

that are available are more akin to the early customer relationship management systems, with which they are sometimes compared. The idea in both cases is to create value by aggregating the multiple interfaces between the host organisation and the partner or customer concerned. Early in the development cycle of customer relations management systems they appeared to be simple aggregation tools which took multiple snapshots of customer interactions (usually using some form of spreadsheet analysis) and aggregated them. This appears to be very much the current level of PRM development, with little if any intelligence embedded in the systems themselves.

Evidence from the Database suggests that communication is generally acknowledged as one of the most important CSFs in the Operational dimension (cited by 67% of the alliance executives interviewed). Often there was regular and effective communication between the individuals specifically responsible for a relationship, but more often than not that communication did not extend beyond those individuals (further levels of communication were absent in 72% of the cases analysed). In the best relationships (those scoring 75/100 or higher), both/all organisations participating in the relationship recognised the value of both internal and external communication, and had developed appropriate internal and external communication programmes, including identification of the key stakeholders on each side and a description of their relative roles and responsibilities, along with a formal diary or current chart of the meetings that were to be held. These communication programmes allowed participants to understand what information they should expect as a result of those meetings.

As noted above, the best communication programmes identified at least three key categories of stakeholder: (1) operational management, (2) multi-relationship management and (3) strategic management. In the best relationships, not only was the communication good between all three levels within each organisation, it was equally good (that is, appropriate) from one organisation to the other at the differing levels. This meant that the senior executive sponsor was able to have a good overall view of the relationship which was fundamentally in sync with the day-to-day feelings of the operational management team responsible for it.

The best communication programmes generated a communication matrix (see Figure 11.3), which was used as the backbone for the governance model: issues were passed up the structure, and guidance and direction were passed down, and these issues and solutions were shared with partners.

O44: Quality Review

This common success factor was one of the most rapidly expanding of all those identified in the operational area. As little as three to four years ago the idea of reviewing the quality or effectiveness of a business-to-business relationship was seen as potentially very damaging because it conveyed a message to partners that they or your own organisation were remiss in certain key respects. However, there is clear evidence from the latest research that the adoption of a formal quality review process (sometimes called a healthcheck or audit) is now rapidly becoming the norm.[9]

---

9   See Ard-Pieter de Man and Geert Duysters, *The Third State of Alliance Management Study*, Maastricht: NSI/Universiteit Maastricht, 2009: www.duysters.com/Downloads%20managerial/ASAP%20survey.pdf (accessed 8 April 2014).

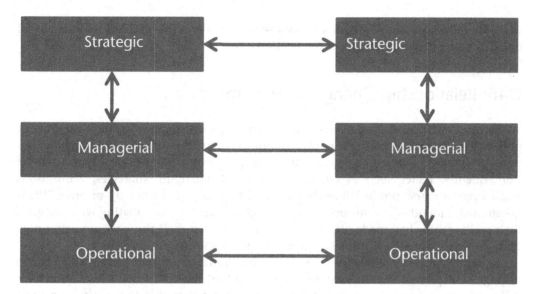

Figure 11.3 Communication matrix

In addition, there is compelling evidence that the conduct of such a process significantly enhances a relationships chances of success. The desire for a business relationship appraisal process appears to be driven by both internal and external factors. The internal factor is the desire of senior management to check on the appropriateness of the actions to generate commercial return, and the external factors appear to be based on the need to conduct regular audits of key relationships as a result of the US Sarbanes-Oxley Act, the Enron scandal and other high-profile audit failures.

It is evident from the annual ASAP conferences that a regular healthcheck conducted through a formal quality review meeting (usually annually) is becoming standard practice in a wide range of sectors (see, for example, the ASAP conference 2004 Metrics Track delivered by Procter & Gamble, Eli Lilly and Cisco Systems).

O45: Memorandum of Understanding and Principles or Alliance Charter

The existence of an MOUP in a strategic alliance relationship is a surprisingly good litmus test of both the effectiveness and maturity of the relationship. Such a document (which is variously described as: a charter, a code of behaviour, a partner plan or a partner programme) should not be legally binding and should concern itself with those factors which form the backbone of a significant strategic alliance relationship (for example, governance structure, communication, key stakeholders, vision, business value proposition(s), communication matrix, project-specific issues and so on).

The existence of an MOUP is one of the most frequently occurring CSFs in the Operational dimension, and it is also the one that is most well received by all levels of management. Operational managers welcome it because it gives them a context within which to perform their day-to-day duties and a set of rules to live by, and senior executives welcome it because it gives them an easy-to-read (usually a five-page document) way of understanding the current state of the relationship.

O46: Relationship Change Management

While most alliances have a defined change management process for the initiatives or projects that are run as part of the relationship, very few (according to the Database, less than 15%) have a defined change management process for the relationship as a whole. Consequently, issues such as changing personnel, changing strategies, acquisitions and mergers or new product launches all tend to take the alliance by surprise. When questioned, individuals from such alliances had no means of articulating what progress their relationships had made other than generalities such as, 'I think we are better now than we were before,' or 'I think key people understand each other better.'

In a small minority of relationships in which a formal or informal relationship change management process was in existence, it was noticed that the value the relationships delivered was enhanced and lasted longer. It appears that this CSF is the one most important in enabling relationships to endure the stresses and strains of the dynamics of modern-day business life.

O47: Operational Metrics

We noticed that in some organisations, while there were sets of strategic or cultural metrics which were used to measure the relationship in general, separate and often simpler sets of operational metrics were also in use. This was most frequently the case in high-tech relationships, where such factors as number of days trained on partners' products or services, number of opportunities in the pipeline, leads generated by partners and proposal wins were all recognised as specific operational indicators of the success of the relationship.

O48: Business-to-business Operational Alignment

As was the case with cultural alignment, many organisations did not pay sufficient attention to integrating of the intent of the relationship into each partners' operational units. In the most outstanding cases the relationship resulted in a 'zippered' interaction between many different operational levels in both/all partners.

However, in the lesser-performing relationships there was a good alignment between the intent or desire of both alliance partnership teams, but this often hardly ever reached the operational units necessary to execute on the relationship. For example, the corporate alliance teams at the head offices of a large hardware company and a large software company planned, designed, negotiated and signed an excellent theoretical strategic alliance relationship which would have benefited both organisations through the development of specific breakthrough solutions utilising the hardware and software of both organisations. However, neither party took the trouble to sell the relationship to the national sales teams in Europe, the Middle East and Africa which would be responsible for marketing the solutions. Consequently, there was an inordinate delay of six to nine months when no sales were made. The joint marketing team for the relationship seemed to believe that it was sufficient simply to inform the local sales units that the relationship existed for the extra sales to flow. This was obviously not the case. In the better-performing organisations a great deal of time and effort is devoted to persuading local sales units about the benefits they will gain from selling combined products and services (for example, bonuses and commission).

O49: Exponential Breakthroughs or Innovation

This CSF is often associated with the management buzzword 'innovation and business sustainability'. It refers to the ability of partners to generate new and exciting business value propositions through a defined and repeatable process within the context of the relationship. We observed that a very small minority of organisations had anything resembling a formal process for this until two to three years ago. However, this CSF is another which is rapidly gaining prominence in the better-performing organisations (for example, Reckitt Benckiser, Procter & Gamble, SAP and IBM). Many organisations are now looking to external third-party advisers to help them shape a breakthrough process which will enable them to bring new products and services to market more quickly and more effectively.

O50: Internal Alignment

This CSF is closely related to O48, 'Business-to-business operational alignment', and often goes hand-in-hand with it. Whereas business-to-business operational alignment considers the alignment between the parties to a relationship, O50 focuses at the efforts organisations make to ensure internal alignment in order to take advantage of the products and services generated by the relationship more effectively within their own go-to-market processes.

Organisations that had devoted specific resources to this area showed a high leverage of value to effort (that is, the resources they devoted to communicating internally, giving presentations and persuading staff both verbally and by adapting compensation plans, paid for themselves many times over in terms of extra products and services sold). This was seen as a high leverage point by a large number of the senior executive sponsors questioned (> 67%).

O51: Relationship Development Plan

There was a marked absence of formal relationship development plans among the alliance professionals in the Database (<13%). This in part appears to be the result of the level of maturity of the alliance professionals' thinking. Many believed that collaboration and partnering was based on personal contact and regular interaction with key stakeholders in partner organisations, and that a project plan would simply get in the way, serving as a barrier to the necessarily fluid and nebulous networking required for success.

There is also a second and more pragmatic reason why many alliance professionals felt that they could not develop a relationship development plan: many of them felt that the majority of their role was taken up with tactical efforts of 'doing rather than planning' (this was particularly true of those alliance professionals who were handling more than one strategic alliance at once).

Whatever the reason, there is clear evidence that the existence of a formal relationship development plan, no matter how brief and no matter how limited, contributes very greatly to the operational success of strategic relationships. Such a plan very often goes hand-in-hand with the communication matrix mentioned in the section on O43, 'Communication', above. Indeed, among the relationships examined where there was a relationship development plan, in the overwhelming majority of cases significant attention was also devoted to communication (>97%).

O52: Issue Escalation

Issue escalation appears to be a well-understood and well-practised procedure in most project management relationships, especially in the high-tech sector, but it is rarely formally recognised in strategic alliance management. In the majority of cases where we questioned strategic alliance professionals about it, the most common answer was: 'That is part of my job, it is my job to make sure that issues get sorted.'

Where a relationship issue escalation process existed, it usually reflected the types of issue that arose (for example, technical issues would be escalated through the appropriate technical channels, commercial issues would be escalated to the executive sponsor, and relationship issues would be escalated to the strategic alliance manager). Most organisations did not have a formal issue escalation process in their strategic alliance relationships. In those relationships where issue escalation took place effectively, there was usually evidence of senior executive support, good communication and a formal quality review.

Special Strategic Alliances

CHAPTER

12 *Co-opetition: Sleeping with the Enemy*

One of the most difficult strategic alliance types to manage involves collaboration with an existing or potential competitor, referred to as 'co-opetition'. The opportunities and challenges presented by this approach offer us a good framework to examine the fundamentals of complex business-to-business collaborations.

The old view of competition was relatively simple and based in large part on the five forces analysis conducted by Michael Porter.[1] An organisation knew who its customers were and how to get to them, and it knew its competitors that were trying to take its customers away. In part, this industry model was based on the 'big is good' notion – that organisational size and complexity could be used as an effective barrier to entry. That model appears no longer to be valid. Nowadays, small, agile organisations have developed business value propositions which are more closely in tune with consumers' needs, and through collaborative relationships with other suppliers and competitors they have nibbled away market share from the big players.[2]

The Cold War is an outmoded concept, and so are the old views of competition. Organisations that business leaders once thought of as foes have now become allies, and vice versa. The idea that market share is a pie, and that the bigger a slice a company can take the less that remains for its competitors, is now outdated. Of the top 100 companies by capital value we surveyed in November 2006, only five did not see strategic alliances as a business imperative over the next ten to twenty years.

Organisations are increasingly polarising into three camps when it comes to deciding on competitive strategy. There are those that hunker down in their market sectors, hoping to establish an unassailable competitive position through industry specialisation. Then there are those that aggressively seek out face-to-face confrontation with clear rules of engagement in multiple market sectors: 'In any confrontation there is a winner and a loser, and the trade off is exact – what I win I win from you, so that my gain is directly linked to your loss.' Finally, there are those that have a more flexible policy. These organisations are coming to realise that there can be multiple winners, and that effective players take the view, 'I want to win, but I don't insist that you lose.'[3]

---

1   Michael E. Porter, 'How Competitive Forces Shape Strategy', *Harvard Business Review* 57, no. 2 (March–April 1979): 137–45.

2   Adrian J. Slywotzky, *Value Migration: How to Think Several Moves Ahead of the Competition*, Boston, MA: Harvard Business School Press, 1995.

3   Dudley Lynch and Paul Kordis, *Strategy of the Dolphin: Scoring a Win in a Chaotic World*, London: HarperCollins, 1989.

What is Driving Co-opetition?

Strategic alliances are sweeping through nearly every industry and are becoming an essential driver of superior growth. The value of alliances is estimated to reach $30 trillion–50 trillion within five years. Peter F. Drucker[4] has observed that not only is there a surge in alliances, but 'a worldwide restructuring' is occurring in the shape of alliances and partnerships.

Recent surveys by Booz Allen[5] have revealed the following:

- More than 20% of the revenue generated by the top 2,000 US and European companies now comes from alliances, and this is predicted to increase in the near future.
- These same companies earn higher returns on investment and returns on equity from their co-opetitive alliances than from their core businesses.
- Leading-edge alliance companies are grouping their alliances in a concentrated manner, thus creating a string of interconnected relationships that allows them to overpower the competition.
- The traditional 'command and control' organisational model is inadequate to manage complex sets of relationships formed outside the direct control of a corporation.

The co-opetition model is based on the concept of mutual benefit, whereby organisations move from adopting a central position to a more co-operative role. The alliance is at the centre, rather than one or other of the partners, and the customer relationship often shifts from an individual company to the alliance as a whole. Typically, we find that companies that have adopted the co-operative model do so to outflank the competition and substantially raise the competitive bar. The most distinguishing feature of the co-opetitive model is that no single partner is in control, and all work together to raise the competitive bar to prevent new entrants.

There are certain environmental conditions that favour the formation of co-opetitive alliances and explain the increase in co-operation over the last decade:

- Competitive boundaries have blurred as technological advances have created crossover opportunities, merging formerly distinct industries.
- Advances in communications (voicemail, email and e-business) and the trend towards global markets have linked formerly disparate products, markets and geographical regions, and have facilitated the open communication essential between partners.
- Intensifying competition and increasingly demanding customers require improved capabilities across the board, and few companies have the time or resources to either develop these themselves or acquire them.
- There is an insatiable drive for high technological standards and compatibility in a globally linked world.

---

4   'What Executives Should Remember': a compilation of Peter Drucker articles for the *Harvard Business Review*, 2006: http://dev.europepmc.org/abstract/MED/16485812/reload=2;jsessionid=x6PHxqsWZXHhaGMLQMlv.0.

5   John R. Harbison and Peter Pekar, Jr, *A Practical Guide to Strategic Alliances: Leapfrogging the Learning Curve*, McLean, VA: Booz Allen & Hamilton, 1998: http://www.boozallen.com/media/file/A_Practical_Guide_to_Alliances.pdf.

- A growing number of companies have successfully scaled the alliance learning curve and established a global body of expertise to ensure successful alliance formulation and execution.

Studies have revealed that in 1985 only 26% of the revenue of the top US companies came from their core businesses. Diversification was still the standard of the day. By 1998 this had all changed. Today we find that core alliances generate over 60% (in the USA) and 67% (in Europe) of these companies' revenue. It is essential to effectively identify, protect and enhance one's core business without giving up the key elements of the value chain where one's core is not positioned. As competition intensifies, alliances fill in capability gaps to protect the core business.

Fifteen years ago US companies produced only 14% of their revenue overseas. Most US companies saw competition as confined to the US borders. However, today 35% of US revenue (and 45% of European revenue) comes from international sales – making all firms vulnerable to threats from global players, especially from experienced co-operative international partners.

Research and development took a back seat in the early 1980s, with only about 2% of revenue spent on it. By 1995 a dramatic change had occurred, with nearly 6% of revenue allocated to R&D in the US and Europe. ASAP believes that this change was directly related to the increased importance of new product development to companies' competitive positions. Since 1990, our surveys have shown that new products have accounted for a steady stream of over 20% of revenue every two years. Accommodating such rapid innovation has put pressure on management to act faster and smarter with fewer resources – hence the move toward co-opetitive alliances.

Recent studies by Booz Allen & Hamilton[6] have revealed the link between growth and market capitalisation. Table 12.1 illustrates what the high-performers can achieve.

Table 12.1 Growth and performance figures of co-opetitive organisations, 1991–2001

	Annual rates of growth			Ten-year cumulative growth		
	Shareholder returns	Earnings	Revenue	Shareholder returns	Earnings	Revenue
90th percentile	23.7%	25.9%	21.1%	841%	997%	678%
80th percentile	19.1%	17.8%	13.3%	573%	516%	347%
50th percentile	12.7%	9.6%	8.5%	331%	251%	226%

Source: Booz Allen & Hamilton: http://iveybusinessjournal.com/topics/strategy/equity-alliances-take-centre-stage#.U4DJE_ldVqU.

Note: Shareholder returns reflected stock price appreciation plus dividend reinvestment, adjusting for stock splits.

6   Marc Margulis and Peter Pekar Jr., 'Equity Alliances Take Centre Stage,' *Ivey Business Journal*, May / June 2003: http://iveybusinessjournal.com/topics/strategy/equity-alliances-take-centre-stage#.U4DJE_ldVqU.

Clearly, they generate growth, but that growth also translates into high shareholder returns and earnings. It is not surprising that these companies have much higher price/earnings ratios and market capitalisations than their competitors or the market in general.

The majority of these top performers are among the leading alliance companies, and they experience significantly higher return on investment from their alliances than from their core business, gain a higher percentage of their revenue from alliances, and earn 70% more return on shareholder equity than their competitors which have fewer alliances. Research by Bharat Anand and Tarun Khanna of Harvard Business School and the Yale School of Organization and Management shows that alliances outperform mergers in terms of stock market value creation, as Case Studies 16 and 17 show.

Case Study 16: AOL

In June 1999 AOL announced a major alliance with DirecTV to provide broadband access to AOL customers, and in the following weeks the market value of AOL increased $21 billion. In contrast, when AOL announced its proposed merger with Time Warner in January 2000, its market capitalisation dropped $39 billion.

Alliances tend to raise both partners' market value, while acquisitions tend to raise the market capitalisation of the acquiree and lower that of the acquiror.

Case Study 17: TriStar Pictures

In the 1980s CBS, Columbia Pictures and HBO entered a co-opetitive alliance to form a film company and studio, TriStar Pictures, with an initial investment of $300 million. Through TriStar, HBO gained access to an additional source of feature films, CBS obtained a toehold in cable TV services and a source of feature films for commercial broadcasting, and Columbia Pictures gained access to new distribution channels and extra studio capacity when space was scarce.

Although TriStar operated separately from its parents, it did not have its own distribution system. Its parents distributed TriStar's films through their own distribution systems, thus raising the effectiveness and productivity of the partners. TriStar's movies were made, sold and distributed through TV, cable and cinemas in a much more seamless way, which helped to establish to cable and made HBO the dominant force in the paid cable field. Table 12.2 shows the capabilities each partner brought to the alliance.

Table 12.2   Case Study 17: TriStar Pictures

Capabilities	HBO	Columbia	CBS	Alliance	Observations
		Tradeables			
Creative art	25%	50%	50%	75%	All capabilities
Production	25%	50%	50%	75%	existed to some extent within
Theatre distribution	0%	50%	25%	75%	the individual partners – sharing
Consumer promotion	25%	50%	75%	75%	alone created value Improved
Cable marketing access	50%	0%	25%	75%	production asset value of Columbia Realised
Video distribution	0%	50%	25%	75%	maximum value for entertainment/ movie
Broadcasting	0%	0%	75%	75%	Archive for all parties
Consumer access	25%	50%	75%	75%	Improved audience and reach

Source: Booz Allen Hamilton: http://iveybusinessjournal.com/topics/strategy/equity-alliances-take-centre-stage#.U4DJE_ldVqU.
Note: All % figures refer to the ability of the unit to perform the described function.

Co-opetition requires a different business model. While the relative size of the partners may differ, they are equals at the points of intersection (specific product or services provided to the marketplace). All the partners are working towards the same goal, but the day-to-day running of the alliance is not under direct control of any one partner.

Ray Noorda, founder of the networking software company Novell, was probably responsible for coining the term 'co-opetition', which has quickly been adopted as a new model for doing business as we move towards increased competition through mass globalisation and multi-channel marketing. Some of the dilemmas and challenges presented by this new model are discussed below.

Situation 1: External Market Changes

Your key supplier is acquired by the competition. Let's say apparel competitor A decides to buy a textile plant to start manufacturing its own clothes – the same plant from which you buy apparel to distribute.

Your competitor could decide to restrict its supply of products to you, but by doing so it would lose out on the wholesale business. Similarly, you could live in fear of your competitor, or work with it to improve manufacturing efficiency and thus drive down the cost of your supply chain. However, doing this would also improve your competitor's supply chain.

Situation 2: 'Borrowing' an Established Distribution Network

You want to sell products internationally, but don't have as strong a distribution network as one of your key competitors.

Do you try to build a distribution network from scratch, or do you find a way to work with your competitors to share and enhance the existing distribution network for mutual advantage?

Situation 3: Change in Manufacturing Strategy Creates New Customers

You want to expand into alternative distribution channels.

What happens when you start manufacturing your own products and begin to look for alternate channels of distribution, including those organisations that previously used to manufacture for you? At one point you considered these companies competitors. Are they now potential customers?

Situation 4: Rationalising Supply Chain Costs

Two competitors in a diminishing market sector generate competitive advantage by rationalising their manufacturing capabilities to combine their production plants into one large and highly efficient facility. Not only does this allow economies of scale, it allows both parties to reduce the costs of R&D by sharing the function. This in turn means that other players in the sector are driven to use the same facilities, with the first two players taking a premium from the other competitors for the use. In some situations this results in 'supply chain islands' being formed, where the efficiency and effectiveness of the supply chain is all that matters, not who is actually in the chain. In these circumstances, the most damaging position is to be outside any of the chains.

Situation 5: Compensating for Inadequate Products

Chrysler, one of the largest automobile manufacturers in the world, had a reliability problem with its engine assembly line and needed a better engine for its cars quickly. Instead of waiting to fix the problem (which might have taken many years of R&D work), the company entered into a partnership with a competitor, Mitsubishi (which had a superior assembly capability), to supply the engines for Chrysler cars.

Situation 6: Disintermediation

Probably the most significant development in collaboration in recent years is disintermediation, where manufacturers use the Web to sell directly to customers and therefore have little need for complex relationships with distributors.

However, a complexity on the original simple model is that many manufacturers found that some of their traditional distributors had stronger relationships with customers and were far better at servicing their needs using 'back-end' processing technologies. Many manufacturers have therefore reverted to doing what they do best (manufacturing) and viewing distributors as partners once more, as Case Study 18 explains.

Case Study 18: iGo

Although iGo started as a catalogue reseller of other manufacturers' products, it is now a multi-channel marketer that designs, distributes, and manufactures accessories for mobile technology products such as laptops and wireless devices. This evolution has brought it more competition from other manufacturers selling direct to customers.

iGo could consider laptop manufacturers IBM, NEC, and Acer as threats to its accessories business. These manufacturers produce their own lines of accessories and can sell them directly to their laptop buyers. However, through a series of negotiations, and in the true spirit of co-opetition, iGo views these manufacturers as partners: 'They refer their customers to iGo to service and supply accessories that they've discontinued; occasionally. they'll even refer buyers to us to service current models.' These referrals enable iGo to reach a much broader audience with less advertising expense. In return, IBM, NEC, and Acer can provide a higher degree of service and ultimately retain more customers: for example, IBM customers can contemplate purchases confident that they will be able to obtain the accessories they needs even if the item is discontinued.

Now that iGo also manufactures its own line of branded products, it sells them through alternative distribution channels, including stores and other companies' catalogues. This has forced iGo to look at its traditional competitors as partners. For example, Xtend Micro Products, based in Newport Beach, California, is one of iGo's well-respected competitors that sells a similar, but in some cases superior, line of power supply products and accessories such as in-flight/auto adapters, batteries and chargers for laptops. Xtend had established strong, exclusive relationships to supply its in-flight adapters to major airlines and offered its products in computer catalogues.

iGo was suddenly faced with the question, 'Do we spend the next six months developing our own line of similar products to compete with Xtend, or do we acquire Xtend?' It decided to acquire Xtend Micro Products in a stock transaction in August 2000, essentially making Xtend a part-owner, or partner, with a stake in iGo.

Particular Problems with Co-opetition

Successful alliances or partnerships all rely to a larger or smaller extent on a number of identified best practice principles, attitudes and management structures. Alliance Best Practice has developed the full list of these elements over the last ten years. From that extended list we have identified those aspects which are particularly important in any collaborative relationship with potential competitors.

BUILDING AND MAINTAINING INTERNAL ALIGNMENT

This means having a systematic process for identifying key decisions and stakeholders, and informing, consulting or negotiating with each stakeholder as appropriate. The benefits include; ensuring durable, value-enhancing decisions, reducing the time necessary for sound decision making, enabling different functions or regions to plan to respond to impacts, increasing the likelihood of meeting commitments or avoiding making commitments that can't be met, and avoiding partner confusion.

HAVING A PROCESS FOR DUE DILIGENCE

This means systematically evaluating the characteristics of a potential partner in an agreed manner. The ASAP due diligence model is based on a '3D fit' approach which considers alignment or fit in three specific dimensions: strategic, operational and cultural. Organisations need to understand and take relationship compatibility into account when evaluating potential partners, to avoid problems stemming from poor relationship fit or planning how to mitigate them. Clearly, in some cases this will not be possible since situations may arise where the parties' options are limited. But at least an awareness of the possible danger areas will help prospective partners to conduct the negotiations as efficiently as possible. Having a robust process for due diligence will help partners to anticipate and prepare for relationship challenges and allow them to leverage differences (often the driving force behind partnering in the first place) to enhance the quality and creativity of joint work.

DEVELOPING A GOOD WORKING RELATIONSHIP WHILE NEGOTIATING A WIN/WIN DEAL

During partnership negotiations, focusing equal and separate attention on both the substantive aspects of the deal and the working relationship necessary to implement it is essential. This approach allows negotiators to create a negotiation environment that enables the creation of value-maximising deals. It builds a foundation for working well together upon which to launch the partnership, and creates excitement and a buzz about the choice of partner and the likely value of the relationship, which will be necessary to sustain motivation levels throughout the vicissitudes of the relationship.

ESTABLISHING A COMMON VISION

It is imperative that prospective partners clearly understand both the personal and organisational reasons why the alliance is in their best interests. This view must be capable of being expressed as a commercially viable vision identifying common strategic goals and agreed processes to achieve them. In addition, agreement on common metrics of performance ('How will we know when we have succeeded?') is crucial for reporting to senior management.

ACHIEVING EXPONENTIAL 'BREAKTHROUGH' PERFORMANCE STANDARDS

Alliances must be charged with achieving exponential advances, because all the parties will wish to see a competitive return and hope to share in additional value created. This does not necessarily mean that the partners will have to compromise: each can get exactly what it is looking for, and something else of value will be left over for them to share as long as the returns are exponential. This is usually achieved by setting challenging breakthrough goals, establishing small breakthrough project teams to establish credibility, seeking early gains integrated with stretching targets, and rewarding innovative thinking rather than punishing it.

HAVING A ROBUST, INTEGRATED, ALLIANCE METRIC FRAMEWORK

Unless the alliance is constantly measured against objective criteria set at the beginning of the project, success will be hard to define. The metric sets must encompass not just substantive, but also relationship elements. It will not always be possible to express performance on relationship issues empirically. It is important that the parties agree on the metric dimensions early and look for a balanced set of metrics that rewards behaviour as much as results. The alliance metric sets must then be integrated with the business key performance indicators.

THE EXISTENCE OF A DEFINED PROCESS

A defined process for alliance formation and management must exist for the alliance to have any chance of success. Without a formal process, time lost, ambiguity and conflict through misunderstanding will cripple the emerging relationship. It is important to agree on a defined process at the start, including common terminology for stages, phases, outputs and deliverables, as well as consistent and integrated team roles.

ALLIANCE REWARD SYSTEM TIED INTO THE DIAGNOSTICS AND METRICS SYSTEM

It is imperative that the right kinds of behaviour and results are suitably rewarded. Without defined rewards, alliance initiatives become 'business as usual', and energy, creativity, innovation and commitment are lost. However, it is not necessary, or even recommended, for the reward system to comprise only cash incentives. Promotion, qualification, peer group elevation and recognition will go a long way to institutionalising the benefit of being associated with an alliance programme. The parties should celebrate success openly and fulsomely, and integrate alternative methods of compensation. It is preferable to make an alliance the fast-track business unit that every ambitious employee wants to belong to.

ESTABLISHING COMMON GROUND RULES FOR WORKING TOGETHER

Having a standard approach to conducting joint planning for how partners will work together and manage their relationship is crucial operationally. Both/all parties need to build an understanding about their partner(s) and their partners' culture and policies. They need to agree on specific relationship goals. They should jointly plan ways of achieving relationship goals in the light of similarities and differences. These measures will all mitigate the likelihood that problems will arise and maximise the likelihood that they will be handled effectively when they do. Finally, they will enhance the ease of decision making over time.

HAVING DEDICATED ALLIANCE MANAGERS

Dedicating and enabling a person to be specifically responsible for managing the relationship side of each significant alliance will significantly enhance the chances of success. This will ensure that relationship management is given focused time and attention and ensure effective implementation of ground rules/protocols for working together. Having dedicated alliance managers helps to co-ordinate communication between the partners, and managers can spot potential conflicts early on, and thus take prompt remedial action. Alliance managers can mediate disputes and gauge and track the health of the working relationship over time.

HAVING COLLABORATION SKILLS IN ALLIANCE EMPLOYEES

Routinely investing in maintaining, updating and instilling skills (for example, joint problem solving, conflict resolution, how to conduct difficult conversations) that enable all employees involved in alliance to work effectively with partner team members is fundamental to building collaboration capability. It is important to ensure that collaboration skills exist at all points of interaction between the partners, including at the working level, to enhance the extent to which partners can truly maximise the value realised during alliance implementation. Partners should be encouraged to deal with conflicts and difficult issues in ways that enhance, rather than detract from, the working relationship.

HAVING A COLLABORATIVE CORPORATE MINDSET

Consistently thinking in terms of the good of the alliance rather than the good of the company's individual interests is an indication of the maturity of the collaborative relationship. Collaborative companies underscore the importance of employing collaboration skills, which ensure effective and consistent application of alliance processes, tools and skills. Maintaining a collaborative mindset enables alliance employees to deal with uncooperative partners and ensures that alliance managers are not the only ones taking a global perspective.

MANAGING MULTIPLE RELATIONSHIPS WITH THE SAME PARTNER

Having a corporate-wide ability to identify, discuss, track and manage the numerous and often complex interconnections between partners – such as when partners are also competitors, partial owners, suppliers and/or customers – is obviously crucial in complex collaborative relationships. Excellent collaborative organisations ensure that appropriate differences in how each facet of a relationship is perceived and managed are communicated and understood across the relationship. They ensure that difficulties in one part of a relationship do not create negative consequences for others, and they enable joint gains through a global view of the relationship rather than a parochial, division-based view.

ALLIANCE REWARD SYSTEM TIED INTO DIAGNOSTICS AND METRICS SYSTEMS

Reward systems must be viewed from the perspective of partners, and should be integrated seamlessly into the diagnostic '3D fit' of the alliance programme and the metrics used for measuring success. They must be measured as viewed by the other partner(s), and financial indicators alone are insufficient. Reward systems must take account of performance over the long term and include non-financial indicators.

AUDITING ALLIANCE RELATIONSHIPS

Monitoring and reporting on the health of the working relationship between alliance partners through the use of a formal mechanism, process or standard procedure of some kind significantly increases the chances of success. Identifying simmering/underlying conflicts, negative perceptions or relationship risks prior to their undercutting the relationship and ensuring that they are addressed constructively has been shown to be indicative of successful long-term synergistic collaborations.[7] Identifying ways in which relationship protocols concerning strategy, management or working together are leading to conflict and providing the foundation for adjustments is critical in building a collaboration that can reinvent itself over time. When applied across multiple relationships, auditing can identify organisational barriers to effective partnering.

MANAGING CHANGES THAT AFFECT THE ALLIANCE

Having the ability to anticipate change as early as possible and discussing and planning, collaboratively for its implications leads to continuous improvement and a 'learning alliance' ethos. Line managers should be sensitive to reorganisations and/or departures of key personnel. They should mitigate negative effects of downsizing, mergers or strategic restructuring and adapt to competitive or regulatory environment changes. During the life of the relationship, both/all partners will need to collaborative to expand, contract or shift the focus of the relationship as appropriate.

Three Specific Keys to Successful Co-opetitive Partnerships

All of the factors above are clearly important in collaborative relationships, but some key generic actions stand out as essential.

DEFINE THE GOALS OF PARTNERSHIP

This point may seem self-evident, but it is surprising how many alliances ASAP has seen where this fundamental issue has not been addressed with clarity at the outset. Do you want to expand your distribution outlets? Do you want to reduce costs in your supply

---

7   Fourth State of Alliances Study: http://www.strategic-alliances.org/content/tag/4th-state-of-alliance-management.

chain or your sales and/or marketing functions? Do you want to introduce new and innovative products or services? Both/all parties should be clear from the start what the alliance offers them commercially. However, in addition, the parties should ensure that there is a clear and recognisable commercial benefit for the other party or parties. Without this, the collaboration will fail.

ESTABLISH AN OPEN RELATIONSHIP AND DIALOGUE

Both/all parties must be frank in delineating areas in which they plan to compete with their partner(s). For example, Company A may say that a particular account is off limits but the rest are open to competition, and in exchange will promise not to go after Company B's top five accounts. Clarify from the outset that certain proprietary or competitive information is private, and will remain so.

ESTABLISH CHECKPOINTS ALONG THE WAY

External conditions, such as the emergence of new competitors in the market, or internal conditions, such as management, often change. These factors could alter the direction of the company or the patronage of certain customers and therefore affect the purpose of the partnership, so you should continually re-evaluate the relationship.

Partnering with the competition, if done properly, allows each company to focus on its core strengths, reap added sales and still make money, all while keeping customers happy by offering the best quality and range of goods and services.

The high-tech sector has made stunning commitments to the future of alliances. Nearly every company in this sector sees substantial opportunities for growth through alliances: 92% of them have said that alliances are important to their present and future growth. The Independent Directors Council (IDC) estimates that third parties influence over 60% of the $88.7 billion software market (IDC meeting, San Jose, 25 March 2003).[8]

Today, companies face a curious dilemma. On the one hand, vendors are expected to form alliances to leverage other firms' resources to achieve their corporate objectives. As a vice president of alliances for a billion-dollar software firm put it: 'We can expand operations off balance sheet.' On the other hand, alliance partners' activities are sometimes considered extraneous, and may be difficult to evaluate and justify. Partners may operate quite differently from the vendors, creating significant cultural conflict.

In these tight financial times, marketing and sales organisations have been cut to the bone, and vendors are reluctant to spend money on alliances without being able to exercise considerable control and being assured of a positive outcome. A $200 million communications software firm expressed this as: 'We keep resources tight until we've defined and proven success.' Nor are customers completely sold on alliances. According to *Getting Partnering Right*, 70% of end user customers feel that partnering leads to lower service levels.[9]

As an industry leader in multimedia software observed: 'Buyers are only one bad decision away from losing their jobs.'

---

8   http://www.idc.com.

9   Neil Rackham, Lawrence Friedman and Richard Ruff, *Getting Partnering Right: How Market Leaders are Creating Long-term Competitive Advantage*, New York: McGraw-Hill, 1996.

CRITICAL ISSUES IN IT ALLIANCES

Most vendors try to do too much with alliances

Some have hundreds if not thousands of partners. Vendors may offer dozens of marketing and sales programmes, many of which are of little value to their partners. They begin the fiscal year with a long list of deliverables, and then try to accomplish everything, regardless of the possibilities of success. As one hardware executive told his marketing and sales staff: 'Treat this like a 15 million-dollar company. Don't ask me for the resources of a billion-dollar company.'

Alliance programmes do not fit with a company's business strategy and plans

Alliance programmes are often treated as isolated entities, separate from other sales and marketing activities, so they are not sufficiently funded or supported by the firm's executives. A vendor may be well-positioned in the marketplace because of its offerings, reputation and size. It sets certain expectations in the market about its business and offerings, and ensures there are capabilities in place to achieve market expectations. In many cases, however, that same company launches an alliance programme that does not comply with these expectations, and fails to fulfil the market commitment.

Many companies do not monitor alliance programmes effectively

The fact is, most alliance programmes are not monitored, and companies don't know whether their programmes are succeeding or failing. Alliance programmes aim to increase leveraged revenue, complete or extend product offerings, create demand for joint solutions, achieve market share and increase sales coverage. However, most firms only measure customer revenue; they are rarely able to tell whether a transaction was aided or leveraged by a partner. If vendors do apply non-revenue metrics (and most do not), they typically measure leads from marketing programmes, transaction profiles, in-house training or partner training.

Many vendors use the wrong role models for alliances

Vendors often model their alliance programmes on industry leaders and well-known companies whose business goals and models may differ dramatically from their own. The two companies most frequently cited in our survey as having exemplary alliance programmes were IBM and Siebel. While both have superb programmes, these are applicable to every company. IBM, for example, sometimes conducts several days of joint planning prior to signing an alliance agreement, and conducts in-person planning sessions on an ongoing basis to keep close tabs on its partners. Not every firm has the organisation or budget to do this for every partner.

KEY OBSERVATIONS

Goals

The key goals companies identified for alliances were 'revenue', 'partner alignment', 'complete or extend product', 'create demand' and 'achieve market share'. Though the best alliance organisations have a broad range of goals, interviewees considered revenue the bottom line in alliance partnerships. As one person remarked: 'If there's no ability to drive revenue for both parties, you don't have the basis for the relationship.' But can revenue goals be achieved without focusing on other business goals as well?

Strategies

The leading alliance strategy was to combine an extended whole product (a complete solution for customers) with collaborative sales (co-sales to joint customers). Companies also favoured strategies based on the judicious use of resources, such as applying significant resources only to certain alliance types or to a handful of top partners.

Success factors

Companies considered relationship planning and training the most important common success factors. Factors related to relationship building and joint planning focus on establishing and broadening alignment with the partner(s) and developing joint plans that assign resources and set milestones, whereas training and marketing support address the development of partner expertise and revenue-readiness.

Alliance mistakes

Vendors indicated that the most common alliance mistakes were 'lack of focus', 'inadequate joint planning' and being 'overly tactical'. Many also cited internal imbalance as a problem. Vendors were highly aware that in order to achieve success they must maintain a sharp focus while balancing strategic and tactical requirements. As the vice president of a leading enterprise software company remarked: 'You need to be stra-tactical.'

Organisation

Vendors showed a strong predilection for locating the alliance function within the sales department, but were split as to where alliance managers should be located – headquarters, the field, or both.

Multinational alliances

Our international interviewees were quite vocal about the need to survey local country markets and understand local alliance requirements and capabilities. Single partners will not necessarily function well in every country or geography; the partner's strengths, weaknesses, market share and capabilities can vary dramatically. Vendors felt that local vendor and partner organisations should be trained and empowered to manage global alliances within their geography.

Measurement

The companies surveyed were consistent only in measuring customer revenue; many did not effectively track revenue leveraged from sell-with alliances. For this reason, vendors' alliance measurements were typically disconnected from their plans and actions. Without effective metrics, they often could not discern the level of their partners' success, and were unable to justify corporate investment in alliances. One executive expressed this as: 'If it's worth doing, it's worth measuring.'

PUTTING IT ALL TOGETHER: A PRACTICAL CASE STUDY

Case Study 19 is reproduced with the kind permission of Jeremy Cox at The Wisdom Network.[10]

Case Study 19: The Ludlow Sausage Company – Winning the Co-opetition Game

When Tesco, a major UK retailer, gained planning permission to open up a shop in the rural town of Ludlow in Shropshire, five family butchers which had served the local population for generations found their businesses at risk. These five firms, which normally competed with each other for local trade, were persuaded by the mayor, Graeme Kidd, to collaborate, not only to protect their businesses, but also to reach out to new customers. This case study describes the progress made towards establishing a successful online retail business and identifies some of the key lessons learned, particularly the importance of creating a collaborative network to generate value for customers – in this case, between competitors.

Background

Ludlow in Shropshire is an old and extremely picturesque town in one of the most rural parts of England. In recent years it has established a reputation among food critics for the quality of its produce. It has three restaurants with Michelin stars, and has held a thriving annual food and drink festival for over ten years. Graeme Kidd, the current mayor and founder of The Ludlow Sausage Company, helped to set up this food festival.

In the early 1990s Tesco applied for planning permission to build a supermarket on the site of Ludlow's auction yard, located in the town, but away from the retail centre of Ludlow. Concerns were raised that local retailers serving the population of 10,000 would lose a significant share of their trade to the national retailer. It was felt highly unlikely that any successful challenge could be mounted to prevent Tesco from establishing the retail outlet in Ludlow.

The Ludlow Chamber of Trade was evenly divided as to whether an in-town Tesco store would bring trade into Ludlow or merely wreak havoc on existing retail businesses. Kidd was

---

10   www.thewisdomnetwork.com.

among those who took the pragmatic view that Tesco was coming to town in any event, and would provide additional employment to the community.

In 1995, Kidd and small group of local businesspeople set up the Ludlow Marches Food and Drink Festival.[11] This event featured 'sausage and ale trails', which aimed to stimulate experimentation among the conservative populace by encouraging them to visit and sample products in the premises of the local butchers and pubs. Being creatures of habit, most of the town's residents tended to visit the same shops, potentially missing out on the choices available.

The idea of getting the butchers to work together to establish a sausage trail proved very popular among local people and festival visitors, and it has become one of the main attractions on the food festival programme. The butchers, having competed for generations, were not natural allies in this new venture. Nevertheless, they were persuaded to support the festival, and from the start it was a resounding success. Each year now, the butchers produce and cook some 3,000 assorted sausages just for the festival. Six or seven years down the line, the food festival became a major landmark on the gastronomic landscape: in 2003 it attracted over 17,500 visitors to the town.

As the owner of a Web authoring company, Kidd came up with the idea of establishing a trading company and Internet retail outlet for the five family butchers in Ludlow. This would help to build the identity of Ludlow as a source of good-quality food, and also had the potential to significantly increase the customer base for what were essentially retail businesses relying on local traffic.

Having established the principle of co-operation among competitors, Kidd felt it was a logical extension to bring them together under one trading umbrella – The Ludlow Sausage Company. The first challenge was to set up a meeting between them all to discuss and agree to the formation of the co-operative venture. Business meetings were not the norm among these family butchers, but they agreed to co-operate in the production and packing of sausages and meats which would be sold online via the website www.theludlowsausage.co.uk.

Kidd, who still runs his small but successful Web authoring company, had researched e-commerce and online retailing as part of a long-term assignment as a contributor to an IT magazine, and was very well placed to design the business model and map out its processes and infrastructure requirements. His research had covered some 150 food websites and a variety of online retailing packages. The one he opted for was Actinic, the 'shop in a box', which was sufficient for their needs and cheap.

Establishing the Business by Degrees

The butchers had no experience of the Internet, and Kidd was cautious about raising expectations too high and promising too much too soon. He raised a small budget, including a grant of £10,000 from AWM, the regional development agency, and designed a simple process readily understood by the butchers and which could be conducted without upsetting their normal routine. The Ludlow Sausage Company website would attract buyers, who could either choose a standard offering of a small hamper of sausages or make up their own selection and then place their orders. Kidd would then pass the orders on to the butchers, place the produce in standard sausage presentation pallets and vacuum-pack them. Kidd had sourced 10,000 pallets at a good commercial price, and each butcher would provide a 'module' of sausages which could be packed easily into the pallets. These pallets were then assembled into the hamper orders placed by customers.

---

11   www.foodfestival.co.uk.

Kidd also designed the website to make it simple to understand and navigate, and also to exude the typically friendly Shropshire humour. This would minimise lost orders and nurture a relationship with customers.

Market Testing
Kidd made the decision to start slowly in order to prove the viability of the website and ordering process. Promotion was carried out using public relations tactics rather than paid-for advertising. Through his contacts as a former business journalist, his first port of call was the *Guardian* newspaper's food section. This generated the first few online orders and confirmed that the ordering and fulfilment process worked.

Positioning
There is a growing appetite for food which is of high quality and known provenance. The Shropshire heritage coupled with Ludlow's new-found fame as one of the few towns outside London with Michelin-starred restaurants provided a credible backdrop to the claims that sausages and other provisions from The Ludlow Sausage Company would be of the highest quality.

Early Mistakes and Lessons
While firms like easyJet, Ryanair, lastminute.com and Amazon had built their success on the offer of low prices, for quality products price is not the key differentiator. Kidd was paying the butchers the same price for their sausages as would be paid by Ludlow town shoppers. Initial orders had too small a mark-up to cover the costs of packing and distribution. For each order there was a minimum overhead of £11 (reduced later to £7 – see 'Cost Reduction' below), so once he'd paid the butchers, the £20 normal charge for a pack of sausages contributed no margin at all. The minimum price was raised to £25, and to his surprise this had no impact on the volume of orders received, which continued to grow without interruption.

The second mistake was to pack and ship orders on a daily basis. This proved uneconomic. Now orders are packed and shipped on Wednesdays. Customers who want the hamper to arrive on a particular day, such as birthday, pay a premium. Again, Kidd found that this did not detract from the customer experience.

Promotional Strategy
Once the business was running effectively, Kidd felt confident enough to increase the promotional push. Apart from well-placed articles in the national press, The Ludlow Sausage Company also appeared at several food and drink fairs.

The first of these was the Royal Show, an annual food fair at Stoneleigh Park in Warwickshire. This show sells itself to exhibitors on the basis that approximately 120,000 ABC1 category wealthy visitors will appear: 'The Royal Show is a lifestyle exhibition for those who appreciate quality of life and have a passion for the countryside ....' In the event, this proved disappointing, as The Ludlow Sausage Company was seen as just another of the many catering companies which were exhibiting.

A greater success was appearing at a beer festival in Shrewsbury sponsored by the Campaign for Real Ale (CAMRA). Beer and sausages are natural allies, and while people queued up to sample some of the hundreds of beers on offer, their friends or other family members bought 'rounds' of sausages.

Alliance Strategy

While firms will often focus their attention on their own IT infrastructure, processes and internal capabilities, the imaginative use of alliances to create and deliver value to customers at a profit is often overlooked.

Increasing Penetration and Enhancing the Product Range
Spurred on by the success of the CAMRA event, Kidd formed an alliance with the local brewery, Hobson's. A sausage was specially commissioned which contained Hobson's beer, intended to be promoted through the network of pubs Hobson's delivers to directly. Hobson's Ale was also a complementary addition to the range on the website. This increased The Ludlow Sausage Company's reach via Hobson's pub distribution channel and also provided the brewer with an additional low-cost outlet. Critical to the success of this alliance is the fact that both parties have gained from it.

Cost Reduction
One of the major items of cost, a mentioned earlier, is distribution. Small firms lack the buying power to gain the advantage of lower shipping costs. When The Ludlow Sausage Company was established, the typical courier costs per order were £11. Kidd knew the owner of a small Italian car parts importer, and suggested that together they could increase their buying power by sharing a courier account. Again, both would gain from the arrangement. This enabled Kidd to reduce the average cost from £11 to £7, which, together with the minimum order price increase from £20 to £25, ensured that the profit margin improved significantly.

Future Extension of the Range
Ludlow is also twinned with St. Pietro Cariano, outside Verona in Italy. On a recent visit to the owner of a vineyard which produces 10,000 bottles of high-quality red wine, Kidd agreed plans to offer this wine for sale via The Ludlow Sausage Company website.

Future Strategy
Kidd admitted that much of the strategy had been developed on the fly rather than through any deliberate and well-thought through plan. One of the key considerations going forward concerns which customers to seek. To date, customers have mainly been individuals ordering on their own behalves. Increasingly, he is seeing a trend towards company offices consolidating orders to reduce their overall prices, as word of mouth spreads within firms. He will also make a decision about supplying commercial customers such as restaurants, but may well have to adjust the pricing strategy.

A further decision to be made will be to either limit the scope of the company to Ludlow but extend the range, or to replicate the company under a different brand name in other regions of the UK, or to sell his know-how to others better placed to forge the appropriate alliances with food producers, suppliers and distributors.

Key Lessons

What makes this case study so interesting is that with very few resources it was possible to generate a successful business and overcome potential problems. While technology is important to provide the infrastructure for an online business, The Ludlow Sausage Company would not have flourished without collaboration from suppliers and distributors and changes in behaviour:

- The butchers, who had competed for generations, now banded together, motivated in part by a desire to protect their businesses from a much larger potential competitor.
- Sensitivity to their needs to carry on their normal business with minimum interruption was required.
- Trust was essential between the parties, so that each could leverage its own skills without having to be involved in every decision Kidd made.
- Research was important – not only to select an appropriate infrastructure, but also to provide a simple and compelling website that would attract customers and make it easy for them to place orders.
- The whole product includes the experience. What makes The Ludlow Sausage Company so attractive goes beyond its products to its friendliness and local country humour. A website which was purely functional would not have delivered this experience.
- Don't always go for a low price. Where quality matters, people are prepared to pay. This is only reasonable, as the time, care and attention which goes into the creation of these products should be justly rewarded. Those customers fixated on price are more likely to shop at Tesco.
- Kidd agreed that carried out periodically, proper planning would have made the company more effective that much sooner. As the business grows, and now that it is at something of a crossroads, the need for planning is greater.
- Alliances are critical, and can be used to:
  - develop customer value, in this case for The Ludlow Sausage company, the butchers and Hobson's;
  - lower costs to serve customers, in this case, through the alliance with the Italian car parts importer;
  - increase market access, in this case through the alliance with Hobson's;
- Pay attention to presentation. Kidd was able to portray the spirit of The Ludlow Sausage Company as friendly, local, with generations of experience and a sense of humour. Indeed, he developed a brand identity for the company which allies with and helps to extend Ludlow town's brand as a quality food and drink destination.
- Get it right first time. While mistakes were made, these were minor, and did not detract from the overall customer experience. Experimentation coupled with low-intensity promotion allowed Kidd to iron out any wrinkles. Once the basic capability was in place and proven, he could then fine-tune some of the processes to improve the viability of the business without sacrificing customer value.

Conclusions

Strategic alliances are sweeping through nearly every industry and are becoming an essential driver of superior growth. The value of alliances is estimated to range between $30 trillion to $50 trillion within five years.

More than 20% of the revenue generated from the top 2,000 US and European companies now comes from alliances, with more predicted in the near future.

These same companies earn higher returns on investment and returns on equity from their co-opetitive alliances than from their core businesses.

Leading-edge alliance companies are grouping alliances in a concentrated manner, thus creating a string of inter-connected relationships which allows them to overpower the competition. In many cases these interconnections include direct competitors.

The traditional 'command and control' organisational model is inadequate to manage a complex set of relationships outside the direct control of the organisation.

Typical issues driving this new model of co-opetition include the need to:

- respond to external market changes;
- tap into established distribution networks;
- adapt manufacturing strategies to win new customers;
- rationalise supply chain costs;
- compensate for inadequate products;
- practise disintermediation.

Successful deployment of this new strategy is dependent on a wide range of factors, but three particular imperatives can be identified:

1. Define the goals of partnership.
2. Establish an open relationship and dialogue.
3. Establish checkpoints along the way.

In the IT sector (the leading-edge user sector) there are specific problems:

- Most vendors try to do too much with alliances.
- Alliance programmes may not fit with a company's business strategy and plans.
- Many companies do not effectively measure alliance programmes.
- Many vendors use the wrong role models for alliances.

The key goals companies in our survey identified for alliances were 'revenue', 'partner alignment', 'complete or extend product range', 'create demand' and 'achieve market share'.

The leading co-opetitive strategy was to combine an extended whole product (a complete solution for customers) with collaborative sales (co-sales to joint customers).

Companies considered relationship, planning, and training the most important common success factors.

Vendors in our survey indicated that the most frequent alliance mistakes were 'lack of focus', 'inadequate joint planning', and being 'overly tactical'.

Vendors we surveyed showed a strong predilection for locating the alliance function within the sales department, but were divided as to where alliance managers should be located – headquarters, the field, or both.

The companies surveyed were consistent only in measuring customer revenue; many did not effectively track revenue leveraged from sell-with alliances.

13 *Insource/Outsource/ Smartsource*

Companies are increasingly frustrated by the following conundrum.

Information technology is not the core of their business, so they will never be world-class at IT. However, IT is a critical enabler of business performance, and therefore a crucial tool for success for almost every organisation. Previous thinking suggested that companies should either insource IT (do it themselves) or outsource it (pay someone who is world-class to do it for them). But these simple options mean that they either perform the function badly or give away control of the prime business driver.

A new paradigm is evolving in which companies 'smartsource' their IT supply chains. This involves establishing collaborative alliances with a range of chosen suppliers with a view to improving performance without losing control, then sharing with them the benefits generated.

This chapter describes a consultancy engagement in which best practice alliance formation and management techniques were applied to securing value-added relationships with suppliers in the field of information technology.

Description of the Problem

The organisation concerned is an international retailer best known for clothing and food products, but also operating considerable businesses in financial services, homeware and other general services. The IT function is an integral part of the company. It employed (at the time of this study) roughly 450 permanent employees and approximately 250 contractors, as well as using a large number of third-party suppliers.

The problem was that the organisation had too few internal IT resources to complete the projects demanded by the business. However, some of these projects were time-critical and could not wait. It appreciated the need to use external supplier resources, but it had been through a number of bad experiences with its traditional vendor/supplier relationship model.

In addition, the organisation needed a standard manner of employing supplier resources throughout the enterprise because its control of supplier relationships was generally very fragmented and at a low level. Consequently, the organisation found it difficult to leverage its existing relationships with suppliers in order to add value. In developing a new model, the organisation couldn't rely on suppliers' suggestions about processes for developing relationships because they were universally biased in favour of the suppliers. What was required was an independently validated process based on identifiable best practices. Finally and crucially, the organisation wanted a definable and quantifiable process that didn't take lots of management time to administer.

The Work Conducted

The organisation approached Alliance Best Practice for help in developing a supplier-independent strategic alliance process based on best practice partnership principles.

The conceptual ideas behind strategic alliances were first of all explained to the organisation in workshops using an Alliance Best Practice guidebook.[1] Complementary concepts were agreed and a common set of operating definitions developed to describe parts of the process to be developed (phases, stages, tasks, activities, examples, tools, definitions, templates and models). The approach was then proceduralised and documented as a best practice workbook. The workbook was then integrated with existing initiatives within the organisation:

- ITIL 1 – *The Information Technology Infrastructure Library (ITIL) Supplier Management Process;*[2]
- ITIL 2 – *The Total Acquisition Process (TAP) Services Guide;*[3]
- *Goal Directed Project Management;*[4]
- the *SUMMIT Ascendant Development Environment;*[5]
- results of recent McKinsey research;[6]
- best practice benchmarking research conducted in the USA in 2001;[7]
- results of recent Gartner research;[8]
- Internal Project Management progression standards ('quality gates').

This integration needed to recognise the characteristics, issues and other relevant information (not least political) that currently affected the organisation's management team.

The work was then delivered as a series of outputs, including a documented process, a sub-process flowchart for each phase, template deliverables, a presentation describing the process for internal consumption, structured training on the process, a continuous improvement sub-process and a template project plan. The process was conducted in six phases:

---

1   Association of Strategic Alliance Professionals, *Alliance Formation and Management*, vols 1 and 2, Canton, MA: ASAP, 1999.

2   Central Computer and Telecommunications Authority, *The Information Technology Infrastructure Library Supplier Management Process*, London: CCTA, 1997.

3   Central Computer and Telecommunications Authority, *The Total Acquisition Process Services Guide*, London: HMSO, 1995.

4   Erling S. Andersen and Kristoffer V. Grude, *Goal Directed Project Management*, 2nd edn, London: Kogan Page, 1995.

5   PricewaterhouseCoopers, *SUMMIT Ascendant Development Environment*, London: PWC, 2001.

6   Mani K. Agrawal and Minsok H. Pak, 'Getting Smart About Supply Chain Management', *McKinsey Quarterly* 2, 2001, pp. 2–27.

7   J. Blanchette, *Best Practices in Supply Chain Management and Partnerships*, Chapel Hill, NC: Best Practices LLC, 2001.

8   Gartner Research Corporation, *Supply Chain Collaboration: Lessons from the Leading Edge*, Stamford, CT: Gartner Research Corporation, January 2002.

1. **Planning/start-up** – The project team carried out a review of the existing relationship with the supplier and the nature of the intended future relationship in order to establish objectives.
2. **Defining success** – The project team informed potential partners about the process for creating alliances, ensuring that both the client and supplier had similar expectations .
3. **Operational planning** – This phase defined how the combined supplier/vendor project team would work, agreeing governance processes and deliverables, escalation processes, risk management, project milestones and arrangements for termination of the alliance.
4. **Creating the partnership** – This phase created the partnership, with particular emphasis on negotiation, finalising contracts and communication (internal and external).
5. **Running/managing the partnership** – Once the partnership was up and running, attention focused on training, tracking, corrective action, review, change control, reporting key performance indicators, issues and register management, and reassessing risks.
6. **Reviewing/improving the partnership** – Any process needs ongoing review, so this phase concerned itself with: review, documentation, comparing alliances and partnerships (external and internal) and adopting a methodology for continuous improvement.

The above approach is illustrated in Figure 13.1.

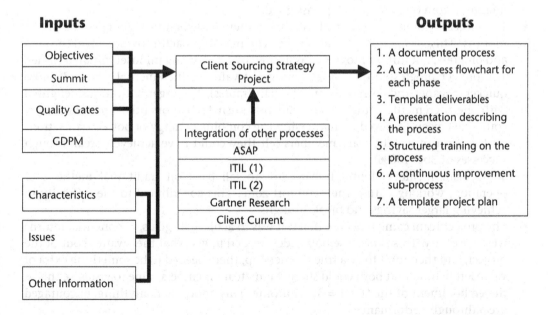

Figure 13.1 Smartsourcing approach, showing inputs, outputs and influencers

The client then chose a specific project which had been causing concern on which to trial the approach.

Results/analysis of the Trial Project

A review of the trial project using the smartsourcing approach reached the following conclusions:

- The approach was very different from the traditional one employed by the organisation. This meant that the amount of time needed for initial instruction and coaching was high compared with traditional vendor/supplier relationship projects. However, the project team recouped this time many times over during the course of the project through the binding effect of thinking of themselves as a single integrated team.
- The approach was sometimes misconstrued as 'motherhood and apple pie'. Some people not directly involved with the project misconstrued the approach as a 'soft sell' of a traditional approach. They did not appreciate the fundamental difference between a collaborative approach and a confrontational one. This was borne out in the way the alliance team members attacked problems. They refused to accept compromise, and sought breakthrough solutions which genuinely provided win–win value, while their traditional colleagues could only conceptualise win–lose commercial agreements where both sides had to compromise to achieve progress.
- There was evidence that some people were psychologically uncomfortable with the concepts explored. In project team slang, 'They didn't get it.' This led to a number of members from both sides being reassigned.
- The project chosen was a difficult one since there had been little progress for twelve months. This was good and bad, in that the new approach provided breakthrough and progress, but further progress was limited by a restricting mindset initiated earlier.
- The project progressed quickly and provided value in incremental terms (30–40% quicker, cheaper and with high-quality deliverables). The organisation was delighted with the incremental progress and did not push for exponential progress, which could have been achieved by harnessing the combined energy of both organisations on the team (privately, team members felt they could have achieved breakthrough successes of 300–400%).
- Some team members found it hard not to fall back on traditional methods of operation, working within their comfort zone. This contributed to the difficulty in achieving larger savings and breakthroughs.
- The project team came to realise that if it was to achieve its goals, exponential returns were necessary. This is because both sides needed to get what they wanted out of the project, and then for it to be a true partnership, there needed to be something extra of value left behind that both could share. Many team members came to visualise this as the embodiment of the '1 + 1 = 3' syndrome. This, more than anything, encouraged breakthrough performance.

Discussion of Some Key Elements of Smartsourcing

At this stage a further examination of the '1 + 1 = 3' synergistic relationship will be valuable. Although specifics will differ from alliance to alliance, the fundamentals remain constant:

- For a partnership or alliance to fully succeed, all parties must associate themselves completely with the new entity created (the partnership or the alliance). If the contributing organisations are successful in achieving this initial state, the increased level of performance exhibited in the pursuance of team goals is truly extraordinary.
- The rewards and returns generated by the relationship need to be exponential, not incremental (measured in terms of hundreds, not tens, of percentage points). This is because by the definition of partnership, all parties get full value from the relationship and there is something of value remaining for them all to share.
- This in turn drives the need to establish breakthrough metrics rather than incremental ones. In dealing with breakthrough performance, some people are psychologically better prepared to accept synergy than others, but all types perform better once they have personally experienced the synergistic '1 + 1 = 3' experience. It appears that more research into the behavioural preferences of standard personality types would increase the effectiveness of alliance teams.
- The approach seems to provide a way of making the term 'smartsourcing' tangible. There is further evidence that European organisations, as opposed to North American ones, are less advanced in their use of alliances as a business tool. This is borne out by the amount and depth of alliance research currently being conducted and applied globally.

The organisation in question entered the smartsourcing debate by looking at a tactical problem in information technology: how to conduct more IT projects with fewer resources without compromising standards of control or quality. It is now re-evaluating the idea based on a strategic overview of how it uses suppliers throughout its entire supply chain. The issue for debate has become how to re-engineer value in its entire supply chains such that extra value is generated in the chain for all contributors. There is ample evidence that this is now a global issue of critical importance, as illustrated by the aggressive search for competitive advantage in IT supply chains:

> ### Consolidation Drives a New Type of Cooperation
> *Gartner Dataquest predicts that the alliances and other cooperative business arrangements that arise from this virtual consolidation will bear a much closer resemblance to keiretsu (a Japanese term denoting a cooperative collection of independent companies) or ecosystems than the bilateral sales and delivery agreements that typify cooperation in IT services today. Strategic relationships among providers in these new IT services 'solution communities' will be multilateral, solution driven and highly interdependent.*[9]

---

9   Christine Adams, *Rethinking Alliances in the Services Value Chain*, Gartner Dataquest Industry Insight Report, Stamford, CT: Gartner Research Corporation, September 2001.

There is a subtle but fundamental distinction between traditional outsourcing and smartsourcing, as shown in Table 13.1.

Table 13.1   The difference between outsourcing and smartsourcing

Traditional outsourcing	Smartsourcing
Non-core functions only	Mission-critical functions considered
Fix immediate problems	Strategic improvements, lifecycle alignment
Usually focused on cost reduction	Usually focused on profit generation
Asset elimination	Asset reallocation and reinvestment
Vendor and supplier have no vested interest in each other's success	Shared risk and reward, commitment to mutual success
Governance is by contract and service level agreements	Co-governance in key strategic areas
Focus is on price point per product offering	Focus on total supply network investment and savings
Price-driven	Driven by total cost and value
Performance indicators are mutually exclusive	Performance indicators linked to total solution meeting client and provider goals
Vendor-based and vendor-driven	
Little incentive for long-term investment	Alliance/partnership-based
Managed at operational level	Incentive systems involve co-investment, productivity improvement and profit sharing
Third parties paid according to savings	Managed at executive level
	Third parties paid according to business performance

We can add certain observations regarding when smartsourcing should be considered. We suggest that smartsourcing is useful in looking at 'shared core' functions (see Table 13.2).

Table 13.2   The distinction between core, shared core and non-core

Core	Shared core	Non-core
Mission-centric	**Mission-critical**	**Mission-peripheral**
The function is *essential* to the organisation's success:	The function is *fundamental* to the organisation's success:	The function is *secondary* to the organisation's success:
• one of the key market differentiators	• closely tied to the core business functions	• useful but not essential
• essence of the organisation's competitive advantage	• not one of the organisation's key market differentiators	• usually a support function
• absolutely integral to support the business mission	• not the essence of the organisation's competitive advantage	• can be provided by a variety of specialists
• the organisation must maintain a world-class competency in order to sustain competitive advantage	• highly integral – must maintain organisational connectivity and tight connection to the organisation and core competencies	• easily separated away from the organisation
	• cannot and must not split the provider functions away from mainstream business	• maintaining a world-class competitive advantage is not of high importance
	• a world-class competency would provide real competitive advantage, but the organisation is not able to justify economically a world-class competency in this area	

Source: Based on original research by Robert Porter Lynch: Warren Company. www.warrenco.com.

Finally, from the results of the programme, we can articulate clear general guidelines for success in smartsourcing:

• Collaboration as a personal commitment is an important principle which must be shared by key team members. People, not processes, make partnerships work.
• Anticipate that it will take management time to make the partnership work – if you can't spare the time, don't start.
• Generate mutual respect and trust, which are essential to the programme – if you don't trust the people with whom you're dealing, don't proceed.
• Remember that both partners must get something out of it (money, eventually) – mutual benefit is vital – but in addition, there should be something of value left over.
• You need to recognise at the outset that prospective partners will probably have to share more (common objectives, team goals, experiences and so on).

- You need to recognise that during the course of collaboration, circumstances and markets change. Recognise your partner's problems and be flexible. Having one happy and one unhappy partner is a formula for failure.
- Appreciate the differences in cultures – don't expect a partner to act or respond identically to you. Find out the true reason for a particular response.
- Recognise your partner's interests and independence.
- Handle the details, even if the arrangement is tactical in one of the candidate's eyes. Your tactical activity may be a key piece in an overall strategic jigsaw puzzle.
- Celebrate achievement together – it's shared elation, and the partners will have earned it!
- Negotiate the ever-changing requirements of the relationship with a strategic view to the future in a co-creative manner that enables innovation and turns breakdowns into breakthroughs.
- Recover development costs to obtain volume/margin benefits by finding larger markets for provider services.
- Resolve unpleasant or contentious issues so that they do not fester and poison the relationship going forward.

What's Happening Elsewhere?

The following is a list of some organisations that have applied the smartsourcing approach during the recent past, showing some of the ongoing results achieved.

ORGANISATION: FORTUNE 500 TELECOMMUNICATIONS COMPANY

Problem

The alignment of a merger and acquisition object had slipped eighteen months due to conflicts with the internal IT staffs of the four companies involved as well as with the supporting IT vendors of the four companies.

Solution

The organisation implemented a smartsourcing approach to assess the current hurdles being encountered by the IT functions, then fast-tracked a self-funding project that implemented the solutions within three-month windows for each phase.

Results

The organisation was able to consolidate three IT data and communication centres into one central site within four months. In addition, it was able to remove 40% of its legacy equipment and software, reduce over-licensing by 35%, retain 90% of its staff and develop a new enterprise outsourcing contract that saved it $10 million a month over the next five years.

ORGANISATION: A $78 BILLION INTERNATIONAL BANK

Problem

The organisation had outsourced all of its glasshouse/back office, communication support and related technical personnel without understanding or applying a strong cross-functional strategic contract and strategic service level agreements.

Solution

The organisation applied smartsourcing programmes that generated a realistic architecture of what the institution should outsource and what it should maintain, at what cost, with realistic expectations of returns.

Results

Through guidance and mediation, the organisation developed new strategic contracts with multiple, large vendors for its outsourced requirements and took back in-house its core competencies that leveraged the institution's competitive edge within the marketplace. The total process was performed within eighteen months and generated an additional 12% in savings using outsourced functions for the client. Moreover, the client increased its transaction rates by 45%, and reduced its transaction costs from $1.65 to $0.84 per transaction while gaining state-of-the-art architecture and e-commerce capabilities.

ORGANISATION: LARGE INTERNATIONAL FAST FOOD RESTAURANT CHAIN

Problem

The organisation had multiple manufacturing plants throughout North America. A benchmarking analysis showed that none of the plants were competitive compared to best-in-class manufacturers. A strategic review indicated that manufacturing was not a necessary core competence.

Solution

The organisation negotiated a strategic sourcing alliance deal with a major competitor that had world-class competencies in manufacturing. Key issues were negotiated, including a long-term global strategy, logistics, supply management, co-ordination of investments and integration of information services.

Results

The roll-out programme proceeded rapidly. After twelve months the programme was nearly six months ahead of schedule. Manufacturing costs were reduced by almost 15%, logistics were substantially improved, and return on assets increased dramatically by closing some plants and shifting ownership of some older ones to the strategic sourcing partner, which proceeded with major upgrades to the facilities.

Smartsourcing Conclusions

Although the term 'smartsourcing' will inevitably continue to mean different things to different people, there is evidence it is being increasingly used in two specific contexts:-

1. The phrase 'insourcing, outsourcing, smartsourcing' describes the means by which organisations can outsource non-core activities while keeping control. A more sophisticated version of this might be the outsourcing of shared core activities.
2. 'Smartsourcing' is generally applied to a situation where an organisation finds value-added methods for improving the way it secures its supply chain. In this context there is plentiful evidence that 'supply chain wars' are already under way in North America.

In both scenarios the common factor is a core element of partnership or alliance, whether it be tactical or strategic.

Smartsourcing as we have described it provides a value-added solution to the question of how to achieve more with the same or fewer resources because, in essence, both parties are 'borrowing' the elements they do not currently have from each other, such as expertise, distribution outlets, products or deployment capabilities.

Major industry analysts are now recommending variations of this theme, both in the IT sector and elsewhere. Prominent among these is Gartner, which seems to view smartsourcing as a credible management technique rather than a passing fad. However, this may have something to do with the fact that outsourcing generally gains ground during recessions, both in terms of debate and work generated.

Evidence from North America suggests that smartsourcing will increase in profile over the course of the next 18 to 24 months as management consultants (particularly IT consultants) seek to sell the idea to European multinational companies. These approaches will probably come through the IT or procurement functions, thus matching twin approaches (1) and (2) in the list above.

Practical evidence from applying the approach suggests that there are some critical do's and don'ts to achieving success. Although not comprehensive, the following list serves as a guide.

Do:

*   Stress the different nature of smartsourcing at an early stage in any project.
*   Generate some hard-edged metrics by which to judge the success of the smartsourcing project – profit, cost reduction, improved quality, reduced time to market, increased market share and IT breakthrough are all good examples.
*   Choose team members carefully – some personality types handle the concepts involved better than others.
*   Stretch the teams involved by focusing on exponential rather than incremental results.
*   Be prepared to integrate the approach into existing initiatives in the organisations involved.

Don't:

- Rely on feelings of camaraderie and friendship alone between the two teams – there needs to be a formal process with defined outputs.
- Set challenging goals from the outset and refuse to settle for incremental improvements.
- Skimp on initial explanations, education and training – the time spent will be paid back many times over by continued rapid progress on the project.
- Neglect the needs of other partners, since their dissatisfaction will sour the relationship early if they feel that benefits are imbalanced
- Let cynicism remain unchallenged – it is very easy for these types of projects to slip back into 'motherhood and apple pie' assignments.

At its best, smartsourcing can deliver the following:

- the highest value creation and lowest transaction costs for both parties over the entire longevity of the contract;
- improved strategic vision;
- flexibility and adaptability in the host organisation;
- a co-operative and co-productive win–win relationship;
- high performance (personal, team and organisational) and increased rapid response;
- continuous innovation;
- total supply chain/network optimisation.

The approach can be applied to a number of functional areas, including manufacturing, distribution, logistics, IT systems, procurement, human resources (some areas), accounting and finance.

Finally, there is evidence that early adopters of this approach are now reaping the benefits, for example:

- Alexander and Alexander
- AT&T Leasing
- Chase Manhattan
- Chevron
- CSST
- Desjardins
- Dow Chemical Company
- Federal Express
- IBM Leasing
- International Quick Service Food Corporation
- Inacom
- Pepsi (North America and International)
- Siemens Corporation
- Taco Bell
- University of Colorado
- USAA
- US Department of Defense

- Warner-Lambert
- Wells Fargo Bank.[10]

10   Source Warren Company, Florida, USA. www.warrenco.com.

PART V

Developing Alliance Capability

CHAPTER 14 *Partnering with SMEs*

The following case studies have been chosen to reflect partnering activities in small to medium-sized enterprises, principally in the UK. Generally, they reflect successful instances of partnering where some considerable obstacles or challenges were overcome. There were a number of reasons for choosing this particular sector:

- to show that partnering is an activity that can be practised by businesses of any size;
- to show how the common success factors recur regularly in practical examples;
- to give a sense for how practitioners deal with everyday problems (wherever possible, in their own words);
- to showcase partnering success stories.

Case Study 20: Mercedes-Benz (UK) Ltd – Alliances in the Supply Chain

Mercedes-Benz (UK) Ltd, is a subsidiary of one of the most prestigious vehicle manufacturers in the world. Mercedes-Benz AG, has recently introduced partnership sourcing into some of its core manufacturing activities.

A few years ago demand on the company's commercial vehicle import centre at Barnsley in the UK was beginning to outstrip capacity, leading to an expansion and rethink of operations. As well as increasing capacity, the company wanted to become faster at developing new solutions and products.

It was an ideal opportunity to seek closer involvement from certain key suppliers. 'The general thrust was to outsource non-core activities, and thereby increase the capacity of existing operations,' said David Duke, Purchasing Manager. 'We chose existing suppliers who had indicated a desire to co-operate in solving our problems.' These included Jost (GB) Ltd and Eberspächer (UK) Ltd – both companies that knew Mercedes-Benz's products and the relevant market.

Jost took on responsibility for designing, developing and installing fifth wheel couplings for commercial vehicle tractor units. Eberspächer undertook a similar role for air and water heaters.

Meanwhile, another partnership with Mailcom resulted from an opportunity identified when reviewing an existing subcontract, of bringing an activity in-house while retaining the benefits of subcontracting. Looking for a company to receive, store, pick and dispatch its marketing and customer information, Mercedes-Benz found Mailcom.

The alliance has:

- cut warehousing and distribution costs by around £70,000;
- reduced lead times by 40%;
- led to a closer working relationship with the users of the system.

Duke believes that the partnerships with Jost and Eberspächer helped the revised operations at Barnsley: 'We've increased capacity, become more flexible and reduced inventory redundancy.'

Case Study 21: BAE Systems – Effective Communication in Alliances (O43)

Kembrey Wiring has a long-standing relationship with BAE Systems (BAES). But until late 1998, when it was awarded Strategic Partnership status with BAES, Kembrey was only one of a number of subcontractors. It was used mainly as a tactical supplier to meet surges in demand across a variety of military aircraft projects. Work was therefore spasmodic, and the relationship was underpinned by a traditional type of contract.

The reason why Kembrey had not been used more frequently was mainly because of its problems in adhering to schedules that were sometimes unattainable and in meeting deadlines. This situation was very much a reflection of the nature of the old-fashioned type of contract, which was specification-driven and did not encourage communication between client and supplier. The reasons for Kembrey's difficulties had never been investigated.

In 1999 BAES was asked to help trial a new Relationship Evaluation Tool (RET), which had been jointly developed by the Department of Trade & Industry (DTI) and the Society of British Aerospace Companies (SBAC) out of the Supply Chain Relationships in Aerospace (SCRIA) initiative – a system to evaluate supply chain relationships that was originally devised within the aerospace industry. It was decided to use the relationship between BAES and Kembrey as a candidate for this work under the guidance of Glenn Whitley, the BAES contract officer responsible.

This was a top-down initiative facilitated by Jeanette Medati, the SCRIA champion within the company. It involved joint workshops between customer and supplier, as a result of which it was possible to identify the root cause of the difficulties.

It was down to one thing – poor communication, both inside BAES and externally to and from the supplier. One individual within BAES had been responsible for writing the work packages against which Kembrey manufactured and supplied components. This person had no experience in writing such packages, but understandably did not want to admit this. He simply did his best. Kembrey struggled to understand the requirement, and in turn did not want to reveal its difficulties to the client, so deadlines for production were missed.

As a result of the evaluation Kembrey offered to show the person concerned how to write work packages. This led to barriers between client and supplier breaking down, with consequent improvements in communications and trust. Thus the partnering relationship began.

Although a partnering relationship is not specified in the contract, nor formalised in any charter or agreement, it is underpinned by joint top-level quarterly review meetings, supported by an informal network of ad hoc joint working groups that take forward particular issues and troubleshoot problems as required. A set of joint values defines the day-to-day working relationship. Part of the partnering initiative includes regular reviews (using RET principles) of the success of the arrangement.

Kembrey can now provide a much more efficient service, with schedules being adhered to and deadlines met. Trust and communications, which were almost non-existent before partnering, have greatly improved, and this has led to a culture of innovation, improvement and a joint approach to seeking better value, based on the sharing of technical information.

Case Study 22: Unimatic and Rockwell Automation – Trust in Strategic Alliance Relationships (Cu31) and Joint Problem Solving (T17)

At the time of this case study, Unimatic was an automation engineering company with £3.6 million annual turnover, specialising in the supply and design of motion control and positioning systems. It had long adhered to a partnering philosophy, developing strong relationships with a few key suppliers.

One such supplier was Rockwell Automation, the giant global provider of industrial automation. Rockwell also had a basic partnering philosophy, and despite its huge size, extended its capabilities through strategic partnerships with a network of specialist local companies.

Rockwell's UK Marketing Manager, Dominic Molloy, said: 'Partnering gives us access to a wider market, bringing innovation and added value to our products through the skills of companies like Unimatic.'

Martin Stevens, Unimatic's Managing Director, explained that the strong association with a quality global supplier like Rockwell adds to Unimatic's credibility, affording access to companies that would otherwise not be open to them. Frequently, Unimatic and Rockwell will meet prospective customers together, demonstrating a level of innovation and service that would not be possible separately.

As a motion systems designer, Unimatic contributes a lot of free consulting upfront, solving problems and sometimes writing software to meet customers' needs, relying on the value of the service provided to win the order. However, there is a danger that the customer may then want to source the parts more cheaply through one of Rockwell's mainstream direct suppliers. When such situations arise, 'We can't, of course, forbid the supplier from selling,' explained Molloy, 'but we make every effort to convince them that the long-term benefits of conducting business with the Unimatic/Rockwell Automation partnering relationship outweigh their short-term interests.'

The strength of the relationship was tested when it had to face such problems. Stevens acknowledged that 'Rockwell has to consider other pressures and priorities, so problems are not always solved to our entire satisfaction. However, openness and honesty are the keys to building trust and as long as we can see real commitment to find a solution, it is appreciated and acceptable. Conversely, if we have not performed, Rockwell's reaction is supportive. They want to find out what's wrong and whether they can help. They approach it as a joint problem.'

'The relationship is very strong as it permeates through both companies,' emphasised Stevens. 'It is implemented by people and their counterparts at different levels – strategic, research, technical, marketing and sales.'

Rockwell has two other Motion Solution providers like Unimatic in other regions, and joint meetings are held with open discussion of aspects such as volume of sales, whether targets have been met, customer complaints, problems with the products, and development and market opportunities. Experience has shown there is greater benefit from sharing knowledge than the perceived danger of loss of commercial advantage.

Hands-on training is another activity often carried out jointly. Rockwell has extensive facilities in Milton Keynes, including a state-of-the-art product demonstration area, to which Unimatic can bring customers. Unimatic is also welcome to use conference rooms for internal or customer meetings.

In hindsight, what would they do differently? 'We could have painted the bigger picture better and earlier to mainstream suppliers,' reflected Molloy. 'And we would commit more time in the early stages,' said Stevens. 'New relationships absorb resources.'

Their key recommendations for others are: be open, don't expect it to be easy, don't walk away from problems, look at the long term, and aim for a win–win.

Case Study 23: Bass Breweries, Open Book Partnering – Due Diligence in Partner Selection (Co2)

Centurion IT Ltd operates in the print management marketplace, working with large organisations, trade unions and not-for-profit groups to provide an outsourced management facility.

Bass Brewers Ltd is the UK's second largest brewer. Its brand portfolio includes Carling, the UK's largest beer brand, Grolsch, Tennent's, Bass Ale, Worthington and Caffrey's.

In 1999, following a strategic review, Bass recognised that there had to be a better way of accomplishing its print purchases than the existing myriad of separate transactions generated by end-users from its different brands located across the UK.

Procurement Manager John Polglass recalled: 'We decided to commission a print management company to act as a one-stop shop for all our print needs from stationery to major point-of-sale material. Following a rigorous selection process, we appointed Centurion.'

This would be an open book partnering relationship with transparency required of both parties. Costs were agreed for all Centurion's relevant resources, with a percentage addition to cover on-costs and profit. Polglass explained: 'We used the standard Bass contract as we considered it unwise to move too quickly away from what we all understood, but this contained a section that evoked the spirit of the relationship and set out the way we intended to work with each other.' In future he would like to think the contract might be different and reflect the way the relationship should work.

Centurion worked hard to identify the key people with whom to network. Sue Lawson, the Account Director, can now point to a dedicated team that understands Bass's requirements, having up to 500 points of contact: 'They know us and feel comfortable picking up the phone to ask for anyone in the team.'

The Account Manager, Tamara Thomson, reflected: 'We spent too long building relationships with some of the agencies, which were often protecting their positions and inadvertently blocking innovation. Once we were able to talk directly to the end users, we understood their requirements more clearly and were able to deliver real benefits and develop trust.'

The process was not without its challenges, particularly in the early stages, and Centurion's Managing Director, Simon Tate, is full of praise for the support received from the key people at Bass: 'They looked on these as joint problems, helping to take the heat out of difficult situations, finding where the blockages were and removing them without trying to apportion blame.' The biggest problem was cultural inertia – resistance to change. Tate added: 'With hindsight, we should have put in more resources at the beginning. In fact, we now feel this is such an important phase that in future we would deliberately over-resource to ensure that our staff were able to cope with the new scenario more easily and to engender immediate confidence from the client's personnel.'

Bass now provides desks for Centurion's people to work with it for part of the week. They are considered part of the team, not just a voice on the phone. Lawson confirms: 'This helped move from responding to what's happened towards anticipating needs.'

All agree there have been significant benefits. Due to changing demand it is difficult to put a figure on the savings, but benchmarking from the early stages indicates some 30% on print in the first year and even greater savings on stationery. Key performance indicators have been identified and are now being monitored by independent auditors.

New initiatives are being developed jointly and with great confidence. One example is a digital asset management system that provides Bass with access to all its imaging, which the partners worked on together with the third party, from the tendering stage through to implementation.

Polglass believes: 'The key to success has been the openness and honesty, from directors through every level in the team, which has led to a genuine culture of trust.'

Case Study 24: Marriott Hotels, Alliances in Affinity Groups – Technical Competence and Cultural Alignment (Cu38)

In the early 1990s Whitbread Hotel Chain's Procurement Director, Brian Crawford, became convinced that one-off competitive tendering was inappropriate for the hotel industry. It took some time to convince all of his colleagues that partnering with selected companies would offer the best long-term value to Whitbread Hotels. But eventually he won the intellectual argument by creating unhappiness with the status quo. Put simply, he proved that there is a better way than the costly and time-consuming tendering system.

His next task was to identify those companies with which Whitbread Hotels should partner. Brian's key criteria included technical competence and cultural alignment. Did the potential partners have the right management philosophy and a willingness to commit resources and staff time? Most importantly, did they have the intellect to produce innovative solutions to problems? Several partnering relationships were established in the mid-1990s, including a very successful one with John Laing plc, before the practice of partnering faced its greatest challenge on 6 January 2000, when Whitbread Hotels acquired the Swallow Group of hotels, nearly doubling the number of its four-star hotels to a total of 60 Marriotts in the UK.

Whitbread Hotels quickly established a Partnered Design and Development Team, managed by Hugh Davies of Buro Four. All of the team members had previous experience of working with Whitbread Hotels. Their brief was to convert as many hotels as possible to Marriott brands (within strict brand standards) in the shortest possible time and within tight budget constraints. Two weeks later, 26 hotels had been identified as suitable for conversion to the Marriott brands (Marriott Hotels, Renaissance and Courtyard by Marriott).

To work alongside Davies and his team, Whitbread Hotels also established the idea of 'Becoming a Marriott' (BAM) and created an in-house BAM team of hotel operations managers and a BAM committee comprised of one representative from each hotel function, including property and procurement. Just over one month after the acquisition, the hotel general managers were advised on the timings for the conversion of their hotels.

The early involvement of the designers, working closely with contractors, key suppliers and hotel management, was essential in successfully driving the £50 million programme. The first ten hotels to convert to Marriotts were completed in just seven months. Close liaison between the teams ensured that there was minimal impact on occupancy or guest satisfaction during the conversion process. Whitbread Hotels calculates that without the early input of the Partnered Design Team, it could have taken 50% longer to convert the hotels, with consequent loss of revenue.

However, the project was not without its problems. Because of the need for speed, the initial survey had not discovered that one hotel had dry rot and needed to have asbestos removed. In addition, the hotel management wanted to install a sprinkler and air conditioning system. This caused great consternation on site. The project managers, AYH, chaired a number of full and frank discussions between the local team members while the problems were reviewed and solutions found. Only occasionally did it prove necessary to refer the problems upwards, and then the ease of access to Hugh Davies ensured that delays were kept to the minimum.

The project is well summed up by David Harris, Operations Director of Pearce Leisure: 'We all knew that the project had to be completed within a limited timescale. It was up to us, as a team, to find the solutions. We accepted that there were bound to be times when some people were going to suffer some pain, but overall, it was worth it. We made money, and the hotels were refurbished to a high standard and in a very short time. Without an effective partnering approach it would just not have been possible.'

Case Study 25: DEK International UK, Smartsourcing Alliance – Cultural Alignment (Cu38)

DEK International UK manufactures high-tech screen-printing equipment which is used in the production of printed circuit boards (PCBs). Typical customers include Ericsson, Siemens and Motorola. Established in 1968, the company operates from a purpose-built factory on an industrial estate in Weymouth, Dorset.

It was a desire to remain on this site that encouraged the company to consider outsourcing some of the processes used in manufacturing its printers. Growth and capacity were more important than costs. Two key suppliers, Lutze (cables) and Metool (drag trains) suggested that DEK should consider outsourcing the wiring jig and loom production to Power Panels of Walsall. DEK's Contracts Manager, Richard Stewart, decided to pursue the suggestion, but rather than concentrate on one firm, he identified eight, including Power Panels, that were capable of undertaking such work. Five were visited before DEK decided on Power Panels. Why Power Panels? 'Because we had a similar attitude towards our work and spoke the same language,' said Stewart.

Stewart and David Fox, the Chairman of Power Panels, quickly put together a management team to oversee the partnering relationship. DEK wanted to minimise disruption, so it was agreed that the move towards total outsourcing would be phased over fifteen months, beginning in the spring of 2000. The management team encouraged contact between the companies at all levels, and eventually, in July 2001, a rolling contract was signed by DEK which ensured that Power Panels would be the sole supplier of wiring jig and loom production for the next three years.

The partnering arrangement ensured that DEK could remain at its current site, maintain its quality standards and, in time, produce cost benefits of around 6% a year. Power Panels, which had previously concentrated on supplying equipment for production plant, was able to enter into a new high-tech area and obtain quality business averaging £5 million a year. The company was also able to advise DEK on ways to improve the quality of the PCB soldering, and with the security of a three-year rolling contract, to invest in new equipment.

To ensure the smooth operation of the partnering relationship, the management team meets at least every two months, alternating between company premises, or when convenient, at the premises of a customer located between Walsall and Weymouth. Both companies' engineers are encouraged to communicate frequently, sometimes daily, on issues of quality and delivery. Because of the working relationships that have developed between each company's employees, most problems are solved quickly, but if they are not, they can be speedily referred upwards to Stewart and Fox.

The major problem facing the partners today is the cyclical downturn in the electronics industry. Stewart is aware that the number of units produced by DEK in 2012 is likely to be well below the levels seen in 2000. This will have an impact on the value of work Power Panels can expect, but the partnering arrangement is seen as a long-term arrangement. Both partners believe that it will help them to weather the storm.

Case Study 26: The Isle of Wight Housing Association – MOUP or Alliance Charter (O45)

The Isle of Wight Housing Association (IoWHA) decided to adopt a partnering approach to the refurbishment of Lukely Court in order to minimise disruption to the residents. The partnering arrangement should ensure that the contract was completed on time, to specification and within budget. IoWHA's Bill Gordon, assisted by DKP, produced a project brief, and four construction companies were invited to tender. Gordon stressed that while cost was a factor in the evaluation, it was by no means the only one. Over 100 different issues were considered, customer care being the most important.

Following the evaluation, Mountjoy was awarded the contract and a project facilitator, Mike Thomas Ltd, appointed. Other companies with which Mountjoy had worked previously and a representative of the residents, Jodie Little, were invited to join the partnering team. The first workshop meeting took place in February 2000, but since most of the participants had little experience of partnering, Thomas began by explaining its basic principles. He encouraged each company to state its objectives for the project. These were then refined into group objectives, and finally, the group's mission statement, the Lukely Court Partnering Charter.

Everyone involved in the project acknowledged that the initial workshop meeting, followed by others at three-monthly intervals, encouraged teamwork and a camaraderie that they had not previously encountered on a construction project. As a consequence, the project was completed on time and within budget, each company's activities were profitable, and most important of all to Gordon, the residents were content.

Most of the major problems were encountered in the early stages of the project, when the group was still coming to terms with the principles of partnering. Traditional methods of supply were sometimes found wanting. Whereas in the past Coastline Windows might have been content to pass on delays from its suppliers, it encountered peer pressure from its partners. Coastline accepted that it would have to rationalise its procurement procedures and adopted a policy of stockpiling the composite doors, which were produced by another supplier.

Rachel Raison of Coastline accepts that while at first she might have found the process of partnering harrowing, Coastline Windows has gained great benefit from the project. Not only was it profitable, but the company has now established close relationships with its partners and she is confident that its enhanced reputation will result in further orders: 'As a company, we are now more customer focused and we feel better for it.'

There were other problems, including site delays caused by the removal firm not moving the residents' personal effects on time. Graham Pengelly of Mountjoy believes that this might have been a less of a problem had the removal firm attended the first workshop, but as communication between the partners improved, there were fewer problems. Those that did arise were resolved quickly and amicably. Each company is now sold on partnering, and they are all looking forward to the next project: 'We became friends and made money. What more can you ask?'

Case Study 27: Consignia, Co-opetition Creating Innovative Products – Exponential Breakthroughs or Innovation in Alliances (O49)

One of Royal Mail's corporate brand colours is red, and it came as no surprise to Consignia's purchasing team when postal workers indicated that they wanted their stormproof coats to include red, rather than the traditional high-visibility colours of orange or yellow.

In March 2000 Consignia's purchasing team, led by Agnes Lyons, issued clear aims and objectives to all their contracted and non-contracted suppliers, detailing a request for the development of a high-visibility red that was compliant to EN471. The waterproof/breathable material had to be lighter in weight than the current fabric and to retain its excellent performance properties. The currently contracted suppliers Porvair and Carrington PF (materials), Feuchter and Sioen, suppliers of cut, make and trim (CMT), together with badge and tape suppliers Quazar and 3M, were invited to participate in the project.

At the first meeting in March 2000 Lyons explained that Consignia expected everyone to work together to achieve success and that all innovative breakthroughs would be shared within the group. No single member would be able to patent the solution it found. This applied to all contracted and non-contracted parties. There was some initial reluctance to proceed under these terms, but after a frank and detailed discussion, each company agreed that it could see the potential benefits of producing the fabric and committed itself to the project. BW Wernafelt, a non-contracted supplier, was the first to achieve the exact shade of red, which set the benchmark for the remaining participants.

It was necessary during the project for Consignia to re-tender the material's specification. To ensure that its requirements and future intentions were fully understood, all documentation subsequently carried a 'development clause' giving clear and precise instructions to suppliers. Following the tender process, WL Gore replaced Carrington PF as one of the contracted suppliers.

It took Porvair and WL Gore eighteen months to perfect the dye, but reduction in the weight of the material quickly followed. The other members of the group were kept informed of developments. This enabled Feuchter and Sioen to make suggestions that would ease the eventual manufacture of the garment. Quazar developed a heat-applied encapsulated logo, which reduced intensive CMT labour and improved the waterproofing properties of the finished garment. The result was the successful production of a lightweight, high-visibility, red stormproof coat fully compliant with EN417 which, following trials throughout the UK, has been used for all such coats issued to postal workers since 2003.

The biggest problem encountered by the partners was fear that a competitor might gain commercial advantage. In the early stages of the project, Lyons and Consignia's Clothing Technical Manager, Graham West, fought hard to encourage trust between the partners. They both agreed that regular progress and review meetings were an essential element in building the trust and co-operation needed to develop this market-leading product, which can now be adapted for a number of markets and other uses.

Case Study 28: British Airways and Astron, Streamlining the Supply Chain – Shared Objectives (S20)

British Airways (BA) used to purchase all its printed products directly, but during the 1990s the airline became increasingly aware that it was time to look for a wider print solution. The objective was to drive efficiencies through a centrally managed solution, and BA approached a number of its key print suppliers to discuss the possibility of forming a partnering relationship. Astron impressed BA with its openness, and especially in the way it was prepared to arrange visits for BA personnel to meet other companies with which Astron had partnering agreements.

As a result of these visits it became clear to BA's management that a partnering agreement with a key supplier could provide the wider print solution for which they were looking. BA subsequently entered into an evaluation process with each of its main suppliers before offering a five-year contract to Astron. According to Linda James, Senior Manager Marketing Procurement, a major factor was the cultural fit between the two companies: 'Our print buying team felt comfortable with Astron's proposal; the company was clearly going in the same direction as BA.' Astron was also strong in its use and development of new technologies, and could clearly give BA good communications with its very best customers.

Over the past ten years BA has developed its partnering relationship with Astron. They have established a joint vision that revolves around the principle of an effective customer/ supplier relationship, where both organisations actively seek opportunities to create added value for the other.

BA's Caroline Zych and Astron's Kay Smith manage the relationship, ensuring that its strategic goals are met. Zych and Smith meet frequently, but every quarter a formal meeting is scheduled where performance is measured and any problems resolved. Smith acts as the dedicated BA account manager and works across the BA organisation to develop products and services that support the business requirement. She is supported by a dedicated BA team back at the Astron head office. Smith and the team collaborate with a diverse range of BA stakeholders around the world. Projects range from the design of prestigious marketing products and the management of high-value tickets through to the international sourcing and inventory management of over 1,500 separate operational items.

BA and Astron have also recognised the importance of a streamlined supply chain, and continually work together to ensure that every aspect of it adds value to BA's business. Mutual collaborations to deliver change have included piloting e-requisition solutions to order routine print items within the UK. Re-engineering products and developing processes and services have cut costs further.

By selecting the company as a long-term partner, BA has enabled Astron to invest in new systems and resources tailored to BA's marketing and operational teams' strategic development. These benefits have then been used by Astron to develop other customers within its portfolio. BA has gained from a number of Astron's innovative ideas and has made considerable financial savings. In the last financial year these amounted to 'double-digit savings on a multi-million-pound contract'.

Case Study 29: British Energy and Eurest, Alliances in Procurement – Senior Executive Support (S25) and Effective Communication (O43)

Faced with an increasingly competitive market, British Energy needed to reduce costs and the procurement team was not exempt. In 2007 its Procurement Director, Brian Rees, embarked on a project to outsource many of British Energy's support services, such as catering, industrial cleaning, lift maintenance and clerical support.

Although Eurest Managed Services (EMS) already undertook some of these services, it faced competition for the new contract. This was to include 23 core services and up to 32 non-core services at each of British Energy's eight nuclear power stations and two administrative centres. Thirteen companies were invited to tender. After an initial sifting process this was reduced to six, and eventually two. Adrian Dyer, Managing Director of EMS, and Rees believe that when it came to the last two, price was not the issue; it was more: 'Can we work with each other? Do we trust each other?' In the final analysis, the fact that British Energy and EMS had been working together for three years proved to be a significant factor.

Since implementation in October 2010, the project has gone extremely well. EMS is on course to meet the target of reducing British Energy's costs by £2 million a year, and in an industry where safety is paramount, all the health and safety objectives are being met. The six-man executive team, which includes both Rees and Dyer, meets every six weeks to ensure that key performance indicators are met. These regular meetings, together with open book accounting, have led to greater trust between the two partners – so much so that, given its greater access to company information, EMS has been able to make further cost saving suggestions to British Energy that will, in turn, help its own business to grow. As Rees said: 'By sitting together, we can make savings.'

But it has not been an easy road to success. Some difficulties have been encountered along the way, particularly in establishing the structure of the partnering relationship. While Dyer and Rees knew what they wanted to achieve, others within their companies, who were used to the more traditional adversarial relationship between customer and supplier, did not. Much time was spent in bringing everyone onside.

The concept of partnering also proved to be too revolutionary for some of the personnel within British Energy, many of whom have been with the company for a long time. Radical change has not been easy to accept. Some of the cost saving measures EMS introduced, like disposable plates in the canteens, were not well received and have had to be discontinued. Both Dyer and Rees acknowledge that it would have been better had more attention been given to selling the relationship to the staff at a much earlier stage in its development. They are now looking closely at implementing training, team building and communication programmes that should help to overcome these problems.

Case Study 30: Alstom and Steelcraft, Power Alliance – Alliances for Cost Reduction (Co7)

Alstom Power UK Ltd manufactures high efficiency gas turbines that are sold worldwide, primarily to the oil and gas industries. Steelcraft, originally part of the Darchem group, is a manufacturer of precision components for the aerospace, nuclear and power engineering industries. The company, which has been a key supplier to Alstom for twenty years, became independent following a management buy-out in 1995.

The initial relationship was limited strictly to that of customer and supplier. Although it was a regular supplier, Steelcraft had to compete for each contract through competitive tendering, but in 1995 the situation changed. With an increasing order book, Alstom required stability in the supply chain and granted Steelcraft preferred supplier status. In the following five years an excellent working relationship developed between the two companies, which resulted in Steelcraft being recognised as one of Alstom's top-performing suppliers.

In the late 1990s, in order to contend with over-capacity in the power market and a strong sterling impacting upon the company's competitiveness, Alstom embarked on a cost reduction programme and the relationship with Steelcraft developed further. The plan was to eliminate over-capacity through outsourcing non-core activities. Alstom was faced with a number of options, including sourcing from low-cost countries, using European sources known to the company or developing relationships with local/UK companies. Concern regarding the complexity of parts being outsourced encouraged the company to look closely at the latter.

In late 1999, Chris Odam, Alstom's Sourcing Director, approached Brian Burgin, Steelcraft's Managing Director, about the possibility of forming a 'partnering relationship'. Since Alstom was responsible for 35% of Steelcraft's turnover of £5 million, Burgin was immediately interested. Several meetings were held, with Alstom openly sharing internal cost data for all the components proposed for outsourcing.

Eventually, terms were agreed that allowed for an immediate reduction of 15% in the price of the components produced by Steelcraft, with a target of a further 15% reduction through both parties working together on design improvements to value-engineer savings. In return, Steelcraft received a five-year contract and financial assistance towards the cost of purchasing raw materials.

The initial plan called for Steelcraft to take over existing employees and equipment within the Alstom facility in Lincoln. This was a cause of some concern for those employees directly affected by the plan, who feared they might lose their acquired rights. To reassure them, Burgin and Odam, assisted by their human resources teams, held regular meetings with both the staff and their trade union representatives.

The arrangements were also a cause of concern for the Steelcraft board, since the company was obliged, under the Transfer of Undertakings (Protection of Employment) legislation, to accept the transfer of the employees as if they remained on Alstom's books. However, the problem soon disappeared because, with ever-increasing order books, Alstom's Operations Director, Brian Stringer, was seeking extra space within the Alstom facility as well as retaining the skilled employees proposed in the Steelcraft transfer. He asked Odam to enquire whether Steelcraft would be prepared to release the Alstom employees scheduled for transfer, and Alstom set about recruiting its own. Faced with this request, Odam and Burgin embarked upon a plan to find suitable premises and 20 skilled workers within the Lincoln area.

While the recruitment and training process was taking its course, purposeful and urgent discussions were taking place within the East Midlands Development Agency (EMDA) and local authorities on the property front. Chris proposed the development of a Technology Park, which could be used by a number of key suppliers to Alstom. A consortium was established, which included Lincolnshire County Council, North Kesteven District Council and the EMDA. Agreement was eventually reached on the development of a three-hectare Technology Park, approximately three miles from Alstom's facility in Lincoln. This facility now houses a purpose-built facility for Steelcraft.

Alstom's public open day was seen as an excellent opportunity to kick-start the recruitment process. Advertisements were placed in the local press inviting interested parties to meet Brian Burgin and his Steelcraft team during. It was a great success, and soon Burgin had all the staff he required. Within weeks, Steelcraft employees were to be found working within the Alstom factory. To ensure quality was maintained and to facilitate integration, Alstom provided a senior engineer to help with the training programme.

Both Burgin and Odam agree that the secret of the partnering relationship's success has been the level of trust between the two companies and their willingness to share problems and to find solutions to those problems. The two meet regularly, at least once a month, and their respective supervisors are encouraged to work closely together to find rapid solutions to any problems that might occur.

Performance indicators are reviewed at regular intervals, and open book accounting is accepted as a matter of course. Burgin acknowledged that when first approached, some of his fellow directors were concerned about the element of risk involved in accepting a 15% reduction in prices, but, as he said: 'To succeed in business, you have to take risks. In return we received a five-year contract from Alstom. Partnering has enabled us to strengthen the bond and to maintain continuity with a valued customer.'

Case Study 31: Sydney Harbour Bridge – Public Sector

The construction of a tunnel to capture and store periodic overflows of storm water and sewage prior to treatment and final discharge to the ocean was a key component of a New South Wales (NSW) Government initiative to clean up the harbours, bays, rivers and beaches of the state. The announcement that the 2000 Summer Olympics would be held in Sydney created an imperative to find and implement a solution within three years. The project was awarded in January 1998, and construction commenced in mid-1998.

The project was deemed infeasible for satisfactory completion within the short timescale using a conventional approach. The Board of Directors of Sydney Water Corporation (SWC) sanctioned an alliance approach based upon the belief that this innovative arrangement would achieve its goals – in particular meeting the deadline imposed by the Olympics – in the most efficient manner. It chose as partners Transfield, Connell Wagner and Montgomery Watson.

The alliance model was chosen because it would create a 'no-blame', 'best for project' culture. It was intended to increase co-operation between the partners, to reduce disputes and to allow a sharing of most of the benefits or costs that might accrue during the project.

The basis of the alliance was a formal agreement which created a single integrated team involving all parties by aligning objectives and taking a win–win integrated team approach to any issues, working though problems and opportunities as they arise, based on a 'best for project' approach. The agreement contained a 'no dispute' clause which ensures the interdependence of the alliance partners is maintained by removing the right to litigation except in the case of 'wilful default'.

The alliance was based on variable cost arrangements that allowed important risks (for example, design and construction) to be pooled or shared.

Three project teams, with specific roles and responsibilities, were involved in co-ordinating the alliance:

1. **Integrated Project Team (IPT)** – An integrated team with all alliance partners represented and headed by the project manager, it was responsible for project delivery.
2. **Alliance Implementation Team (AIT)** – This team managed and maintained the alliance process and comprised the departmental managers in the IPT.
3. **Project Alliance Leadership Team (PALT)** – This team comprised senior executives from the four alliance partners and had the prime responsibility for the creation and direction of a high-performance alliance culture. It also monitored the performance of the IPT and provided guidance and support to the AIT.

The Alliance was based on written principles accessible to all members of staff from senior management to the workface:

- Act in a way that is best for the project.
- Build a champion team which is integrated across all disciplines and organisations.
- Commit to a no-blame culture.
- Use breakthroughs to achieve exceptional results in all project objectives.
- Commit corporately and individually to openness, integrity, trust, co-operation, mutual support and respect, flexibility, honesty and loyalty to the project.
- Outstanding results provide outstanding rewards.

- Deal with and resolve all issues within the alliance.
- Spread the alliance culture to all stakeholders.

The main problems that arose reflected a lack of understanding by the client (the Government of New South Wales) of the nature and implications inherent in setting up and managing an alliance relationship, in particular:

- **Project boundaries** – The SWC did not clearly identify at the start the boundaries between itself and the alliance. This led to various difficulties and misunderstandings. For example, early in the project, SWC's project director was required to perform two arguably conflicting roles – one as a senior client representative and the other as a member of the PALT. Later this arrangement changed, with a SWC general manager taking over the former role allowing the project director to stand back and take a strategic overview.

- **Management and direction** – Since the project was first developed as a concept in early 1997, there had been considerable personnel changes: the SWC had eight directors appointed, and six directors, three managing directors, and one acting managing director retire. Furthermore, the SWC project directors reported to at least five different general managers. All these changes resulted in the scheme becoming the 'orphan' project of SWC – there was therefore no clear 'ownership' of the project for some time.

- **Processes** – There does not always appear to have been a consistent process by which the board considered, monitored and decided on all relevant issues – while some issues were advised to the board for information or decision, on other occasions significant decisions were taken without any reference to the board.

- **Key performance indicators** – A key feature of the alliance was the sharing of a reward pool for performance in excess of expectations. The reward was determined and distributed through five key performance indicators covering cost, time, environment, safety and community margins. While the theory supporting these indicators was developed at the start of the alliance, the defining of specific criteria required in order to apply these key performance indicators was delayed.

The alliance approach lends itself to circumstances where there are legitimate time constraints and where the project is so unusual as to cause uncertainty about the type or extent of risks that might arise. It is designed to nurture a culture that focuses on delivering outcomes and ensuring that all issues are resolved within the alliance. This approach was successful as, from the outset, the team focused on cost and scope of work and collectively solved problems and made decisions. Since the contract was signed there had not been a contract dispute, discussion or claim from any of the parties. Instead, time was spent discussing how to improve the project. This enthusiasm for innovation extended to all 400 team members.

The project also had secondary benefits for alliance members – Transfield, Montgomery Watson and Connell Wagner have put in and won combined bids for other water industry design and construction jobs since that original collaboration.

Case Study 32: Reebok UK and Tibbett & Britten – Improving Distribution in the Supply Chain

Until 1994 Reebok UK carried out its own distribution within the UK. By 1994 it was apparent that the volume of distribution and the expectations of customers exceeded Reebok's capacity to meet those demands and expectations. Reebok decided to outsource the fastest-growing element. Tibbett & Britten Group plc (T&B) was selected as the outsource distribution supplier. T&B had the necessary capacity and professional skills to fulfil Reebok's requirements.

The initial project was so successful that the alliance was extended, in incremental steps, to cover the outsourcing of all Reebok's distribution operations, not only in the UK, but extending to Benelux (the trading co-operation between Belgium, the Netherlands and Luxembourg) and Ireland by early 2001.

Since the mid-1990s the sports and fitness trading situation in the High Street has undergone enormous changes. Many small independent retailers have disappeared, unable to compete with emerging retail giants. Those who remain demand higher standards, more added-value services, and more flexibility and responsiveness from their suppliers. Only those sports brands suppliers willing and able to absorb and respond to these changes can prosper.

Reebok identified service excellence as a valuable differentiator in this challenging and competitive trading environment. It sought a distribution specialist which shared its cultural outlook and determination to succeed. It looked for a partner which had the operational capacity and infrastructure to support challenging business growth, had earned the respect of its competitive peers and provided a route to best practice.

This alliance led to a process of continuous performance improvement that, over the first five years of its life, allowed Reebok to greatly enhance its market share, while at the same time reducing unit operating expenses by as much as 35%.

Complete trust between the partners, with open book accounting, has been established as a prerequisite. T&B has been totally integrated within Reebok's supply chain, customer operations, forecasting and activity processes. Other characteristics are even more profound:

- The alliance is continuous; there is no termination or renewal date.
- T&B participates in Reebok's annual strategic planning process.
- T&B sets its own budgets, targets and key performance indicators.
- T&B determines capital investment programmes.
- T&B handles some commercially sensitive roles, such as managing the samples process and product quality control.

Reebok has reduced the number of transportation suppliers, with the consequent economies of scale this produces. This has, in turn, led to greater efficiency in customer services, as well as in the utilisation of assets and resources.

Enhanced planning has allowed detailed analysis of customer needs, coupled with a three-month rolling forecast and risk assessment, providing maximum flexibility in replenishment.

Since 1999 the distribution centres have managed continuous improvement based on the European Foundation for Quality Management business excellence model.

Assessment centres are utilised to fill all T&B positions. All staff are on performance reviews, with targeted personal development programmes. Structured training and development is conducted at all levels, with an emphasis on high performance. Pay is set within the upper quartile.

The alliance partners review performance monthly, based on only six key performance indicators, covering service, cost and inventory control. Service to the top 15 retail accounts, however, is subject to individual scrutiny.

The benefits of continuity of the relationship between key personnel is fully recognised. Allan Kenny, Reebok's Logistics Director, and Frank Hawes, T&B's Operations Director, have worked together since the start of the project. They recognise that stability and robustness of service operations is important in a constantly evolving environment.

They have learned to respond flexibly to rapidly changing requirements. Because Reebok is an exceptionally customer-focused business, it needs to respond to marketplace needs. There is a constant learning process. Performance took a dip in 1999 when there were problems with inventory control; this had been under-resourced. The problem was addressed, and this is now a major strength and basis for service performance.

Both parties to the alliance recognise that they could not have achieved these results on their own. The strength of the alliance has brought an enormous commitment to people and process management, which has bred confidence throughout the organisations.

Case Study 33: South West Water – Bringing Capital Projects Under Control

In 1995 John Bennett, then Capital Investment General Manager at South West Water, was concerned that most of his company's capital projects were exceeding their planned budget by considerable margins. This was leading to valuable time and resources being used to process claims and counter-claims with contractors. He was convinced that there had to be a better way, and as a result South West Water investigated the potential of a partnering approach to project delivery.

A selection process for partners was implemented, and in the following two years South West Water embarked on six trial projects, each on an individual basis. While the new system produced further efficiency savings and a reduction in contract claims, it was still far from perfect. One project overran by £2 million, and the subsequent review discovered that this had been because each partner had left the initial planning meeting with different views on the project's priorities – and in one case, different specifications. However, it was felt these projects were relatively successful and worthy of extension. From 1997 the partnering relationships were further developed to include linked projects – one team accepting responsibility for two or three separate projects.

Everyone acknowledged that partnering had led to significant improvements in performance, and subsequently they agreed to Bennett's suggestion that they further refine the partnering arrangements for the 2000-2005 capital programme. Bennett's aim was to reduce the number of partners working with South West Water to two civil contractors, two process engineers and four design engineers.

To assist him in the evaluation process following initial selection, he produced a series of exercises designed to establish each company's strengths and weaknesses. He was keen to find companies that had excellent communication between their directors and project managers, and especially those that showed a willingness to become team players. (Technical capability and project experience had already been taken into consideration.)

Members of Bennett's team observed the exercises and produced appraisals of each company's performance. South West Water then entered into individual discussions with the successful companies on margins, overheads and planned efficiency savings as the final stage in the selection process.

Once these had been agreed, the following companies were invited to a workshop to discuss the partnering arrangements for the forthcoming capital plan and dates for delivery: Faber Maunsell, Babtie, Gleeson Construction, Purac, Pell Frischmann Water, Hyder Consulting, Biwater Treatment and Alfred McAlpine Civil Engineering. At this meeting they formed the programme teams and, as a team, agreed on the best method for delivering the capital programme's objectives.

It was decided to split South West Water's geographical area into two sections, East and West. This was to encourage performance comparators and healthy competition between teams. South West Water brokered the marriage of delivery partners, but to ensure that each team would receive an equal amount of work (approximately £80 million), the division was based on a financial rather than a geographical boundary. A steering group was established to define the partnering agreements. Key performance indicators, incentive payment processes and dispute resolution procedures were agreed, and each partner's role was clearly defined. The group took a holistic view across both programmes and agreed to meet every six months to review progress.

To reflect the nature of the project, no lawyers were involved in the drafting of the final agreement because the partners felt that they did not wish to be tied down by a legal document. The steering group is able to change the partnering agreement as and when required. Under the terms of the agreement, if a contract is completed ahead of schedule and under budget, the cost savings are shared between South West Water and the partner(s).

Each contractor/engineer has gained from having a guaranteed five-year contract and has received financial benefit from those projects completed with cost savings. The main benefit to South West Water has been a considerable saving of time and money in resolving outstanding claims, as there are no claims at all. As John Bennett said: 'Partnering has enabled South West Water to reduce its contingency liability for the resolution of claims from £21 million in 1995 to zero in March 2002.' But the partners recognise that further refinements can be made, and to improve communication between them, they are in the process of establishing a virtual company which will enable them to act as one entity. This will come into force for the next three years, and should ensure continuity when key personnel move on, as they inevitably will.

15 *Developing Alliance Programmes*

There are broadly three stages to organisational alliance maturity: opportunistic, systematic and endemic. These three stages are almost always sequential, but there are certain circumstances in which some companies choose not to progress to the next stage, although there are no known instances of companies using a step-through strategy by missing out a stage. We will consider the three stages in order.

Stage I: Opportunistic

Typically, organisations in this stage use partnerships tactically (most often to bid for business which they could not win alone or to force suppliers to collaborate for extra value in the supply chain). Actions and initiatives in this stage are not combined, and projects are driven by internal champions. Success is measured by commercial return or deals, and little if any thought is given to the long-term health of the relationships involved.

Stage II: Systematic

Organisations which enter this stage have recognised the effort they are putting into multiple instances of partnering and have further recognised the value of systematising their efforts. Typical actions include establishing a central strategic alliances planning team, developing common governance procedures, joining external alliance associations, developing common methodologies and toolsets for internal use, and seeking out external best practices. This stage appears to be the longest, includes the greatest number of alliances examined, and appears to be the most common for organisations today.

Stage III: Endemic

This stage includes world-class partnering organisations which have progressed through Stages I and II and have now implanted partnering as the very means by which they do business. In this stage, partnering is not seen as a management fad, but rather as 'the way we do business around here'. Typical actions in this stage are breaking apart corporate partnering teams and repositioning their functions within line management, making collaboration a key skill which is measured in individual appraisal processes, and utilising partnering as a key competitive strategy in multiple functions (for example, sales, procurement, supply chain management, manufacturing, and research and development).

Relationships Examined

Figure 15.1 shows a snapshot of the ABP Database illustrating the number of alliances by the alliance lifecycle stage that they were in when examined (snapshot is April 2014).

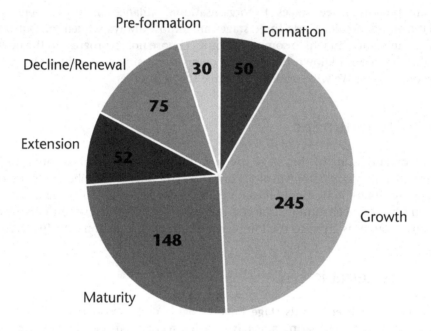

Figure 15.1 Benchmarked companies by stage of organisational alliance maturity

Common Success Factors

Our research into strategic alliances found that certain factors recurred time and again in successful collaborative relationships (see Chapter 1). These factors reappeared more frequently than could be explained by coincidence alone. We noted a number of points of interest.

While not all the factors needed to be in place for a successful relationship, it was observed that the more factors that were present, the more successful the relationship.

Research from Booz Allen Hamilton suggests that the improvement factor can be as much as 700%.

The common success factors appeared to remain consistent over time. Research conducted by Andersen Consulting in 1999 identified 'trust' as a key CSF in strategic alliances, research conducted by Alliance Best Practice in March 2014 once again identified trust as one of the key components in successful alliance relationships. The research also found that the CSFs were not sector-specific: they are equally applicable in all sectors.

Finally, it appears that the incidence and importance of the common success factors changes from stage to stage. Each stage comes with its own challenges and myths, which this chapter explores, but the evidence strongly suggests that paying particular attention to the common success factors accelerates effective progress through each stage.

Stage Drivers

It appears that most organisations choose to enter into alliances for one or more of these reasons:

- **to develop new business** – usually by pitching for a piece of work they would not be able to secure alone;
- **to reduce costs** – many organisations have already squeezed all the cost reductions they can from their supply chain, and many are now turning to collaboration with their suppliers to develop more innovative cost-saving models based on the concept of joint value; partnering appears to be the tool of choice to achieve this;
- **to develop new products and services** – innovation has become an increasingly important business strategy as companies recognise that a growing amount of their business is coming from recently released products and services; this in turn is placing an increasing strain on R&D departments to produce new ideas more quickly; consequently, they are turning to external alliances and collaborations to ease this burden.

Challenges in Stage I

BUILDING BRICKS WITH NO STRAW

This is the syndrome of expecting alliance professionals to be able to develop and manage successful alliance relationships with no support. It was common in our research to find individuals at multiple levels up to and including vice presidents and country managers who were expected to produce outstanding results with no training, partner support systems, methodologies, templates, tools and so on.

The reality is that no matter how good or 'alliance-savvy' an individual might be, he will benefit from being able to rely on an appropriate support infrastructure provided by the organisation.

CONFUSING TERMINOLOGY

In many situations during our research we saw individuals adopting positions and attitudes that were detrimental to the relationship simply because they misunderstood what individuals in their partner organisations meant by key phrases and terminology. This trivial oversight is responsible for massive lost value and time in many strategic alliances.

PROBLEMS IDENTIFYING KEY STAKEHOLDERS

It is amazing how much time it takes organisations to interact successfully with each other. Even in a situation where both/all are fully committed to interaction, the apparently simple process of identifying the right person to speak to is fraught with considerable difficulties which necessarily slow down relationship development.

APPOINTING THE WRONG PERSON TO THE ALLIANCE ROLE

A closely allied problem to the one above involves appointing the wrong type of personality to an alliance role. There is no doubt that some people find it easier to and more natural to act in a collaborative manner than others, so many organisations are wasting a great deal of time and effort asking the wrong types of people to act as alliance managers.

One of the most common instances of this is the appointment of large account salesmen in the high-tech sector to become alliance managers. What they typically find is that the very skills, attitudes and beliefs that made them a success as salesmen are actually a barrier to their becoming successful alliance managers.

SHORT-TERM THINKING

The strategic alliance model is a long-term business model, and while it can produce results quickly, it is also somewhat unreasonable to ask, 'How will this strategic alliance affect my sales this month?'

Challenges in Stage II

The essence of the challenge in Stage II is effective systematisation. There are various internal and external factors at play here, but in addition there are considerable barriers to effective progress.

PARTNERING QUICKLY AND EFFECTIVELY

Organisations are beginning to understand a lot more about each other's ways of working, and this is being recognised as very valuable. The ability of organisations to engage with each other to discover both the core and the context is recognised as a key competitive weapon, and one that leads to an acceleration in the growth of business value . However, the reality of aligning two large organisations is extremely complex and fraught with difficulty. Often a local office doesn't know that any relationship exists at the corporate level.

INVESTMENT REUSE

Organisations increasingly want to reuse the investments they have made in opportunistic deal making initiatives with other organisations. These days, understanding organisations is costly and time-consuming, and many organisations are looking to move effectively and speedily from Stage I to Stage II. The problem is that many of deals agreed in Stage I are designed for a particular situation, and do not lend themselves easily to the concept of methodologies and processes.

PRESSURE TO AUDIT PARTNERING PROCESSES

CEOs worldwide are increasingly under pressure from such aspects as the US Sarbanes-Oxley Act and the fallout from Enron and other such high-profile audit failures, and need to convince both internal and external stakeholders that they have a repeatable and auditable process for this new business model. What they do not have when they enter Stage II is clear and concise language to describe the new business model in terms that shareholders can easily grasp. Consequently, they fall back on grandiose announcements to the press and industry analysts that sound good in theory but are hollow in execution.

RISK MANAGEMENT

Organisations don't want to be held to ransom by individuals who manage very valuable relationships. In the past, when a key person left a relationship, business results would suffer as an individual from the partner had to get to know another key individual replacement. Now systematisation is reducing the dependence on individuals and bringing with it a reduction of business risk which can be measured. However, there is still considerable resistance from some old-style key relationship managers who see their organisational influence and power being eroded by the rigour of the new operating protocols.

COMPARING LIKE WITH LIKE

Systematisation also allows for consistency in comparing one alliance relationship with another, and thus leads to the ability to develop in-house best practice programmes as one business unit learns from another (but see also the 'Damaging Alliance Myths' chapter in this book, in which very many professionals believe it is pointless to compare relationships because 'all alliances are unique').

IT COSTS LESS TO WORK TO A SYSTEM

Invariably, organisations which have considered this question recognise its implicit truth: it costs less in terms of time, money and effort (often all three are linked) to follow a process that has already been defined than it does to invent a new one. The corollary is also true: organisations that use best practices make more money.

CEOS ARE TIRED OF HYPE

Chief executives these days are growing increasingly tired of the hype that surrounds partnering and want to see palpable evidence of its success rather than 'motherhood and apple pie' statements of anticipated value. This attitude is increasingly driving a systematic and coherent approach to alliances. The challenge for most CEOs and CFOs is that there are very few coherent balanced scorecards for alliances. In addition, the tasks of tracking influenced extra revenue or influenced cost savings can be very complex indeed – so complex, in fact, that many just give up and count value twice (for example, the so-called 'double bubble' counting in high-tech companies).

MANAGING MULTIPLE ALLIANCES

One of the biggest problems for many organisations moving from Stage I to Stage II thinking concerns alliance portfolio management. This is because a successful solution involves so many different aspects, a lot of which are beyond individual control: alliance strategy, senior executive support, organisational maturity, partner choice and balance, and so on.

Many organisations solve this problem pragmatically by 'taking the problem offline' – allocating it to a newly formed alliance centre of excellence, which can be either real or virtual. The alliance centre of excellence performs the strategic, integration, standards setting and balancing tasks essential to managing an alliance portfolio successfully. The drawback is that sometimes the centre of excellence becomes isolated from the operational units and is seen as a 'corporate ivory tower', adding no real value, but dictating rules that pose barriers for local alliance practitioners.

LACK OF CONTROL

There is no doubt that some individuals and organisations can tolerate lack of control more easily than others. By its nature a balanced collaboration will have joint control or sometimes shared control between the parties, depending on the situation and context. This aspect of deriving value from a collaborative model is implicit in its nature, and the leading-edge organisations are now experimenting with alliance manager assessment centres which identify those personalities that will feel most at home (and will therefore perform better) in these situations.

ALLIANCE TIERING

The categorisation of alliances needs to be about more than just money. Here are some examples of categories that can be applied:

- The forecast value to your organisation of a strategic partner will exceed $X million over the next five years, either through revenue contribution, cost savings, or a combination of both.
- The relationship content is central to your organisation's group strategy.
- There is a strong board-level focus on the relationship from both companies.

- The relationship has the potential to have a significant impact on your organisation's growth.
- The partner has an industry leadership (or sector leadership) reputation.
- The partner has shown itself capable of successful, multi-faceted relationships across many of your organisation's lines of business.
- The partner appoints a board-level champion for the relationship.
- The partner is prepared to share critical strategic thinking with your organisation.

Challenges in Stage III

TECHNICAL EXCELLENCE IS NOT PARTNERING EXCELLENCE

This problem showed up time and again in high-tech collaborations (but was certainly not restricted to this sector). The problem was that organisations and individuals believed that partners would work with them simply because their products and/or services were of high quality. These individuals misunderstood the nature of alliances in the twenty-first century.

It is true that if an organisation does not have products and services which are fit for purpose, then its chances of partnering success are slim. However, the converse also holds true, and is reflected in the Database: just because an organisation has good products and services does not necessarily make it a good candidate for partnership.

This problem was commonly seen in the software sector, where the opening statement from an alliance executive was often: 'We make good software, so how many licences do you want to sell on?' This is hardly collaborative language, and is actually offputting for the partner as it perceives itself as being downgraded to the role of a reseller of the other's services and products.

EMBEDDING COLLABORATIVE THINKING IN AN ORGANISATION

Just as alliance programme management is the major problem when moving from Stage I to Stage II, embedding collaborative thinking and behaviours is the main challenge facing advanced Stage II companies.

The essence of the problem appears to be that organisations do not put appropriate structures in place to appropriately reward the behaviour they are seeking. The consequence is that lip service is paid to collaborative aspirations while the programmes themselves become enshrined in meaningless PR documents which are not supported by local action.

COLLABORATIVE NEGOTIATION

Negotiation in alliances is not the same as negotiation in other aspects of business life. The difference lies in the distinction between a collaborative and an adversarial approach. In an alliance compromise is failure, while in most normal commercial negotiations compromise is seen as the natural end point achieved in balanced negotiations. For a further and deeper discussion of these distinctions, see the Harvard Negotiation Project, *Difficult Conversations*.[1]

---

1   Douglas Stone, Bruce Patton and Sheila Heen, *Difficult Conversations*, London: Viking/Penguin, 1999.

Conclusions

Our research suggests a number of powerful conclusions that corporate strategists in all business sectors would do well to consider:

Strategic alliances are steadily growing in popularity as organisations discover that they can't just go it alone. This appears to be the case for the very largest corporations (for example, Microsoft, IBM, GE and Eli Lilly) as well as the smallest SMEs.

As the desire to enter partnerships increases, many organisations are now looking to systematise the way they conduct their partnering efforts. Those that do so successfully (using known best practices) enjoy a critical competitive advantage over those that develop in-house programmes.

We can identify three stages of organisational alliance maturity:

- Stage I – opportunistic;
- Stage II – systematic;
- Stage III – endemic.

These stages appear to be sequential, and there are no instances in our research of companies missing out any of these stages. Managing the efficient passage from one stage to another is a considerable challenge since it relies on a complex set of interrelated common success factors which change in emphasis depending on the stage of development.

Strategic alliances remain complex business models to get right, but certain recurring factors are evidently crucial in successful endeavours. There are over 52 of them in five critical dimensions: Commercial, Technical, Strategic, Cultural and Operational. While success in every regard is unlikely, the more attention organisations pay to these factors, the better their results.

To grow their businesses quickly and effectively, CEOs are turning to a third-generation model of business growth: that of ally in the build/buy/ally combination. Strategic alliances help them to achieve this more quickly, with less risk.

There are a number of myths regarding strategic alliances which are not borne out by the research evidence. Some of these myths can be very damaging in developing partnering programmes.

Despite the evidence of best practice, there are quite considerable challenges involved in the successful execution of strategic alliances. Those organisations that develop strategic alliances appear to learn from their experiences and conduct them better as the number increases.

16 *Alliance Standards and Schemes*

There are now a number of alliance standards being developed, both domestically and internationally. Three of the better-known of these standards have been developed and are managed by the Association of Strategic Alliance Professionals, the British Collaborative Relationships Standard (BS 11000) managed by the British Standards Institute (BSI), and The Partnering Initiative (TPI) managed by the International Business Leaders Forum (IBLF). Details of each of these schemes can be found below.

Association of Strategic Alliance Professionals: Certification Programme

The ASAP alliance management certification programme offers members the opportunity to demonstrate their mastery of core alliance skills and the management of all forms of collaborative business relationships. The programme features two levels of certification:

1. **Certification of Achievement – Alliance Management (CA-AM)** – the basic level of certification for up-and-coming alliance professionals;
2. **Certified Strategic Alliance Professional (CSAP)** – the advanced level of certification for seasoned practitioners with a command of the full alliance lifecycle from inception to termination.

Certification has proven valuable for both individuals and the organisations for which they work. Successful alliance managers need to have in-depth knowledge of a wide range of skills, and through certification, they can demonstrate their knowledge of these skills.

In addition, certification represents a level of professional achievement. Becoming certified demonstrates a commitment to the profession. Just as important, Certified Strategic Alliance Professionals are recognised leaders and serve as role models within the alliance management profession.

ASAP's certifications are increasingly recognised as the standard for alliance managers. The certification process examines competence in three critical areas, as shown in Table 16.1.

Table 16.1 ASAP alliance management competencies

Context skills	Core skills	Company skills
Communications skills	Creating strategic alignment	Company strategic imperatives
Conflict resolution	Value proposition development	Industry and technical drivers
Negotiation skills		
Financial management	Governance	Organisational and functional structure
Change management	Alliance metrics setting	
Project management	Operating principles	Company governance
Team management	Joint business planning	Company partnering culture
Leadership through influence	Alliance negotiations	
Problem solving and decision making	Organisational alignment	
	Relationship management	
	Transition	
	Cultural considerations	

ASAP's *Professional Development Guide* provides a definitive compilation of job descriptions and requisite skills and competencies associated with each stage of an alliance professional's career in any industry. If you are an alliance management professional, explore the *Professional Development Guide* to find out whether your capabilities match your title and what you need to learn to advance to the next level. Hiring managers need to cross-reference their alliance management position summaries with the *Professional Development Guide*'s outlines for manager, senior manager, director and vice president-level alliance management positions to ensure the discipline's most current theories, tools, and methodologies are being applied to their partnerships.[1]

Institute for Collaborative Working: BS 11000

The Institute for Collaborative Working (ICW; formerly Partnership Sourcing Ltd) was established in 1990 as a joint initiative between the Department of Trade & Industry (DTI; now the Department for Business Innovation and Skills) and the Confederation of British Industry (CBI). It is totally self-financing, operating as a not-for-profit organisation. The ICW's continuing role is to help organisations, large and small, in both the public and private sectors, to build and develop effective competitive business relationships based upon a collaborative approach.

BACKGROUND TO BS 11000

The journey to BS 11000 began in 2004, when the ICW started to gather together its knowledge to establish a route map for collaborative working, which resulted in the launch of CRAFT, a unique and integrated approach to building and sustaining more effective

---

1   The *Professional Development Guide* can be downloaded from www.strategic-alliances.org/professional-development-guide/ (accessed 8 April 2014).

business relationships. This coincided with a research project, 'Future Connections', highlighting the growth and demand for more complex business operating models moving towards 2020.

Against this backdrop, the ICW was pleased to engage with the BSI to develop a national British standard, initially published as PAS 11000 (2006). The ICW continued its association with the BSI to create a certification scheme, piloted successfully in 2009, then chairing the BSI committee to migrate to BS 11000 whose report was published in 2010.[2]

BENEFITS OF WORKING WITH BS 11000

Collaborative business relationships have been shown to deliver a wide range of benefits, which enhance competitiveness and performance while adding value to organisations of all sizes. The publication of the BS 11000 is a landmark as it is the first national standard in the world. It does not represent a one-size-fits-all solution, but provides a consistent framework which can be scaled and adapted to meet particular business needs.

Collaboration between organisations may take many forms, from loose tactical approaches to longer-term alliances or joint ventures. BS 11000 does not enforce a single rigid approach, and recognises that every relationship has its own unique considerations while harnessing a range of benefits. For those organisations with well-established processes the framework provides a common language that can aid engagement, while for those starting out, the framework creates a road map for the journey.

THE EIGHT-STAGE FRAMEWORK

1. Awareness

Relating effectively with external organisations can be challenging, and can be constrained by internal barriers. It is crucial to ensure that efforts are focused on those relationships where collaboration will deliver real value.

2. Knowledge

Creating effective collaboration requires strategies that are focused on the business objectives and recognise the risks associated with greater integration, including knowledge management and business continuity, underpinned by an exit strategy to identify key concerns.

3. Internal assessment

Understanding the strength and weaknesses of your own organisation is essential if collaboration is to be successful. This includes processes, skills and experience compatible with the desired outcomes.

---

2   http://www.bs11000.com/.

4. Partner selection

Finding the right partner is also essential, but is frequently is based on assumptions that long-standing traditional relationships can simply be adapted. Often this is not the case, so it is important to understand the profiles of the partners you are looking for and how you will evaluate their capabilities to collaborate.

5. Working together

Establishing joint governance for collaborative programmes and integrating this with effective contracting arrangements requires careful attention, taking into consideration the joint objectives and those of the individual partners, and ensuring that the incentives and measurement will support collaborative behaviours.

6. Value creation

The key to maintaining a strong relationship is to ensure that it remains current and drives innovation to bring additional value to the partners through joint continual improvement programmes.

7. Staying together

Joint management is crucial if relationships are to mature and support staff and the business environment. Effective performance and behaviours should be monitored, along with issues and disputes, which will be inevitable, but can strengthen relationships if handled effectively.

8. Exit strategy

Maintaining a joint exit strategy is important to keep the partners focused. At the same time, having clear rules for disengagement will frequently improve engagement throughout the life of the relationship and into the future.

The standards lifecycle model is structured into three phases (Strategic, Engagement and Management) with the objective of creating a robust platform to maximise the benefits of collaborative working by supporting the culture and behaviours necessary to optimise integration.

Case Study 34: Network Rail UK – the Value of BS 11000

'BS 11000 gives us the strategic framework to develop, with our key suppliers, the policies and processes, the culture and behaviours required to establish successful collaborative relations and to drive continual improvement. Maintaining collaborative business relations can only lead to benefits for Network Rail and its suppliers, for the rail industry and for Britain.'
Simon Kirby, Managing Director, Network Rail Infrastructure Projects

Why Certification?

Network Rail is the first organisation within the rail sector to implement and gain certification to the Collaborative Business Relationships standard, BS 11000. The company adopted the standard as a framework for developing the policies and processes, culture and behaviours required to drive continual improvement with key suppliers.

One of the core incentives for the adoption of the standard was Sir Roy McNulty's *Rail Value for Money* study, published in May 2011, which identified greater collaboration between organisations in the industry as one of the means for delivering greater value for passengers and tax payers (see Table 16.2).

Table 16.2   Needs/benefits analysis of BS 11000

Customer needs	Customer benefits
Respond to the rail industry challenge to deliver greater value for money	Contracts and businesses aligned with BS 11000, resulting in a new environment for doing business and reducing costs
Redefine the partnering approach with the supply chain to improve levels of performance, introduce greater levels of innovation and deliver cost efficiencies	Simplified contractual relationships using best practice for collaboration, leading to increased competency and a common language across the supply base
Deliver a significant and growing capital works programme in a safer, quicker and more efficient manner, providing better value for money for the fare-paying passenger and the tax payer	Creation of a blueprint for moving forward through step-by-step projects – BS 11000 encourages an ongoing mentality, a 'lifecycle standard' in which processes continue to evolve

Implementation

In order to identify the corporate changes required to enable the principles of BS 11000 to be put into practice, Network Rail recruited the services of BSI and the ICW, one of the members of BSI's Associate Consultant Programme. The project began with an initial gap analysis workshop to compare the requirements of the standard with existing processes in place. This exposed the corporate changes that needed to be addressed, which in turn generated the Relationship Management Plan (RMP).

Different plans were developed for four different pilot projects since they were at varying stages of development. Since the suppliers had unique needs and aspirations, plans had to be developed for each supplier, and in turn, the suppliers had their own RMPs. One of the fundamental principles behind the collaborative initiative is for clients and suppliers to understand each other's aspirations at a corporate level.

Implementation was not without challenges. The major one was convincing the rail industry that 'Network Rail meant it' as a result of a historical legacy of the rail industry being considered 'uncollaborative'. Where collaboration had previously existed within the industry, it was considered ad hoc and deployed in the wrong places. The organisation also had a major education task to demonstrate to the industry that the standard would in fact help deliver tangible business benefits.

Network Rail has since been working with the Railway Industry Association as well as the BSI and the ICW to provide briefings to the company's supply chain about BS 11000 and the benefits of this approach.

A number of Network Rail's strategic partners are currently engaged with BSI in the implementation and assessment phases of the standard, offering opportunities for best practices to be shared throughout the industry.

The main focus of Network Rail's supply chain arrangements is currently on the use of the alliance, delivery partner and engaging models, which are represented across the following four pilot projects: Crossrail south-east section project (partner Balfour Beatty Rail Ltd); Finsbury Park to Alexandra Palace capacity improvement (partner Balfour Beatty Rail Ltd); Hitchin grade separation (partner HOCHTIEF (UK) Construction Ltd), and Reading station civil engineering works (partner BAM Nuttall Ltd). A fifth project, the Edinburgh to Glasgow Improvement Programme, has now been added to the pilot schemes.

Benefits

Neill Carruthers, Head of Contracting Strategy, Infrastructure Products at Network Rail, said: 'Perhaps the single biggest benefit of working to BS 11000 that Network Rail has realised is the requirement for greater structure and process in the management of the relationship. The requirement to focus on continual improvement and demonstrating value through the collaboration rather than only meeting the project outputs has helped to create a focus on the effectiveness of the relationship for our project teams and its overall contribution to success.'

Jeremy Candfield, Director General of the Railway Industry Association (RIA), which represents the rail supply industry, said: 'Getting supply chain relationships right is fundamental to achieving a more efficient railway. RIA has long been supportive of greater collaboration and transformed supply chain behaviours, and there is a natural fit between BS 11000 and our own Value Improvement Programme initiative in reaching those goals.'

The Future

Network Rail's BS 11000 programme is already being expanded, and other major projects will be added to the initial pilot portfolio. The capital expenditure on these additional projects will increase the overall value of projects working under BS 11000 to almost £3 billion. The next phase of the process will see further training and development within Network Rail as the company investigates the scope for the adoption of BS 11000 within other areas of the business. Kerry Garratt, Product Marketing Manager at BSI, said: 'We are delighted that Network Rail has implemented BS 11000 so successfully and that the standard is providing them with a framework to enhance and improve the structure and processes within their relationships. We believe the standard is being adopted throughout industry because of the benefits that any organisation can realise through the improved management of their business partnerships.'[3]

---

3   More information about BS 11000 can be found at www.bsigroup.co.uk/en-GB/bs-11000-collaborative-business-relationships/ (accessed 8 April 2014).

International Business Leaders Forum: The Partnering Initiative

WHAT IS THE PARTNERING INITIATIVE?

As a not-for-profit organisation, TPI promotes ongoing learning in all aspects of partnering theory and practice, generating a wide range of free source materials. TPI believes that partnering is essential in creating a sustainable world. TPI has over twenty years' experience working at the cutting edge of global partnering needs and emerging trends, and a track record of continuously expanding the theory and improving the practice of cross-sector collaborations. TPI's network comprises seasoned partnership practitioners from across the globe, ensuring a broad range of cultural, industry and sector experience as well as an in-depth understanding of how partnerships function in practice.

TPI understands that one size does not fit all, and adopts a highly individual and adaptable approach. It can broker the valuable connections and experiences that different sectors need. TPI also understands the complexity of partnerships and of organisations. Rather than delivering off-the-shelf services which may not be appropriate, it works in partnership with clients to understand their individual contexts, needs and the most appropriate action to deliver their desired outcomes.

ABOUT THE TPI CERTIFICATE IN PARTNERING PRACTICE

To address the vital challenge of building partnering capacity, IBLF's The Partnering Initiative has launched 'Building Skills and Knowledge for Effective Multi-stakeholder Collaboration', a three-day training programme to develop skills, understanding and knowledge for effective cross-sector partnering.[4] Offering the option to continue to a Certificate in Partnering Practice, the course balances core knowledge with highly interactive experiential learning through role-play, 'serious games' and peer-to-peer exchanges.

Many of today's societal, environmental, business and humanitarian challenges are so complex and interconnected that they can only be tackled by different sectors working together. Local and multinational multi-stakeholder alliances between governments, businesses, civil society bodies and development agencies enable them to pool their resources and competencies to stimulate innovation, maximise impact and ensure sustainability.

However, effective collaboration between stakeholders with different missions, interests, cultures and even vocabularies is difficult to achieve. It requires common understanding across partners, collective leadership, a collaborative mindset, a key skill set, and both strong relationship management and output-focused project management. With these critical elements in place, partnerships can achieve significant impact. Without them, partnerships are likely to under-perform, or fail altogether.

---

4   For more information, see http://thepartneringinitiative.org/.

17 *The Strategic Alliance Professional*

Alliance Best Practice suggests that the competencies of a good strategic alliance manager (SAM) are closely linked to the common success factors of successful strategic alliances. We in ABP believe that an effective SAM needs to be adept in the following three areas:

1. knowledge of alliance best practices and ability to put them into action;
2. personal skills and capability;
3. personal collaborative behaviours and values.

Skills and Capability: Overview

ABP defines external management skills as the ability to implement a range of common success factors in business-to-business relationships, and capability as the ability to recognise which skill is relevant at which time for which type of relationship.

We recognise four distinct types of partnering relationship:

1. **Transactional relationships** – These types of relationships are commonly called vendor or supplier relationships. They are transactional in nature because the common interaction is adversarial, with both/all parties requiring diametrically opposed objectives (highest price versus lowest price, greatest volume versus greatest value add, and so on).
2. **Enhanced relationships** – If the host relationship manager has done his job correctly, then he will have convinced the supplier(s) to add extra value to the relationship *at their own cost and effort*. These situations are often product-, service- or business unit-specific, and are generally conducted as pilots. The key dynamic balance that needs to be maintained here is the ability to generate extra value *for both parties*.
3. **Collaborative relationships** – Assuming that enhanced pilot projects have already been conducted in the relationship, the next step is to combine these disparate activities into a co-ordinated and integrated whole. When this is achieved, we say that the relationship has reached collaborative status (both/all parties are actively looking for collaboration opportunities to add to the existing enhanced projects).
4. **Partnership relationships** – Finally, the host partner may enter into a full partnership with the supplier(s) in which the defining characteristic is shared risk and reward. Typically (although not always), these relationships are highly structured and run as legally binding joint ventures.

Behaviours and Values: Examples

Organisations typically recognise that the behaviours and values set out in Table 17.1 will be helpful in developing external relationship management skills.

Table 17.1 Examples of useful behaviours in conducting strategic alliances

Core behaviours	Partnering behaviours	Company behaviours
Innovation and learning	Dedication to partner success	One team
Work with drive and commitment to results	Cross-functional collaboration	Inspirational leadership
Think globally	Doing more with less	Open communication
Establish plans	Influence others without authority	Challenge ourselves
Demonstrate leadership	Resolve conflicts	Recognising excellence
Act with integrity	Increase and drive partner loyalty	Innovative spirit
Communicate openly, effectively and with trust	Cultural awareness and sensitivity	Best place to work
Manage projects		Care for our customers
Focus on team members		
Organisational sensitivity		

Knowledge of Best Practice and the Ability to Put it into Action

Organisations will typically need to collaborate more closely and more often with a range of chosen external organisations. The nature of these interactions will depend on the classification of the partner(s) identified. This interaction is summarised in Table 17.2, and demonstrates that as the degree of business intimacy increases, so does the commercial value of the relationship to the parties.

Table 17.2 Types of alliance relationships

Transactional	Enhanced	Collaborative	Partnership
Commonly called vendor or supplier relationships	Supplier devotes its own resources to add value to the relationship	Enhanced pilot projects co-ordinate into an integrated whole	Full partnership with supplier(s) entails shared risk and reward
Transactional in nature	Often product-, service- or business unit-specific, and generally conducted as pilots	Both/all parties seeking further collaboration opportunities	Highly structured, legally binding joint ventures
	Generate added value for all parties		

Source: Based on original research by Vantage Partners, LLC.

It is the relationship manager's job (whether part-time or full-time) to maximise the commercial value of these external relationships cost-effectively through active day-to-day strategic alliance management. He achieves this through a defined process of relationship optimisation, which follows this sequence:

1. **Partner identification** – deciding what type of relationship is required in the given situation to achieve the company's goals and objectives;
2. **Baselining** – determining the desired scope of the relationship and the current level of commercial value to both/all companies;
3. **Benchmarking** – comparing the relationship's performance to a collaboration best practice database to determine areas for improvement;
4. **Action planning** – designing an appropriate joint action plan to improve the relationship based on data captured in the benchmarking stage;
5. **Resource allocation** – negotiating resources to execute the agreed joint action plan;
6. **Review** – conducting regular 90-day reviews of the relationship and taking remedial action where necessary.

Skills and Capability: Details

We will now examine the common success factors and the skills required for the four different types of business-to-business collaborative relationship: transactional, enhanced, collaborative and partnership.

TRANSACTIONAL

Developing a business value proposition for the relationship (Co1)

Skill: the ability to create a clear articulation (usually in writing) of the value of the relationship measured in terms of products or services being developed or projects delivered, with particular reference to all partners, the customers, the consumers and the market.

Demonstrating this ability:

- All key stakeholders need to have a common understanding of the value in the relationship.
- The very best business value propositions are 'breakthrough value propositions', in which the capability, service or product being developed is unique and not easily copied by the competition.
- It is important to document the BVP, both to avoid misunderstanding and also to gain commitment to it by working on the document jointly with the partner(s).
- You should consider how others might replicate your BVP. The more effort you put in, the less easy it should be for competitors to replicate it.
- The BVP lies at the heart of any partnership discussion and should be considered first in the Transactional stage. This is the start point for all alliance discussions.

- Typically and traditionally, failure to address this area has been one of the most common reasons for partnership failure.
- Business aggregation is not a BVP – simply because one partner is large and the other partner is dominant in a particular sector does not relieve them of the burden of understanding what specifically they are developing, how the value created will affect the host company, and how the value created will affect the partner(s).
- BVPs need to be developed in the context of the overall strategy of the relationship (see MOUP definition in Appendix 4). They can be developed either top-down or bottom-up (from the strategic or the operational viewpoint).

Conducting partner due diligence exercises (Co2)

Skill: A rigorous understanding of the suitability of potential alliance partners before you enter a relationship with them.

Demonstrating this ability:

- In practice, due diligence will differ depending on the business sector and the type of relationship. However, the core fact remains that devoting at least some time to assessing the suitability of candidate partners before entering into binding discussions with them will be rewarded many times over later in the relationship.
- Sometimes conducting a full formal due diligence process is impossible, in which case the relationship manager must make a judgement call as to how much effort to put into the process, bearing in mind the size of the prize, the state of collaboration knowledge in the partner organisation, the intent of the relationship, and so on.
- Both/all parties should understand that an assessment of how they will work together before they do so is of enormous value. Clearly, it is important that no partner intimidates the other(s) through the use of this process; rather, it is designed to establish how the partners can work together most effectively.
- Just because a partner has a large market share in a particular sector or has some great technology software, hardware or services does not make the partner attractive. Many relationships have suffered from the curse of non-integrated functions or processes, leading to costly and time-consuming failed collaborations.
- A typical due diligence assessment should include the following considerations:
  - **Internal** – How prepared is the organisation for partnership?
  - **External** – How will the market (and other existing partners) react?
  - **Commercial** – Is there money here?
  - **Technical** – Is there alignment of both/all companies' products and services (overlap)?
  - **Strategic** – What is the direction of the partner(s)?
  - **Cultural** – How easy will it be to inter-operate?
  - **Operational** – How will it work country by country or business unit by business unit?

Researching and understanding the partner company market position (T12)

Skill: Understanding the market position of the chosen partner(s), and fully understanding why this is important to the host organisation.

Demonstrating this ability:

- Many partnering organisations do not take enough time to critically examine the current and future market positioning of their prospective partners. This is understandable in fast-moving environments like telecommunications and ICT. However, there are many examples of companies which were not competitors at the outset of a relationship quickly becoming entrenched rivals simply because of a change in strategic direction of one or the other.
- They take the view (sometimes erroneously) that what has gone before will continue into the future. This is very often a dangerous assumption.
- As a relationship manager, you should pay attention to the market position of your prospective partners and regularly assess their technical and commercial excellence. However, more important than this is an understanding of why a particular factor is important to the host company. (See related skills around business strategy formulation and in particular strategic alignment as defined in Appendix 4.)
- Every organisation must develop a clear understanding of its prospective partner market positions and the impact such positioning has on its own operations. These positions should be reassessed regularly to ensure that they have not shifted.
- Partner positions can vary depending on theatre of operation, geography, sales line or technical product line. It is perfectly acceptable to partner with an organisation which has competing products or services. However, the scope definition and articulation of what is (and more importantly what is not) in scope will be critical here.

Articulating the host company market position (T13)

Skill: The ability to articulate the host company's market position in relation to the chosen partner(s), and fully understanding why this is important to the partner(s).

Demonstrating this ability:

- All relationship managers should be able to explain with clarity, simplicity and exactitude the host company's position, including its strategic direction, core values and beliefs, and partnering process.
- This skill is absolutely crucial to attracting and securing the best partner candidates. Organisations which are successful in this area are said to have achieved Partner of Choice (POC) status – other organisations compete to partner with them.
- POC status allows the host company to negotiate the best deals, attract the highest-quality partners and secure advantageous technical or commercial terms.
- Without this key explanation, the partner(s) will not be able to assess the host as a prospective partner effectively, so valuable time may be lost because of potentially confusing and conflicting messages from multiple executives from both/all partners.

- The reality of strategic relationships these days is that 'You have to choose.' This means that it is highly unlikely that any one candidate partner will have the best scores in a multidimensional due diligence exercise. In reality, the relationship manager will need to construct a decision matrix to help to balance the pros and cons of the prospective partner(s).

Developing the relationship's legal/business structure (Co3)

Skill: Developing the most appropriate structure for the relationship given the size, strategy and intended scope. This could be formal or informal and includes identifying: the governance model, key stakeholders, and relationship documentation.

Demonstrating this ability:

- In the Transactional category of partnering, this aspect is extremely important, and it entails the relationship manager negotiating the best terms for the partnership. But note that simple adversarial haggling may be inappropriate and you may want to give the partner(s) the opportunity to impress you with offerings that are beyond the legal contracts or structure. This is unlikely to happen if the partner or partners feel that they have been screwed down to the last penny in an aggressive process.
- Negotiating a global agreement is a time-consuming task, and it is often better to negotiate local agreements as pilots where you can, then later build them up into larger arrangements as the relationship begins to demonstrate its value.
- When you're negotiating, you're not earning! Remember to spend an appropriate amount of time on the negotiating process. If no common structure is agreed, it is unlikely that both/all sides will be prepared to commit to significant investment or growth plans.
- Know when to walk away. It is very tempting, having spent a considerable amount of time or energy on partnership negotiations, to carry on to see them through. But the best partner managers go into negotiation situations with a clear understanding of how long the process should take. If it takes longer, then they are usually prepared to walk away and consider a second-choice partner who may be able to come to an agreement more quickly.
- It is important to know what intentions and objectives you are trying to achieve through the relationship because different types have different optimal structures. For example, a transactional partnership would probably have a simple supplier agreement, whereas a full partnership structure would require a much larger set of complex documentation. It is identified best practice to develop a memorandum of understanding and principles first, to identify such considerations as objectives, revenue streams, costs, key stakeholders and the governance model.
- Different alliances have different purposes (development, R&D, cost reduction and so on). It is likely that the host company's procurement department will have standard templates which could accelerate your efforts here. It is worthwhile keeping up to date with these as they can save you a great deal of time and trouble.
- Bear in mind that a structure that works well for one relationship may not be appropriate for another.

- In many cases in a transactional relationship the need is for speed, as an identified business opportunity might pass the host company by if it takes too much time to come to an agreement. It is here that the factor of business-to-business trust comes into its own.
- The best partnership documents (even transactional ones) have an element of shared risk and reward. This should be carefully built into the overall contractual framework.
- Generally, the evidence suggests that the greater the risk and reward, the greater the payback from the relationship.
- Remember the adage 'form before function', and design your relationship first before involving your legal department.

Developing and implementing a robust set of partner metrics (Co5)

Skill: The ability to construct a formal set of measurements which are accepted by both sides to represent the key performance indicators in the relationship.

Demonstrating this ability:

- You should aim for a relationship balanced scorecard, measuring multiple dimensions of the relationship rather than just commercial or technical factors and service level agreements. For example, a suitable balanced scorecard might involve strategic and operational factors as well as cultural and commercial ones.
- You should distinguish in your scorecards between cause and effect. This is very important, and is often a factor that is missing from traditional transactional supplier scorecards.
- In a best-of-breed scenario, you should also invite your partner(s) to conduct a 360-degree assessment of the host company and how easy or difficult it is to partner with. This will generate an enormous amount of value, not just in the data collected, but also in the act of showing your partner that you are open to constructive criticism.
- Beware! If you do manage to get your partner(s) to give you an honest assessment, you must ensure that you take action as a result of the feedback.
- Organisational culture is both real and notoriously difficult to define. However, its impact can be massive. So even though the task is difficult, you should take pains to include cultural aspects of both individual and company behaviour in your assessments (see 'Behaviours and Values' section below).
- Remember: 'What gets measured gets done.' So be sure to start small and controllable rather than developing something which is unwieldy and incapable of execution from the start.
- When looking at operational metrics, consideration should be given to the following factors:
  - **Control** – Is this factor under our control?
  - **Impact** – Is this a high or a low impacter (see Chapter 5 in particular on scoring the ABP success factors).
  - **Relevance** – How relevant is the factor under consideration given your current situation?

Developing an expected relationship cost/value ratio (Co10)

Skill: The ability to construct a workable expected cost/value ratio for both the host company and its partner(s). The cost/value ratio is defined as the amount each partner receives back for each commercial unit invested in the relationship (for example, financial investment). The key factor of this skill is expectation: the best collaborating organisations know in advance what the cost/value ratio should be for relationships they are managing – not just transactional ones, but also the other partnership types.

Demonstrating this ability:

- This skill is nearly impossible without a good grasp of Co8, 'Commercial benefit', and Co7, 'Commercial cost'.
- Many organisations give up on the process of identifying value and cost, believing it to be too difficult to accomplish. But without applying some commercial and statistical rigour to their relationships, organisations have no way of prioritising investments, spotting under-performing relationships quickly, taking appropriate remedial action and exiting failing relationships if necessary.
- Many organisations are now using the cast/value ration to:
    - satisfy their CEOs that alliances are a valuable commercial model;
    - comparing internal results and taking action accordingly;
    - building business cases to secure investment in alliance relationships'
    - manage internal and external expectations;
    - brief industry analysts;
    - compare similar relationships stage by stage.
- Note that this factor focuses on an *expected* cost/value ratio. This suggests that each partner already has a preconceived figure in mind.

Developing a set of shared objectives for the relationship (S20)

Skill: The discovery and articulation of common and shared high-level objectives that both/all partners seek to achieve as a result of the strategic collaboration.

Demonstrating this ability:

- Unlike mutual needs where there may be disparate requirements from both/all parties to the relationship, it is imperative that both sides are clear about having similar strategic objectives for the relationship.
- It is essential that the high-level (or strategic) objectives of both/all parties are shared and understood by all. Although seemingly obvious, it is remarkable how often this basic tenet is ignored.
- In many cases one or both/all of the partners will have strategic intentions which are not shared with their partner(s). Although this situation may be tolerable in the short term (say eighteen months), in the longer term the differing strategic intentions of the partners will lead to an increasing amount of tension in the relationship, which will inevitably initiate a downward vicious spiral.

- The only practical way to ensure alignment is to run a joint workshop attended by the senior executive sponsors of the relationship to articulate clearly the common goals of the collaboration. That articulation is then recorded in the MOUP.
- Failure to identify any common strategic goals is an early indicator of trouble! The reverse of this is also true – common strategic objectives act like a magnet, drawing the relationship on ever faster towards shared goals.

ENHANCED

Constructing and managing a relationship development plan (O51)

Skill: The construction and active management of a relationship development plan.

Demonstrating this ability:

- Relationship managers need to be clear about the distinction between a project plan, which delivers elements of value for the relationship, and a relationship development plan, which delivers enhancements to the relationship over a given period. The purpose of a relationship development plan is to identify all the CSFs relevant to the intended type of relationship and to ensure that they are all in place and operating at near maximum efficiency. Since not all the CSFs can be achieved immediately and since there is a critical dependency between many of them, there is clearly a need for a set plan to accomplish this objective.
- Many alliance professionals believe that collaboration and partnering is based on personal contact and regular interaction with key stakeholders in the partner organisation(s), and that a development plan will simply impose a barrier to the fluid and nebulous networking necessary for success. Evidence from multiple successful relationships shows the contrary. The simple truth is that relationships don't manage themselves, they need to be managed actively, and the best way to do this is through a relationship development plan:
  - Identify where you are now in relationship terms according to an objective standard.
  - Decide what type of relationship you would like, bearing in mind constraining factors.
  - Identify the key CSFs that will lead you to that desired point.
  - Identify milestones along the way that will allow you to determine whether you are making progress.
  - Develop and document a joint relationship development plan in order to achieve this.
  - Review the plan regularly.
- Relationship managers should be aware of a seductive 'activity trap' here. Evidence from experienced professionals shows that many of them felt that the majority of their role was taken up with tactical efforts of 'doing rather than planning' (this was particularly true of relationship professionals who were handling more than one partnership at once). The temptation to fall back on activities and firefighting is very strong, particularly when there is organisational pressure to be seen to be 'doing something'. However, the relationship manager should remember at all times that he is the conductor of the orchestra, not one of the musicians.

- There is clear evidence that the existence of a formal relationship development plan, no matter how brief and no matter how prescribed, contributes greatly to the operational success of strategic relationships. Such a plan very often goes hand-in-hand with the communication matrix mentioned earlier, often supplying the milestones and activities that provide the content of the messages.

Designing and implementing an issue escalation process (O52)

Skill: The ability to design, implement and manage an issue escalation process suited to the size and complexity of the relationship, with regard to the number of identified key stakeholders.

Demonstrating this ability:

- Aspects of issue escalation in relationship management are not dissimilar to those in project management. In both cases the intention is the same – to provide a process whereby issues can be addressed and resolved at the most appropriate (usually lowest) levels of the relationship.
- The greatest danger in this area is that all managerial and operational members of the relationship pass all issues to the steering group for resolution. This is a mistake. The purpose of the steering group is to set strategy and to be a court of last call, not to be used as a 'squabble shop'.
- A suitable escalation process needs to be defined at various levels within the relationship: strategic, managerial and operational. Although the exact definition of each of these levels varies from relationship to relationship, the underlying structure is sound and can be used by host company relationship managers.
- It is a mistake in this area to try to force issues into categories which are too simplistic (for example, technical issues, quality issues, or client or customer issues). In reality, it is likely that relationship issues will most often be a combination of a number of these factors.
- Issues are best resolved as a joint process involving both/all parties to the relationship. This procedure provides a practical way to increase the degree of communication and build trust.
- There is a strong temptation for relationship managers to avoid the construction of such a process in favour of a mindset which says, 'This is just part of my job.' This is another mistake.
- Research shows that most organisations do not have formal issue escalation processes in their strategic relationships, whereas a sizeable majority of successful strategic relationships did ensure that such processes were in place. The conclusion is obvious: the construction of a suitably scaled and sensitively managed escalation procedure contributes to relationship success.
- In those relationships where issue escalation took place effectively there was usually evidence of senior executive support, good communication and a formal quality review. These factors appear to co-exist very happily with each other.

Developing relationship communication plans (O43)

Skill: The ability to: design, implement and manage both internal and external communication plans to support the relationship. 'Internal' here means internal to the host company, and may include confidential information which may not be shared with the partner(s). 'External' means those plans that are shared with the partner(s) and external analysts.

Demonstrating this ability:

- This skill is not simply a matter of effective communication – that skill is covered under basic or fundamental skills. The skill we are discussing here is the ability to put together plans and communicate of key messages about the relationship at agreed and planned intervals that enhance the relationship's performance.
- Many relationship managers are frustrated when part-time or occasional members of the relationship team (on either side) make comments or commit actions which are not in keeping with the spirit of the relationship. However, these same relationship managers have often not put in place plans to communicate to relationship contributors what exactly is the spirit of the relationship.
- There is often regular and effective communication between the individuals specifically responsible for the relationship, but frequently that communication does not extend beyond those individuals. For this reason, a considered plan is required to scope and scale the amount of internal and external communication necessary.
- Such communication programmes include an identification of the key stakeholders on each side and a description of their relative roles and responsibilities, as well as a formal diary or current chart of the set meetings that are to be held. In addition, these communication programmes give individuals an understanding of what information they should expect as a result of such meetings.
- The best communication programmes identify at least three key categories of stakeholder – strategic, managerial and operational – and produce communication messages suitable for each of them. Note that the type and content of each message is different in each case. In the more formalised relationships a matrix exists that similar to the example shown in Table 17.3.

Table 17.3   The three levels of strategic alliance communication

Level	Communication type	
	Internal	External
Strategic	Steering group minutes and decisions	Annual briefings
Managerial	MOUP outputs	Quarterly bulletins
Operational	Weekly reviews	None

- In best practice relationships, good communication exists between all three levels within each organisation, but it is equally appropriate between the differing levels in the partner organisations. This allows the senior executive sponsors to develop an effective overview of the relationship which is fundamentally in sync with the day-to-day feelings of the operational management team responsible for the relationship.
- The best communication programmes generate a communication matrix which is used as the backbone for the governance model. These matrixes are generally be similar to the example in Table 17.3, but identify the individual key stakeholders (from the MOUP) and the part they play in the relationship.

Conducting quality reviews (O44)

Skill: The ability to review of the quality of the outputs of a relationship on a regular predefined basis.

Demonstrating this ability:

- This ability is closely aligned to the ability to conduct annual relationship audits. However, quality reviews are most often conducted on a quarterly basis and will normally only involve the managerial levels in the relationship.
- In order to conduct a quality review, both/all parties need to define the constituent factors of 'quality'. These may differ from relationship to relationship, and may include such aspects as products, services, communication, trust, support, commercial value and speed of progress.
- This CSF is one of the most rapidly expanding of all those identified in best-of-breed relationships. As little as three to four years ago the idea of reviewing the quality or effectiveness of the outputs of a relationship was seen as potentially very damaging because it implied that either the partners or the host organisation were remiss in certain key aspects. This is no longer considered to be the case.
- There is clear evidence from a large number of successful strategic relationships that the adoption of a formal quality review process (sometimes called a healthcheck) is rapidly becoming the norm and is contributing greatly to relationship success. This appears to be driven by both internal and external factors. The internal factors include the desire of senior management to check on the appropriateness of the actions to generate commercial return. The external factors appear to be based on the need to conduct regular audits of key relationships as a result of the US Sarbanes-Oxley Act, Enron and other high-profile audit failures.
- It is evident from the annual ASAP conferences that regular healthchecks are becoming standard practice in a wide range of sectors.

Designing and implementing an MOUP or Alliance Charter (O45)

Skill: The ability to run a workshop comprising key stakeholders of both sides with the sole objective of constructing a memorandum of understanding and principles or alliance charter for the relationship.

Demonstrating this ability:

- Documentation differs from one in strategic relationship to the other, and many organisations have a number of aspects of an MOUP (variously described as; a charter, a code of behaviour, a partner plan or a partner programme) in their existing legal and non-legal documents. However, there is overwhelming evidence from best practice partnering organisations that the creation of a single, brief document that articulates the key aspects of the relationship is of crucial value.
- A typical MOUP would be five pages long and include a half-page description of the following aspects:
    - vision of the relationship;
    - business value proposition(s);
    - relationship scope;
    - key metrics;
    - governance
    - key stakeholders;
    - relationship development plan;
    - communication programme(s);
    - relationship change management;
    - key documents/contracts.
- The existence of an MOUP in strategic collaborative relationships is a surprisingly good litmus test of both the effectiveness and the maturity of the relationship.
- Such a document should not be legally binding and should concern itself with the factors which will form the backbone of a significant strategic relationship set out above.
- The existence of an MOUP is one of the most frequent CSFs in the Operational dimension. In addition, it is the one that is most welcomed by all levels of management. Operational managers welcome it because it gives them a context within which to perform their day-to-day duties and a set of rules to live by, and senior executives welcome it because it gives them a brief, easy-to-read way of understanding the current state of the relationship.

Developing and implementing an alliance reward system (Co6)

Skill: The ability to design and implement a system or process in which individuals are rewarded appropriately for good collaborative behaviour.

Demonstrating this ability:

- Relationship managers and organisations alike need to recognise that there will be times (usually not very often) when the needs of the relationship outweigh the immediate needs of one party or another. In such situations the most effective partnering behaviours favour what is best for the relationship rather than what is best for the organisation in isolation. A collaboration reward system is designed to highlight such situations and reward organisations and staff who make appropriate decisions.

- The reward type can be commercial or non-commercial, and may be large and small depending on the size and complexity of the relationship. However, it must be capable of recognising both the organisations and individuals involved. Examples include:
  - only allowing organisations to vote for their partners' employees;
  - providing team rewards in the form of meals (anything from a pizza in the office to formal restaurant outings);
  - commercial bonuses based on the revenue impact of the relationship.
- Examples are plentiful in this area, but the key skill of the relationship manager is to pick a type of reward that which is sympathetic to and in harmony with the commercial and cultural goals of the particular relationship.
- This skill is intimately related to Co5, 'Key metrics', and O47, 'Operational metrics'.
- As a simple guide, decide what factors are important , then embed the appropriate incentives to achieve them.
- It is at the operational level where the grandest partnering schemes and strategies need to be implemented, because this is where the on-the-ground work gets done. Paying attention to financially insignificant but impactful rewards for collaborative behaviour can have a massive effect on the success or otherwise of a relationship.
- It is counterproductive if the executive team of any of the partners talks a good game of relationship inter-operation while rewarding direct sales and confrontational behaviour.

Establishing business-to-business operational alignment (O48)

Skill: Aligning the host organisation's operational business units with the operational business units of the other partner(s) in the relationship.

Demonstrating this ability:

- A relationship manager can't rely on contracts to make people speak to each other. The existence of agreed forms of interaction and behaviour will help, but it is the relationship manager's job to ensure that positive and constructive interactions are occurring at each of the three levels in the relationship – strategic, managerial and operational. Probably the most important of these three areas is operational, because this is usually the level at which the work is actually being conducted.
- As is the case with cultural alignment, many organisations don't pay sufficient attention to integrating the intent of the relationship into the partners' operational units. In the most notable cases this relationship results in a 'zippered' interaction between many different operational levels in both/all partners.
- However, in lesser-performing relationships there is usually good alignment between the intent or desire of both/all senior partnership teams, but this hardly ever reaches the operational units necessary to execute on the relationship. For example, two corporate alliance teams at the head offices of a large hardware and a large software company respectively planned, designed, negotiated and signed an excellent theoretical strategic alliance relationship which would have benefited both organisations through the development of specific breakthrough solutions utilising both companies' hardware and software. However, neither party took the trouble to convey the importance the relationship to the sales teams in the countries in

Europe, the Middle East and Africa which were responsible for selling the solutions. Consequently, there was an inordinate delay of six to nine months with no sales made. The joint marketing team for the relationship seemed to believe that if it simply informed the local sales units that the relationship existed, extra sales would flow automatically. This is clearly not the case, and the better-performing organisations devote a great deal of time and effort to persuading local sales units of the value they will see individually from selling the combined products and services of the relationship (for example, in terms of bonuses and commissions).

Conducting alliance audits/healthchecks (Co4)

Skill: The ability to construct and conduct a formal review of the relationship on an annual basis. The audit will normally take at least 2 weeks to conduct and question all key stakeholders to the relationship from both/all sides. It will most often be followed by an MOUP workshop to ratify and reset the relationship strategy.

Demonstrating this ability:

- Relationships are organic in nature, which means that they are subject to change because of influences such as strategy, management changes, and internal and external factors. Formal reviews according to a predetermined timescale (usually annually) allow this to be accommodated.
- This skill is closely associated with O44, 'Quality review', and 045, ' Memorandum of understanding and principles or alliance charter'.
- The MOUP agenda can be used as the questioning structure for the relationship audit (see 'Running a MOUP Workshop' available from the Alliance Best Practice website at www.alliancebestpractice.com).
- Senior executive support from one side or the other can increase the value of such periodic healthchecks significantly. If the senior executive sponsor from one side shows an interest in the results, it is likely that the senior executive sponsor from the partner side will take a similar interest. This in itself creates a virtuous circle: if those involved in the relationship know that the results of the audit are going to receive such high-level attention, they are likely to complete the exercise more rigorously than if this were not the case. Consequently, it is highly recommended that relationship managers take the time to explain to senior executives why regular audits are such an important factor in the continuous relationship improvement cycle.
- Such audits should not comes as a surprise to anyone. They should be planned well in advance and should have some clear areas for investigation. As suggested earlier, these could be the same ones that make up the MOUP agenda, but this does not have to be the case and it is perfectly acceptable for one or both parties (preferably both) to the relationship to agree a key set of questions which will form the basis of the audit.
- It is important that the scoring of the questions should be as objective as possible. To this end, it may make sense to ask an independent entity to conduct the audit process. This could be a member of the auditing group of one of the parties or an external organisation.
- The questions that form the basis of the audit should be agreed in advance and adhered to on a regular basis – they should not change every year because this will

make comparisons difficult. The purpose of the exercise is to illustrate the progress made and make the connection between 'doing the right things' and 'getting the right results'.

- Meetings between senior executives from time to time when they happen to be in the same physical location are not relationship audit reviews. Many organisations use a different terminology to describe the exercise, fearing that 'audit' is too threatening a term. This is entirely acceptable as long as the distinction is maintained between an annual review that resets strategic expectations and measures objective progress year on year, and a regular relationship healthcheck that takes place quarterly and reviews the action plans already set in place by the annual review.
- Meetings to review the audit findings should seek input from all three levels of key stakeholders: strategic, managerial and operational. They should also take place at the same time each year, acceptable to both sides. In a perfect world (although this is not always possible) this would be at the end of the financial year of both/all parties.
- The audit results should be shared with the highest governance group in the relationship (the relationship steering committee, if it exists).
- Templates exist to suggest the correct procedures and formats for conducting such reviews and reporting the findings (see the Alliance Best Practice Database at www.alliancebestpractice.com).

COLLABORATIVE

Collaborative process for negotiation (Co9)

Skill: The ability to negotiate collaboratively rather than adversarially with partners. This means negotiating with the best interests of the relationship in mind rather than the position of one's own company. The main skill of collaborative negotiation lies in negotiating the best possible commercial terms while avoiding damaging the relationship.

Demonstrating this ability:

- The first important point to note is that collaborative (or co-collaborative as it is sometimes known) negotiation is not the same as traditional adversarial negotiation. Adversarial negotiation generally relies on a 'win–lose' paradigm, while collaborative negotiation relies on both sides referring to or bearing in mind an outside agency which is of greater importance than the individual deal itself – in our context, the relationship.
- The concept here is that there will be multiple negotiations in a relationship, sometimes taking place almost daily. The critical need is for the negotiations to take place in such a way that the two parties maintain their mutual respect for each other during the process.
- It often helps if both sides agree a process for this type of negotiation which leaves both sides free to concentrate on the quality of their interactions while at the same time following a pre-set formula or process to ensure fairness for both sides.
- One of the conundrums posed by this type of negotiation is the classic example sometimes called 'the prisoners dilemma'.

- Another useful insight into this area can be gained from studying game-playing strategies, particularly negotiation game strategies between teams.
- Many people wrongly feel that you can either have a good relationship or you can have a good commercial deal. Research has proven that this is not the case – in fact, the reverse is often true: the better the relationship, the better the commercial deal is for both sides.
- Good indicators of collaborative negotiation include one side looking to help the other not lose money on a deal, compensating for unit price reductions with volume orders, transparent pricing models and open book accounting.
- Negotiate as if you will have to implement the deal yourself.
- Beware of 'shipping in' different teams for negotiation and execution.
- Collaborative negotiation is sometimes used in the Cultural dimension, but appears in this section because it has such a powerful effect on the commercial value of the deals which are agreed.
- It is one of the most important high impacters identified in partnering best practices, and is a key indicator of organisational cultural style and collaboration effectiveness.
- See the following additional resources available from the Alliance Best Practice website at www.alliancebestpractice.com:
  - Managing Both Substance and Relationship
  - Approaching Persuasion as Joint Problem Solving
  - FAQs on Improving Organisational Capacity to Negotiate
  - Improving your company's return on negotiation
  - The point of the deal.

Developing and implementing risk sharing strategies (S23)

Skill: The ability to recognise the nature and degree of risk in a collaborative relationship/venture and devise suitable executable strategies for sharing that risk with partners in an equable way.

Demonstrating this ability:

- Risk sharing between partners does more to build the business-to-business trust factor than almost any other alliance best practice. Sometimes risk sharing is impossible because of company policies or internal rules, but where it is possible it is a powerful driver of close organisational alignment and support.
- Strategies to address CSF S22, 'Tactical and strategic risk', and S23, 'Risk sharing', are clearly intimately linked, as without the first the second is impossible. The reason they are separated in alliance best practice terms is that it is surprising how often organisations have one and not the other.
- Many organisations identify risk in their collaborative relationships, but fewer further refine their understanding to encompass tactical and strategic risk, and fewer still have a formal risk mitigation and sharing process in place to deal with the different types.
- The most frequently cited commonly understood risk was 'the risk of losing money or wasting time'. ABP identifies in addition:

- **Market risk** – Will the market continue to provide opportunities that enable you to sustain growth? (Beware of entering new markets with new products utilising new technology – 'compounded risk'.)
- **Competitive technology risk** – Will a competitor develop a technology that will make yours obsolete? Are margins sufficient in the event of a price war? Are the technologies supporting your value proposition approaching obsolescence in the sort or medium term that may eliminate or reduce the benefits you seek from the alliance?
- **Co-operative environment risk** – What are the chances someone or something (a partner, government, subcontractors, transportation and so on) will stop or slow down the venture?
- **Management risk** – Are sufficient personnel available to carry out the venture? Can the necessary resources be obtained in a timely and cost-effective manner?
- **Political risk** – Are there governmental regulations, now or pending, that will interfere with success?
- **Resources risk** – Will the supply of materials or products remain available? Will the partners have the financial, human and intellectual resources required?
- **Capital risk** – Will inflation, exchange rates or government policy have an effect on the investment's value?
- **Prospective partner risk** – Is the prospective partner strong enough to withstand competitive pressures? Will it be stable and co-operative in the long term? Will it maintain a strategic perspective?
- Each of the above risk categories should be assessed closely in a collaborative relationship, and either ruled out or addressed.
- Additional resources in this area:
  - See Critical List Analysis Checklist (available from the Alliance Best Practice website downloads section).

Securing senior executive support (S25)

Skill: The ability to generate senior executive support for the relationship both inside the host organisation and its partner(s).

Demonstrating this ability:

- During the research to develop the ABP Database, the need to secure senior executive support was recognised in an overwhelming majority of cases (93%). However, the majority of senior executives interviewed paid only lip service to the role of the executive sponsor.
- It is usually too easy for senior executives to claim to be supporting a relationship without actually committing to action.
- There are very few organisations that adopt a formal job description for the role (9%), and of those that do, only a handful require a senior executive to sign off on the objectives, duties and responsibilities specified in such a job description (see Senior Executive Job Description, available from the downloads section of the Alliance Best Practice website at www.alliancebestpractice.com).

- At the same time, there are a number of natural 'alliance champions' who experience great frustration because they are unaware of how to contribute to the success of the relationships in question.
- All too often, senior executive support is reduced to personal 'chemistry' between top executives on both/all sides of relationships. This is fine while it lasts, but if one of the individuals involved leaves, the relationship will suffer.
- The best examples of senior executive support seem to go hand-in-hand with regular (six-monthly) executive briefings at which the senior executive of one or sometimes both/all sides drives a formal agenda which includes not just operational but also strategic issues. We observed that in these cases there was a greater sense of integration and coherence between the operational teams on both/all sides of the relationship.
- The practice also developed into a virtuous (though threatening) circle. Typically, this was demonstrated by the operational teams on both sides contributing more and more planning time for these meetings (10–15 days was not unusual) to avoid being shown up in front of their own senior executives and being personally and professionally embarrassed.
- The logical steps to improve senior executive support are as follows:
  - Identity a range of suitable senior executives and nominate them in the MOUP.
  - Brief senior executives on the nature of the role and their duties and responsibilities.
  - Encourage senior executives to hold regular yearly or twice-yearly relationship strategy meetings.
- Best-of-breed examples include the IBM Partner Executive Programme (PEP).

Developing business-to-business trust (Cu31)

Skill: The relationship manager needs to be able to increase the degree to which the organisations involved in an alliance trust each other to deliver on their commitments, progressing it from the personal to the organisational level.

Demonstrating this ability:

- This area is one of the most hotly debated aspects of best practice partnering. For many years trust was seen as a soft skill which could not be proceduralised, much less taught as a skill or improved. Nowadays, though, that perception is changing radically – see, for example, work done in this area by (among others) Paul Lawrence and Robert Porter Lynch of Harvard Business School,[1] and also the Accenture Thought Leadership Group[2]).
- Current thinking suggests that business-to-business trust is founded on far more than just corporate morality – it depends on predictable outcomes, good communication, mutual respect, clear understanding of the culture of one's own organisation and that of the partner(s), senior executive support, clear governance processes and so on.
- The key aspect of this skill for relationship managers is that it needs to be to be replicable – the trust needs to exist between the organisations rather than the people involved (although it often grows out of personal chemistry between individuals).

---

1   http://www.systemoftrust.com/html/articles.html.

2   http://www.accenture.com/Microsites/change-management/Pages/latest-thought-leadership.aspx.

- Trust is a high impacter, but is the result of a number of low impacters, such as communication, information sharing and quality delivery.
- Business-to-business trust is far from common, and no organisations identified in the Database had a formal or credible business-to-business trust building model. This is due in no small part to the fact that the essence of organisational trust is widely misunderstood.
- Paradoxically, the impact trust can have on relationships was almost universally identified as a common success factor (94%), with many individuals able to cite quite clearly the commercial value of developing trust, for example: 'It helps you negotiate the natural ups and downs of the relationship more easily. Your partner doesn't immediately reach for the contract when you don't deliver and he tries to see why this problem might have occurred rather than blaming individuals.'
- An increasing degree of attention has been paid to this important area in the recent literature on partnership management (see particularly 'Lost in Translation' by Fons Trompenaars and Peter Williams,[3] 'Strategic Alliances between American and German Companies: A Cultural Perspective' by Khaled Abdou,[4] and 'Managing Cultural Differences in Alliances' by Pablo C. Biggs).[5]
- There is no doubt that many organisations are now beginning to wake up to the hidden impact cultural misalignment can have and are developing a language to describe organisational diversity in a way which allows them to address the differences (for example, BT, SAP, Siemens Communications, Air France, Delta and Capgemini).

Identifying and controlling destructive organisational cultural issues (Cu37)

Skill: The ability to identify undesirable personal or organisational cultural traits and to eradicate them from the relationship.

Demonstrating this ability:

- In every strategic relationship there exist some specific aspects of one or both/all the organisation's cultures which can lead to problems: the nature of communication, organisational arrogance or aggression, or organisational attitudes towards escalating problems (in some organisations doing so seems perfectly reasonable, while in others it is seen as a fast track to proving that you can't do your job and can lead to an early exit from the organisation). Whatever the particular instance, there was a high prevalence in the Database of specific cultural issues causing specific problems (over 86%).
- Common undesirable cultural traits include arrogance, poor communication, an overly tactical focus, lack of planning, lack of listening, a blinkered approach and too close a focus on personal or organisational goals. To overcome such issues, the relationship manager must first air them with the partner(s), seeking to agree on a common definition of which traits are unacceptable. This allows the relationship manager to add desirable and undesirable traits into the MOUP in a defined manner (the P in

---

3   http://hbr.org/2011/04/lost-in-translation/ar/1.
4   http://www.emeraldinsight.com/journals.htm?articleid=868870.
5   http://www.myalliances.com/resources/578-managing-cultural-differences-in-alliances.

MOUP), and consequently to develop a governance procedure for when these traits are identified. Note that this is planned ahead of time (before problems arise).

Formal joint planning (O42)

Skill: The ability to collaborate to construct a formal plan to improve the effectiveness of the relationship over time, including both revenue and resourcing aspects.

Demonstrating this ability:

- This formal relationship plan is not a business plan or an individual project plan, rather it involves a conscious effort by the relationship manager to construct a plan to help make the relationship more effective over time.
- Many organisations do not invest in their relationships, yet still expect them to deliver increasing value. This is both illogical and damaging because relationships do not manage themselves.
- Many organisations fail to value their partners' investments in the relationship.
- In those relationships that have a formal relationship plan, we noticed that the CSF scores were significantly higher (73%). In addition, this CSF was often misconstrued – for example, in the high-tech sector many alliance professionals who claimed to have formal business plans in fact just had forecasts of new business rather than a balanced plan showing both investment and revenue returns.
- The existence of a well-defined and formal relationship plan was a feature of a minority of the alliances examined (< 23%). However, where one did exist, it was apparent that the alliances had a longer and a more trouble-free existence.
- Factors that usually command a great deal of attention in a relationship plan include communication, trust, metrics, operational alignment, internal alignment, business-to-business alignment, cultural impact, strategic direction and vision.

Developing internal alignment (O50)

Skill: The ability to organise interactions within the host organisation so that it is able to function effectively in the partnering process, sometimes expressed as becoming 'easy to partner with'.

Demonstrating this ability:

- The relationship manager must be able to effectively implement a process to identify key decisions and issues related to the partnership.
- It is necessary to identify the relevant internal stakeholders in various departments and how they contribute to the alliance, consulting with them to ensure they are appropriately informed and involved throughout the lifespan of the partnership.
- This capability is fully instituted when it is both consistently applied to all phases of a partnership's life span and includes explicit guidelines for maintaining internal alignment as changes affect the relationship.
- This was one of the least frequently implemented aspects of best practice in the Database, but paradoxically, it was regularly seen as the most important.

- In most cases this alignment is performed by individual relationship champions through their own personal efforts, sometimes by visionary senior executives, but most often through informal mechanisms such as casual hallway conversations and periodic ad hoc update emails.
- This skill becomes particularly important when companies expand both domestically and globally, and as relationships became more complex over time, respondents reported that it grew increasingly difficult to achieve internal alignment. Companies reported that with such growth, it could prove impossible to ensure that all stakeholders' views were taken into account, some functions might be asked to make sacrifices with which they did not agree for the good of the organisation, and it was increasingly likely that important stakeholders would be overlooked.

Valuing relationship assets (T11)

Skill: Developing a clear understanding of the commercial value of the assets generated by the relationship as all parties to the relationship express them. Typically (although not universally), the measure of such value will be commercial.

Demonstrating this ability:

- This area is intimately associated with Co7, 'Commercial cost', Co8, 'Commercial benefit', and Co10, 'Expected cost/value ratio'.
- Both/all partners need to feel that they are receiving equal and reciprocal amounts of value in any balanced collaboration.
- Jointly developed valuable assets are a key indicator of a true strategic relationship, and are usually a necessary prerequisite to continuing or increased investment in the relationship by one or both/all sides.
- Identification the value of assets is usually a two-stage process:
  - **Stage 1** – hard assets are identified and quantified (for example, marketing funds, R&D facilities, personnel, and products or services produced);
  - **Stage 2** – soft assets are identified and quantified (for example, intellectual property rights, client mindshare and knowledge transfer).
- This process is extremely important as it identifies any actual or perceived differences in value provision in the relationship.
- Without this process, deep-seated but unspoken disquiet can ferment into active discouragement and sabotage.

PARTNERSHIP

Establishing shared control (T18)

Skill: The ability to devise governance strategies which allow the other partner(s) an agreed degree of control over the direction and strategy of the relationship.

Demonstrating this ability:

- Balance is critical in strategic partnerships, and nowhere more so than in the area of shared control. Sharing a degree of control with its partner(s) enables an organisation to give a concrete demonstration of the collaboration ethic. However, the key skill is to balance the degree of control to cede with the need to avoid compromising organisational goals.
- If organisations can master the sharing of this critical feature of the relationship, then the chances of success are massively enhanced. This does not necessarily mean that both sides always exercise the same degree of control in the relationship. Sometimes one of the partners necessarily has a greater degree of ownership of the issues than the other(s). However, in all the best practice partnering cases both/all partners came to an agreement about the level of shared control in the relationship.
- Control can be exercised by the most appropriate partner at the most appropriate time, and that degree of control can shift between them depending on the types of issues faced, the stage of the relationship, the stage of an individual project and so on. This may involve conceding control at key moments in the relationship to a partner which has a better grasp of the current situation or a greater ability to effect meaningful breakthroughs.
- Organisations do this because they expect (and receive) the same courtesy from their partners if such needs arise later in the relationship.
- This area is intimately associated with Co7, 'Commercial cost', Co8, 'Commercial benefit', and Co10, 'Expected cost/value ratio'.

Developing business-to-business strategic alignment (S26)

Skill: The ability to align the business strategy with that of the chosen partner and vice versa (that is, to ensure that the partner business strategy is aligned with the business vision, particularly as it relates to O2ville).

Demonstrating this ability:

- This CSF was the least in evidence in the Database. The power of this CSF becomes apparent when one considers that organisations typically invest marketing funds, time and energy in areas which are in sync with their strategic direction. Hence, by choosing areas that are aligned with this, the host company may be able to tap into additional resources, budgets and investment funds.
- It is typified by organisations sharing strategic direction with each other on such issues as: technical/business direction, R&D and market research.
- Most organisations operate to a timescale of only twelve to eighteen months, and if they have a strategic plan for the relationship, it is constructed from significant initiatives rather than a consideration of classical strategy-affecting issues such as political, economic, social, technological considerations.
- High-tech alliances, particularly between software companies and systems integrators, exhibited a lower instance of this factor in general. However, 'alliance fortresses' are increasingly developing in which adherence to a common strategic purpose or concept is a prerequisite for membership of the partner ecosystem.

Creating a common relationship vision (S30)

Skill: Creating a shared vision for the relationship which drives the partnership towards a desirable goal for both/all organisations. The best relationship visions inspire partners to ever-greater levels of performance in pursuit of overarching strategic goals.

Demonstrating this ability:

- It is by no means easy to develop such a vision, especially in the telecommunications and high-tech sector, where commercial goals and market share tend to represent the only types of vision acceptable to senior executives.
- The existence of a defined vision was absent in the majority of cases examined in our research – in fact, it was formally present in less than 12% of the relationships in the Database. However, this did not mean that individuals on each side of relationships couldn't articulate in their own words 'what the relationship is all about'. This is a critical test of the relationship manager's powers of communication and visioning skills.
- Best practice in this area suggests that the existence of a compelling vision can have a galvanising effect on the mechanics of the relationship.
- Examples of commercial visions include 'increasing market share by 10%', 'offering a genuine choice in a Microsoft-dominated sector' and 'providing the best entertainment venue in the world'.

Personal collaboration skills (Cu33)

Skill: The use of accumulated personal business skills to improve the efficiency and effectiveness of the relationship being managed. Examples include communication skills, interpersonal skills, listening skills, influencing skills, persuasion and collaborative negotiation.. This section is concerned only with those which are specific to partnering or crucial to partnership success.

Demonstrating this ability:

- Very few organisations currently have coherent and integrated programmes to develop collaboration skills, although many have individual training courses for aspects of the collaboration skill set, such as negotiation, interpersonal skills, 360-degree review, project management, influencing skills and mediation. This is in many respects surprising given that there is a clear, strong causal link between the collaboration skills of key stakeholders and the success of collaborative relationships. The reason for this might be that no association or trade body has sufficiently articulated a comprehensive framework of skills to describe the competencies of professional collaboration. However, the evidence suggests that such initiatives are now gaining ground – for example, the ASAP certification programme and the underpinning competencies framework (see Alliance Competency Framework articles on the ASAP website).[6]

---

6   www.strategic-alliances.org.

- The Association of Strategic Alliance Professionals now offers two inter-related qualifications to alliance and partnering executives: CSAP and CA-AM.[7]

Establishing and maintaining business-to-business cultural alignment (Cu38)

Skill: The ability to recognise diverse cultural types and to plan and execute an integration strategy which allows the partners to operate together to create added value while not detracting from the uniqueness of each.

Demonstrating this ability:

- Many institutions that recognise organisational culture as an in-house enabler or barrier to progress with partnership have developed their own language to describe their own cultural norms. It is relatively common these days to see organisations taking pains to explain their cultural heritage to organisations with which they collaborate. They use this internal language as a framework to identify to potential partners the culture with which they will be aligning, and they actively encourage partners to consider their own organisations' culture along similar lines.
- There is good evidence that such active and early cultural alignment helps to minimise the delays, misconceptions and damaging perceptions commonly found in the Cultural dimension.
- Many organisations that do not already have a cultural alignment language or framework are now turning to external advisers to help them with the situation (for example, SAP and Siemens and Air France and Delta).
- For further information, see, for example, the Corporate Identity Compass tool.[8]

Relationship change management (O46)

Skill: The ability to design and implement relationship change management processes which allow the business-to-business relationship to adapt smoothly to unexpected changes in personnel, procedures, policy, strategies and so on.

Demonstrating this ability:

- While most alliances have a defined change management process for the initiatives or projects that are run as part of the relationship, very few (<15%) appear to have specified a change management process for the relationship itself. Consequently, issues such as changing personnel, changing strategies, acquisitions and mergers or new product launches tend to take the relationship by surprise. When questioned, individuals from such relationships had no means of articulating what progress the relationships had made other than by repeating team generalities such as 'I think we are better now than we were before,' or 'I think key people understand each other better.'
- In a small minority of relationships in which a formal or informal relationship change management process was in existence, we noticed that the relationships enjoyed

---

7   www.strategic-alliances.org.

8   www.identity-compass.org.

elongation or extension of the value they delivered, and in general were valuable for longer.

- It appears that this factor is the one most responsible for enabling relationships to endure the stresses and strains of the dynamics of modern-day business life.

Creating innovative breakthroughs in the relationship (O49)

Skill: The ability to design and implement processes and systems which lead to new product or service in a replicable and cost-effective way.

Demonstrating this ability:

- It is no longer sufficient for experienced relationship mangers to recognise innovation and creative thinking when they see it. There is now a need for them to be able to design processes and procedures that create such innovation quickly and efficiently. Thankfully, these processes are generally very simple, and almost all are based on derivatives of the brainstorming workshop approach.
- The advantage a relationship manager enjoys over his in-house colleagues is that he can call on the creative input of an external organisation – the partner – which often generates remarkably creative thinking as it may have a different corporate mindset.
- This CSF is the one most often associated with the management buzzword 'innovation and business sustainability'. This generally refers to the ability of organisations to generate new and exciting business value propositions through a defined and repeatable process within the context of the relationship.
- A very small minority of organisations had anything closely resembling a formal process for this until two to three years ago. However, this factor is another which is rapidly gaining prominence in the better-performing organisations (for example, Reckitt Benckiser, Procter & Gamble, SAP and IBM).
- Many organisations are now engaging external third-party advisers to help them to shape a breakthrough process which will allow them to bring new products and new services to market more quickly and more effectively. It seems this external help is required in the form of objective facilitation rather than any groundbreaking approaches developed by the external consultancies.

Establishing a relationship management centre of excellence (Cu35)

Skill: Developing an actual or virtual centre of alliance excellence within the relationship manager's area of influence, allowing best practice principles and practices to be shared openly between non-competing units of the host and the partner organisation(s).

Demonstrating this ability:

- The centre of excellence consists of an actual or virtual group of people tasked with developing, coaching and implementing alliance and partnering standards, enabling access to and integration with identified external best practice standards and bodies.
- Best practice examples include both back-office and front-office functions. The front-office function usually concerns itself with providing value to the wider community of full-time and part-time relationship managers, while the back-office function focuses on enforcing agreed organisational standards in partnering.
- There is overwhelming evidence from the Database that when organisations begin to share alliance knowledge, performance increases markedly (for example, with an incidence of 46%, performance improvement increased by 87% on average).
- These centres of excellence are by no means all physical entities, some are virtual groups of staff from multiple disciplines. Neither are all of them formally established – some were clearly set up as a result of common observation of need: 'We started a regular teleconference call once a month to share experiences on our relationships. To be honest, at first it was just a chance to share frustrations, but pretty soon people began to share experiences or tips and tricks that had worked well for them that others could use. We started to share documents and templates, and it really helped with our day-to-day jobs.'
- There is a common misconception in high-tech partnerships that centres of excellence formed to test technical solutions are the same as alliance centres of excellence. This is clearly erroneous, although there are aspects of technical collaboration that share common best practices with collaborative relationships, such as communication models, operating protocols and budgetary sign-off.

Capability

Table 17.4 illustrates the levels of capability required in each of the four partnership types.

Table 17.4   Example of a skills matrix evaluation for alliance relationship managers

	Individual contributors				Team managers	
	Entry	Beginner	Intermediate	Advanced	Manager	Executive
Transactional						
Developing business value propositions for the relationship (Co1)	0	1	2	3	4	4
Conducting partner due diligence exercises (Co2)	1	2	3	4	4	4
Researching and understanding partner company market position (T12)	2	3	4	4	4	4
Articulating host company market position (T13)	1	2	3	3	4	4
Developing the legal/business structure (Co3)	0	1	2	3	4	4
Developing and implementing a robust set of key metrics (Co5)	0	1	2	3	4	4
Developing an expected relationship cost/value ratio (Co10)	1	2	3	4	4	4
Developing a set of shared objectives for the relationship (S20)	2	3	4	4	4	4
Enhanced						
Constructing and managing a joint relationship development plan (O51)	0	0	1	2	3	4
Designing and implementing an issue escalation process (O52)	0	0	1	2	3	4
Developing relationship communication plans (O43)	1	1	2	3	4	4
Conducting quality reviews (O44)	0	0	1	2	3	4

Designing and implementing an MOUP (O45)	0	0	2	3	4
Developing and implementing an alliance reward system (Co6)	0	0	2	3	4
Establishing business-to-business operational alignment (O48)	0	1	3	4	4
Conducting alliance audits/healthchecks (Co4)	1	1	3	4	4
Collaborative					
Developing a process for negotiation (Co9)	0	0	1	2	3
Developing and implementing tactical and strategic risk mitigation strategies (S22)	0	1	3	4	4
Securing senior executive support (S25)	0	0	2	3	4
Developing business-to-business trust (Cu31)	0	0	2	3	4
Identifying and controlling destructive organisational cultural traits (Cu37)	0	1	3	4	4
Formal joint business planning (O42)	0	1	3	4	4
Developing internal alignment (O50)	0	1	2	3	4
Valuing relationship assets (T11)	0	0	1	2	3
Partnership					
Establishing shared control (T18)	0	0	2	3	4
Developing business-to-business strategic alignment (S26)	0	0	1	2	3

Table 17.4 Example of a skills matrix evaluation for alliance relationship managers *continued*

	Individual contributors				Team managers	
	Entry	Beginner	Intermediate	Advanced	Manager	Executive
Creating a common relationship vision (S30)	0	0	0	1	2	3
Personal collaboration skills (Cu33)	0	0	1	2	3	4
Establishing and maintaining business-to-business cultural alignment (Cu38)	0	0	0	1	2	3
Managing relationship changes (O46)	0	0	1	2	3	4
Creating exponential innovative breakthroughs in the relationship (O49)	0	0	0	1	2	3
Establishing an alliance centre of excellence (Cu35)	0	0	0	1	2	3

Key:
Level 0 – skill not required or not present.
Level 1 – required but not essential skill.
Level 2 – required skill with reasonable level of performance.
Level 3 – skill important to the position; employee needs to demonstrate consistent good performance.
Level 4 – skill required for the position; consistent high level of performance essential.

Behaviours and Values: Details

CORE BEHAVIOURS/VALUES

Table 17.5 shows the core behaviours and values that successful relationship managers draw on.

Table 17.5 Examples of core behaviours and values for alliance managers

Behaviour/value	Definition
Innovation and learning	Desire to constantly improve
	Passionate curiosity to try new approaches
	Always willing to consider and accept new ways of working
	Recognition that lifelong learning is a journey, not a destination
Work with drive and commitment to results	Hard-working
	Demanding of self and the team
	Expects the best results
	Unwilling to settle for second-best
Think globally	Constantly aware of the 'big picture'
	Aware of own actions and how they impact the strategic goals of the relationship
	Sees the interaction between multiple tactical initiatives
	Constantly looking for synergy in interactions
Establish plans	Recognises the need for structured planning
	Able to create suitable levels of plans relevant to the scale of the task
	Pragmatic timekeeper who knows how long tasks and activities really take
	Methodical, paying close attention to detail
Demonstrate leadership	Able to command respect through knowledge and attitude
	Communicates vision well
	Able to combine views of both the host and the partner(s)
	Involves team members in strategic decisions and communicates implications well
Act with integrity	Demonstrates consistency in actions and approach
	Exemplary personal habits
	Not afraid to communicate bad news
	Prepared to be accountable for team performance

Table 17.5 Examples of core behaviours and values for alliance managers
continued

Behaviour/value	Definition
Communicate openly, effectively and with trust	Communicates with clear and simple language at an appropriate level of detail
	Seeks and gives effective feedback on previously communicated issues
	Consistent with communication messages regardless of level or organisation involved (host or partner)
	Takes the time to explain the need for actions as well as the action itself
	Involves all team members in communication appropriate to their level and role
Manage projects	Schedules tasks in appropriate order
	Able to multi-task
	Clear understanding of mutual interdependency
	Comfortable dealing with large amounts of data
Focus on team members	Consensual leader who seeks team members' opinions
	Actively seeks team input and takes demonstrable action on the outcomes
	Passionate about people development
	Good delegater
Organisational sensitivity	Understands host organisational culture well
	Aware of political tensions within own and partner organisations
	Keeps in touch with multiple functions and departments
	Wants to know what is going on in the organisation
	Aware of organisation's initiatives and priorities

PARTNERING BEHAVIOURS

Table 17.6 Examples of partnering behaviours and values

Behaviour/value	Definition
Dedication to partner success	Desire to see the partner succeed
	Always looking for additional opportunities for the partner
	Keen to find senior executive champions for the partner in the host organisation
	Constantly communicates good news and success stories about the partner

Behaviour/value	Definition
Cross-functional collaboration	Involves all relevant departments and functions in the relationship
	Explains the involvement of everybody in the team, both inside and outside the organisation
	Seeks out new functions as they become available and incorporates them into team briefings
	Aware of cross-functional dynamics, both within the host and partner organisation(s)
Doing more with less	Revels in using leverage to achieve breakthrough results elegantly
	Takes pride in over-achieving with limited resources
	Treats lack of resources as a challenge, not a setback
	Acutely aware of the power of synergy and possible valuable overlaps in the relationship teams
Influence others without authority	Persuasive communicator
	Listens well and combines others' goals and ambitions with those of the relationship
	High personal credibility and natural authority
	Subject matter expert on collaboration and partnering
Resolve conflicts	Good facilitator
	Can see many points of view in any issue
	Body language demonstrates active listening
	Prepared to make a stand when the issue is right
	Unwilling to go back on previous commitments
Increase and drive partner loyalty	Takes time to ensure the host is easy to work with
	Introduces partner(s) to multiple levels of interaction in the host
	Secures valuable payback for partner(s) on successful completion of joint objectives
	Showcases the partner(s) regularly to host staff and management
Cultural awareness and sensitivity	Understands the organisational culture of both the host and partner(s) well
	Sensitive to those aspects of both which are deeply held and important
	Able to explain the importance of aspects of organisational culture to both the host and the partner
	Comfortable with other national, geographic or religious cultures
	Copes well with diversity

TYPICAL COMPANY BEHAVIOURS

Table 17.7 Examples of typical company core behaviours

Behaviour	Definition
One team	Proud of a diverse ethnic, cultural and social make-up
	Passionate and knowledgeable about all products and services
	Always thinking of the big picture – outside own team, department and so on
	Collaborative and co-operative
Inspirational leadership	Confident, insightful and visionary
	Authentic, honest, caring and supportive
	Involving and inclusive
	Respects and values others' contributions
	Leads by example
Open communication	Honest, open, trusted and credible
	'We say what we mean' – simple, clear and jargon-free
	Approachable, always willing to listen and give feedback
	Engaging and personal
Challenge ourselves	Adaptable, flexible and keen to learn/grow
	In touch with own strengths and development areas
	Supportive, always willing to share skills and experiences to promote staff development
	Challenging, determined to grow and develop as one team
Recognising excellence	Appreciative and aware of each partner's contribution
	Knows what motivates host and partner(s) and what makes them tick
	Clear, transparent and fair about what great performance means
	Personal and thoughtful in rewarding and recognising staff performance
Innovative spirit	Passionate about developing new services, applications and new businesses
	Bold, not afraid of risk or failure
	Inquisitive, persistent and tenacious about new solutions
	Rewards and encourages innovation
Best place to work	Proud to be part of the organisation
	Committed to doing what's right for customers, society and partners
	Highly motivated and passionate about organisation's activities
Care for our customers	Accountable and responsible for exceeding customer expectations
	Obsessive about what customers value most
	Empowered to develop positive emotional relationships with customers

Alliance Skills

Table 17.8 Alliance skills by relationship type

Transactional	Enhanced	Collaborative	Strategic
Developing business value propositions for the relationship (Co1)	Constructing and managing a relationship development plan (O51)	Developing and managing collaborative negotiation processes (Co9)	Establishing shared control (T18)
Conducting partner due diligence exercises (Co2)	Designing and implementing an issue escalation process (O52)	Developing and implementing risk sharing strategies (S23)	Developing business-to-business strategic alignment (S26)
Researching and understanding the partner company market position (T12)	Developing relationship communication plans (O43)	Securing senior executive support (S25)	Creating a common relationship vision (S30)
Articulating the host's market position (T13)	Conducting quality reviews (O44)	Developing business-to-business trust (Cu31)	Personal collaboration skills (Cu33)
Developing the relationship's legal/ business structure (Co3)	Designing and implementing an MOUP or alliance charter (O45)	Identifying and controlling destructive organisational cultural issues (Cu37)	Establishing and maintaining business-to-business cultural alignment (Cu38)
Developing and implementing a robust set of key metrics (Co5)	Developing and implementing an alliance reward system (Co6)	Formal joint business planning (O42)	Managing relationship changes (O46)
Developing an expected relationship cost/value ratio (Co10)	Establishing operational business-to-business alignment (O48)	Developing internal alignment (O50)	Creating exponential innovative breakthroughs in the relationship (O49)
Developing shared objectives for the relationship (S20)	Conducting alliance audits/healthchecks (Co4)	Valuing relationship assets (T11)	Establishing a relationship management centre of excellence (Cu35)

18 *Collaboration: The Future*

I have spent what seems like the best part of my life observing the development of strategic alliances and those groups determined to instil this newborn management science with a degree of rigour and respectability. In fact, it has only been 12 years, and at times I need to remind myself of that fact, especially when I attend conferences and see that the same topics (and sometimes the same speakers) are on the agenda as appeared in my first alliance conference back in 2001! At times it feels like I and many of my visionary colleagues are swimming against the tide of popular management thinking in proposing quality standards and a greater degree of systematisation in this area.

But then I open a newspaper or turn on a radio, and the need for business-to-business collaboration screams out at me. One example from the many that I can recall stands out as a stark illustration of the power of alliances to achieve the unachievable.

It was March 2008, I was driving up the M1 motorway in England, and the radio was tuned to BBC Radio 4's news programme. The first item was about the massively overdue and over-budget Wembley Stadium. The interviewer had just asked a representative from the Australian consortium responsible for the rebuild why the project was over-running. The response was:

> *In all honesty I don't know. We had rock-solid contracts in place and fearsome penalty clauses. We subdivided the tasks and made sure that none of the suppliers could communicate with each other for fear that they might collude in developing sub-standard processes. At the end of the day, none of that helped and we ended up getting further and further behind schedule, all despite our extensive command and control procedures in place.*

The very next item covered the successful launch by Her Majesty the Queen of the new Terminal 5 at Heathrow Airport – in many respects a similar capital-intensive and highly sensitive national development project. But here the terminal was opening on time and within budget. The interviewer asked a representative of the British Airports Authority (BAA) what was the secret. His answer was:

> *We faced many problems with Terminal 5, and we were under severe public and governmental pressure. We had environmental issues to consider, and we were using state-of-the-art technology and techniques to achieve our goals. Given that scenario, traditional procurement models just couldn't deliver what we wanted. We needed a new model to achieve our goals. We found it through open and honest inter-firm collaboration. We set simple and flexible open guidelines at the beginning, and were keen to explain to every supplier that we worked with what our vision was. After that, we left it mostly to them to come up with the solutions. In fact, we solved some engineering problems that I thought were impossible to solve through collaboration alone. It was amazing!*

I can think of no better example of the sea change in inter-business relationships and the power of strategic alliances than these two statements. One of my original mentors in this area, Robert Porter Lynch of the Warren Company, is fond of saying: 'Collaboration has the power to solve all the world's problems.' I'm not sure that I believe him, but when I hear reports like the one above, I start to wonder!

What I do know is that the pressure to collaborate has never been higher, and it's getting stronger by the year. The current recession in Western Europe and in other parts of the world is forcing companies to leverage the resources of partners to greater and greater effect, and at the same time I hear from respected commentators that one of the fundamental reasons for the recent global financial meltdown was the lack of business-to-business trust between major players in the banking sector.

I can only see business alliances increasing in value and scope, and similarly I can see the standards required among alliance managers growing daily. I think the situation is similar to that in the project management industry twenty years ago. At that time there were no standards and no generally accepted certifications of competence. People were allocated large and complex projects on the basis of their experience and their ability to deliver results.

Twenty years later, I can see evidence that new standards have come into place, driven by the industry association. I can see that project managers now need to be qualified with certifications, and they also use common tools to help them in their jobs (software programs like Microsoft Project Manager and processes like Prince II).

I can foresee a similar trend in strategic alliances developing over the next ten years. Already we have a global industry association, the Association of Strategic Alliance Professionals, and a large number of tools and processes developed by the more forward-thinking companies and consultancies. We have a certification process which enables aspiring alliance managers to gain suitable qualifications (such as the ASAP certifications of CA-AM and CSAP). Organisational standards are beginning to appear with the introduction of BS 11000, the standard for Collaborative Business Relationships, which will very soon will become a recognised international standard, and finally we have a respected and powerful group of international business leaders who are using alliances as a tool to achieve business sustainability.

All of these initiatives give me hope for the future, hope for a more connected economy, one in which the needs of individual companies are respected not because of their size, but for the priceless contribution they can make to the vision of the alliances in which they are partners.

And as to why we haven't seen meteoric progress over the last ten years, I have come to believe that it has something to do with the phenomenon that Malcolm Gladwell identified in his book *The Tipping Point*.[1] In it he mentions the prerequisites for a successful breakthrough in thinking. These include time and external pressures as well as the quality and attractiveness of the message, but they also include the role of what he calls 'mavens' – people who network passionately to secure extended support for a concept they believe in.

If I have any aspiration in writing this book, it is that Alliance Best Practice will be seen as a vehicle for the dissemination of quality standards in business-to-business collaboration and that I can do my part by serving as a maven to spread the word as far

---

1   Malcolm Gladwell, *The Tipping Point: How Little Things Can Make a Big Difference*, London: Little, Brown, 2000.

and as wide as I possibly can that strategic alliances, when executed well, are the most elegant business model available.

Appendix 1:
About Alliance Best Practice

Alliance Best Practice is a research and benchmarking consultancy specialising in business-to-business collaborations based in the United Kingdom. Its partners and associates are a group of independent alliance experts who each specialise in certain aspects of strategic alliance formation or management. Its goal is to increase the knowledge and subsequent adoption of proven best practice principles for its clients. To support it in this endeavour it has researched strategic alliances deeply and maintains the ABP Database of observations of alliances in action gained from many leading-edge partnering organisations. This Database currently contains over 200,000 entries.

We welcome contributions from anyone who would like to submit research for consideration for inclusion in the Database or from organisations which would like to be benchmarked. Please email all enquiries in the first instance to info@alliancebestpractice. com, or if you would like further insights from the Database, please visit our website at www.alliancebestpractice.com.

If, after having read this book, you feel that you would like further information about the subject of strategic alliances and the role they can play in organisational growth and development, then please feel free to contact me at Mike.nevin@alliancebestpractice.com. We are constantly developing the ABP Database, and actively welcome the contributions of any practitioners, academics or consultants active in the area of business-to-business collaboration today.

Appendix 2:
The Alliance Best Practice Database

Alliance Best Practice Ltd has been examining the common success factors that feature in successful strategic alliances since 2002. During that period we have constructed the ABP Database to organise our findings.

Originally, the Database was used as a repository of results to allow organisations to benchmark their alliance performance against a group of similar alliances in their sector. However, as the size and complexity of the Database grew, we were able to spend more time examining the trends and insights provided by the data, so the Database now enables us to make statistically supportable statements regarding what works and what does not work in business-to-business alliances.

The Database contains over 200,000 observations of alliances in action captured between 2002 and 2014, and the data capture process is ongoing. The Database's structure is relational and built around 52 defined common success factors in strategic alliances. As a consequence, it represents a searchable source of pragmatic alliance best practice experience; so far (May 2014), there are over 600 in-depth diagnostic assessments of strategic alliances in the Database.

The Database's development was based on primary, secondary and ongoing research in the following three stages.

Stage 1:

- secondary research;
- investigation of over 27,000 international strategic alliances;
- discovery of the 52 common success factors.

Stage 2:

- primary research;
- validation of the research with over 300 active practitioners;
- development of the benchmarking tool;
- over 600 applications of the benchmarking tool.

Stage 3:

- ongoing research;
- segmentation of the Database;
- derivation of insights based on trends that became apparent;
- identification of commercial value.

The Database is unique because from the beginning it took a proprietary route by asking the same questions consistently of every alliance ABP observed.

Of course, many organisations conduct partner assessments or healthchecks yearly or twice-yearly, but these tend to allow the participants to define their own categories based on questions such as:

- How do you think the alliance is performing?
- Do you think the alliance is progressing satisfactorily?
- What do you think is going well or badly regarding the alliance?
- Are you currently happy or unhappy with the alliance?

The problem with such systems is that they are overly subjective in nature and are very difficult to compare with each other.

Alliance Best Practice took a different route: having identified a common or repeating set of success factors, we used these to assess the degree of best practice in action in a given relationship. We did this by turning each factor into a question. Hence the CSF of trust became the question: 'Does business-to-business trust exist in this alliance relationship?'

In the early days of constructing the Database our questions were limited to binary responses of 'yes' or 'no', so the advice we were able to give was restricted to identifying those CSFs which were absent and recommending their adoption. However, as the Database grew we were able to use the earlier responses to further refine our questioning as we became more granular and accurate in our scoring of the factors. Very soon we were able to identify not just whether a factor was present, but also how effectively (on a scale of 0–100) it was performing measured against the earlier benchmarking we had conducted.

Today the ABP Database of over 200,000 observations allows us to be extremely sophisticated in our scoring techniques. Not only can users of the Database determine which factors are performing well and which are not, but they can also receive advice as to what other organisations have done in the past to maximise their scores in those categories. This is what we in Alliance Best Practice mean by 'standing on the shoulders of giants': current Database users are benefiting directly from the experiences of the companies which have gone before them.

Alliance executives typically use the ABP Database to assess relationship potential or organisational alliance maturity as follows:

Relationship Potential:

- How does a single relationship benchmark against other similar best practice alliances?
- Is there unrealised commercial potential in the relationship?

Alliance Capability:

- What is the current stage of alliance maturity in our organisation?
- What challenges will we face in the near future, and what successful strategies have other organisations used to make progress quickly?

In our experience there are three critical elements driving the desire of companies to benchmark their alliance relationships:

Rationalisation:

- The vast majority of companies are reassessing their strategic alliances and are concentrating their resources on a smaller number of them.
- This means that a relatively small number of companies will be significant 'winners'.

Risk:

- Companies want to know whether any of their strategic relationships are at risk.
- If they are, they also want to know what they can do about it.

Return:

- In the current tight economic climate, companies want to know that they are receiving the appropriate commercial return from their partnering efforts.

Currently, over 300 organisations are represented in the ABP Database (see Appendix 3), and the largest individual business sector represented in the Database is high-tech, as shown in Figure A2.1.

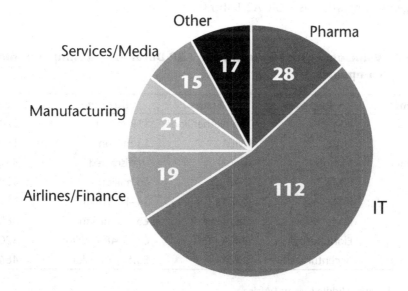

Figure A2.1 ABP Database breakdown by sector

Here are comments from some of these organisations about the ABP Database:

'We have been able to assess accurately our capabilities as matched against a world-class database. This has allowed us to be realistic in our growth ambitions and also to avoid making the common mistakes made by others in our situation, thus saving a considerable amount of time and money.'

'We have accelerated our understanding of the gaps in our knowledge and processes through the initial diagnostic. This has enabled us to remedy those gaps much more quickly than would otherwise have been possible.'

'It has been established that the database has saved us over three man years' effort by giving us already developed templates, tools and methodologies on which to build our thinking.'

'The database has allowed us access to pragmatic evidence of best practice which has been crucial in developing the strategic presentations that have guided our development thinking. Knowing the actions, trends and intentions of our competitors and alliance partners has allowed us to position our alliance strategies to best effect with minimal effort.'

'The database research has allowed us to differentiate our alliance strategy to best effect, making us an attractive partner to our key collaborators (Microsoft, IBM, Oracle, SAP and HP).'

Using the ABP Database and the principles it embodies has been extremely valuable for a wide range of companies, as Table A2.1 shows.

Table A2.1 Value generated by using the ABP Database – a sample of high-tech companies

Clients	Partners	Scope	Baseline	Increase
Capgemini	IBM	The Netherlands	$19 million	270%
Unisys	EMC	EMEA	$3 million	180%
Capgemini	Microsoft	Global	Undisclosed	340%
Oracle	IBM	Germany	€6 million	400%
Cognos	IBM	EMEA	$4–14 million	350%
Oracle	IBM	Germany	€6–23 million	380%
BT	Eight partners	EMEA	£150–480 million	320%
Micro Focus	Accenture	EMEA	£3.5–17 million	486%

Note: EMEA = Europe, Middle East and Africa.

Objective scoring of alliance relationships in the collaborative portfolio of companies is a very valuable exercise when it is backed up by hard evidence of how to make the journey most effectively and efficiently, as illustrated in Figure A2.2.

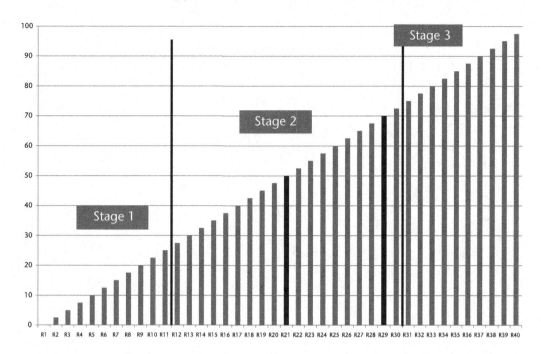

Figure A2.2 Alliance benchmark extract (example)

Appendix 3:
Companies in the Alliance Best Practice Database

Accenture, Adobe, Adva, Aenis, Agilisys, Air France, AirPlus, Alcatel Lucent, Alterian, Alzus, AMD, Amdocs, Amec, Amey, Amgen, AMP Capital, ANA, APC, Apple Inc, Ariba, Arqiva, Arriva, Arrow, Aruba Networks, Ascent Media, Associated Business Leaders LLC, Astellas, AstraZeneca, AT+T, Atos Consulting, Atos, Attenda, Autonomy, Avanade, Avaya, Avis, AXA, Axiom, Axon Global, BA, BAA, BAE Systems, Detica, Balfour Beatty, Bank of America, BASF,Basilica Consulting, Battelle, Bax Global, Bayer Healthcare, Bayer Schering Pharma, BBC Corporation, BCX, BDO Unicon, BEA, Bearing Point, Bechtel, Bell Canada, Biogen Idec, Biovail Pharmaceuticals, BMC, BMI, BNP Paribas, Boehringer Ingelheim, Borland, BP Oil and Gas, Bristol-Myers Squibb, British Library, Brocade, BT, BT Global Services, Buckland Austin, Business and Decision, Business Objects, CA Technologies, Cable and Wireless, CACI, Capgemini, Capita, Cardinal Health, Carillion, Carlson Wagonlit, Caterpillar, CellTech, Cephalon Europe, CGI, CH2M Hill, Check Point Software, Chordiant, Ciber-Novesoft, Ciena, Cisco, Citrix, Claranet, Cloudera, Cognizant, Cognos, Colt Telecom, Computacenter, Continental Airlines, CSC, CSG International, Csiper, Cubist Pharmaceuticals, Datawatch, Delaware, Dell, Deloitte, Delta, Deutsche Bank, Diagonal Consulting, Dimension Data, Disney, Dr Reddy's, DSM, DST Global Solutions, Dundas and Wilson, Dupont, DWF, Ebay, EBRC, EDS, Eisai Inc, Eli Lilly, EMC^2, Endo Pharmaceuticals, Epiphany, Equinix, Ericsson, Ernst & Young (E&Y), Everis, Everything Everywhere, Exact Software, Exel, Experian, Exponent, Fidessa, Flexera Software, Fluid Software, Fluor, Fontline, Fontworkx, Forest Laboratories Inc, Fujitsu, GE Capital Finance, GeneMedix, Genentech, Genesys, Genset, Genstruct Inc, Genzyme, Getronics, Givaudan, Glades Pharmaceuticals, GlaxoSmithKline, Google, Hewlett Packard, Hitachi Consulting, Hitachi Data Systems, Hoffmann-La Roche Ltd, i2 Technologies, IBM, IBS, IDS Sheer, Imbercal, ImmunoGen Inc, Imperial Tobacco, Indra, Infor, Informatica, Infosys, Intec, Integralis, Intel, Intentia, Interserve, Ipsen, ITS, Jacobs Engineering, Japan Corporate Bank, Jarvis, JBoss, Juniper Networks, KAI Pharmaceuticals, Kalamazoo, Kana, Kaspersky, Keane, King Pharmaceuticals, KLM, Kofax, KPMG, Kronos, Kuehne & Nagle, Kyowa Hakko Kogyo Co Ltd, Laing O'Rourke, Lawson, Lenovo, Logica, Logicalis, LTSB, Lufthansa, Mahindra Satyam, Manhattan, Mannkind Corporation, Marks and Spencer, Maxygen Inc, McAfee, Merck, Micro Focus, Microsoft, MicroStrategy, Minster Law, Misys, Mitie, Ministry of Defence (MOD), Motorola, Mouchel, Mphasis, MSG, NCR Corporation, NEC, NetApp, Netsuite, NextiraOne, nFocus, Nokia, Nokia Siemens Networks, Nordea, Nortel, Northwest Airlines, Norwich Union Life, Novaquest, Novartis, Pharmaceuticals, Novell, Noven Pharmaceuticals Ltd, Novo Nordisk AS, NTT Data, Nuance Software, O2, O2 Telefonica, Omax Auto, Omega Signs, Opentext, Oracle, Organon, OSI Pharmaceuticals inc, Otrum, Panduit, Pegasystems, Perceptive Software, Peregrine, Pfizer, Philips, PLM,

Polycom Inc, Procter and Gamble, Progress Software, Pronto Software, Protein Design Labs, Purdue Pharma LP, PwC – PricewaterhouseCoopers, Qgenisys, Qliktech, RBS, RCC, Reckitt Benckiser, Red Hat, Redpoint Bio Corporation, Reneuron, Response Biomedical Corporation, Ricoh, Rider Levitt Bucknall, Rifcon, RIM - Research in Motion, Roche Pharmaceuticals, Roiter Zucker, Rolls Royce, Royal Bank of Scotland (RBS), RSA, RWD Technologies UK Ltd, Sage, Salesforce.com, Samsung, Sanofi Pasteur, Sanofi-Aventis, SAP, Sapient, SAS Institute, Satyam, SCC, SCH, Schering Plough, Schneider-Electric, Scottish Widows, Serco, Shavlik Technologies, Shiongi & Company Ltd, Shoretel Inc, Siebel, Siemens, Signify, Singapore Airlines, Skyteam, Software AG, Sophos, Sprint, SPSS, SSA, Staffware, Star Alliance, Starbucks, Steljes, Stem Cell Sciences, Steria, StorageTek, Success Factors, SugarCRM, Sun Microsystems, Sungard, Symantec, Symphony, T Mobile, Takeda Pharmaceuticals, Tandberg, TAP Pharmaceutical Products Inc, Tata Communications, Tata Consulting Services (TCS), TDG, Tech Data, Telmex, Telus, Teradata, Tertagenetics Inc, Tessella, Thomson Reuters, Tieto, TNT Express, Triple Point Technology, T-Systems, Tubelines, UBS, uLogistics, Unilever, Unipart Logistics, Unisys, United Airlines, Veeam, Verity, Verizon, Vignette, VMware, Vodafone, WebMethods, Websense, Wipro, Withy King, Wyeth Pharmaceuticals, Wyse, Xansa, Xchanging, Xerox, Xerox Services, Yahoo, Zebra, and Zurich Financial Services.

Appendix 4:
Definition of Terms

Definition of terms lies at the heart of understanding.

Plato

ABP Alliance Best Practice Ltd, a research consultancy dedicated to identifying and implementing proven best practices in strategic alliances.

ABP Framework The collection of alliance best practice documents compiled by Alliance Best Practice Ltd, including case studies, white papers, presentations, methodologies, questionnaires and training materials.

Alignment The degree to which both/all partners in a relationship agree on a common score for selected CSFs. Alignment in the ABP Model refers to a situation in which the scores are 5% or less apart. Misalignment refers to a situation in which the partners' scores are 50% or more apart.

Alliance A business-to-business relationship in which there is a high degree of collaboration.

Alliance Balanced Scorecard A well-known approach in general management areas thanks to the work of Kaplan and Norton,[1] among others. It identifies key performance indicators and their structure in a balanced reporting set, including, for example: leading and lagging indicators, internal and external factors, and long-and short-term factors

Alliance Best Practice The conscious use of identified common success factors in sequence to achieve superior competitive performance in alliances.

---

1   Robert S. Kaplan and David P. Norton, *The Balanced Scorecard: Translating Strategy into Action*, Boston, MA: Harvard Business School Press, 1996.

Alliance Control   Strategies designed to deliver the correct degree of control required in relationships. This relates to the entire structure of guidance rules and regulations published by both/all partners to ensure appropriate governance of the relationship. These will vary in complexity and degree of depth depending on the value or potential value of the relationship in question, but typically include attitude to risk, risk sharing, key stakeholders' roles and responsibilities, systems of control and the MOUP.

Alliance Maturity   An indication of an organisation's attitude to partnering, reflected by a score of 0–100 in three stages:
Stage 1 = 0–25 Opportunistic
Stage 2 = 25–75 Systematic
Stage 3 = 75–100 Endemic.

Alliance Operation   Addressing senior management's commitment, determining the calibre of resources devoted to the alliance, linking budgets and resources with strategic priorities, measuring and rewarding alliance performance, and assessing its performance and results.

Alliance Process   The completion of structured tasks in a defined order to achieve an alliance goal, for example discovering new partners, optimising a partnership relationship, or developing a new set of partner products or services.

Alliance Relationship   A relationship in which one or more parties share one or more of the following: costs, benefits, customer knowledge, production capability, market intelligence and intellectual property rights.

Alliance Termination   Winding down an alliance, for instance when its objectives have been met or cannot be met, or when a partner adjusts priorities or reallocates resources elsewhere.

Balance of Trade   The flow of value between two transactional partners in a case where each partner 'buys from' or 'sells to' the other.

Best Practice   Synthesised common sense.

Business Excellence   The original name of the model developed by the European Foundation for Quality Management which seeks to show business owners the interactions between leadership, resources, processes and results which successful companies employ to grow their business.

Business Intimacy	The degree to which two or more organisations share complex or sensitive information and/or develop joint operating procedures.
Business Intimacy Spectrum (BIS)	An expression of the degree of business intimacy in an alliance relationship, from low to high, for example: Transactional, Enhanced, Collaborative or Partnership.
Collaborative Relationship	The development of a group of inter-related enhanced relationships with a common purpose, goal, go-to-market model and strategy.
Contract Negotiation	Determining whether all parties have realistic objectives, forming high-calibre negotiating teams, defining each partner's contributions and rewards as well as protecting any proprietary information, addressing termination clauses, penalties for under-performance, and ensuring that arbitration procedures are clearly stated and understood.
Control Questions	A paired set of questions in the ABP benchmarking questionnaire. The results are compared to verify data integrity. For example, if the answer to one paired question was high, then the score of the second paired question should be equally high. If it is not, then the answer to both is regarded as somewhat suspect, therefore reducing the data integrity score below 100%.
CSF	Common success factor – an element of a strategic alliance which contributes significantly to the success of the relationship.
Data Integrity	The quality of the data captured in an ABP benchmarking questionnaire. The integrity is expressed as a score out of 100.
Desired Outcome	The output of successful alliance relationships, for example: cost-effective revenue, business growth, new products and services, entry into new markets, cost reductions and quality improvements.
Dimension	A grouping of the common success factors according to their nature. Five distinct dimensions are identified in the ABP framework: Commercial, Technical, Strategic, Cultural and Operational.

Due Diligence	All the investigations organisations need to undertake to reassure themselves that a candidate would make a suitable partner. Typically, this includes factors such as commercial resilience, strategic direction, technical quality, cultural alignment, operational structure and customer attitude. Aspects specific to the host company include organisational customer focus, the business language used and the proposed use of the host organisation's brand.
Enhanced Relationship	A transactional relationship in which one or more parties enhance the basic offering by adding something of specific value to the other party or parties, which in turn increases the value of the product or service to the eventual consumer.
External Relationship	A relationships between one organisation and another. Some of these relationships may be collaborative, in which case they are usually defined as either alliances or partnerships.
Going Native	Demonstrating too much preference to a partner's views or needs to the detriment of the organisation's own position.
High Impacter	A CSF whose impact is high but which usually takes time to show results (for example, Cu31, 'Business-to-business trust').
Incremental Revenue	Revenue developed as a result of the relationship that would not otherwise have existed.
Internal Alignment	All those activities, efforts and communications an organisation undertakes to clarify to its own staff the nature and purpose of an alliance. Typically, the greater the degree of internal alignment, the easier the organisation is to partner with. It usually involves areas such as sales, marketing, finance, internal audit, technology and field operations.
Key Metrics	The key performance indicators alliance managers choose to measure in particular relationships.
Key Performance Indicator	A best practice success factor that can be clearly measured and has been shown to have a great impact on results: for example, trust, cultural alignment, commercial return, cost/value ratio or dispute resolution processes.

Low Impacter A CSF which has a low impact but which takes less time to show its results (for example, Co1, 'Business value proposition').

Misalignment A situation in which both/all partners are more than 50% points apart in their assessment of a CSF.

MOUP Memorandum of understanding and principles – a document explaining the guiding principles and operating procedures for a relationship, covering such as vision, business value proposition, governance model and key stakeholders.

Mutual Needs Needs from a relationship that are identical for all the partners involved. This is by no means a common occurrence because in most cases different partners will have different needs, but when the needs are truly identical, the power and impact of the relationship is significantly enhanced and the chances of success are far greater.

Partner Assessment Analysing a potential partner's strengths and weaknesses and developing strategies to accommodate each partner's management styles, preparing appropriate partner selection criteria, understanding a partner's motives for joining an alliance and addressing resource capability gaps that may exist for a particular partner.

Partnership A particularly advanced form of business-to-business collaboration which has a high degree of business intimacy. Typically, these types of alliances are between vendors and suppliers and the goal is enhanced service provision (for example, Telefonica UK has a range of partnerships with selected key suppliers, including IBM, HP, AEG, Sky, Vodafone and Carillion).

Primary Research The collection of original primary data, often undertaken after a researcher has gained some insight into an issue by reviewing secondary research or by analysing previously collected primary data. It can be accomplished through various methods, including questionnaires and telephone interviews in market research, or experiments and direct observations in the physical sciences.

RACI Responsible, Accountable, Consulted and Informed – the role a key stakeholder will play in either an optimisation process or a benchmark review.

Relationship	An arrangement between two or more organisations that may or may not be an alliance relationship, defined depending on the model adopted: for example, Transactional, Enhanced, Collaborative and Alliance.
Relationship Intimacy	An expression of the degree of business intimacy between two or more organisations, usually associated with the Business Intimacy Spectrum. More details areavailable from the Alliance Best Practice Database at www.alliancebestpractice.com.
Secondary Research	Also known as desk research, this involves the summary, collation and/or synthesis of existing research, as opposed to primary research where data is collected from, for example, research subjects or experiments.
Statistically Significant	In statistics, especially in statistical testing, a result is statistically significant if it is unlikely to have occurred by chance, hence providing enough evidence to reject the hypothesis of 'no effect'.
Strategic	Having a major impact on a business or a significant business department through factors such as commerciality, innovation, business breakthrough, developing new markets or new customers in existing markets. Generally (though not always), 'strategic' indicates a degree of importance or value in an alliance relationship.
Strategic Alliance	A formal or informal relationship between two or more parties to pursue a set of agreed goals or to meet critical business needs while remaining independent. 'Strategic' in this phrase denotes the importance of the relationship. These types of relationships are usually business-critical.
Strategy Development	Studying an alliance's feasibility, objectives and rationale, focusing on the major issues and challenges and developing resource strategies for production, technology and staff. It requires alignment of alliance objectives with the overall corporate strategy.
Synergy	A situation in which both/all parties in an alliance receive more value than it costs them to contribute. Usually this cost/value ratio arises because of the particular appropriateness of the partners involved.

Transactional Relationship   A relationship between a supplier and a buyer where goods or services are exchanged for value (usually commercial value).

Appendix 5:
Further Reading

Adarkar, Ashwin, Asif Adil, David Ernst and Paresh Vaish. 'Entering Emerging Markets: Must They be Win–lose?', *McKinsey Quarterly* 4, November 1997.

Aharoni, Yair, ed. *Coalitions and Competition: The Globalization of Professional Business Services*, New York: Routledge, 1993.

Anand, B.N. and T. Khanna. 'Do Firms Learn to Create Value? The Case of Alliances', *Strategic Management Journal* 21, 2000, pp. 295–315.

Anderson, Erin. 'Two Firms One Frontier: On Assessing Joint Venture Performance', *Sloan Management Review* 31(2), 1990, pp. 19–30.

Bazerman, M. 'Why Negotiations Go Wrong', *Psychology Today*, June 1986, pp. 54–8.

Bell, Chip R. *Customers as Partners: Building Relationships that Last*, San Francisco, CA: Berrett-Koehler, 1994.

Bell, Chip R. *Managers as Mentors: Building Partnerships for Learning*, San Francisco, CA: Berrett-Koehler, 1998.

Bleeke, Joel and David Ernst. 'Is Your Strategic Alliance Really a Sale?', *Harvard Business Review* 73, January–February 1995, pp. 97–105.

Brandenburger, Adam M. and Barry J. Nalebuff. *Co-opetition*. New York: Currency/Doubleday 1996.

Bridges, William. *Managing Transitions: Making the Most of Change*, New York: Perseus Books, 1991.

Brown, Shona L. and Kathleen M. Eisenhardt. *Competing on the E4: Strategy as Structured Chaos*, Boston, MA: Harvard Business School Press, 1998.

Carlisle, J. and N. Rackham. *The Behavior of Successful Negotiators: A Report*, Purcelleville, VA: Huthwaite, 1994.

Chesbrough, Henry W. and David J. Teece. 'When is Virtual Virtuous? Organizing for Innovation', *Harvard Business Review*, January–February 1996, pp. 66–73.

Christensen, Clayton. *The Innovator's Dilemma*, New York: HarperBusiness, 2000.

Cialdini, R. *Influence: Science and Practice*, New York: HarperCollins, 2000.

Conger, J.A. 'The Necessary Art of Persuasion', *Harvard Business Review*, May–June 1998.

Corey, Raymond E. *Technology Fountainheads: The Management Challenge of R&D Consortia*, Boston, MA: Harvard Business School Press, 1997.

Corporate Executive Board, Corporate Strategy Board. *Institutionalizing Alliance Capabilities: A Platform for Repeatable Success*, Washington, DC: Corporate Executive Board Corporate Strategy Board, 2000.

Das, T.K. and B.-S. Teng. 'Managing Risks in Strategic Alliances', *Academy of Management Executive* 13(4), 1999, pp. 50–62.

Davenport, Tom. *Process Innovation*, Boston, MA: Harvard Business School Press, 1993.

DeKluyver, C.A. *Strategic Thinking: An Executive Perspective*, Upper Saddle River, NJ: Prentice Hall, 2000.

Doyle, Michael and David Straus. *How to Make Meetings Work*, East Rutherford, NJ: Berkley Publishing Group, 1993.

Doz, Yves L. and Gary Hamel. *Alliance Advantage: The Art of Creating Value Through Partnering*, Boston, MA: Harvard Business School Press, 1998.

Drucker, Peter Ferdinand. *Managing for Results*, New York: HarperBusiness, 1993.

Ernst, David and Tammy Halevy. 'When to Think Alliances', *McKinsey Quarterly* 4, Winter 2000.

Ertel, Danny. 'Turning Negotiation into a Corporate Capability', *Harvard Business Review* 77(3), May–June 1999, pp. 69–78.

Ertel, Danny and Mark Gordon. *The Point of the Deal*, Cambridge, MA: Harvard University Press, 2007.

Ertel, Danny, Jeff Weiss and Laura J. Visioni, *Managing Alliance Relationships: Ten Corporate Capabilities*, Boston, MA: Vantage Partners, LLC, 2001.

Fischer, Roger, William Ury and Bruce Patton. *Getting to Yes: Negotiating Agreement Without Giving In*, New York: Penguin Books, 1991.

Geis, George T. and George S. Geis. *Digital Deals: Strategies for Structuring Partnerships*, New York: McGraw-Hill, 2001.

Gomes-Cassares, Benjamin. 'Alliances and Risk: Securing a Place in the Victory Parade', *Financial Times*, 9 May 2000.

Gomes-Casseres, Benjamin. 'Group Versus Group: How Alliance Networks Compete', *Harvard Business Review* 72, July–August 1994, pp. 62–74.

Gomes-Casseres, Benjamin. 'Joint Ventures in the Face of Global Competition', *Sloan Management Review* 30, Spring 1989, pp. 17–26.

Gomes-Casseres, Benjamin. *The Alliance Revolution: The New Shape of Business Rivalry*, Cambridge, MA: Harvard University Press, 1996.

Hamel, Gary, Yves Doz and C.K. Prahalad. 'Collaborate with Your Competitors and Win', *Harvard Business Review* 67(1), January–February 1989, pp. 133–9.

Hammond, John S., Ralph L. Keeney and Howard Raiffa. *Smart Choices: A Practical Guide to Making Better Decisions*, Boston, MA: Harvard Business School Press, 1998.

Handy, Charles. 'Trust and the Virtual Corporation', *Harvard Business Review* 74, May–June 1995, 65–71.

Harbison, John R. and Peter Pekar *Smart Alliances: A Practical Guide to Repeatable Success*, San Francisco, CA: Jossey-Bass, 1998.

Harrington, H. James. *Business Process Improvement*, New York: McGraw-Hill, 1991.

Hock, Dee. *Birth of the Chaordic Age*, San Francisco, CA: Berrett-Koehler, 1999.

Hughes, Jonathon and Jeff Weiss. *Making Partnerships Work: A Relationship Management Handbook*, Boston, MA: Vantage Partners, LLC, 2001.

Hwang, Peter and Willem P. Burgers. 'The Many Faces of Multi-firm Alliances: Lessons for Managers', *California Management Review* 39(3), Spring 1997, pp. 101–17.

Johnson, Spencer. *Who Moved My Cheese?*, New York: Putnam, 1998.

Kanter, Rosabeth Moss. 'Collaborative Advantage: The Art of Alliances', *Harvard Business Review* 72(4), July–August 1994, pp. 96–108.

Kaplan, Robert S. and David P. Norton, *The Balanced Scorecard: Translating Strategy into Action*, Boston, MA: Harvard Business School Press, 1996.

Katzenbach, Jon R. and Douglas K. Smith. *The Wisdom of Teams: Creating the High-performance Organization*, New York: HarperBusiness, 1994.

Kogut, Bruce. 'Joint Ventures: Theoretical and Empirical Perspectives', *Strategic Management Journal* 9(4), July–August 1988, pp. 319–22.

Kogut, Bruce. 'Why Joint Ventures Die So Quickly', *Chief Executive*, May–June 1998, pp. 70–73.

Kotter, John P. *Leading Change*, Boston, MA: Harvard Business School Press, 1996.

Kouzes, Jim and Barry Posner. *The Leadership Challenge*, San Francisco, CA: Jossey-Bass, 1996.

Kurtzman, Joel. *Thought Leaders: Insights on the Future of Business*, San Francisco, CA: Jossey-Bass, 1998.

Leeke, Joel and David Ernst. *Collaborating to Compete*, New York: Wiley, 1993.

Lorenzoni, Gianni and Charles Baden-Fuller. 'Creating a Strategic Center to Manage a Web of Alliances', *California Management Review* 37, Spring 1995, pp. 146–63.

Luehrman, Timothy. 'Strategy as a Portfolio of Real Options', *Harvard Business Review* 76, September–October 1998, pp. 89–100.

Maister, David H. *Managing the Professional Service Firm*, London: Free Press Business, 1997.

Mandell, Lewis. *The Credit Card Industry: A History*. Boston, MA: Twayne, 1990.

Marks, Mitchell and Phillip Mirvis. *Joining Forces: Making One Plus One Equal Three*, San Francisco, CA: Jossey-Bass, 1998.

Mnookin, Robert H., Scott R. Peppet and Andrew S. Tulumello. 'The Tension between Empathy and Assertiveness', *Negotiation Journal* 12(3), July 1996, pp. 217–30.

Moore, Geoffrey. *Inside the Tornado*, HarperCollins, 1999.

Moore, Geoffrey. *Living on the Fault Line: Managing for Shareholder Value in the Age of the Internet*, New York: HarperBusiness, 2000.

Moore, Geoffrey and Regis McKenna. *Crossing the Chasm: Marketing and Selling High-tech Products to Mainstream Customers*, New York: HarperBusiness, 1999.

Morrison, Terri, Wayne A. Conaway, George A. Borden and Hans Koehler. *Kiss, Bow, or Shake Hands*, Avon, MA: Adams Media, 1995.

Murnighan, J.K. and D.E. Conlon. 'The Dynamics of Intense Work Groups: A Study of British String Quartets', *Administrative Science Quarterly* 36(2), June 1991, pp. 165–86.

Nadler, Gerald and Shozo Hibino. *Breakthrough Thinking: The Seven Principles of Creative Problem Solving*, 2nd edn, Roseville, CA: Prima Publishing, 1998.

Nanda, Ashish and Peter J. Williamson. 'Use Joint Ventures to Ease the Pain of Restructuring', *Harvard Business Review* 73(6), November–December 1995, pp. 119–28.

Nohria, Nitin et al. 'Colliers International Property Inc.: Managing a Virtual Organization', Harvard Business School Case no. 396-080.

Ohmae, Kenichi. 'The Global Logic of Strategic Alliances', *Harvard Business Review* 89(2), March–April 1989, pp. 143–54.

Rackham, Neil, Lawrence Friedman and Richard Ruff. *Getting Partnering Right: How Market Leaders are Creating Long-term Competitive Advantage*, New York: McGraw-Hill, 1996.

Reich, Robert and E. Mankin. 'Joint Ventures with Japan Give Away Our Future', *Harvard Business Review* 64(2), March–April 1986, pp. 78–86.

Rousell, Charles. 'The Science of Alliances: Making an Exit', *Accenture Outlook Point of View*, July 2001.

Schneider, Susan and Jean-Louis Barsoux. *Managing Across Cultures*, Upper Saddle River, NJ: Prentice Hall, 1997.

Segil, Larraine. *Intelligent Business Alliances*, New York: Random House, 1996.

Senge, Peter M. *The Fifth Discipline: The Art and Practice of the Learning Organization*, New York: Currency/Doubleday, 1994.

Senge, Peter M., Art Kleiner, Charlotte Roberts, Rick Ross and Bryan Smith. *The Fifth Discipline Fieldbook: Strategies and Tools for Building a Learning Organization*, New York: Currency/Doubleday, 1994.

Silkenat, J. and J. Aresty. *The ABA guide to International Business Negotiations: A Comparison of Cross-cultural Issues and Successful Approaches*, 3rd edn, Chicago, IL: American Bar Association, 2009.

Spekman, Robert E. and Lynn A. Isabella. *Alliance Competence: Maximising the Value of your Relationships*, New York: Wiley, 2000.

Suen, Wilma W. 'Alliance Strategy and the Fall of Swissair', *Journal of Air Transport Management* 8(5), 2002 pp. 355–63.

Teisberg, Elizabeth O. 'Why Do Good Managers Choose Poor Strategies?', Harvard Business School Case no. 9-391-172, 5 March 1991.

Thomas, R. Roosevelt Jr. *Redefining Diversity*, New York: Amacom, 1996.

Trompenaars, F. *Riding the Wave of Culture: Understanding Diversity in Global Business*, 2nd edn, New York: McGraw-Hill Professional Publishing, 1997.

Ury, William. *Getting Past No: Negotiating Your Way from Confrontation to Cooperation*, New York: Bantam Doubleday Dell.

Vengel, Alan A. *The Influence Edge*, San Francisco, CA: Berrett-Koehler, 2001.

Ward Biederman, Patricia and Warren G. Bennis. *Organizing Genius: The Secrets of Creative Collaboration*, New York: Perseus Books, 1998.

Whetten, David A. and Kim S. Cameron. 'Principles for Managing Meetings', in *Developing Management Skills*, 2nd edn, New York: HarperCollins, 1991.

Yoshino, Michael P. and U. Srinivasa Rangan. *Strategic Alliances: An Entrepreneurial Approach to Globalisation*, Boston, MA: Harvard Business School Press, 1995.

Zook, Chris and James Allen. *Profit From the Core: Growth Strategy in an Era of Turbulence*, Boston, MA: Harvard Business School Press, 2001.

Useful Websites

www.alliancebestpractice.com
www.alliancesphere.com
www.alliancevista.com
www.amazonconsulting.com
www.pslcbi.com
www.strategic-alliances.org
www.thepartneringinitiative.com
www.vantagepartners.com
www.warrenco.com

Appendix 6:
Useful Additional Resources

The following resources are available for download from the Alliance Best Practice website at www.alliancebestpractice.com.

- Alliance Best Practice Taxonomy
- How to Run an Alliance Best Practice VST Exercise
- About Equinix
- Why Partner with Equinix?
- How Collaboration Technologies are Improving Process, Workforce and Business Performance
- Steelwedge Partner Programme Guide
- Why the Hybrid Cloud Makes Sense
- An Explanation of the Alliance Best Practice Alliance Benchmarking System
- S21 Developing the Scope for a VST Alliance Optimisation Exercise
- Identity Compass
- Alliance Balance Scorecard Example
- Example Internal Communication Plan
- Alliance to Win Factsheet
- Alliance to Win Overview
- Business Value Proposition
- BVP Workshop
- Delivering an MOUP Workshop
- Tieto Partner Selection Criteria
- The Alliance Best Practice 52 Common Success Factors
- A Lens on Cooperation
- Example Alliance Benchmark Report - High Tech
- The VST Value Proposition
- VST Example Proposal
- VST Programme Overview
- Example VST Report Progress Summary
- Enterprise Level Partnering
- Examples of Value Baselining in Strategic Alliance Relationships
- Relationship Optimisation
- Scoring the ABP Common Success Factors CSFs
- Alliance Benchmarking Factsheet
- What is Alliance Benchmarking
- Initiating a Strategic Alliance Using an MOUP
- MOUP Pre-Workshop Briefing Document

- VST Value Proposition
- VST v CHAMP Feature Comparison
- VST Training Course for Channel Executives
- VST One Day Course Outline for Alliance Executives
- VST Methodology 2 Slide Pack
- VST Methodology 2 Slide Pack
- VST Dashboard
- VST Case Study Short
- VST Briefing Pack for Senior Executives Version 3.0
- VST Briefing Note for Partners
- VST Bridge to Value FAQ
- VST Alliance Sales Methodology
- VST Methodology Version 9.0
- Scoring the Alliance Best Practice Common Success Factors (CSFs)
- The Alliance Best Practice Benchmarking Questions
- VST Briefing Pack for Senior Executives Version 2.0
- IBM CEO Study 2012
- An example VST Rollout Programme Version 1.0
- The Tieto VST Methodology Version 10.0
- Cu 36 Developing Decision Making Processes
- Cu 31 Developing Business-to-Business Trust
- Cu 33 Developing Collaboration Skills (Advanced)
- Cu 33 Developing Personal Collaboration Skills
- S30 Developing a Common Vision
- C09 Negotiation Training by Lifecycle Stage
- Cu 38 Developing Business-to-Business Cultural Alignment
- O39 Developing and Executing an Alliance Best Practice Process
- O42 Developing a Joint Business Plan
- O43 Developing and Executing Communication Programmes
- Alliance Management Salary Review and Benchmark 2012
- Example Alliance Scorecard
- Common Success Factors in Strategic Alliances
- Alliance Scorecard Example
- Influencing the Key to Successful Business Relationships
- MOUP Template for Go To Market (GTM) Alliances
- Procurement Driven Growth
- The New Deals
- The Alliance Sales Methodology
- An Examination of the Build Buy Ally Growth Model
- Alliance Culture – It's in the DNA!
- Activating Agility
- Innovation through Collaboration
- Capitalising on Complexity the 2010 IBM CEO Study
- Sponsorships as Strategic Alliances
- Linked In Guide
- The Right Way to Think About Alliances
- The Partnership Charter

- Third State of Alliance Management Study May 2009
- Managing Alliances in a Recession
- Little Red Book on Building Alliances
- Building Trust and value in Strategic Alliances
- Building Relationship in Your Supply Chain
- The Power of Virtual Collaboration
- ABP One Day Training Course
- Summary of ABP Training Courses
- Alliance Negotiation Training
- Project Plan for Relationship Optimisation Programme
- Executive Sponsor Job Description
- ABP Template Relationship Optimisation Report for two Partners
- Alliance Capability Assessment Diagnostic Template
- Scoring the ABP Common Success Factors
- MOUP Briefing Pack
- Reviewing a Strtegic Alliance using an MOUP Workshop
- Initiating a Strtegic Alliance using an MOUP Workshop
- High Tech MOUP Example
- MOUP Questionaire
- MOUP Project Plan
- Alliance Best Practice Joint Business Plan
- MOUP Scoping Template
- Template External Communication Plan
- Alliance Best Practice Framework
- External Communication Template
- Alliance Best Practice Framework
- The Collaboration Advantage – Customer Focused Partnerships in a Global Economy
- An Introduction to Alliance Best Practice

Example of a Typical ABP Alliance Excellence Set of Benchmarking Questions

These questions would be benchmarked against the entries in the Database to allow companies to assess their Alliance Maturity as against the Alliance Maturity Model™ (AMM™)

Table A6.1 Typical ABP benchmarking questions

1. Leadership	2. Resources	3. Alliance processes	4. Key metrics	5. Key results
1A: Attitude	2A: People	3A: Partner recruitment	4A: Commercial	5A: Gross partner revenues
1B: Commitment	2B: Procedures	3B: Onboarding	4B: Technical	
1C: Guidance	2C: Programme	3C: Healthchecks	4C: Strategic	5B: Partner of choice statistics
1D: Structure	2D: Products	3D: Relationship optimisation	4D: Cultural	5C: Cost of alliance sales
1E: Global/ regional interaction	2E: Platform	3E: Demotion/ exit	4E: Operational	5D: Cost/value ratios
				5E: Alliance excellence programme milestones

Module 1: Leadership

1A: ATTITUDE

- What is the attitude of the senior executive team to partnering and alliances generally in your company? Can you illustrate this with some quotations or examples?
- Where does partnering sit in your company (for example, in sales, marketing, corporate planning)?
- At what level is the most senior alliance-focused person in your organisation?
- What is the degree and depth of local alliance leadership:
  - in your corporate function?
  - in the field?
- Is there a global alliance management function (for example, either a team or an individual who has management responsibility for alliances generally)?
- Is there a recognised career path for alliance executives within your organisation?
- Is there a job description available for alliance or relationship managers in your company?
- How are individual business units/geographies/countries/product lines within your company incentivised to 'sell' alliances?

1B: COMMITMENT

- How do the senior executives in your organisation show commitment to the concept of strategic alliances?
- How many partner events do your senior executives attend per year?
- Do your senior executives sponsor an alliance relationship?
- What resources do your senior executives allocate to alliances on an annual basis?

- Do your senior executives regularly sign a senior executive alliance sponsor job description?

1C: GUIDANCE

- Does your organisation have a formal alliance review board that monitors and validates the alliance strategy?
- Is there a partnering vision in your organisation which is commonly available to all staff?
- Is there a formal alliance strategy which is written down in your company?
- Is there a generally recognised process of executive sponsoring for strategic alliances?
- Does your organisation have a formal partner enablement programme which is supported by senior executives from multiple divisions?

1D: STRUCTURE

- How is the alliance function structured in your organisation?
- How are alliances reported in the annual report in your company?
- What is the communication matrix between, for example, sales, marketing, R&D and production that allows cross-functional alliances to operate?
- How are the most common alliances structured?
- Is there a formal process of segmenting alliances?
- What is the difference in structure between different alliance segments?
- How many partners does your organisation have in each of its segment areas or levels?

1E: GLOBAL/REGIONAL INTERACTION

- Is there an alliance centre of excellence in your organisation?
- If so:
  - Which function does the centre of excellence report to?
  - How do the alliance managers in the field receive support from the centre of excellence?
  - How does the centre of excellence ensure adoption of company standards by alliance managers in the field?
- Does your company have a chief alliance officer? If so in which function is the post located?

Module 2: Resources

2A: PEOPLE

- Does your organisation have a formal alliance training programme?
- How does your company recruit alliance managers? How does this differ from the recruitment process for other staff?
- What is the alliance culture within your organisation that individuals have to understand in order to be successful?

- Is there a process of individual alliance personality profiling in your organisation? If so, against what database are the results profiled?
- Is there a process or system for identifying team collaboration potential?
- Is there a recognised alliance centre of excellence? Is there more than one? If so, how many?
- Do you train your partners in your alliance processes?

2B: PROCEDURES

- Does your organisation have a formal alliance governance processes?
- If so, does it define alliance rules of operation that must be followed by your company's alliance personnel?
- Does your organisation conduct executive reviews in which the executive sponsors of alliance relationships conduct high-level relationship examinations on a regular basis?
- Does your company conduct alliance audits? If so, what issues are covered?
- How is the alliance audit conducted (By whom and when? Time-based or activity-triggered?)?
- Does your organisation conduct regular alliance healthchecks on a quarterly basis?
- What does your organisation recognise as 'alliance governance'? What is covered by this term?
- Does your company have a common alliance taxonomy of terms and words used in alliance business?
- What would lead to an alliance manager being sacked?

2C: PROGRAMME

- Does your company have a formal programme for alliance development?
- What are the milestones of objectives in your global/regional/country alliance programmes?
- Do you have a formal alliance programme manager?
- To whom does the alliance programme manager report?

2D: PRODUCTS

- Does your organisation regularly produce new products and/or services with partners?
- Is there a defined process for producing these products/services?
- Do you insist that field sales staff sell these products/services?
- Do you have a tracking system for these products/services?
- Do you have a data store, knowledge store or database of these offerings? If so, is it accessible to the partners through a portal?

2E: PLATFORM

- What resources are available to alliance staff in your organisation?
- Does your company have a defined alliance storehouse of data that alliance executives at all levels can access?

- Does your organisation have an automated alliance management system that helps company staff to perform their day-to-day functions?
- Does your company have a defined alliance toolset that employees can use to speed up their alliance activities?
- How does an alliance manager in the field receive support from your organisation?
- What alliance processes are available for individuals to use?
- What alliance training is available to your organisation's staff?
- What technology support systems are in place in your organisation to help accelerate and automate the process of alliance management?
- How are alliances reported in your organisation?
- Is there an alliance-specific application available to alliance executives in your organisation?
- What is the interaction between the alliance-specific applications and the other corporate applications in your company (for example, human resources, accounting, finance, sales)?
- How are alliance meeting usually conducted in your organisation (What types of technology are used – telephone, videoconferencing, telepresence, webinars?)?

Module 3: Alliance Processes

3A: RECRUITMENT

- Do you have a standard partner/alliance recruitment process?
- Is the process automated?
- Does the process co-ordinate with your alliance management systems and processes?
- How often do you recruit partners?
- What categories of due diligence do you use to choose partners?

3B: ONBOARDING

- Do you have a formal onboarding process for partners?
- Do you have an induction process for new partners?
- Do you produce any induction packs for new partners?
- Do you have internal and external documentation for onboarding partners?
- How long does your onboarding process take?

3C: HEALTHCHECKS

- Do you have a formal alliance/partner healthcheck process?
- If so:
  - How often do you run the process?
  - Who conducts the process?
  - What happens to the output of the healthcheck?
  - Is the healthcheck 360 degrees? Do you share the results with partners?

3D: OPTIMISATION

- Do you have a formal optimisation process for your alliance relationships?
- If so:
  - How long does your optimisation process take?
  - Who are the key stakeholders in the optimisation process?
  - What results have you achieved with your optimisation process?
  - Who conducts the optimisation process (Is it one-sided, or do both parties contribute?)?

3E: DEMOTION/EXIT

- Do you have a formal alliance/partner demotion and/or exit process?
- If so:
  - What triggers the process?
  - How do you explain the process to partners?
  - What explanatory information exists for partners to explain the process?

General process questions

- Does your organisation have a standard partner selection approach?
- Is there a defined partner programme?
- Who has responsibility for the different types of alliances in your organisation?
- Is there a joint business planning process in your organisation for individual alliances?
- What are your organisation's country-specific alliance policies (if any), and how do they differ from corporate standards?
- What types of rewards/bonuses are available for alliance managers?
- What is the process for knowledge exchange between alliance managers?
- Is there a channel conflict identifier process?
- Is there a buy–build–partner decision methodology in operation?
- Is there an alliance regeneration programme?
- Is there an alliance IT management system (sometimes called a partner relationship management system)?
- Are there any identified best practice alliance processes and procedures?
- Are the following processes in existence in your organisation (that is, are they documented and followed regularly):
  - developing an alliance business value proposition?
  - partner due diligence programme?
  - alliance structure assessment?
  - alliance audit?
  - alliance balanced scorecard development?
  - compensation plan review?
  - cost of alliance sales model?
  - alliance business case builder?
  - alliance healthcheck?
  - asset valuation analysis?

- alliance output market assessment?
- alliance strategy development?
- MOUP alliance review/instigation?
- alliance healthcheck/MOUP review?
- alliance risk analysis?
- alliance decline/renewal analysis?
- senior executive job description?
- alliance healthcheck?
- developing an alliance centre of excellence?
- alliance process development?
- developing a relationship business plan?
- developing a communication programme?
- capability healthcheck?
- relationship change management programme?
- developing an integrated set of operational metrics?
- developing an alliance strategy?
- developing a relationship project plan?
- developing an alliance governance model?
- relationship optimisation?
- capability building?
- relationship refresh?
- diagnostic/healthcheck?
- tiering programme process?
- designing an alliance manager assessment programme?
- delivering an alliance manager assessment programme?
- online alliance manager assessment?
- CSAP coaching?
- CAAM coaching/guidance?

Module 4: Key Metrics

4A: COMMERCIAL

Note: These questions are directed at individual alliance relationships.

- Do you have an identified business value proposition for the relationship?
- Have you conducted due diligence to identify suitable candidate partners? If so, what criteria were used?
- How did you arrive at the optimum legal/business structure?
- Do you regularly perform a relationship audit with this partner?
- What are the key metrics that drive this relationship?
- Do you have a relationship reward system linked to key metrics?
- What is the commercial cost of this relationship?
- What is the commercial benefit of this relationship?
- What process for negotiation was employed in developing this relationship?
- What is the expected cost/value ratio of this relationship?

4B: TECHNICAL

Note: These questions are directed at individual alliance relationships.

- Have you performed a valuation of the assets of this relationship?
- What is the partner company market position? Why is this important to you?
- What is the host company market position? Why is this important to the partner?
- What is the market fit of the proposed solution?
- To what extent does your product fit with your partner's product/service offerings?
- Are there clearly identified mutual needs which are satisfied in the proposed relationship?
- What is the process for team problem solving?
- How will control be shared and exercised in the relationship between the contributing parties?
- What is the degree of partner accountability, and how is this expressed?

4C: STRATEGIC

Note: These questions are directed at individual alliance relationships.

- Are there common and shared specific objectives for the relationship?
- What is the scope of the relationship, and how has this been arrived at?
- What degree of tactical and strategic risk is involved in this relationship? What happens if it doesn't go ahead?
- How is the risk shared by all parties?
- What exit strategies have been identified?
- What support is there from senior executives in your organisation for this relationship? How is this evidenced?
- What degree of business-to-business strategic alignment exists, and what measures were used to ascertain this?
- How does this relationship fit the strategic business path?
- Do you have any other relationships with the same partner?
- What common ground rules of strategic operation have you agreed with the partner?
- Is there a common vision on all sides of the strategic intent of this relationship? If so, can you articulate it in your own words?

4D: CULTURAL

Note: These questions are directed at individual alliance relationships.

- What is the degree of trust in the relationship? How is this evidenced?
- What is the level of maturity of alliance thinking in your organisation?
- What degree of collaboration skills exist in this relationship on both sides? How have these skills been applied?
- Is there a dedicated relationship manager identified to work on this alliance from both sides?

- Is there a dedicated alliance department in your organisation to whom you can turn for help in this and other alliances?
- How long is the decision making process in your partner's organisation? How does this compare with decision making in your own organisation?
- Are there any other cultural issues which get in the way of business as usual?
- What degree of business-to-business cultural alignment exists, and what measures were used to ascertain this?

4E: OPERATIONAL

Note: These questions are directed at individual alliance relationships.

- Do you have a defined alliance process?
- How long has it taken you to get to where you are now in the alliance relationship? Where is that?
- How far away from revenue generation are you currently?
- Do you have a formal business plan for the relationship?
- What elements of communication are present? How many meetings and with whom?
- Do you have a process for an ongoing healthcheck of the alliance (for example, a 90-day review)?
- Does a relationship charter or MOUP exist? How was it signed?
- What is the relationship change management process?
- What operational alliance metrics do you use, as opposed to strategic or scorecard metrics?
- What degree of business-to-business operational alignment exists, and what measures were used to ascertain this?
- Do you have a process for generating exponential breakthroughs or innovation in the relationship?
- What degree of internal alignment exists? How is this evidenced?
- Do you have a formal relationship project plan written down?
- How are issues escalated?

Module 5: Key Performance Results

5A: GROSS PARTNER REVENUES

- How are partner revenues reported in your annual results?
- Do you practice 'double counting' when it comes to alliances?
- Do your partner revenues differ in any material way from your normal business results?
- Do you comment separately in your annual return on partner performance?
- What percentage of gross revenues do your partner revenues represent?

5B: PARTNER OF CHOICE STATISTICS

- Do you conduct a 'Partner of Choice' programme?

- If so:
  - Do you measure the programme formally?
  - What are the key metrics for the programme?
  - How does the programme co-ordinate with your other existing alliance/partnering processes?
  - How do your Partner of Choice statistics inter-relate with your other alliance statistics?

5C: COST OF ALLIANCE SALES

- Do you regularly measure the cost of alliance sales?
- If so:
  - What categories of measurement do you have for alliance sales?
  - Do your categories reflect both direct and indirect costs?
  - Do you include cross-charging in your alliance cost model?
  - Do you have an explanatory document which explains in detail how you calculate your alliance cost figures?

5D: COST/VALUE RATIOS

- Do you have a concept of alliance cost/value in your organisation?
- If so:
  - Is it widely appreciated and used?
  - What are the factors that go into calculating the alliance cost/value ratio?
  - Is the cost/value ratio used in personal assessment forms?
  - How is the cost/value ratio expressed (Percentage figures? 40% Payback figures? 15:1?)?

5E: ALLIANCE EXCELLENCE PROGRAMME MILESTONES

- Does your organisation have a formal 'Alliance Excellence' programme?
- If so:
  - How is the programme defined?
  - Does the programme have a formal programme manager? If so, is the role full-time?
  - What are the key milestones of the programme?
  - What is the anticipated timescales for the programme?

General Questions

- What are the key indicators of success in your strategic alliance relationships?
- How do the key indicators link to your strategic business goals?
- How will you measure the effectiveness of the best practice partnering programme?
- How will you measure the effectiveness of the alliance centre of excellence in your organisation?

- What does the top-level reporting dashboard look like for:
  - your organisation?
  - your alliance(s)?
- What is the link between the strategic issues measured in the top-level dashboard and the operating-level metrics used by your business on a daily basis for:
  - your organisation?
  - your alliance(s)?

Index

Printed in the United States
by Baker & Taylor Publisher Services